For Shay

from one who greatly respects
your mother's enthusiasm for
history and Corbow,

Wrigley

Labour and working-class lives

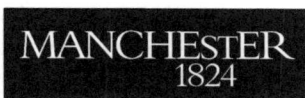

MANCHESTER
1824

Manchester University Press

To Chris Wrigley:
an inspiration behind more than four decades of research and
publication into modern British, European and global history

Labour and working-class lives

Essays to celebrate the life and work of Chris Wrigley

Edited by

Keith Laybourn and **John Shepherd**

Manchester University Press

Published by Manchester University Press
Altrincham Street, Manchester M1 7JA

www.manchesteruniversitypress.co.uk

British Library Cataloguing-in-Publication Data
A catalogue record for this book is available from the British Library

Library of Congress Cataloging-in-Publication Data applied for

ISBN 978 1 7849 9527 0   hardback

First published 2017

Typeset in Garamond
by R. J. Footring Ltd
Printed in Great Britain
by CPI Group (UK) Ltd, Croydon, CR0 4YY

Contents

Editors and contributors

Editors

Keith Laybourn is Professor of History and the Diamond Jubilee Professor of the University of Huddersfield, and a Fellow of the Royal Historical Society. He has known and worked with Chris Wrigley for nearly thirty years. He has written and edited extensively on British labour history, social policy, women's history, the history of voluntary organisations and policing history. He published *The General Strike* with Manchester University Press in 1993 and many books on the rise of labour, including *The Rise of Labour* (Arnold, 1988) and *Under the Red Flag* (Sutton, 1999). With David Taylor he published *Policing in England and Wales 1918–1939: The Fed, the Flying Squad and Forensics* (Palgrave, 2011) and his own most recent book is *The Battle for the Roads of Britain: Police, Motorists and the Law c. 1890s–1970* (Palgrave, 2015). He edited the *Annual Bulletin of Historical Literature* (1999–2010) for the Historical Association, is an Honorary Fellow of the Historical Association and is President of the Society for the Study of Labour History (2012–).

John Shepherd is Visiting Professor of Modern History at the University of Huddersfield and a Fellow of the Royal Historical Society. He has worked in polytechnics and universities and was Visiting Professor, Co-founder and Joint Director of the Labour History Research Unit at Anglia Ruskin University, Cambridge. His publications include *George Lansbury: At the Heart of Old Labour* (Oxford University Press, 2002, 2004), *Britain's First Labour Government*, with Keith Laybourn (Palgrave, 2006, 2013) and *Crisis? What Crisis? The Callaghan Government and the 'Winter of Discontent'* (Manchester University Press, 2013, 2015). He edited with Chris

Wrigley *On the Move: Essays in Labour and Transport History Presented to Philip Bagwell* (The Hambledon Press, 1991) and also jointly edited with Jonathan Davis and Chris Wrigley *Britain's Second Labour Government 1929–31: A Reappraisal* (Manchester University Press, 2011). Currently he is completing for Manchester University Press a biography of Dr Jon Cruddas MP, former Shadow Cabinet member and Head of Labour's Policy Review, 2012–15.

Contributors

Joan Allen is Senior Lecturer in Modern British History at the University of Newcastle. She is a member of many history committees, including the Steering Committee History UK, the Executive Committee of Newspaper and Periodical History, the Library Committee of the Institute of Historical Research and the Executive Committee of the Society for the Study of Labour History. She has research interests in Victorian society and politics, nineteenth-century British radicalism, and especially Chartism, for which she is the co-convenor of the Chartist Conference. She has written many articles and published a range of books, including the monograph *Joseph Cowen and Popular Radicalism in Tyneside 1829–1900* (Merlin Press, 2007); she has also edited a number of books, including (with Owen Ashton) *Papers for the People: A Study of the Chartist Press* (Merlin Press, 2005) and (with Richard Allen) *Faith in Our Fathers: Popular Culture and Belief in Post-Reformation England, Ireland and Wales* (Cambridge Scholars, 2009). She is currently writing a book on the Catholic press.

Kenneth D. Brown is Professor Emeritus in History at Queen's University Belfast and was Pro-Vice-Chancellor from 2001 to 2009, when he retired. He has ranged widely over British labour, business and religious history and written on British and Japanese economic and social development. He is currently finishing a new biography of Herbert Gladstone. Among his publications are *Essays in Anti-Labour History* (Macmillan, 1974), *A Social History of the Nonconformist Ministry in England and Wales, 1800–1930* (Oxford University Press, 1988), *The British Toy Business: A History Since 1700* (Hambledon Continuum, 1996) and *Factory of Dreams: A History of Meccano Ltd, 1901–1979* (Crucible, 2007).

Malcolm Chase is Professor of Social History at the University of Leeds. He has written extensively on British Labour history and Chartism and is currently researching self-improvement, popular reform and public good in the mid-nineteenth century. His publications include *The People's Farm: English Radical Agrarianism, 1775–1840* (Oxford University Press, 1988), *Early Trade Unionism: Fraternity, Skill and the Politics of Labour* (Ashgate, 2000), *Chartism: A New History* (Manchester University Press, 2007) and

1820: Disorder and Stability in the United Kingdom (Manchester University Press, 2013).

Dick Geary is Emeritus Professor in History at the University of Nottingham and has specialised in European labour movements and the intellectual history of Marxism. He has specialised in German history and is also researching the history of slavery. His publications include *European Labour Protest 1848–1929* (Croom Helm, 1981), *Karl Kautsky* (Manchester University Press, 1987), *European Labour Politics from 1900 to the Depression* (Palgrave, 1991), *Hitler and Nazism* (Routledge, 1993) and (with Stephen Hodkinson), *Slaves and Religions in Graeco-Roman Antiquity and Modern Brazil* (Cambridge Scholars, 2010).

Kevin Jefferys was formerly Professor of Contemporary History at Plymouth University. He is an expert in British labour history, Churchill and the Second World War, and the history of sport in Britain. He has published many articles and books. The latter include *Churchill Coalition and Wartime Politics 1940–1945* (Manchester University Press, 1991), *Retreat from the New Jerusalem: British Politics 1951–1964* (St Martin's Press, 1997), *Anthony Crosland* (Metro Books, 1999), *Finest and Darkest Hours: The Decisive Events in British Politics from Churchill to Blair* (Atlantic Books, 2002), *Politics and the People: A History of British Democracy Since 1918* (Atlantic Books, 2007) and *Sport and Politics in Modern Britain: The Road to 2012* (Palgrave Macmillan, 2012), for which he won the Lord Aberdere Literary Prize in 2013.

Nicole Robertson is Senior Lecturer at Sheffield Hallam University, where she specialises in nineteenth- and twentieth-century British history, researching the co-operative movement, white-collar workers, the history of retailing and consumer society. Her current research focuses on workplace politics among white-collar workers in Britain between 1920 and 1970, and examines the rise of the British workplace, unemployment, gender, politics, professionalisation and identity. She is a former PhD student of Chris Wrigley. Her publications include *Consumerism and the Co-operative Movement in Modern British History: Taking Stock* (edited with Lawrence Black; Manchester University Press, 2009), *The Co-operative Movement in Britain: Minding Their Own Business* (Ashgate, 2010), a contribution to the *The Second Labour Government 1929–31: A Reappraisal* (Manchester University Press, 2011) and articles in *Business History* (2012) and *Labor History* (2014).

Janet Shepherd writes on modern social history. She gained her PhD at London Guildhall University (part-time) on pauper education in nineteenth-century England and has taught in London, Cyprus and

Cambridge. She has contributed nine entries to the *Oxford Dictionary of National Biography* (Oxford University Press, 2004) and her recent publications include *The 1950s Home* (Amberley Publishing, 2017), *Britain in the 1920s* (Shire, 2010), *Britain in the 1970s* (Shire, 2012) and *1950s Childhood* (Shire, 2014), all jointly with John Shepherd. Her current research interests centre on modern British social history and children's literature. She is the daughter of Dr Ernest Seeley (1900–89), General Secretary of the ATTI union and a leading member of the Progressive League for fifty years.

Andrew Thorpe is Pro-Vice-Chancellor and Executive Dean (Humanities) and Professor of Modern British History at the University of Exeter. Among his publications are *The British General Election of 1931* (Clarendon Press, 1991), *The British Communist Party and Moscow, 1920–1943* (Manchester University Press, 2000), *Parties at War: Political Organization in Second World War Britain* (Oxford University Press, 2009) and *A History of the British Labour Party* (Palgrave Macmillan, 4th edition 2015). His most recent publication, co-edited with Richard Toye, is *Parliament and Politics in the Age of Asquith and Lloyd George: The Diaries of Cecil Harmsworth, MP, 1909–1922* (Royal Historical Society, 2016). He is currently working on the life and political career of Labour leader Arthur Henderson (1863–1935).

Noel Whiteside is Professor of Comparative Public Policy at the University of Warwick and has been awarded a Visiting Professorship at SSEE (Smith School of Enterprise and Environment), Oxford University. She is a contemporary historian of social and public policy development with specific interests in labour markets and the construction of social dependency in comparative (European) perspective. Her recent books include *Pension Security in the Twenty-First Century: Redrawing the Public–Private Divide* (edited with Gordon L. Clark; Oxford University Press, 2000, 2005), *Britain's Pensions Crisis: History and Policy* (edited with Hugh Pemberton and Pat Thane; Oxford University Press, 2006), *Transforming European Employment Policy: Labour Market Transitions and the Promotion of Capability* (edited with Ralf Rogowski and Robert Salais; Edward Elgar, 2011), *Casual Labour* (Oxford University Press, 1986) and *Bad Times: Unemployment in British Social and Political History* (Faber & Faber, 1991). She has also contributed to three of Chris Wrigley's edited books.

Matthew Worley is Professor of Modern History at the University of Reading specialising in twentieth-century British politics. His particular interest is in the inter-war British labour movement and he has written on the Labour Party, communism in Britain and Europe, and the far right. He is currently researching the link between politics and youth culture in the 1970s and 1980s, paving the way for a book to be published by Cambridge University Press in 2017. His books include *Class Against Class: The Communist Party in Britain Between the Wars* (I. B. Tauris, 2001), *Labour Inside the Gate: A History of the Labour Party Between the Wars* (I. B. Tauris, 2005), *Oswald Mosley and the New Party* (Palgrave Macmillan, 2010) and (with E. Smith) *Against the Grain: The British Far Left from 1956* (Manchester University Press, 2014).

Chris Wrigley: a tribute

PROFESSOR THE LORD HENNESSY OF NYMPSFIELD, FBA

Chris Wrigley is a reason to be cheerful. He has shown his own generation of scholars and the younger ones whose development he has nurtured how to live a historical life to the full. In an era when ever more of the poetry of university life has been crowded out by the plumbing (to use a distinction made by the political scientist Trevor Smith, himself a former vice-chancellor), Chris has shown it is possible to combine a quartet of virtues: being a highly productive scholar at the top of his game; a good citizen within his institution; a cherished teacher at all levels; *and* a natural and generous practitioner of reaching out to a wider audience, not least through his beloved Historical Association.

As if these accomplishments were not impressive enough, Chris has also found time to live a public and political life of real and sustained political engagement. Had he won a seat for Labour in the 1980s, how the party would have been enriched in the House of Commons. But think of the books we might have had to forgo. Though maybe not. Chris could well have combined, like Roy Jenkins or Roy Hattersley, a writing life with a routine determined by the division bell and the constituency surgery.

As I write these thoughts on the last day of 2016, Chris and his work are an exemplar in an important and time-specific fashion. In the United Kingdom and further afield, this is not a progressive, centre-left, hour. Nor is it a climate in which trade unionism will naturally flourish. Now that the antagonistic gene within the British labour movement's genome is flowing mightily and disruptively once more with almost certainly considerable electoral consequences to come in England and Wales and no sign of a revival in Scotland, it is important that the Wrigley *oeuvre* is not forgotten – that the generations to come do not despair but realise instead that though there are no iron laws of history, the British labour tradition has a rich and usable past on which it can draw for both practical and inspirational purposes.

As this collection of essays shows, Chris Wrigley has been – and will remain – a very special guide and a lustrous beacon, a living exemplar that meticulous scholarship can be blended with a political and public life to the mutual flourishing of both.

Peter Hennessy
South Ronaldsay, Orkney
New Year's Eve 2016

Chris Wrigley: a personal reflection

PROFESSOR MARGARET WALSH

Chris Wrigley is very well known as a historian of labour and of industrial relations, as well as a historical biographer and an avid acquirer of history volumes. In this last capacity, he has a reputation for having a jam-packed university office that has not only amazed numerous students but has been and remains infamous among colleagues, past and present, and new appointees. (The studies at home are no less full!) He has been active and held positions in several academic organisations, including the Historical Association, the Society for the Study of Labour History and the Economic History Society. As well as mentoring many PhD students, he has given many academic papers in the UK, Germany, France, Italy, Sweden, South Africa and Brazil. Since his retirement he has retained his long-standing commitment to his local branch of the Historical Association and remains active on the committee of the Nottingham branch. He also serves on the Board of Trustees of the Arkwright Society at Cromford, Derbyshire.

But there has always been time for other activities and pastimes, some of which are not so well known. Since his undergraduate days, Chris has been a solid supporter of the Labour Party and was very active in local government in the 1980s when he was at Loughborough University. Then he served on both the Charnwood Borough Council and the Leicestershire County Council and stood as a candidate for Parliament in 1983 (Blaby) and in 1987 (Loughborough). Since moving to the University of Nottingham in 1988, he has opted only to stand regularly for potential losing seats on the Rushcliffe Borough Council. He has, however, maintained his interest in and acute commentary on politics and current affairs.

Rock and roll has been a lifelong passion and he is a walking encyclopaedia on this genre of music, as well as being a jazz enthusiast. His collection of vinyl and CDs rivals that of his books. He has also attended classical concerts, both in Birmingham and in Nottingham, though his dislike of opera remains constant. Shellfish is also a lifelong passion! Travel for pleasure has been another notable feature of his 'other life'. As well as visiting many European countries he turned to long-distance travel and his holidays have included memorable visits to Peru, Costa Rica, Namibia, Botswana, Zambia, Madagascar, China, Vietnam and the United States, and cruises to the Arctic, the Antarctic and the Galapagos Islands. Home territory has not been neglected in Chris's travels. Holidays have brought stays in new parts of all the countries in the United Kingdom while Ramblers 'away weekends' have instigated a different type of appreciation of the natural landscape of England. Indeed, activity in the local branch of the Ramblers has involved not only greater familiarity with the East Midlands, but also the capacity to find and lead walks. Retirement only brings greater involvement in a variety of activities as well continuing research on the late-twentieth-century British coal industry.

Maggie

Acknowledgements

Any academic publication owes a great debt to the generosity of others, and this is no exception. The editors would like particularly to thank the University of Huddersfield for financing the time of one of them to undertake the preparation and editing of this volume. Colleagues and ex-colleagues, such as Sarah Bastow, Barry Doyle, David Taylor and Paul Ward, have been encouraging in this project and Neil Pye and Chris Ellis, former students, have been particularly helpful in offering advice. John Shepherd would also like to thank members of the Lansbury family (separately acknowledged in his chapter) and particularly Dame Angela Lansbury, CBE, for interviews. Andrew Thorpe would also like to thank John Edmonds, Billy Hayes and other attendees for their comments on an earlier version of his chapter at the History and Policy Trade Union Forum meeting 'The Labour Party and the trade unions', at King's College London, in March 2012.

Many thanks must go to Tony Mason (Senior Commissioning Editor) and Alun Richards (Editorial Assistant) at Manchester University Press, and Ralph Footring, our copy-editor, for their help in preparing this book. Without their careful guidance, and that of the rest of the MUP staff involved, this book would have been a long time in production.

The various contributors have cited their sources throughout and thanked individual libraries and private collections for the use of their material. In all chapters there has been fair dealing and none contains any substantial amount of material from any secondary source. We would particularly like to acknowledge Charles Gladstone for the use of the Herbert Gladstone material in the chapter by Professor Kenneth Brown and the Controller of Her Majesty's Stationary Office (Norwich) for permission to make the occasional quote from crown copyright material. Like the National Archives, whose sources have occasionally been used, the Controller gives automatic right to quote from government documents as long as proper attribution is made. Darren Treadwell of The People's History Museum provided us with permission to quote from the records it holds for the Labour Party and the Communist Party of Great Britain. Stefan Dickens of the Bishopsgate Library in London approved the use of the George Howell collection. Anna Towlson of the British Library of Political and Economic Science approved the use of branch minutes of the Independent Labour Party (ILP) and records of the National Administrative Council of the ILP it holds in its collection. James King of the Modern Records Centre at the University of Warwick permitted the use of the records of the Friendly Society of Ironfounders. Northumberland Records Office and Mark Cordell of Tyne and Wear Archives and Museums have indicated their approval to use the records of various co-operative groups in the north-east of England, their use of which also falls within fair dealing. James Goddard of the Trades Union Congress Library agreed to the use of its collections at London Metropolitan Library. We would like to thank Girton College for permission for the selective use of material from the Barbara Wootton papers.

Every effort has been made to trace copyright holders and to avoid any infringement of copyright. However, we apologise unreservedly to any copyright holder whose permission has been inadvertently overlooked.

Among the individual contributors, Dick Geary would like to thank (apart from Chris), Richard Evans and Klaus Tenfelde, who both stimulated his interest in British and German social history. Matthew Worley thanks Andrew Pearmain, Lucy Robinson, Evan Smith, John Street, Mike Waite and David Wilkinson for their helpful comments on his chapter. John Shepherd is grateful to the late Professor John Postgate, the literary executor of the Lansbury and Postgate papers, deposited in the British Library of Political and Economic Science. The BLPES has also approved direct quotations from all its primary collections under the terms of fair dealing.

Finally, the editors would like to thank the contributors to this volume, who have produced the fruits of their research in honour of Professor Chris Wrigley. Many of them have been his colleagues or students. Others have worked with him on various projects and know and appreciate the contribution he has made to the study of modern British, European and global history.

Abbreviations

AEU	Amalgamated Engineering Union
ALRA	Abortion Law Reform Association
ASE	Amalgamated Society of Engineers
ASSET	Association of Supervisory Staff, Executives and Technicians
ASTMS	Association of Scientific, Technical and Managerial Staff
AWCS	Association of Women Clerks and Secretaries
BLPES	British Library of Political and Economic Science
BMA	British Medical Association
CCCS	Centre for Contemporary Cultural Studies (University of Birmingham)
CND	Campaign for Nuclear Disarmament
CPGB	Communist Party of Great Britain
ELFS	East London Federation of Suffragettes
FPSI	Federation of Progressive Societies and Individuals
FSIF	Friendly Society of Ironfounders
HHM	Holyoake House, Manchester
ILP	Independent Labour Party
IMF	International Monetary Fund
LCC	London County Council
LHASC	Labour History Archive and Study Centre
LRC	Labour Representation Committee
LSC	London Society of Compositors
MFGB	Miners' Federation of Great Britain
MLRC	Marriage Law Reform Committee
MRC	Modern Records Centre
NCA	National Co-operative Archive

NEDC	National Economic Development Council
NF	National Front
NFWW	National Federation of Women Workers
NLC	National Liberal Club
NUC	National Union of Clerks
NUGMW	National Union of General and Municipal Workers
NUM	National Union of Mineworkers
NUR	National Union of Railwaymen
PL	Progressive League
PLAN	Journal of the FPSI and PL, with full name sequentially *Plan: For World Order and Progress* (April 1934–September 1939), *Plan Bulletin* (October 1939–December 1941), *Plan* (January 1942–June 1948), *Plan: For Freedom and Progress* (July 1948–1990), *Plan* (1990–2002) and *Progressive League Newsletter* (2002–05)
PLP	Parliamentary Labour Party
RAR	Rock Against Racism
RMT	National Union of Rail, Maritime and Transport Workers
RPC	Revolutionary Party Committee (of the ILP)
SDF	Social Democratic Federation
SDP	Social Democratic Party
SFC	Socialist Film Council
SL	Socialist League
SPD	Sozialdemokratische Partei Deutschlands (German Social Democratic Party)
SWP	Socialist Workers' Party
TGWU	Transport and General Workers' Union
TNA	The National Archive
TUC	Trades Union Congress
WBCG	Workers' Birth Control Group
WCG	Women's Co-operative Guild
WEC	War Emergency Committee (formerly the War Emergency Workers' National Committee)
WFL	Women's Freedom League
WLL	Women's Labour League
YCL	Young Communist League

Introduction

KEITH LAYBOURN and JOHN SHEPHERD

For more than four decades, Professor Christopher Wrigley, affectionately known as Chris, has been a leading authority on British labour and trade union history, and nineteenth- and twentieth-century British history more generally, with much of his writing in the form of biography. Chris is one of the most influential British historians to have emerged since the Second World War and his ubiquity has earned him the reputation of being almost a Renaissance-like figure in the range and depth of his historical study and understanding of, and influence on, modern British and European history. Chris is a gifted historian, a dedicated researcher, a first-rate lecturer, a caring tutor, a generous and indeed supportive and self-effacing colleague, as well as a close friend of many historians, including those who have contributed to this volume.

Chris was born in 1947 and raised in Woking. He was educated at Goldsworth Primary School, Woking, and Kingston Grammar School before going to the University of East Anglia, where he obtained his BA. In 1968 Chris registered at Birkbeck College, London, where Professor Eric Hobsbawm supervised his doctoral research on Lloyd George and the labour movement with special reference to 1914–22. Chris's choice of this particular interest had developed from his close links with A. J. P. Taylor and with the availability of the Lloyd George papers at the Beaverbrook Library. His pioneering PhD was published in 1976 as *David Lloyd George and the British Labour Movement*.[1]

---

1 Chris Wrigley, *David Lloyd George and the British Labour Movement* (Hassocks: Harvester, 1976).

In 1987, Chris married Margaret (Maggie) Walsh, the distinguished Professor of American Studies at the University of Nottingham, whose work on women and cars in the United States is innovative. Maggie has acted as the locus of Chris's life in recent years. How many times must Chris have said to colleagues and friends 'Don't tell Maggie' when he was eating a particularly calorie-rich bun? Of course, Maggie was not to be deceived and was always aware of Chris's foibles.

Chris began his teaching career at Queen's University Belfast, where he was Lecturer in Economic and Social History between 1971 and 1972. He then moved to Loughborough University as Lecturer in Economic History between 1972 and 1978, subsequently becoming Senior Lecturer in Economic History between 1978 and 1984 and Reader between 1984 and 1988. He became Reader in Economic History at the University of Nottingham in 1988 before being raised to Professor of Modern British History in 1991, holding the post until 2012, when he became an Emeritus Professor. He acted as Head of the School of History and Art History between 2000 and 2003.

Chris has played many roles in connection with his academic career. He was a Team Assessor (History) for Teaching Quality Assessment for the Higher Education Funding Council for England (HEFCE), 1993–94, a member of the History Panel, HEFCE, for the Research Assessment Exercise in 1997 and 2001 (to assess and grade the academic standards of the various higher-education institutions for the distribution of state research money), and a member of the History Panel of the Economic and Social Research Council (ESRC) between 2002 and 2005. Chris has been President of the Historical Association (1996–99), a Vice-President of the Royal Historical Society (1997–2001) and a member of the Council of the Historical Association (1980–2008). He was on the Executive Committee of the Society for the Study of Labour History from 1983 to 2005, and was its Vice-Chairman between 1993 and 1997 and Chair between 1997 and 2001. Since 2012 he has been honoured by being made one of the five Vice-Presidents of the Society. Chris was also awarded an honorary LittD by the University of East Anglia in 1998. He was also editor of *The Historian* (published by the Historical Association) from 1993 to 1998 and since 1998 has been the editor of a history series of books with Ashgate. He was on the Council of the Economic History Society from 1983 to 1992, in 1994, and again from 2000 to 2008, has been on the editorial board of *History Today* since 1992, and has been a member of the History Sub-committee of the Research Assessment Exercise. Chris has also been a trustee of the Sir Richard Arkwright Cromford Mill Trust since 2012, formerly being a member of its Consultative Council between 2011 and 2012. There is, indeed, almost a breathless quality about the range of Chris's academic roles, which he has combined with an active political career.

Chris was a Labour member of Leicestershire County Council between 1981 and 1989, acting as Labour Chief Whip in 1985 and 1986, and leader of the Labour group between 1986 and 1989. He was also a Labour member of Charnwood Borough Council between 1983 and 1987, acting as deputy leader of the Labour group. During this period he contested two general elections, being Labour candidate for Blaby in the 1983 general election, where he gained 6,838 votes (12.2 per cent) for third place, and contesting Loughborough in the 1987 election on behalf of the Labour and Co-operative Party, coming second, with 14,283 votes (24.5 per cent).

Despite his Emeritus status, Chris is still writing up his historical research (as discussed here) and is politically active in his support for the Labour Party and his vehement opposition to recent Conservative governments. On 13 June 2013 he was one of about a hundred historians, from all levels of education, who signed a letter published in *The Independent* condemning the narrow and triumphalist projection of British history then being recommended by Education Secretary Michael Gove and Prime Minister David Cameron, who wished Britain to be presented in the school history curriculum as 'a beacon of liberty for others to emulate', in contravention of the Education Acts of 1996 and 2002, which require a balanced and broadly based system. With others, Chris did not support the idea of such an Anglocentric history which was practically ignoring the role of women and non-white ethnic groups. This reflects Chris's heart-felt interest in the study and practice of gaining and maintaining democratic rights in Britain, and his on-going desire, particularly through the Historical Association, to encourage sixth-formers and undergraduates to appreciate their importance in a Britain where there are growing constraints being imposed upon the agencies of democratic rights and free speech by the Conservative governments of David Cameron and Theresa May.

Chris Wrigley is primarily a judicious empirical historian who has studied and researched, although not exclusively, nineteenth- and twentieth-century British history. His work requires some delineation largely because its broad range resists neat categorisation. He has focused upon the political process in Britain, from the mid-nineteenth century to the present, and reflects this in his interest in political parties, prominent political figures and the lives of those who worked within the parties of labour, the trade unions and other groups that represented the emerging labour movement. In essence, this has meant that he has worked in five main, often overlapping, areas of historical research: the trade unions and industrial relations; the Labour Party, the co-operative movement and the working classes; biographical studies of British political and literary figures; business history; and, finally, the international impact of the First World War and related issues such as the history of the Jewish people.

It was as a historian of British twentieth-century trade union history that Chris first came to academic attention. He has re-examined the way in which the new, more general, trade unionism of the late 1880s and early 1890s emerged and has offered an examination of the way in which British trade unions became more varied, democratic and professional in the twentieth century than their sectional, skilled and amateur predecessors. Indeed, his book *British Trade Unions Since 1933* (2002) examines the corporate bias of trade unions as they increasingly worked with the government and employers after the Second World War.[2] Chris's closely related work on industrial relations has been primarily on Britain between 1875 and the present day, as can be seen in the three volumes he edited of *A History of British Industrial Relations*.[3] He has also edited many other works and essay collections, and written numerous articles, as the select list of his publications published at the end of this volume indicates. These include a Festschrift for Philip Bagwell, edited with John Shepherd, entitled *On the Move: Essays in Labour and Transport History Presented to Philip Bagwell* (1991).[4] This range of work on trade unions and industrial relations has acted as an anchor through much of his multifarious research activities, although he extended his interest into European labour history and industrial relations in his jointly edited book *The Emergence of European Trade Unionism* (2004).[5]

Although Chris has written extensively on the British Labour Party, the co-operative movement and May Days, and co-edited *Britain's Second Labour Government, 1929–31* (2011),[6] much of his work has been presented through the prism of biographical history. This is evident in his *David Lloyd George and the British Labour Movement* (1976), *Lloyd George and the*

---

2   Chris Wrigley, *British Trade Unions Since 1933* (Cambridge: Cambridge University Press, 2002).

3   Chris Wrigley (ed.), *A History of British Industrial Relations 1875–1914* (Hassocks: Harvester, 1982; also University of Illinois Press, 1982); Chris Wrigley (ed.), *A History of British Industrial Relations 1914–1939* (Brighton: Harvester, 1988); Chris Wrigley (ed.), *A History of British Industrial Relations 1939–1979* (Cheltenham: Edward Elgar, 1996).

4   Chris Wrigley and John Shepherd (eds), *On the Move: Essays in Labour and Transport History Presented to Philip Bagwell* (London: The Hambledon Press, 1991).

5   Chris Wrigley, J.-L. Robert and A. Prost (eds), *The Emergence of European Trade Unionism* (Aldershot: Ashgate, 2004).

6   John Shepherd, Jonathan Davis and Chris Wrigley (eds), *Britain's Second Labour Government, 1929–31: A Reappraisal* (Manchester: Manchester University Press, 2011).

Challenge of Labour (1990) and *Arthur Henderson* (1990).[7] In these books his research has focused on the tense relationship between the liberal and progressive politics of Britain and the emergence of the labour movement, and the relations between William Gladstone and David Lloyd George and the emergence of the Labour Party. Chris, in examining the emergence of the Labour Party and trade unions, in all their forms and along all their various avenues in Britain, has suggested that it was part of a powerful radical tradition, whether or not it was driven by a socialist or labourist tradition.

Equally important has been Chris's biographical works on other major figures of the twentieth century. The biography *A. J. P. Taylor: Radical Historian of Europe* (2006) and a baker's dozen of edited collections of Taylor's academic and journalistic work have formed a very substantial part of Chris's corpus of work.[8] Chris was a close friend of A. J. P. Taylor, the 'TV don' and one of the leading historians of diplomatic history, and worked with him in compiling a bibliography of Taylor's work.[9] Chris obtained privileged access to some of Taylor's archive after his death, from which he has traced his ideological evolution from Victorian liberalism to Marxism and then the Labour Party as Taylor, 'the troublemaker', continued his lifelong interest in 'the Truth'. What Chris revealed is that Taylor's anti-German sentiments sprang partly from his reaction to the writings of Lewis Namier, a historian of eighteenth-century British history. Chris argued that Taylor felt that history should be written as a novel, and reflected that Taylor had no faith that history could inform and shape the attitudes of future generations. Chris has also written a book on Winston Churchill (2006) and an article on Churchill and trade unionism.[10] He has also written on literary figures such as Beatrix Potter and William Barnes, the poet.[11]

---

7 Chris Wrigley, *David Lloyd George and the British Labour Movement* (Hassocks: Harvester, 1976); Chris Wrigley, *Lloyd George and the Challenge of Labour* (Brighton: Harvester-Wheatsheaf, 1990); Chris Wrigley, *Arthur Henderson* (Cardiff: University of Wales/GPC, 1990).

8 Chris Wrigley, *A. J. P. Taylor: Radical Historian of Europe* (London: I. B. Tauris, 2006). The other books are listed at the end of this volume in 'A select list of the publications of Chris Wrigley'.

9 Chris Wrigley (ed.), *A. J. P. Taylor: A Complete Bibliography* (Hassocks: Harvester, 1980).

10 Chris Wrigley, *Churchill* (London: Haus, 2006); Chris Wrigley, 'Churchill and the trade unions', *Transactions of the Royal Historical Society*, 6(11) (2001), 273–93.

11 Chris Wrigley, 'Hill Top, Beatrix Potter and a tale of much merchandise', *The Historian*, 52 (1996), pp. 14–17; *William Barnes: The Dorset Poet* (Wimborne: Dovecote Press, 1984); Chris Wrigley, William Barnes and rural Dorset', in B. Jones (ed.), *William*

Interspersed with the above work has been Chris's interest in business history and a research interest in the British Industrial Revolution, as well as his work as a trustee in connection with Cromford Mills, where he has organised conferences and publications. Chris has written extensively on the Ministry of Munitions, the wool and coal industries and, more recently, on the tobacco industry and the First World War. He has also worked on studies of the international economy, notably based upon an understanding of the First Word War. Chris's range of interest and expertise is clearly wide and ever-expanding, as he has recently moved his research interest to the history of the British coal industry since the early 1980s, and a study of mid-twentieth-century rural communities. The depth, width and indeed iconoclastic nature of his work, amply illustrated in the select publication list at the end of this volume, have greatly shaped the way in which modern British history has been interpreted. The ubiquitous nature of Chris's work makes it difficult to encompass all of his research interests into one volume of essays. However, since so much of his work has been about working people, socialism and trade unionism, this collection of essays has been gathered together under the title *Labour and Working-Class Lives: Essays to Celebrate the Life and Work of Chris Wrigley.*

The purpose of this collection is to reflect upon the wide range of Chris Wrigley's research and publications over the years, in the study of the various aspects of British labour history, his dominant interest. These essays have been written by some of the leading scholars of labour history. There is no single defining theme but a set of themes revolving around the British labour movement and the lives of those connected with it. There is biography, one of Chris's main interests, in the shape of George Howell and Herbert Gladstone, both of whom helped determine the way in which the labour movement would develop in the mid- and late nineteenth century, and the early twentieth century – Gladstone through his attempts to stem or divert the growth of the Labour Party. There is trade union history. There is the socialist and progressive reaction to the second Labour government's demise in 1931, through the studies of the Independent Labour Party and the Progressive League. There are essays on various aspects of working-class lives and cultures. These raise a number of points and various questions: Was British working-class culture less organised than that in Germany? How did the world of female clerkship develop? Did the trade union relationship sustain the growth of Labour? How did the next generation of the Lansbury family, after George Lansbury, adapt

---

Barnes 1801–1886: A Handbook (Dorchester: William Barnes Society, 1986), pp. 25–8; Chris Wrigley, 'William Barnes: paternalism and nineteenth century socialism', *Somerset and Dorset Notes and Queries*, 32(323) (March 1986), 483–6.

to the new position of Labour in the early twentieth century? And, finally, must Labour lose?

Malcolm Chase's essay on George Howell stems from Chris's interest in the pre-history of British trade unionism and examines different interpretations of the formation and emergence of trade unions. Howell, in his various writings, argued for the accepted view of the mid-nineteenth century that trade unions had their origin in Anglo-Saxon rights and in the emergence of the medieval guilds, which distinguished between skilled and unskilled workers. However, the Webbs saw them emerge somewhere around the beginning of the eighteenth century and, in setting up the new orthodoxy of the late nineteenth century and the early twentieth century, the Webbs influenced a historiography and explanation which Malcolm Chase, among others, now challenges, on the basis of recent research which has revealed the legacy of the guilds.

Kenneth Brown's examination of the appointment of Herbert Gladstone as Liberal Chief Whip in 1899 reflects Chris's interest in political figures connected with progressivism and the labour movement. Herbert Gladstone was much denigrated by his contemporaries, such as Lloyd George, as a lightweight figure, a dwarf in politics very much in the shadow of his famous father. However, Kenneth Brown reveals that others have recognised Gladstone's qualities and that he was the right person to be Liberal Chief Whip in 1899, when the Liberal Party was, as he was, in something of a political wilderness. Faced with a divided Liberal Party, with declining income, as well as his own family responsibilities, Gladstone emerges as the right person to revive Liberal fortunes – especially as he was one of the few prominent Liberal politicians of the 1890s to recognise the importance of independent labour representation in Parliament. Ultimately, of course, he was an important figure in brokering in 1903 a secret parliamentary pact with Ramsay MacDonald, of the Labour Representation Committee, which paved the way for Labour to win twenty-nine, soon to be thirty, parliamentary seats and the revival of the Liberals to 400 seats in 1906. This might have led the Liberal Party to accept a cuckoo in the nest but the action seemed right at the time.

Joan Allen also focuses here upon the labour alliance but through the initiative of the co-operative movement to form the Co-operative Party in 1917, with its obvious links with Labour that were formalised in the 1920s. While this has often been seen by historians, such as G. D. H. Cole, as an immediate reaction to conditions in the first World War and lacking in class consciousness in any real sense, Joan Allen sees it much more as a long-term product of the radicalisation of a membership which was gradually unwinding its links with liberalism, much along the lines suggested by Sidney Pollard (see chapter 3). Examining the branches of the

Co-operative Party in the north-east of England, she argues that while there might have been some disagreement about establishing a political party for the co-operative movement, and difficulties with the local constitutions of co-operatives, which were not geared to providing money for political activities, it is clear that was, for a long time, the direction that co-operative societies in the north-east were drifting towards in a region where working-class solidarity always counted. There was not the diffidence towards political action and class consciousness in the co-operative movement which some writers have suggested.

Noel Whiteside, reflecting upon Chris's interest in industrial relations, is concerned with the way in which state insurance for the unemployed, under the 1911 National Insurance Act, forced the trade unions to make adjustments to their visions of how they treated the unemployed. Before the 1911 Act there was immense diversity and variation in how the trade unions supported their members and controlled the labour market through the provision of benefits for the unemployed. However, the 1911 Act imposed a rigidity on unemployment, by imposing a limit on benefits to 15 weeks per year, with those falling out of benefit being unfortunate rather than long-term unemployed. Although the new state scheme was in many instances run by trade unions, their previous flexibility in providing benefits to a more liberally defined unemployed, and in allowing local branch variation, was replaced by the state's insistence on uniformity and centralisation.

Continuing with the subject of trade unionism, Andrew Thorpe examines the long-established and continuing relationship between the trade unions and the Labour Party. He argues that while both organisations have changed over the years, and despite the contentious nature of the alliance, the relationship has proved enduring and profitable because it has made them stronger together than apart. In particular, he examines the origins of this relationship, how it was introduced and how it has intruded into the policy, membership, party structure and parliamentary leadership of the Labour Party. Only one of Labour's six Prime Ministers, James Callaghan, has come from a trade union background but the others, often coming from a socialist background, have had to come, as Callaghan did, to an arrangement with the trade union movement within the context of what Lewis Minkin referred to as a contentious alliance (see chapter 5).

The essay by Keith Laybourn deals with one of the major turning points in inter-war British labour politics, the disaffiliation of the Independent Labour Party (ILP) from the Labour Party in 1932. He suggests that this was a result of the tensions that had been building up since the beginning of the inter-war years, rather not simply a product of a last-minute campaign by prominent and leading members of the ILP driven by the concern to speed up the socialist revolution. They might have felt that a workers' revolution was required to replace the Labour Party approach of administering capitalism and seeking its reform but this was not a view held by most in the Labour Party, or possibly even the majority of ILP membership in 1932, most of whom were ready to accept conventional and disciplined politics. In the end, however, petulance, rather than sensible decision making, drove the ILP out of the Labour Party in a brief moment when a minority of disaffiliationists gained control of the ILP.

The theme of labour's fragmentation in the 1930s is partly continued by Janet Shepherd in her study of the Progressive League, which was first formed in 1932 by progressives, socialists and liberals, such as Cyril Joad, Aldous Huxley, Bertrand Russell and H. G. Wells. Relatively little-known, and rising to a membership of only 600 at its height, the Progressive League was primarily concerned to promote the cause of sexual revolution in Britain in the mid-twentieth century, raising issues such as birth control, eugenics, abortion reform, marriage reform, the legalisation of homosexuality and the reform of the Obscenity Acts. Committed to the idea that its supporters should support measures that would improve the happiness of all mankind, it also advocated the individualist view that all those who supported it should make their own judgements about what was right. Disunity was often evident, but Janet Shepherd believes that it represented more than simply voices in the wilderness. She considers that the League contributed significantly to the debates, particularly in the 1950s, about marriage, homosexuality, abortion and what constituted obscenity, many of which came to some type of more progressive conclusion in the 1960s. The League's willingness to challenge sexual conventions, and willingness to act as Daniel in the lion's den, meant that it did exert some influence.

Turning to Chris Wrigley's interest in labour lives, Dick Geary, in a far-ranging essay, contrasts the lives of the British and German working classes in the late nineteenth and early twentieth centuries. He suggests the notion that there were marked differences between the two. Britain emerges as a more liberal society, in which in religion, societies and leisure brought the working classes and the middle classes close together. The standard of living of the British working class was higher than the German, their housing provision better – encouraging domesticity – and their absorption of the growing leisure industry more marked. In contrast, the German state was far more interventionist and presided over workers living in greatly overcrowded tenements, in a low-wage economy in which consumption taxes, in the absence of an effective income tax, bore deeply upon them. In this climate, the German Social Democratic Party (SDP) throve and produced its own range of independent, rather than commercially run, leisure activities. Although seriously challenged by the Catholic Church and employers, the SDP became much more class conscious. Driven from a home life, workers aired their grievances in the pubs, which Karl Kautsky referred to as 'the solitary bulwark of the proletarian's freedom' (see chapter 8). Dick Geary contrasts the class-conscious tension in Germany against the more liberal, less class-conscious culture of Britain.

Focusing upon one group of workers, Nicole Robertson deals with the Association of Women Clerks and Secretaries (AWCS), which emerged in 1912 from earlier roots to become an all-female trade union representing lower-middle-class female clerks. Concentrating upon the First World War and the immediate post-war years, she establishes that female clerkship was already well established before the Great War, that the AWCS fought against unemployment and the inequalities of pay but gradually became much more involved in the wider fight for equality and justice for women, and was part of a feminist movement which did not, as many writers have suggested, fall away during the First World War and after. Above all, Nicole Robertson's work challenges the view that there was a lack of collective identity and action among the lower middle classes in early-twentieth-century Britain.

George Lansbury, the leader of the Labour Party from 1932 to 1935, and his wife Bessie had twelve children, ten of whom survived into adulthood and many of whom played a significant role in the history of the British labour movement in the early and mid-twentieth century. This Lansbury generation is the focus of the essay by John Shepherd, whose monumental study of the life and political career of George Lansbury is well known and highly respected. In the early 1920s, members of the Lansbury family for a time became members of the Communist Party of Great Britain – a factor that weighed against their father's inclusion in Ramsay MacDonald's first Labour Cabinet, in 1924. Others became important pioneers in various campaigns in working-class politics, including women's enfranchisement, birth control and the reform of abortion law. Altogether, they created something of a memorable Lansbury Labour dynasty in the East End of London, as well as in national political life. Nevertheless, what emerges from John Shepherd's detailed and meticulous work is that, although the influence of this Lansbury generation was noteworthy in Labour politics, they never reached the political heights of their popular father. Like Herbert Gladstone, the subject of an earlier essay, they played a very important role but in the shadow of their father's dominating presence.

Matthew Worley's interests in the Communist Party of Great Britain (CPGB) and popular music were greatly stimulated by Chris Wrigley's well known interest in popular music and the fact that Chris supervised him for his PhD on British communism. Matthew Worley's essay offers a fascinating insight into how the CPGB and the Young Communist League sought to engage with punk music at a time when the party was losing membership rapidly, in the decade or so before the collapse of communism in Eastern Europe and the Soviet Union. Stimulated by the writings of Martin Jacques, and other prominent members of the CPGB, the attempt to embrace the anti-commercial music establishment of the emerging youth culture in the 1970s led to serious debate within the CPGB between those still committed to mass class conflict based upon industrial struggle as a basis of political consciousness (economism) and those who sought to enact the 'cultural turn', by embracing gender and race as well as class. The CPGB failed in its efforts, and was rather less successful than the Socialist Workers' Party with its 'Rock Against Racism' campaign, but at least there was a vibrancy of campaigning within a declining organisation which did make an impact upon subsequent interpretations of punk rock and youth culture.

Finally, returning to the theme of Labour disunity, Kevin Jefferys addresses the long-lasting question 'Must Labour lose?' This has been an intriguing political question ever since it was first posed in 1960 by Mark Abrams and Richard Rose (see chapter 12). Examining the post-war record of the Labour Party, alongside that of the Conservative Party, Kevin Jefferys questions the inevitability of Labour's decline through a detailed examination of the political results since 1945. Instead of Labour's inevitable decline, he suggests that there is a pattern to the Labour Party's successes and defeats – they have been conditioned by the economic circumstances, the performance of the Conservative Party and the leadership of the Labour Party. In the end, he argues that Labour may not always lose but that, given the gap between the opinion about the leadership in the party and the electorate in the country, it may be some time before Labour regains power.

It has been said that, of all viable literary genres, the Festschrift is the most corpse-like, often being little more than a mere ritual valediction, the scholars' equivalent of the cut-glass decanters and carriage clocks which once formalised retirements in other professions, whereby the recipient is eased out of the grove of academe to the golf course and the rose garden. All too often, such works are as dull and as lifeless as a marble monument, being too impersonal either to satisfy or to stimulate. However, it is hoped that this volume has avoided most of the dangers inherent in this genre and is a worthy testimony to the immensely lively and productive work of Chris Wrigley. There are two grounds for such hope. First, it is now several years since Chris's retirement and there has been time to reflect upon his contribution to the study of history. Secondly, the essays have been written by a varied body of long-established historians intermingled with a group of people whom grant-awarding bodies refer to euphemistically as 'mid-career historians', some of whom have been Chris's PhD students, offering the kernel of their research. Therefore, as might be expected, these essays come from the top drawer.

Finally, it is apparent from Chris's on-going list of publications that he is neither grizzled nor confined to his rose garden or the golf course, although prone to exotic holidays from which fly an impressive array of postcards. Given his continued research, writing and supervision, and his other historical interests at Cromford Mills, the idea of 'retirement', as far as Chris is concerned, is a bit of a misnomer. Everyone connected with the production of this book joins together in hoping that Chris's 'semi-retirement' lasts for many more years. Meanwhile, we offer these essays to him with gratitude, respect and, above all, deep affection.

1

George Howell, the Webbs and the political culture of early labour history

MALCOLM CHASE

George Howell (1833–1910) was the epitome of a nineteenth-century auto-didact, having received an indifferent education, largely part-time, that ended when he was twelve. Successively a ploughboy, apprentice shoe-maker and from the age of twenty-two a bricklayer, he doggedly built a career in labour movement politics, first achieving public prominence as Secretary of the London Trades' Council in 1861–62. He established a reputation as an exceptionally energetic administrator while the Secretary (1865–69) of the Reform League. Howell was the League's only paid official. Subsequently he became Secretary of the Parliamentary Com-mittee of the Trades Union Congress (1871–75), in which capacity he was closely involved in discussions around the 1871 and 1876 Trade Union Acts. After three attempts to be elected to Parliament, he was finally suc-cessful for the north-east division of Bethnal Green in 1885, a seat he held as a 'Lib–Lab' for a decade.

His career was not without controversy, marked out almost from the start as politically astute but cautious and over-respectful of middle-class Liberalism. In itself that might not have fatally corroded his reputation; but historians, not least his only biographer, Fred Leventhal, have also emphasised that his was a career built on 'self-interest and diligence', never outgrowing 'the cautious radicalism of his early years'.[1] Howell's avowed

---

1 F. M. Leventhal, 'Howell, George (1833–1910)', in Joyce Bellamy and John Saville (eds), *Dictionary of Labour Biography, Volume II* (London: Macmillan, 1974), pp. 187–95 (193); F. M. Leventhal, *Respectable Radical: George Howell and Victorian Working Class Politics* (London: Weidenfeld & Nicolson, 1971), p. 217; F. M. Leventhal, 'Howell, George (1833–1910)', *Oxford Dictionary of National Biography* (Oxford: Oxford University Press,

stance as an 'Advanced Liberal' (the self-description he gave to *Dod's Parliamentary Companion* on arriving at Westminster) allegedly made him an anachronism, out of step with a new generation of working-class radicals, advancing under Fabian tutelage towards socialism.[2] The best that the Webbs ever wrote of him was that he was an expert manipulator.[3] Beatrice and Sidney's vicar-apostolic, Royden Harrison, advanced the case against Howell further in the 1960s, arguing that Howell disregarded class loyalty and personal probity in pursuit of his political career.[4] There Howell's reputation largely rests, although a few commentators have been less condemnatory.[5] It is not the purpose of this chapter to unpick the case against, or to rehabilitate, Howell. Instead, it examines George Howell's historical writings and considers how far these reflected his political views and shaped his contemporary reputation. The chapter concludes by pondering what light their reception throws upon the subsequent historiography of labour.

Briefly, George Howell published three substantial historical works, all with leading publishers. *The Conflicts of Capital and Labour, Historically and Economically Considered, being a review of the Trade Unions of Great Britain, showing their origin, progress, constitution, and objects in their political, social economical and industrial aspects*, was published by Chatto & Windus in 1878. In 1891, midway through his parliamentary career, *Trade Unionism New and Old* was issued by Methuen. Finally, in retirement Howell wrote the two-volume *Labour Legislation, Labour Movements and Labour Leaders*, published by Fisher Unwin in 1902. Although a prolific author, George Howell wrote only two other volumes, both legal textbooks, one of which was co-authored.[6] This suggests that Howell

---

2004; online edition, January 2012, at http://o-www.oxforddnb.com.wam.leeds.ac.uk/view/article/34025, accessed 13 November 2015).

2 Michael Stenton and Stenton Lees (eds), *Who's Who of British Members of Parliament, Volume II: 1886–1918* (Hassocks: Harvester, 1978), p. 182.

3 Sidney Webb and Beatrice Webb, *The History of Trade Unionism* (London: Chiswick Press, 1894), p. 473.

4 Royden Harrison, *Before the Socialists* (London: RKP, 1965), especially pp. 143–6 and 202–5. See also the same author's 'Practical, capable men', *New Reasoner*, 6 (autumn 1958), 105–19, especially 111–15.

5 A. D. Bell, 'Administration and finance of the Reform League, 1865–67', *International Review of Social History*, 10 (1965), 385–409, defends Howell from Harrison's charges, insisting that 'no evidence in the [Reform] League records suggests dishonesty on Howell's part' (p. 398). Mark Curthoys, *Governments, Labour, and the Law in Mid-Victorian Britain: The Trade Union Legislation of the 1870s* (Oxford: Clarendon, 2004), pp. 8–10, 95–6, 157–9.

6 George Howell, *A Handy-Book of the Labour Laws … With introductions, notes and … forms, for the use of workmen* (London: Macmillan, 1876); Herman Cohen and George

regarded his work as a historian as particularly significant. Reinforcing that sense, his prolific writing for serial publication included a preponderance of historical work, including 'A history of factory legislation' and 'A century of social and industrial legislation'.[7] Howell was also the first biographer of Ernest Jones, the leader of the Chartist movement in its later stages and subsequently a prominent radical liberal, work that was serialised in 1898 by the *Newcastle Weekly Chronicle*. In addition, he wrote a substantial (but unfinished at his death) history of the London Working Men's Association.[8]

The extent of Howell's emotional investment in his historical writing is evident in his diaries and unpublished autobiography. He repeatedly fussed over the progress of each project, negotiations with publishers, and reactions to his work once published. To give just one example: his diary for the months February–May 1902 charts the progress of *Labour Legislation*, from the moment the advanced copy arrived from the printer ('delivered by post at 10^{40}' he recorded in a diary entry written twenty minutes later on 22 February). Howell dissected each review, for example from the *Daily Chronicle* (which claimed he misspelled 'Tolpuddle'), the *Atheneum* ('good, but just a little carping'), the *Daily News* ('excellent in tone and treatment, discriminating, yet most complimentary') and the *Manchester Guardian* ('by an ignorant, and evidently spiteful, writer. I think I could name him – a low vulgar brute – has always been'). That October, looking back on the sixty reviews published so far, Howell noted with quiet hyperbole: 'It has been, I think, the best reviewed book of the century'.[9]

Labour Legislation was no ephemeral publication, but comprised over 500 pages, in two volumes. It had been commissioned by Fisher Unwin, one of the leading serious publishers of Edwardian England, for 'The Reformer's Bookshelf', a series that included Samuel Morley's *Life of*

Howell, *Trade Union Law and Cases: A Text Book Relating to Trade Unions and to Labour* (London: Sweet & Maxwell, 1901).

7 Howell Collection (hereafter HC), Bishopsgate Institute, London, 6/69, 'A history of factory legislation' (cuttings from *Social Notes*, 20 May–30 June 1881); HC 6/134, 'A century of social and industrial legislation' (assembled from the Co-operative Wholesale Society *Annual*, 1894); see also HC 6/146, 'Labour legislation during the queen's reign' (unattributed press cuttings, 1897).

8 HC 10/3/1, bound volume of cuttings, 'Ernest Jones, the Chartist: poet and orator, patriot and politician', from the *Newcastle Weekly Chronicle*, January–October 1898. *A History of the Working Men's Association from 1836 to 1850* (Newcastle upon Tyne: Graham, [1970]), assembled by D. J. Rowe from the uncompleted manuscript and from some of Howell's articles in *Reynolds's Newspaper*.

9 HC 5/1/5, Autobiography, Volume E, section L, entries for 22 February, and 3, 16 and 23 March 1902, and entry for 'natal year Oct 5th 1901 to Oct 5th 1902'.

Cobden and volumes by L. T. Hobhouse and H. W. Massingham (editor of *The Statesman*). A second edition was issued in 1905. Howell's earlier books were similarly weighty: *Trade Unionism New and Old* had been commissioned by Methuen to launch its 'Social Questions of Today' series (subsequent contributors included J. A. Hobson and G. J. Holyoake). *The Conflicts of Capital and Labour* appeared under the imprint of Chatto & Windus, a prestigious house whose reputation rested mainly on literary works (including such canonical Victorian authors as W. S. Gilbert, Ouida, Algernon Swinburne and Wilkie Collins). A further indication of contemporary perceptions of Howell as an authoritative historian was unwittingly provided by Beatrice Webb herself, in relating how, while writing *The History of Trade Unionism*, she and Sidney visited the Bodleian Library in search of source material. They were received by Bodley's librarian himself, 'with a discourtesy, not to say downright rudeness.... He, finally, repelled our enquiries with the remark that we should find all we required in Howell's *Conflicts of Capital and Labour*!'[10]

What might it have been about Howell's 1878 book that so impressed Bodley's librarian? *Conflicts* was not the 'exceedingly turgid' commercial disaster Leventhal supposed.[11] It was a treatment of workers' organisations, commencing with the argument that they first emerged in Anglo-Saxon England as the growing complexity of urban societies rendered family and kinship (hitherto 'the natural foundation of all social relations') no longer an effective regulator of behaviour. Called frith-guilds, they established 'a mutual responsibility as close as that of the old, and a protection even more complete and thorough'.[12] From this, initially pagan, beginning emerged the religious, social and craft guilds of the Middle Ages. From the fifteenth century, craft guilds (Howell argued) were subject to growing internal stress. This he ascribed to three linked processes: first, the escalating marketisation of trade; second, the growing tendency for journeymen to be excluded from the internal governance of their guild; and third, journeymen's diminishing opportunity to become masters on their own account. In consequence, 'special fraternities' of journeymen began to emerge. 'The origin of the modern trade unions from the journeymen fraternities may be inferred from many peculiar circumstances, as well

---

10 Beatrice Webb, *Our Partnership* (eds Barbara Drake and Margaret Cole) (London: Longmans, 1948), p. 87.

11 Leventhal, *Respectable Radical*, p. 196.

12 George Howell, *The Conflicts of Capital and Labour, Historically and Economically Considered, being a review of the Trade Unions of Great Britain, showing their origin, progress, constitution, and objects in their political, social economical and industrial aspects* (London: Chatto & Windus, 1878), pp. 3–4.

as the striking similarity of many of their features in several important respects.' These 'peculiar circumstances', argued Howell, derived primarily from the decay of apprenticeship and the efforts of the state to arrest apprenticeship's decline, notably by the Statute of Artificers of 1563 ('the 5th of Elizabeth'). The 'striking similarity' was most obvious in the language and ritual of guilds and the early trade societies. Howell was unequivocal: trade unions were 'successors to the old gilds' and 'modern trade-unionism cannot be properly understood or rightly appreciated except by careful study of their early prototypes'.[13]

He would later argue in the fullest statement of his political philosophy that unions encapsulated the principle that 'regulation originated with the *governed* rather than with the governors…. [E]arlier interference with labour was *by mutual consent and arrangement* in the old guilds'.[14] Indeed, in the history of labour, the 'two great forces … constantly at work, mostly at variance' had been 'legislation and associative effort. The latter is perhaps the older of the two', Howell surmised.[15] Trade unions constituted the best compromise between anarchy and coercion. As John Saville long-ago summarised Howell's stance: 'society has only the choice between freedom of contract and coercive status, and any infringement of the former can only lead to the extension of the latter'.[16] Howell's historical perspective concerning the antiquity of associational activity was a riposte to the prevalent view that English common law upheld freedom of trade as a central and inherent principle. This, for example, was the argument forcibly made by Sir William Erle, the judge who had presided over the notorious Wolverhampton tin-plate workers' strike case in 1851 (ruling that non-violent tactics, peaceful picketing included, constituted a criminal conspiracy to restrain trade) and who also controversially chaired the 1868 Royal Commission on Trades Unions.[17]

In the second and subsequent parts of *Conflicts*, Howell traced the shifting allegiances of the state as it sought initially (in the interests of public order) to protect journeymen but then, increasingly, to uphold the

---

13 Howell, *Conflicts*, pp. 9–105, quotations from pp. 9, 73 and 79.

14 George Howell, 'Liberty for labour', in Thomas Mackay (ed.), *A Plea for Liberty: An Argument Against Socialism and Socialistic Legislation* (Oxford: Oxford University Press, 1891), pp. 109, 111 (present author's emphases).

15 Quotation from HC 6/152, 'Industrial progress by legislation and association', [unpublished?] MS (1900).

16 John Saville, 'Unions and free labour: the background to the Taff Vale decision', in Asa Briggs and John Saville (eds), *Essays in Labour History* (London: Macmillan, 1960), p. 320.

17 William Erle, *The Law Relating to Trade Unions* (London: Macmillan, 1869), pp. 1–55, 58–9, 73, 76–7; Curthoys, *Governments, Labour, and the Law*, pp. 30–1, 83–5, 101–2.

freedom of employers to engage whatever workers they wished for the lowest wages possible. Howell analysed the impact of this shift on various occupations, grouping them into three categories: 'trades subject to the Statute 5th of Elizabeth' (especially woollen industry workers, hatters, ship-wrights and tailors); 'trades incorporated by charter' (hosiery and cutlery); and 'trades not under legal restrictions' (principally calico, silk and cotton). Howell then traced the evolution of statute law regarding the combination of workers, culminating 'after a contest of nearly one hundred years' in the final repeal of the 5th of Elizabeth in 1814. 'Political economists assert that labour is a commodity, and that it is governed by natural laws like any other commodity', Howell commented at this juncture, but 'in all other cases the price of commodities is fixed by the seller, not the buyer; why is this refused in the case of labour?'[18]

The central theme of *The Conflicts of Capital and Labour, Historically and Economically Considered* was the uneven and heavily contested evolution of common law and parliamentary statute, as they impacted on workers' capacity to determine the price of their labour: 'From 1349, the date of the Statute of Labourers, to 1824 [the repeal of the Combination Acts], a period of 475 years, all legislation affecting labour was in its essential character in restraint of freedom of contract, labour being fettered by regulation and the labourer denied the rights of association'. Furthermore, the 1824 legislation offered only brief respite. An amending act the following year meant that for a further half-century, trade unions operated in a legal penumbra. As Justice Erle's judgement in the 1851 Wolverhampton tin-plate workers' case showed, trade union officers and members remained vulnerable to 'persecutions' (Howell's term): six men had been sent to prison on that occasion, their sentences upheld on appeal. The contemporary message was clear: any labour legislation that rested on coercion could be shown to rest on principles that had not only failed in the past but which had been productive only of social tension and antagonism:

> Repressive laws are ineffectual, as well as dangerous and oppressive; their effect is demoralising on the mind; men's ideas of right and wrong become confounded, until a sense of injustice brings about the worst evils of violence, even to ferocity.[19]

In addition to this central thesis, Howell interweaved into *Conflicts* separate chapter-length historical treatments of apprenticeship and

---

18 Howell, *Conflicts*, p. 113.
19 HC 6/146, 'Legislation during the queen's reign' (1897), fol. 1, unattributed press cutting dated 25 May 1897; Howell, *Conflicts*, pp. 141 and 146.

technical education, piecework, hours of work and overtime, the federation of trade unions, conciliation and arbitration, co-operation and industrial partnership and friendly societies. His subsequent books on labour history refined and extended his historicised understanding of why trade unions had emerged; but mainly they concentrated on updating and filling out the depiction and analysis of the contemporary labour movement. The historical section of the 1891 *Trade Unionism New and Old* was shorter than *The Conflicts of Capital and Labour*, the bulk of the later work being devoted to analysing the new unionism of the 1880s. In *Labour Legislation* (1901) the historical treatment was broadened to depict social history more generally, while at the same time incorporating personal reminiscences by the author. Unlike the rest of his historical output, however, *Labour Legislation*'s two volumes were unreferenced and carried no bibliography. This was unfortunate for Howell's posthumous reputation, since the book was widely regarded, then and later, as a crowning achievement in the career of its almost septuagenarian author.

Howell's concept of trade unions 'as successors to the old gilds' is open to criticism on a number of grounds. He exaggerated the extent to which economic activity in medieval and early modern towns was subject to guild control. His account was largely unmindful of the mining and metals industries; and he asserted, rather than provided firm evidence for, the continuity of guilds and unions. However, his history was neither haphazardly assembled nor a romantic story of labour's resistance to capital. Throughout the first part of *Conflicts*, and in its introduction and bibliography, Howell warmly acknowledged as the source for his evidence and argument an 1870 publication of the Early English Text Society on the early English guilds.[20] He was particularly indebted to an essay, 'On the history and development of gilds, and the origin of trade unions', contributed to the volume by the German political economist Lujo Brentano, based on extensive research undertaken by the latter in Britain in 1868–69. Brentano was a widely acknowledged writer on trade unionism, in both Britain and Germany, and is an author in whom there has been a revival

---

20 [Joshua] Toulmin Smith (ed.), *English Gilds. The Original Ordinances of more than One hundred Early English Gilds ... from Original MSS. of the Fourteenth and Fifteenth Centuries. Edited, with notes, by the late Toulmin Smith ... with an Introduction and Glossary, &c., by his daughter Lucy Toulmin Smith. And a Preliminary Essay in Five Parts, on the History and Development of Gilds, by Lujo Brentano* (London: Trübner, for the Early English Text Society, 1870). Brentano's essay was also issued as a free-standing pamphlet, *On the History and Development of Gilds, and the Origin of Trade-Unions* (London: Trübner, 1870).

of interest in recent years.[21] A historicist, Brentano believed that the laws operating in and on society were to be discovered by historical investigation. His key German-language work on trade unionism (which developed a case study of the British experience at its heart) refers explicitly to a 'historical law, that the dissolution of an old order will in the absence of constraint at all times necessarily call forth the same organization in the form of guilds among the victims of the consequent disorganisation'.[22] Trade unions, Brentano concluded were '[i]n their origins and functions the guilds of the present day. Like the former guilds English trade unions are no more than organizations of self-help by those with interests in common, intervening whenever State action fails to meet their common needs either totally or in part'.[23]

The attractions of this line of argument for Howell is a point to which this study will presently return. Howell freely recognised, however, that at a number of points Brentano's research was refuted in the editorial apparatus supporting the reprinted texts, prefacing which the German's essay had appeared. The editor in question was Joshua Toulmin Smith, a leading proponent of the campaign against state centralisation in Victorian Britain. Toulmin Smith saw in Anglo-Saxon England the fount of English liberties, and 'local Self-Government' as a force to keep in check the incursion of the state upon those liberties.[24] On these points of debate Howell, while conceding his debt to Brentano, generally preferred Smith's inter-

---

21 E. P. Hennock, 'Lessons from England: Lujo Brentano on British trade unionism', *German History*, 11(2) (April 1993), 141–60. See also James J. Sheehan, *The Career of Lujo Brentano: A Study of Liberalism and Social Reform in Imperial Germany* (Chicago, IL: Chicago University Press, 1966); Lawrence Goldman, 'Civil society in nineteenth-century Britain and Germany: J. M. Ludlow, Lujo Brentano, and the labour question', in José Harris (ed.), *Civil Society in British History: Ideas, Identities, Institutions* (Oxford: Oxford University Press, 2005); and James Thompson, 'The reception of Lujo Brentano's thought in Britain, 1870–1910', unpublished paper, University of Bristol archive depository at http://rose.bris.ac.uk/dspace/handle/1983/915 (accessed 3 May 2009).

22 Lujo Brentano, *Die Arbeitergilden der Gegenwart* (Leipzig, 1872), vol. 2, p. 315, translated and quoted by Hennock, 'Lessons from England', p. 149.

23 Brentano, *Arbeitergilden*, vol. 2, p. 326, translated and quoted by Hennock, 'Lessons from England', p. 150.

24 Joshua Toulmin Smith, *Local Self-Government Un-mystified. A vindication of common sense, human nature, and practical improvement, against the manifesto of centralism put forth at the Social Science Association* (London: Stanford, 1857), p. 37. See also O. Anderson, 'The political uses of history in mid nineteenth-century England', *Past and Present*, 30 (1967), 87–99; and O. Anderson, 'Smith, Joshua Toulmin (1816–1869)', *Oxford Dictionary of National Biography* (Oxford: Oxford University Press, 2004; online edition 3 May 2009, at http://o-www.oxforddnb.com.wam.leeds.ac.uk/view/article/25873, accessed 13 November 2015).

pretation. The extent to which the distinctive anti-centralisation doctrine propounded by Toulmin Smith influenced Howell is beyond the scope of the present study. However, it can only have intensified Howell's advanced anti-statist liberalism; as he commented in 1891, 'according to the new gospel of socialism ... manhood is to be crushed out of humanity, and the State is to regulate the desires, attainments, and needs of all, individually and in concrete'.[25]

This nuanced use of Brentano was overlooked by the Webbs, who, in their *History of Trade Unionism*, dismissed George Howell as a historian of pre-industrial labour, on the grounds that his work was 'a close paraphrase' of Brentano's essay, 'practically the whole of which appears, often in the same words, as Mr. Howell's own'. In the Webbs' opinion, the only value of Howell's work lay in it being a 'thoroughly practical exposition of the Trade Unionism of his own school and time'. The implication was clear: as a historical study it was negligible. More recently, in the official biography of the Webbs, Howell's historical efforts were swatted aside as 'simply a plagiarism from Brentano'.[26]

The status of Howell's research profoundly mattered to the Webbs. Although his works were included in the bibliography of their 1894 *History of Trade Unionism*, they were in a real sense a significant rival to the Webbs' study. First, not only was *Conflicts* the most substantial study of trade union history to have appeared prior to their own, but it too bore the authority of emanating from within the labour movement. Second, Howell's use of Brentano reinforced a critical point of interpretational difference. The Webbs sought to demarcate trade unions from guilds, ideologically and chronologically. In their view, the Industrial Revolution and the class society it engendered constituted a profound discontinuity with all that had gone before: 'We assert, indeed, with confidence that in no case did any Trade Union in the United Kingdom arise, either directly or indirectly, by descent, from a Craft Guild'.[27] Furthermore, Sidney and Beatrice Webb rested their definition of 'trade union' on the principle of permanency – that is to say, trades combinations and organisations of an earlier period had little if any claim on the attention of the labour historian. Institutional continuity through to contemporary trade unionism was crucial. These are important claims, the significance of which needs to be examined.

---

25 Howell, 'Liberty for labour', p. 139; see also Howell, *Conflicts*, p. ix.
26 Webb and Webb, *History*, pp. x and 12; Royden J. Harrison, *The Life and Times of Sidney and Beatrice Webb, 1858–1905: The Formative Years* (Basingstoke: Palgrave, 2000), pp. 217–18.
27 Webb and Webb, *History*, p. 14.

Howell, like Brentano before him, never went so far as to state that there was a direct or, as it were, 'genetic' descent linking trade unions and guilds. In this respect he stopped well short of George Unwin, writing in the early 1900s, as well as certain modern historians of trade unionism (E. P. Thompson and the present author, for example), who have argued that clear examples of continuity can be identified.[28] Long before the Webbs set enduring parameters for subsequent trade union history with their insistence upon the principle of permanency, Howell himself had been clear that early trade unions were 'temporary' and that 'the first permanent trade union' was the Brief Institution, an organisation linking textile workers in the West Country and Yorkshire's West Riding at the turn of the eighteenth century.[29]

It is not the purpose of this chapter to adjudicate between the schools of thought of Beatrice and Sidney Webb, and Lujo Brentano and George Howell in the matter of historical accuracy. It is necessary, however, to register why this difference mattered. Howell, following Toulmin Smith and the Anti-Centralisation Union, which he had founded, was subscribing to a refinement of the long-established popular notion of the Norman yoke – a belief that a wide range of fundamental liberties were established under the Anglo-Saxons but then suppressed or severely curtailed by the 'alien' Norman invasion of 1066, to which also could be traced the institution of the aristocracy. Although politically most potent in the seventeenth century, the idea of the Norman yoke was a long time dying. It remained a notable ingredient in the politics of early nineteenth-century radicalism and Chartism; and its subsequent decline was both uneven and has been exaggerated by historians.[30]

---

28 George Unwin, 'A seventeenth-century trade union', *Economic Journal*, 10 (September 1900), 394–403; and George Unwin, *Industrial Organization in the Sixteenth and Seventeenth Centuries* (Oxford: Clarendon Press, 1904); E. P. Thompson, *Customs in Common* (London: Merlin, 1991); Malcolm Chase, *Early Trade Unionism: Fraternity, Skill and the Politics* (2000; new edition London: Breviary, 2012), pp. 2–53; Malcolm Chase, '"A sort of Corporation (tho' without a charter)": the guild tradition and the emergence of British trade unionism', in Ian A. Gadd and Patrick Wallis (eds), *Guilds and Association in Europe, 900–1900* (London: University of London Centre for Metropolitan History, 2006), pp. 187–98.

29 See, for example, the assemblage of undated and unattributed cuttings from Howell's journalistic output, HC 6/39, 'Trade unionism' (1878), fol. 4. For the Brief Institution see Adrian Randall, *Before the Luddites: Custom, Community and Machinery in the English Woollen Industry, 1776–1809* (Cambridge: Cambridge University Press, 1991), pp. 131–48.

30 Chase, *Early Trade Unionism*, pp. 5, 176; Paul Readman, *Land and Nation in England: Patriotism, National Identity, and the Politics of Land, 1880–1914* (Woodbridge: Boydell, 2008), pp. 138–42, 156–7.

The concept of the Norman yoke was precisely the kind of woolly, unscientific thinking that Fabian historians were intent on rooting out. For them, refuting this concept was more than an issue of historical accuracy. It had always been closely associated with anti-statist positions, as part of a cumulative argument that the powers of the British state (and the frequency with which it intruded into the lives of its subjects) had progressively extended since the Conquest and needed to be reversed. The Fabian conception of the state was not one where government governed lightly: there was a fundamental point of political difference here between the advanced Liberal George Howell and the socialists Sidney and Beatrice Webb. For Howell, trade unions served to stave off socialism and consolidate individualism. Trade unionism was a means – or rather *the means* – through which to realise liberal reform and social cohesion.

Howell even went so far as to deny British Conservatism's customary 'claim to a monopoly of the legislation connected with factory legislation'. Such laws, he argued, were the product of a natural national sentiment and in reality constituted

> the outgrowth of a pre-existing state of things, and of previous enactments for the regulation of apprentices, wages, hours of labour, and methods of work, dating back to the reigns of Plantagenets and Tudors. These, again, were partly due to the old guild-system which in still earlier times governed trade, and regulated labour.[31]

Endemic social unrest earlier in the nineteenth century provided a historical window, Howell thought, onto the fate of a society where trade unionist activity was barely tolerated, if at all. A similar interpretation had been specifically applied to the Chartist period by Brentano, although it is doubtful whether Howell (who did not read German) was aware of this.[32] Biographical accounts of Howell routinely note that he had been a Chartist: in 1848 he joined a National Charter Association branch in the Somerset village where he worked for a time as an apprentice shoemaker. However, the significance of this phase in his life for his later career has never been teased out. 'No more than an adolescent fancy', Leventhal calls it.[33] Howell

31 HC 6/69, 'History of factory legislation', fol. 2.

32 Lujo Brentano, 'Die Englische Chartistenbewegung', *Preussiche Jarbücher*, 33 (1874), 431–47 and 531–50. The first English-language study to discuss Brentano's interpretation of Chartism was by his pupil, Gerhart von Schulze-Gaevernitz, *Social Peace: A Study of the Trade Union Movement in England ... translated by C. M. Wicksteed, and edited by G. Wallis* (London: Swan Sonnenschein, 1890).

33 Leventhal, *Respectable Radical*, p. 7; and see also Leventhal's entry for Howell in the *Dictionary of Labour Biography*, p. 187, which closely mirrors the entry for Howell in Joseph

himself barely discussed it in his published work.[34] Lecturing in 1896 on the progress of the working classes during Victoria's reign, he confined his coverage of Chartism to recommending Carlyle's essay of the same title and a comment that Disraeli's novel *Sybil* 'has always been a favourite of mine'.[35] It is clear that even in 1848 Howell had little sympathy for the politics of direct action and was drawn instead to the example of William Lovett and the London Working Men's Association (the historian of which he aspired to be). Far more significant, however, was a Chartist-related episode from his childhood, virtually ignored by Leventhal.[36] In 1839–40 his family lived briefly in South Wales while his father, Edwin, worked as a stonemason on a reservoir in the Afon Lwyd valley. The Howells rented a house facing onto the Monmouthshire Canal between Pontnewynydd and Pontypool. From there, on 3 November, the six-year-old George Howell witnessed at first hand the march of ironworkers and miners out of Pontypool to join the ill-fated Newport Rising. Not only that, but the young carpenter George Shell, the most widely lamented and subsequently celebrated of the Chartist rebels who died at Newport, was a close friend of the Howell family.[37] In the extensive drafts of his unpublished autobiography, George Howell left several accounts of this friendship. The earliest begins with statement that Shell 'lodged with us, or in the same house, I forget which':

> He often used to take me on his knee at meal times and would dance me up and down as I sat astride of his foot. On the very morning before he left on his fatal expedition he kissed me tenderly as if I were his own…. The long procession passed our door. I was taken out to see the men as they marched by … George Shell … stepped out of the ranks to kiss me and to shake hands with old friends and neighbours…. On the following day as I came home from school I heard the news, for I saw George's brother (so I was told) crying and raving like a madman at the news of George's death. I cried too, many cried, it was an ill-starred day for many in that place.[38]

O. Baylen and Norbert J. Gossman (eds), *Biographical Dictionary of Modern British Radicals, Volume III: 1870–1914, A–K* (Hemel Hempstead: Harvester, 1988), p. 463.

34 The sole exception was a short article, 'Labour politics, policies and parties', in *Reynolds's Newspaper*, 4 June 1905.

35 Unattributed cutting in HC 6/139.

36 Leventhal, *Respectable Radical*, p. 2.

37 Colin Gibson, 'George Shell's letter revisited: some perspectives on its use at the Monmouthshire Chartist trials', *Gwent Local History*, 116 (2014), 33–49; D. J. V. Jones, *The Last Rising: The Newport Insurrection of 1839* (Oxford: Clarendon, 1985), pp. 33, 97–8, 107–9, 155–6, 205; Malcolm Chase, *Chartism: A New History* (Manchester: Manchester University Press, 2007), pp. 111, 113–14, 116–17, 120.

38 HC 5/1/1, Volume A, 'Autobiography of a toiler', fols 27–8. Although written in later life, Howell based this version of his life on transcripts of letters written to a friend in

Subsequent versions of the autobiography omitted the reference to Shell living in the same house as the Howells, but all included a vivid account of how he had paused at their home as the march headed to Newport.[39] A whole instalment of Howell's biography of Ernest Jones was also centred on the incident.[40] Hardly less significantly, Howell believed his father was almost caught up in the movement. 'Mother expected to find father in the procession, for some of the men were pressed into it unwillingly.' However, Edwin Howell had not been able to find his way home across the hills because of thick fog. In no less than five versions of his auto-biography Howell recounted at length his memories of the Newport Rising, emphatically describing it as 'ill-considered, badly conceived, and recklessly planned', but also as 'the one great event which I can recollect'.[41] He cannot have been unaware (from his extensive reading in adult life as well as his interest in the history of Chartism) of how Shell's death had met an outpouring of grief and poetic eulogy that extended beyond his native Pontypool. This episode was the root of Howell's lasting anxiety about (and antipathy to) the efficacy and consequences of any indus-trial protest that originated outside the disciplinary framework offered by trade unionism. As a member of the Reform League's executive in 1867, for example, he opposed the organisation of regular demonstrations in Trafalgar Square. He also regarded the Hyde Park demonstration of 6 May that year with such deep misgivings that he put in place financial arrange-ments to support his wife in the event of his arrest and imprisonment.[42]

While the Webbs regarded Chartism as part of the discredited 'revo-lutionary period' of labour history, they never denied its importance or effaced its existence. This stemmed from their insistence that the Industrial Revolution changed everything. They were clear that trade unionism was solely the product of modern industrialisation. Its authority rested on its very modernity, and its probity on having evolved as labour's front line of defence against the depredations of industrial capitalism. For Howell, on the other hand, the authority of trade unionism derived in substantial part from its antiquity, and its probity from its having evolved out of

---

America, 1870–75 (annotation on folio a). For a detailed analysis of Howell's memories of 1839 see Malcolm Chase, 'A new account of George Shell and the Newport Rising', *Gwent Local History Journal*, 119 (2016), 19–26.

39 HC 5/1/1, Volume A, 'From ploughboy to Parliament. The story of an active, arduous and strenuous life', fol. 15; HC 5/1/1, Volume A, 'Rough draft of autobiography birth to 1855', fols 8–10; HC 5/1/2, Volume B, 'Memoirs of a busy life, 1896', fols 5–6, 10–13; HC 5/1/3, Volume C, 'Autobiography of a toiler', fols 5–7.

40 HC 10/3/1, 'Ernest Jones, the Chartist', chapter 18.

41 HC 5/1/1, Volume A, 'Autobiography of a toiler', fols 27 and 28.

42 Leventhal, *Respectable Radical*, pp. 89–90.

institutions that had themselves emerged because of the moral imperative in early urban society to restore the functions of that most natural of social institutions, the family. In the broad sweep of labour history, seen through Howell's generous optic, Chartism was an irrelevant, temporary blip. It is very telling that in writing the history of the London Working Men's Association, Howell stalled in 1838, leaving it uncompleted from precisely the point that Chartism commenced.

Trade unionism was therefore a force for social cohesion, a means to integrate workers into society. In adhering to this belief Howell was following closely the thought of the Christian socialist J. M. Ludlow, Secretary to the 1870 Royal Commission on Friendly Societies and from 1874 the Chief Registrar of Friendly Societies. (Ludlow in turn was Brentano's main contact point with British intellectuals, and was the person to whom the German dedicated his essay 'On the history and development of gilds, and the origin of trade unions'.[43]) *The Progress of the Working Class* – the highly influential labour history of the 1832–67 period that Ludlow wrote with the Owenite socialist Lloyd Jones – offered such a detailed account of the progress of social cohesion achieved through working-class self-help that, in it, Chartism virtually disappeared from view, appearing merely as 'a form of violence, [which] was a miserable failure'.[44]

So, were trade unions a necessarily assertive response by labour to the Industrial Revolution and the political establishment, as the Webbs argued? Or were they, as Howell passionately believed, part of the historic fabric of society, descended from economic institutions – the guilds – that had once harmoniously united employer and employed, and protected the interests of consumers through their role in apprenticeship training and product quality control? Beatrice and Sidney Webb's belief was that trade union interests were to be vigorously pursued, against an increasingly outdated form of political and economic authority. For Howell, by contrast, trade unions were to be patiently advanced, including through reasonable dialogue with employers, who, in time, might be partners in economic enterprise. He conspicuously dedicated *The Conflicts of Capital and Labour* to the woollen manufacturer, newspaper proprietor and Liberal MP Samuel Morley, 'a large employer of labour, and one who has at all times taken the deepest interest in all questions appertaining to the welfare of the working classes'.[45] Diligence and dogged reasonableness were the qualities he esteemed most in any labour organisation.

---

43 Goldman, 'Civil society in nineteenth-century Britain and Germany', pp. 97–113.
44 J. M. Ludlow and Lloyd Jones, *Progress of the Working Class 1832–1867* (London: Strahan, 1867), p. 296, see also pp. 88, 98 and 294.
45 Howell, *Conflicts*, p. v.

For example, 'its quiet persistent action', he wrote of the Amalgamated Society of Railway Servants, 'has done much to better the condition of railway employees'.[46] Similarly, he characterised the 1871 and 1876 Trade Union Acts as the outcome of 'constitutional and methodical' organisation. 'The public mind was educated by meetings, lectures, publications, annual congresses, deputations to ministers, and interviews with members of Parliament, and by debates, bills, and petitions'.[47]

There is no doubt that the sections on medieval and early modern times of Howell's historical works stuck closely to Brentano's schema. But the extent to which they did was not so egregious that it prevented Brentano from cordially corresponding with Howell, counting him among 'meine Freunde' in his autobiography, or inviting him to advise and attend a conference of the Verein für Sozialpolitik (Germany's economics association), of which he was a founder member.[48] The economic historian H. S. Foxwell (an indefatigable bibliomaniac who assembled both London University's Goldsmiths' and Harvard's Kress libraries) was another correspondent and warm admirer.[49] We should note, too, the extent to which his contemporaries accepted the essence of Howell and Brentano's argument, for example H. de Beltgens Gibbins, author of influential school textbooks, and Margaret Fothergill Robinson.[50] Arnold Toynbee was similarly indebted, although he inclined to view co-operative societies as the fullest heirs to the guild tradition, as were the economists William Ashley and Alfred and Mary Marshall.[51] Frederic Harrison, the leading

---

46 Howell, *Trade Unionism, New and Old*, p. 138.

47 Howell, *Conflicts*, p. 126.

48 HC 1/27, Brentano to Howell, 25 May and 28 August 1890; HC 1/29/part 1, Brentano to Howell, 15 August 1892; Lujo Brentano, *Mein leben im Kampf um die soziale Entwicklung Deutschlands* (Jena: Diderichs, 1931), p. 49.

49 Foxwell was instrumental in organising a testimonial fund for Howell in 1904 and persuaded Campbell Bannerman to award him a Civil List pension in 1906. Leventhal, *Respectable Radical*, pp. 213–14, 254n22.

50 Henry de Beltgens Gibbins, *The Industrial History of England* (London, 1890), p. 26; and see M. Epstein, 'Gibbins, Henry de Beltgens (1865–1907)', in *Oxford Dictionary of National Biography* (Oxford: Oxford University Press, 2004, online edition at http://o-www.oxforddnb.com.wam.leeds.ac.uk/view/article/33384, accessed 13 November 2015); Margaret Fothergill Robinson, *The Spirit of Association. Being some account of the gilds, friendly societies, co-operative movement, and trade unions of Great Britain* (London: Murray, 1913) and see obituary in *The Times*, 7 March 1914.

51 Arnold Toynbee, *Lectures on the Industrial Revolution in England* (London: Rivington, 1884), pp. 178, 222; William Ashley, *Surveys: Historic and Economic* (London: Longmans, 1900), p. 259; Alfred Marshall and M. P. Marshall, *Economics of Industry* (London: Macmillan, 3rd edition, 1885); and Thompson, 'The reception of Lujo Brentano's thought in Britain', pp. 26–30.

Positivist and member of the 1867–69 Royal Commission on Trade Unions, declared *The Conflicts of Capital and Labour* 'quite invaluable' and was instrumental in securing the publication of a second edition in 1890.[52]

Nor, among those most sympathetic to trade unionism, was Howell alone in his interpretation of the early history of association. Even John Burnett, soon to become labour correspondent to the Board of Trade, although rejecting the proposition of a connection between guilds and trade unions, called for the extension of conciliation boards 'in the spirit of the old guilds … for the good of the trade at large', adding that 'the cultivation and development of the modern guild on these lines should be a task reciprocally undertaken by unions of masters and men'.[53] As early as 1861, J. M. Ludlow had argued that 'the trade society of our days is but the lop-sided representative of the old guild, its dwarfed but legal heir', also emphasising 'the fact of the trade societies' struggle, being … five centuries old'.[54] Howell himself may have initially been prompted to seek out Brentano's work on reading the winner of the Trades Union Congress's 1875 prize essay competition. This cited Brentano, albeit without submitting his ideas to detailed scrutiny.[55] The work of a young Leeds lawyer, William Trant, the essay helped promulgate Howell's thesis, firstly when an extended edition was published in 1884, and then through several US editions published by the American Federation of Labor.[56] Samuel Gompers, founding President of the Federation, himself credited the 'clear-cut analysis of trade unionism' offered by the Brentano–Trant–Howell axis as having influenced his thinking more 'than any other economic dissertation with the exception of Professor Thorold Rogers' *Six Centuries of Work and Wages*'.[57]

---

52 HC 1/27, Harrison to Howell, 18 March 1890; George Howell, *The Conflicts of Capital and Labour, Historically and Economically Considered* … (London: Macmillan, 2nd edition, 1890).

53 John Burnett, 'Trade unions as a means of improving the conditions of labour', in J. Oliphant (ed.), *The Claims of Labour* (Edinburgh, 1886), pp. 7–8, 36 (7–39). I owe this reference to Thompson, 'The reception of Lujo Brentano's thought in Britain', pp. 23–4.

54 J. M. Ludlow, 'Trade societies and the Social Science Association: part first', *Macmillan's Magazine*, 3(16) (February 1861), 316; and J. M. Ludlow, 'Trade societies and the social Science Association: part second', *Macmillan's Magazine*, 3(16) (February 1861), p. 362.

55 'Ithuriel' [William Trant], *First Prize Essay on Trades Unions* (Glasgow: William Love, 1875), pp. 8 and 12.

56 William Trant, *Trades Unions: Their Origin and Objects, Influence and Efficacy* (London: Kegan Paul, 1884); William Trant, *Trade unions: Their Origin and Objects, Influence and Efficacy* (New York: American Federation of Labor, 1888); William Trant, *Trade unions: Their Origin and Objects, Influence and Efficacy* (New York: American Federation of Labor, 6th edition, 1893).

57 Samuel Gompers, *Seventy Years of Life and Labor* (New York: Dutton, 1957), pp. 174–5; cf. Gompers' remark, 'thousands of copies have been distributed gratuitously', to

It is therefore worth taking Howell seriously as a labour historian, for the insight this throws on contemporary labour politics, on the evolution of the historiography of British labour and, even, for its intrinsic merits as history. Modern scholarship has to a significant extent vindicated Brentano's and Howell's perspective on guilds' origins, influence and longevity.[58] The dismissal of pre-industrial labour associations by the Webbs has similarly been challenged. Edward Thompson called for 'the Webbian walling of off trade unionism proper from guild traditions' to be dismantled as early as 1968.[59] In 1979 the distinguished labour lawyer Otto Kahn-Freund offered the view that the customs and regulations around British trade unionism 'must be seen as a survival of the very deep-seated pre-capitalist guild spirit'.[60] However, it was only in 1981 that the path-breaking work of John Rule began dismantling the Webbian walls; and the publication of Thompson's own detailed work on the field had to wait until the appearance of his collection *Customs in Common* ten years later.[61]

John Rule especially has illuminated how, far beyond the so-called Industrial Revolution, there existed a profound sense among artisans of possessing a property in skill and, in consequence, a considerable cleavage in labouring identities between 'skilled' and 'unskilled'. This cleavage is everywhere apparent in Howell's thinking. For example, it reinforced the Junta's hostility to those trade unions that lay outside the amalgamated societies.[62] Howell was a classic example of a workman who had 'pursued

Trant, 16 May 1889, reprinted in Stuart B. Kaufman, *Samuel Gompers Papers, Volume II* (Chicago, IL: University of Illinois Press, 1987), pp 205–6.
58 Steven A. Epstein, *Wage Labor and Guilds in Medieval Europe* (Chapel Hill, NC: University of North Carolina Press, 1991); and Steven A. Epstein, 'Craft guilds in the pre-modern economy: a discussion', *Economic History Review*, 61(1) (2008), 155–74; Derek Keene, 'English urban guilds, c. 900–1300: the purposes and politics of association', in Ian A. Gadd and Patrick Wallis (eds), *Guilds and Association in Europe, 900–1900* (London: University of London Centre for Metropolitan History, 2006), pp. 3–26; Bo Gustafsson, 'The rise and economic behaviour of medieval craft guilds: an economic–theoretical interpretation', *Scandinavian Economic History Review*, 35(1) (1987), 1–40; Jan Lucassen *et al.*, *The Return of the Guilds*, supplement 16 of *International Review of Social History*, 53 (2008). See also Antony Black, *Guilds and Civil Society in European Political Thought from the Twelfth Century to the Present* (London: Methuen, 1984).
59 Quoted in *Bulletin of the Society for the Study of Labour History*, 17 (autumn 1968), 20.
60 Otto Kahn-Freund, *Labour Relations: Heritage and Adjustment* (Oxford: British Academy, 1979), p. 41.
61 John Rule, *The Experience of Labour in Eighteenth-Century Industry* (London: Croom Helm, 1981); E. P. Thompson, *Customs in Common* (London: Merlin, 1991).
62 The Junta was the name given by Sidney and Beatrice Webb to the salaried trade union secretaries in mid-Victorian politics based in London. This influential group included William Allen (Engineers), Robert Applegarth (Carpenters), Danile Guilde (Iron-founders), Edwin Coulson (Bricklayers) and George Odger (London Trades Council).

knowledge under difficulties'. He was impatient with those who would leap over the exacting sacrifices of self-help and instead make demands for immediate concessions from employers and the state: 'sooner or later, if the claims put forward are reasonable and just, they will be granted by the Legislature'. By 1891, and the publication of his *Trade Unionism New and Old*, this attitude had crystallised into a considerable hostility to the New Unionism. Howell cheerfully acknowledged that almost anything he wrote would 'as a matter of course' be 'severely handled in the Socialist and New Unionist newspapers and publications'.[63] It is pertinent to note in this context that Brentano found the New Unionist-inspired strike wave of the 1880s reminiscent of Chartism.[64]

Effectively, the Webbs' 1894 *History of Trade Unionism* was an extended footnote to the Fabian manifesto of the previous year, *To Your Tents, O Israel!*, which had called for labour to disassociate from the Liberal Party.[65] The corpus of historical work by Howell was in turn an irresistible target, suspect not only factually but methodologically and politically as well. A critical evaluation of George Howell's not inconsiderable output as a labour historian therefore underlines that the writing of history was an important part of the cultural context in which the labour politics of the period were worked out. The initially positive reception of Howell's historical endeavours, and their subsequent demise, is explicable in the changing political culture of the labour movement in the late nineteenth and early twentieth century.

Acknowledgements

Chris Wrigley helped shape my thinking about the 'pre-history' of trade unionism when he was the very supportive editor of my contribution in 2000 to 'Studies in Labour History', the Society for the Study of Labour History's book series. This particular research on Howell was first presented to the conference 'Trade Unions in British History', held at the University of Leeds in May 2009. I am grateful to all who participated for their interest and encouragement. Most recently I have benefited from very helpfully comments on this chapter by Shirley Chase and Richard Whiting.

---

63 Howell, *Conflicts*, p. 146; HC 5/1/4, Autobiography, Volume D (1860–96), L/xii; and see an almost identically worded comment in L/ix.

64 Hennock, 'Lessons from England', p. 154.

65 *A Plan of Campaign for Labor: Containing the Substance of the Fabian Manifesto Entitled 'To Your Tents, O Israel!',* Fabian Tract 49 (London: Fabian Society, 1894).

2

The appointment of Herbert Gladstone as Liberal Chief Whip in 1899

KENNETH D. BROWN

In 1922 David Lloyd George described Herbert Gladstone, with whom he was then locked in a struggle for both the soul of Liberalism and control of the Liberal Party, as 'the best living embodiment of the Liberal doctrine that quality is not hereditary…. There is no more ridiculous spectacle on a stage than a dwarf strutting before the footlights in garments he has inherited from a giant.'[1] It was typical Lloyd George, clever, spiteful and completely overshadowing Herbert Gladstone's own quietly understated response. Lloyd George's vindictiveness was unwarranted, but his standing as the man who had won the war ensured that his particular version of history, including the slur on his former colleague, would stick. One acolyte, for instance, claimed that Lloyd George's efforts to reunite the Liberal Party after 1921 had been frustrated by a 'small group of embittered men' like Gladstone, who had used H. H. Asquith as a front to cover their own disintegrative activities.[2] Certainly history was not subsequently very kind to Herbert Gladstone. In the autobiographies of his political contemporaries he tends to appear but fleetingly, if at all. Even in his own published memoir he is something of a peripheral figure, since his book was conceived primarily as a defence of his father, whose reputation, whether political or personal, he defended vigorously in print and even

---

1 Quoted in P. Rowland, *Lloyd George* (London: Macmillan, 1975), p. 581.
2 H. Henderson-Livesey, *The Intrigues of Abingdon Street* (n.d.). A copy survives in the Flintshire Record Office, Glynne-Gladstone MSS 1976, hereafter cited as FRO GG MSS. The papers are catalogued but have no folio numbers. They are cited here by kind permission of Charles Gladstone.

in court.[3] Of course, as Lloyd George was really implying, albeit in an unnecessarily nasty way, it was never likely that the son's public career would or even could match up to that of a father who was four times Prime Minister and who dominated British politics for much of Queen Victoria's reign. Perhaps this helps to explain why almost alone of his contemporaries in the Campbell-Bannerman and Asquith administrations the younger man has failed to attract modern biographers, even though as Home Secretary he occupied one of the three great offices of state in one of the outstanding administrations of the twentieth century. Even relatively minor ministerial colleagues like Charles Masterman, C. P. Trevelyan, Sidney Buxton, Reginald McKenna and John Burns found their later chroniclers.[4] Herbert Gladstone's sole monument in the graveyard of history, however, remains the now very dated and always rather dry tome commissioned by his wife shortly after his death in 1930 and written by an undistinguished Oxford historian, Charles Mallet.[5]

In more general historiography, too, he has remained a marginal figure. His time as Under-Secretary at the Irish Office is usually submerged beneath the broader considerations given to the development of his father's policies on Ireland.[6] Lacking the personal charisma of many of his colleagues, his quietly enlightened administration of the Home Office between 1906 and 1910 tends to be overshadowed by the overtly more spectacular work of Winston Churchill and Lloyd George, although it has to be said that neither of the latter was exactly a reluctant self-publicist, even during their years of political adolescence before the First World War. Thus, writing in 1936, R. C. K. Ensor labelled Gladstone as one of the two weakest ministers in the Liberal government of 1906.[7] Some forty years later, one of the pioneers of welfare history, Roy Hay, suggested that Gladstone's officials limited his effectiveness by immersing him in administrative detail.[8] The

3 H. J. Gladstone, *After Thirty Years* (London: Macmillan, 1928).
4 E. Hopkins, *Charles Masterman (1873–1927): Politician and Journalist. The Splendid Failure* (Lampeter: Edwin Mellen, 1999); A. J. A. Morris, *C. P. Trevelyan, Portrait of a Radical* (Basingstoke: Palgrave Macmillan, 1979); D. Waley, *A Liberal Life: Sidney Earl Buxton, 1853–1934* (Hassocks: Newtimber Publications, 1999); M. Farr, *Reginald McKenna: Financier Among Statesmen, 1863–1916* (London: Routledge, 2007); Kenneth D. Brown, *John Burns* (London: Royal Historical Society Studies in History, 1977).
5 C. Mallet, *Herbert Gladstone: A Memoir* (London: Hutchinson, 1932).
6 A notable exception is A. B. Cooke and J. R. Vincent, 'Herbert Gladstone, Forster and Ireland, 1881–2', *Irish Historical Studies*, 17 (1970–71), 521–48.
7 R. C. K. Ensor, *England 1870–1914* (Oxford: Oxford University Press, 1936), p. 406. The other failure in Ensor's judgement was John Burns.
8 J. R. Hay, *The Origins of the Liberal Welfare Reforms, 1906–1914* (1975; Basingstoke: Palgrave edition, 1983), p. 39.

fact remains, however, as others have pointed out, that under his leadership the Home Office generated more legislation than any other government department between 1906 and 1908: without its contribution the Liberal record under Henry Campbell-Bannerman would have been sparse indeed.[9] It is also the case that in the more strident versions of suffragette history, Gladstone the Home Secretary is too often portrayed merely as the unthinking personification of officialdom, the creature of oppressive male government, notwithstanding both his own belief in the case for extending the franchise to women and his persistent efforts to mitigate the treatment of those suffragettes imprisoned for unlawful activities.

Leaving the Home Office in 1910 to take up the post of Governor General in the newly established Union of South Africa inevitably meant that Gladstone moved out of the immediate gaze of British public interest, almost a case of out of sight, out of mind – apart from a brief flurry of press publicity generated by the Rand strikes of 1913 and 1914. By and large, later historians of South Africa have either ignored him – in the relevant chapters of works by E. A. Walker and by R. Davenport and C. Sanders he is scarcely mentioned – or have dismissed him – G. B. Pyrah described him as 'habitually weak and insipid'.[10]

While the first stance may accurately reflect the essentially decorative and ceremonial role of the Governor General in the South African constitution, in Gladstone's case the second does an injustice to his frequent backstage interventions and advice, which did much to stabilise the volatile components of the Empire's newest member. Concurrent with his Governor Generalship, Gladstone was also High Commissioner for Britain's sub-Saharan colonies of Bechuanaland, Swaziland and Basutoland, 290,000 square miles of territory which were home to a handful of Europeans and some 620,000 Africans. For good measure, the High Commissioner was also the monarch's official representative in Southern Rhodesia, where 24,000 European settlers, mainly British, exercised a near feudal oversight of some 746,000 natives through the medium of the British South Africa Company. Here again, the standard work on British policy towards these protectorates is unfair to Gladstone in arguing that his disagreements with Colonial Office policy were based

---

9 See J. Grigg, 'Liberals on trial', in A. Sked and C. Cook (eds), *Crises and Controversy* (Basingstoke: Palgrave Macmillan, 1976), p. 25; M. Pugh, *Lloyd George* (London: Routledge, 1988), p. 34.

10 E. A. Walker, *A History of Southern Africa* (London: Longmans Green & Co., 1968); R. A. Davenport and C. Sanders, *South Africa: A Modern History* (Basingstoke: Palgrave Macmillan, 5th edition, 2000); G. B. Pyrah, *Imperial Policy and South Africa, 1902–1910* (Oxford: Greenwood Press, 1955), p. 25.

on his failure to understand it, for the evidence more strongly suggests that he opposed it on principle.[11] All things considered, therefore, there is much to justify John Grigg's comment that Herbert Gladstone deserves to be rediscovered.[12]

Virtually the only part of Gladstone's career that has attracted more substantial interest from later historians was his role as Liberal Chief Whip between 1900 and 1906: indeed, it is probably true to say that his papers provide a fuller insight than anyone else's into the activities of a party whip. The climax of this work came, of course, in the sweeping electoral victory of 1906, when 400 Liberal MPs were returned to the House of Commons, a majority over the Unionists of 243. It was a stunning achievement and the Liberals' best result since 1832, but while Gladstone's various contributions, whether raising funds, finding candidates, assigning constituencies or holding the party together during the Boer War, have generally been acknowledged, even that recognition has sometimes appeared grudging, even critical. This is particularly so where, as is often the case, the Liberal victory is presented as being pretty much inevitable, the only possible consequence of Conservative fragmentation and the unpopularity of the various measures passed by the Tory government between 1900 and 1905, especially the espousal of tariff reform, which, as Michael Bentley puts it, effectively removed any need for the Liberals to think.[13] The author of the definitive study of the 1906 election, A. K. Russell, is similarly circumspect in pointing out that while the Liberal victory certainly owed something to Gladstone's management, it must also be seen in the context of the poor state of the Unionist Party machine, both local and national, and of the difficulties created by the activities of Liberal Unionist organisations.[14] Yet while a Liberal win in 1906 appeared highly likely to contemporaries, no one, including Gladstone himself, could have anticipated its sheer magnitude, for in the days before the advent of scientific opinion polls there was no way of estimating with any accuracy the outcome of an election. In his own private list of predictions, he did correctly forecast the result in over 350 seats but the Liberals also captured thirty-two seats where he expected certain defeat and another fourteen which he thought it likely they would lose. It seems somewhat churlish, therefore, to gloss over the crucial contribution Gladstone made to the 1906 election triumph by his

11 R. Hyam, *The Failure of South African Expansionism* (London: Macmillan, 1972).
12 J. Grigg, 'Herbert Gladstone', in A. Horne (ed.), *Telling Lives: From W. B. Yeats to Bruce Chatwin* (London: Macmillan, 2000), p. 168.
13 M. Bentley, *The Climax of Liberal Politics* (London: Hodder Arnold, 1987), p. 109.
14 A. K. Russell, *Liberal Landslide: The General Election of 1906* (Newton Abbott: David & Charles, 1973), p. 5.

steady and time-consuming work in organising the party electorally and in wearing down the government in the House of Commons by his effective handling of his own party members. Indeed, it was precisely because of this contribution that he was requested by the Independent Liberals to oversee their election campaign in 1922.

In his own reflections on the outcome of the 1906 election Gladstone gave pride of place to the pact he had negotiated with the Labour Representation Committee (LRC), which facilitated the return to the House of Commons of thirty or so Labour Members. Yet even this has been turned against him by later critics, some on the grounds that the Liberals would probably have won every seat in which they stood aside for an LRC candidate, some because the pact allowed the Labour Party cuckoo into the Liberal nest, from which it eventually ousted its host.[15] The first group, however, credit him with a foresight which neither he nor anyone else possessed, for he could not have known in advance of the election that the Labour Members would merely supplement rather than actually secure a Liberal majority, particularly as by 1906 the Liberals had, with a brief interval between 1892 and 1895, been out of power for the best part of twenty years; the second group of critics tend to ignore all sorts of uncertainties about the health of the Edwardian Liberal Party and the significance of contemporary social changes which were potentially generating support for the Labour Party, uncertainties around which the debate has been detailed and long running.[16]

In 1930, the Liberal activist and journalist J. A . Spender wrote approvingly of Gladstone's work as Chief Whip, describing it as the rendering of a 'signal service' to the party, and, later, more detailed analysis of that service certainly led to a growing appreciation of Gladstone's contribution to Liberal Party fortunes before 1906.[17] By 2004, Colin Matthew felt

---

15 R. Douglas, *The History of the Liberal Party* (Madison, NJ: Fairleigh Dickinson University Press, 1971), pp. 3, 90; G. R. Searle, *A New England? Peace and War, 1868–1918* (Oxford: Oxford University Press, 2004), p. 359; I. Machin, 'Herbert Gladstone', in D. Brack (ed.), *Dictionary of Liberal Biography* (London: Politico's Publishing, 1998), p. 125.

16 The debate could be said to have been sparked into life by T. Wilson, *The Downfall of the Liberal Party, 1914–1935* (London: Fontana, 1965 and 1968 editions; and a new Faber & Faber edition 2011). It lasted a long time. See K. Laybourn, 'The rise of Labour and the decline of liberalism: the state of the debate', *History*, 80 (1995), 207–26.

17 J. A. Spender, *Sir Robert Hudson* (London: Cassell & Co., 1930), p. 63. See H. W. McCready, 'Chief Whip and party funds: the work of Herbert Gladstone in the Edwardian Liberal Party, 1899 to 1906', *Canadian Journal of History*, 6 (1971), 285–303; F. Bealey, 'Negotiations between the Liberal Party and the Labour Representation Committee before the general election of 1906', *Bulletin of the Institute of Historical Research*,

justified in describing him as an 'outstanding whip', a judgement with
which other recent writers have generally concurred, albeit with varying
degrees of enthusiasm.[18] Not all of Gladstone's contemporaries, however,
were so sure, certainly in the earliest days of his tenure. In describing
him as the only weak minister in the Campbell-Bannerman government,
Philip Snowden certainly believed that his appointment had been the
reward for his work as head of Liberal organisation rather than a mark
of any fitness for office.[19] Keir Hardie described Gladstone in 1900 as a
person of 'barely average capacity', a somewhat ungracious observation,
given Gladstone's long advocacy of independent labour representation in
Parliament.[20] Henry Labouchère was even more blunt, confiding to his
fellow radical, Charles Dilke, that Gladstone was 'a hopeless head whip.
A mere fly on the Parliamentary coach.'[21] Beatrice Webb, meeting him
in 1904, concluded that he was a lightweight and dismissed him as a
mere party wire-puller.[22] Yet Webb's judgement of Gladstone, as of most
people she met, was based solely on the extent to which he shared her own
ideas and aspirations: this was, after all, the same woman who earlier had
confided to her private diary that Campbell-Bannerman was 'quite stupid',
Asquith was lacking in leadership qualities, Edward Grey was merely slight
and R. B. Haldane had no grasp of everyday reality.[23] Her assessments also
tended to be characterised by a marked absence of empathy, something
of an oddity in a woman so sensitive to her own emotions and frailties.
In other words, she regarded politicians merely as actors, without any
consideration of the person behind the role. Yet both her judgement and
the insensitive approach on which it was based do seem to have influenced
later interpretations of Gladstone's work as Chief Whip, in the sense
that no one has troubled to consider the personal qualities and private

29 (1956), 261–74; F. Bealey, 'The electoral arrangement between the Labour Representation Committee and the Liberal Party', *Journal of Modern History,* 28 (1956), 353–73;
T. O. Lloyd, 'Lib–Labs and unforgiveable electoral generosity', *Bulletin of the Institute
of Historical Research,* 48 (1975), 255–59; T. O. Lloyd, 'The whip as paymaster: Herbert
Gladstone and party organisation', *English Historical Review,* 89 (1974), 785–813.

18 H. G. C. Matthew, 'Gladstone, Herbert John, Viscount Gladstone', in *Oxford Dictionary of National Biography* (Oxford: Oxford University Press, 2004). For another
favourable assessment see M. Pugh, *The Making of Modern British Politics, 1867–1939*
(Oxford: Wiley-Blackwell, 1993), p. 98.

19 P. Snowden, *My Autobiography* (London: Ivor Nicholson & Watson, 1934), vol. 1, p. 126.

20 *Labour Leader,* 27 January 1900.

21 C. Dilke Papers, British Library (BL), Add MSS 43902, fol. 208, H. Labouchère to C.
Dilke, 30 October 1900.

22 Passfield Papers, British Library of Political and Economic Science, 1/2/5, B. Webb,
Diary, 8 June 1904.

23 *Ibid.,* 28 February 1902.

circumstances which determined both the decision to offer him the job and his acceptance of it. After all, it was highly unusual for the Whip's position to be offered to an individual who had held a Cabinet post and who stood as high in the party as Herbert Gladstone did in 1899.

After filling minor posts in his father's governments of 1880–86 and 1892–94, he was in that last year promoted to Cabinet rank as First Commissioner of Works by Lord Rosebery when he succeeded the older Gladstone as Prime Minister. By this time the young Gladstone was widely recognised as an advanced and vocal champion of Home Rule, a subject on which he had acted both as a sounding board for his father's developing views and as his go-between with the Irish nationalist Members of Parliament. As he himself later put it, he was very much at the centre of party affairs and of course still in daily contact with his father.[24] Herbert may have been a reluctant and infrequent contributor to parliamentary debates, but the force of his platform oratory during his first election campaigns had astonished his sisters and thereafter he was always much in demand as a speaker at Liberal meetings around the country. In the course of the 1890s he also took a lead in arguing the case for greater labour representation in Parliament and in trying to shift the Liberal stance on licensing reform. It was in recognition of both his standing and his platform gifts that in December 1891 he was one of a small number asked by the then Chief Whip, Arnold Morley, to assist the Liberal candidates in the London County Council elections, with a view to enhancing the party's parliamentary prospects in the capital.

That a man of such pedigree, position and experience should accept the post of Chief Whip was widely regarded as a retrograde step, as is evident from the numerous letters Gladstone received when news of his appointment became public. An old acquaintance, J. F. Leese, the Member for Accrington, referred to it as 'an unselfish and self sacrificing' step, and Gladstone's constituency chairman and mentor, James Kitson, took a similar view, telling him that he was the right man for the job even if he was making a sacrifice.[25] Another local party member, Joseph Henry, thanked him for putting the party's interest above his own.[26] Loulou Harcourt offered condolences to him and congratulations to the party for

24 Viscount Gladstone, 'The Chief Whip in the British Parliament', *American Political Science Review*, 21 (1927), 525.

25 H. J. Gladstone Papers, BL Add MSS 46017, fols 153–4, J. F. Leese to H. J. Gladstone, 15 April 1899; H. J. Gladstone Papers, BL Add Mss 46028, fol. 100, J. Kitson to H. J. Gladstone, 16 April 1899.

26 H. J. Gladstone Papers, BL Add MSS 46036, fol. 68, J. Henry to H. J. Gladstone, 14 April 1899.

his self-sacrifice in taking on this 'hardest and most thankless of all har-
ness'.[27] Pressed by both the new Chief Whip and Campbell-Bannerman,
just recognised as the new party leader, to contest North-East Manchester
in the general election of 1900, Augustine Birrell was reluctant, since
the seat had never been won by a Liberal, but he felt constrained to
accept, he said, because 'both men's sacrifices for the party have been so
great that I could not for very shame turn a deaf ear to what they had to
urge'.[28] Even Gladstone's own mother confided to Lord Rosebery that
the position of Whip was 'hard upon him' and the former Liberal leader
himself admitted in the midst of the 1900 general election campaign that
none had a harder or more thankless task than the new Chief Whip.[29]
Why then did Cambell-Bannerman offer him the job and, equally, why
did Gladstone accept it?

The immediate cause of the vacancy in the Liberals' parliamentary organisation was the untimely death on 5 April 1899 of Tom Ellis, promoted
to Chief from Second Whip by William Gladstone some five years before.
Campbell-Bannerman wasted no time in consulting senior party figures
about a replacement and then offered the post to Gladstone a week after
Ellis's demise. An internal promotion might have seemed the obvious
way to fill the vacancy but Campbell-Bannerman, like Gladstone himself,
seems to have had a low opinion of the other Liberal whips. Furthermore, the new leader had acquired his own role as recently as February,
unelected and emerging only because Lord Harcourt had had enough of
Rosebery's constant interventions from the sidelines, while the only other
viable contender, Asquith, preferred for the time being to concentrate
on his legal work. Given his own rather insecure position, Campbell-
Bannerman therefore wanted a man whom he both knew and trusted and
whose politics were like his, broadly faithful to William Gladstone's own.
Herbert fitted the bill on every count.

He had briefly been Campbell-Bannerman's Financial Secretary at the
War Office in 1886 and the two men had developed an easy rapport.
Prior to that Herbert had served in his father's administrations, first as an
unpaid and then a salaried Lord of the Treasury or junior whip, despite the
misgivings of some Liberal leaders that this would be seen as nepotism on

---

27 H. J. Gladstone Papers, BL Add MSS 45997, fol. 18, L. Harcourt to H. J. Gladstone, 16
April 1899.

28 Birrell Papers, Liverpool University Library, MS 10.2, fol. 6, Newspaper cutting dated 3
January 1900.

29 Rosebery Papers, National Library of Scotland, MS 10015, fol. 136, Catherine Gladstone
to Lord Rosebery, 9 May 1899; H. J. Gladstone Papers, BL Add MSS 45986, fol. 43,
Lord Rosebery to H. J. Gladstone, 5 October 1900.

the part of the Prime Minister. It seems that his main task in these roles was to act as his father's go-between with the Irish nationalists, but inevitably he gained some insight into the routine work of the Whips' Office and this, combined with his daily contact with his father, had served to move him close to the centre of party affairs.

The fact that he had such experience probably explains why, early in 1891, Arnold Morley had invited him to chair the National Liberal Club's political committee, a task, he said, which needed a strong man capable of maintaining effective links between the party leaders in Westminster and their organisational headquarters in Parliament Street. Interestingly, the National Liberal Club had been established in 1882 by Herbert's father as a centre for active Liberal workers but, as George Bernard Shaw later noted, it seems that virtually every member had parliamentary aspirations and thus this work also brought Gladstone into daily contact with many of the party's rank and file, as well as its MPs.[30] Although he was replaced as chair of the political committee by Henry Labouchère in 1897, when the radical wing of the party captured control of the Club, Morley was subsequently very flattering about Gladstone's success in drawing individuals together. In part this was a reflection of his genial personality and the well developed social skills which made him a much sought-after travel companion and guest at social gatherings. In part it reflected the fact that while his own political convictions were strongly held, he was always prepared to subordinate them to the wider interests of the party, taking a lead, for example, in dropping Home Rule as a practical political proposition after 1894 and also in seeking to shift the Liberal position on the local veto. Similarly, while he was no imperialist, those in the party with such leanings probably realised that he was the least unsympathetic Chief Whip they were likely to get under Campbell-Bannerman.

Such considerations, then, lay behind the Liberal leader's decision to offer the post to Herbert. But the latter's initial response was cautious. He was happy enough, he assured Campbell-Bannerman, that he would be permitted to retain his freedom of thought on key political issues but he pointed out that other commitments, such as his various company directorships and the maintenance of the family estate at Hawarden, would also make demands on his time. Above all, he said in letter to Campbell-Bannerman on 12 April 1899, 'the frail condition of my mother

---

30 'I have never yet met a member of the National Liberal Club who did not intend to get into parliament.' G. B. Shaw, 'The case for equality. Speech at a National Liberal Club debate in 1913', cited in J. Fuchs (ed.), *The Socialism of Shaw* (New York: Vanguard, 1926), p. 58.

is my first duty'.[31] On the same day, he confided in his sister that Ellis's unexpected death had hit no one harder than himself because he was being pressed by party leaders to take on the Chief Whip's work. The pressure, he said, was 'too great to resist even were I disposed to refuse ... nothing can be more repulsive to me than much, perhaps most, of the work & it means to me an absence of freedom practically till the end of the next Liberal Gov't'.[32]

Gladstone's biographer later asserted that he accepted the post because it allowed him to escape the burden of speaking in the House of Commons.[33] It is true that Gladstone had never felt at ease in the House and his reluctance to participate extensively in its debates dates from the start of his parliamentary career. He was so in dread of making a fool of himself that he avoided giving his first speech for almost a year. Although his rather wooden address on British policy in India passed off better than he had anticipated and attracted the plaudits conventionally afforded to maiden speakers, he clearly found the whole exercise something of an ordeal. The formality and convention of the House, which was not short of first-rate orators, intimidated him. As a member of the government, his handling of parliamentary questions was initially uncertain and if it improved somewhat over time he tended generally to be a responsive speaker, rarely taking the initiative in debate except on matters Irish. He was much more relaxed and consequently a much better performer on the public platform, where he found the freedom and passion he could not summon up in Westminster, and as a result he was much in demand. His parliamentary reticence did not go unnoticed by his mother, who referred to it more than once, and she was not alone. 'I have often wondered', wrote one of Herbert's constituents to him in 1897, 'why you don't participate more in debates in the Commons. Your position warrants it and if you don't you may be put to one side when the party comes to power.'[34]

Mallet's suggestion is further borne out by the fact that once he became Chief Whip, Gladstone spoke rarely in the House, only once in 1901 and not at all in either of the two following sessions. But as is clear from a letter he sent to his sister-in-law, there was more than just parliamentary reticence behind his decision to accept the job, a post which he might legitimately have regarded as being beneath him. 'In the matter of whips',

---

31 H. Campbell-Bannerman Papers, BL Add MSS 41215, fols 66–7, H. J. Gladstone to H. Campbell-Bannerman, 12 April 1899.

32 FRO GG MSS 989, H. J. Gladstone to Maud Gladstone, 12 April 1899.

33 Mallet, *Herbert Gladstone*, p. 173.

34 H. J. Gladstone Papers, BL Add MSS 46036, fol. 61, J. Henry to H. J. Gladstone, 4 March 1897.

he wrote, 'we are in such a desperately bad way that it does not appear to me that I have any option'.[35]

Gladstone was, above all things, a faithful son and he was dismayed by the current state of the party which the father on whom he doted had effectively created. *The Times* was hardly a disinterested observer but its diagnosis of the Liberals in 1894 – 'chaotic … fettered in all sorts of informal ways by all sorts of incompatible engagements and destitute of any coherent body of conviction or any intelligible principle of action' – was certainly confirmed in the second half of the decade.[36] Still divided over the unresolved issue of Irish Home Rule, which had caused the secession of the Liberal Unionists in the 1880s, the party lacked stable leadership after Gladstone's resignation in 1894. His immediate successor, Rosebery, was by turns diffident and hyperactive, while his imperialist sympathies were too much for many Liberals, including Herbert Gladstone himself, and caused a further fissure in the party. Undermined from within by the hostility of Harcourt, who led the Liberals in the Commons, and then heavily defeated in the election of 1895, Rosebery gave up the leadership in October 1896. Reluctantly, Harcourt took over but was unable to bring the Liberal factions together and he resigned in December 1898. On the other wing, the radicals, although lacking effective leadership and internally divided between traditionalists and modernists, provided a constant irritant as they sought to gain control of party organisations and commit the party to a more advanced programme. Talk of programmes of any sort also exposed a tactical division among Liberals, with those who blamed the electoral defeat of 1895 on the Newcastle programme urging a reversion to single-issue politics.

Rising interest in the matter of working-class representation in Parliament was another source of Liberal dissension and one that was brought into sharper focus after 1893, when the Independent Labour Party was established. This was a subject on which Herbert Gladstone's own views had already ruffled the feathers of some of his senior colleagues. An article he drafted in 1892, for example, was too advanced for Arnold Morley, who showed a copy to John Bryce. He did not like its tone either, and suggested that it be published only if amended to remove wording apparently favouring the establishment of a separate labour party.[37]

All in all, therefore, given the lack of Liberal cohesion after 1895, it is hardly surprising that party organisation was also something of a shambles.

---

35 H. J. Gladstone to Maud Gladstone, 12 April 1899, FRO GG MSS 989.

36 *The Times*, 5 March 1894.

37 The article, suitably revised, was published as H. J. Gladstone, 'The Liberal Party and the Labour Party', *Albemarle Review*, 52 (February 1892).

Many of its wealthiest donors were Liberal Unionist in sympathy and their reluctance to support the current leadership meant that resources for an election were inadequate: indeed, the Liberal Central Association's income when Gladstone took over as Chief Whip was barely sufficient to cover running costs and it fell by 14 per cent in the year prior to the 1900 general election. Small wonder that he had few illusions about the party's prospects in that contest.

A year or two into his new role, Gladstone in a speech at Leeds likened himself to the party's valet, adding that while it was difficult to serve the Liberals when they lived in so many different habitations, he was determined to re-unite them. By the time he made this pronouncement, the divisions had been aggravated by the onset of the Boer War, but the wish to restore unity was a powerful consideration behind his acceptance of Campbell-Bannerman's offer. Personal considerations worked in the same direction, since he viewed the post as an opportunity to rediscover a sense of purpose and focus which had become increasingly diffuse since his father's withdrawal from public life in 1894: as a parliamentary col-league put it, the job would give him 'the regular occupation' for which 'I think you have been rather longing'.[38] While William Gladstone's decision to retire was perfectly understandable for a man of eighty-four and indeed had long been expected by the family, its actual occurrence was for Herbert, as his father noted in his diary, 'sad for him and hard on him'.[39] Their personal and political closeness is evident on many pages of the outgoing Prime Minister's diary. For Herbert, this retirement meant the loss of his mentor, the man whom he admired above all others, for whom he had acted as political secretary, through whom he had gained an early insight into the workings of the political establishment, and with whom he had talked incessantly about most of the major issues of the day, not least of course Home Rule. Normally unflappable, he later wrote with some emotion to his father that he could not 'tell you all that is in my heart to say. I'm gradually escaping the darkness which your retirement has cast about me. Whatever the future may bring forth, nothing in this world can bring to me the joy and pride with which for fourteen years I have worked for you, with you, under you.'[40] Such was the impact on him psychologically and emotionally that he was left feeling utterly deflated

---

38 H. J. Gladstone Papers, BL Add MSS 46017, fol. 154, J. F. Leese to H. J. Gladstone, 15 April 1899.

39 H. G. C. Mathew (ed.), *The Gladstone Diaries, Volume XIII: 1892–1896* (Oxford: Claren-don Press, 1994), W. E. Gladstone's diary entry for 9 January 1894.

40 Mary Drew Papers, BL Add MSS 46225, fol. 157, H. J. Gladstone to W. E. Gladstone, 3 April 1894 (copy).

and flat, telling Eddy Hamilton that he had lost all interest in politics and did not much care if he gave them up or they gave him up.[41]

Although the stimulus of promotion to the post of Commissioner of Works doubtless afforded some diversion, the relief was short-lived, partly because the government lasted only until 1895 but mainly because Herbert was increasingly absorbed by the care needs of his father, whose remarkable constitution was at last began to fail. Increasingly, Herbert had to divide his time between London and the family home at Hawarden and also to ensure that someone, usually a sibling but later a live-in housekeeper, was always on hand to take care of physical wants. If a change of scenery was recommended as potentially beneficial for the parents, then someone needed to travel and stay with them. Sisters Helen and Mary and brother Harry all willingly took on a share of the actual work, but the burden of responsibility seemed to fall most heavily on Herbert, probably because he had no family of his own to consider. From Cowes, where rather against his better judgement he took his parents for a break in January 1898, he wrote to Harry that their father 'has gone down in spirit and it left me lower than I would like to admit…. The really trying part just now is the unknown future and anxiety from day to day, how he & to a less extent she [Herbert's mother] will get through it.'[42] The emotional and psychological strain this imposed was evident in one of Mary's letters, written in April 1898. She recounted that her ailing father had asked for Herbert and Harry. Told that they were both away for a day or two, he 'sighed heavily. Both Henry and Herbert gone. Dreadful.'[43] By this time W. E. Gladstone's facial cancer, diagnosed in 1897, was approaching its inevitable outcome and there was the added pressure of having to handle the constant press enquiries and speculation about the health of such a prominent public figure. Herbert was particularly concerned to ensure that every member of the family stuck to the same agreed line. After Gladstone's death in May 1898, Herbert and Harry together took on the by no means insignificant task of organising a state funeral at Westminster Abbey. Even then, Herbert could not escape his father's shadow, for there were extended and sometimes strained discussions as the family sought to identify the biographer who could do justice to its patriarch. Long-standing colleague and friend John Morley was an obvious choice but Herbert and Harry both feared that, as a dogmatic atheist, Morley would not be able to deal satisfactorily with the religious faith which had been so central to their father's life and which they both shared. In the midst of these sometimes

41 E. Hamilton Papers, BL Add MSS 48664, E. Hamilton's diary, 4 July 1894.
42 FRO GG MSS 878, H. J. Gladstone to H. N. Gladstone, 16 January 1898.
43 FRO GG MSS 949, Mary Drew to H. J. Gladstone, 13 April 1898.

fraught discussions, Mary announced that she was proposing to publish her correspondence with Lord Acton. Herbert was outraged, believing this to be premature and a betrayal of family confidentiality, fearing that it would detract from the official biography. He was, he told Harry, dead against this 'bombshell'.[44] All things considered, it was small wonder that Herbert, who had struggled with his father's retirement from politics and then had to deal with the grief, no less powerful because expected, of the final separation, seems to have been left emotionally drained and rudderless. 'I feel', he told fellow Liberal G. O. Trevelyan, 'like a plant torn up by the roots yet unable at present to measure the infinitely great change which must & will overshadow our lives here'.[45]

Nor did the pressure on Herbert ease after his father's death, for his mother, too, was also failing and in September 1898 he confessed to Harry that he was 'dispirited' by the reports he had received on her condition.[46] On one of his increasingly frequent trips to Hawarden he arrived to find that Catherine had had a 'very bad day indeed – the worst I have experienced. She wouldn't leave me alone at all & got much excited.... She wd not eat much & could not work either fork or spoon.'[47] Catherine Gladstone had always doted upon her younger sons, referring to them as her 'sugar plums'. As the last born, Herbert had been the favourite and her emotional attachment to him seems if anything to have deepened as old age inevitably reduced the circle of her other relationships. When either of the boys wrote to Catherine, Helen said 'it counts 10 at least!'[48] On another occasion Catherine dictated to her a letter for Herbert in which 'the only instruction I have is to tell you how much she lives on yr letters'.[49] Now, Herbert was an enthusiastic and generous letter writer but even he quailed when told that the more he and Harry wrote, the better. It did not much matter what he said, since it was the mere fact of having a letter that was important to Catherine.[50] Doubtless this was why he had told Campbell-Bannerman that, in accepting the post of Chief Whip, it had to be understood that his mother was a priority. As it happened, Catherine survived his elevation by only a year or so. Her death in June 1900, however, added further to the weight of personal emotional stress

---

44 FRO GG MSS 878, H. J. Gladstone to H. N. Gladstone, 29 July 1898.

45 Trevelyan Papers, Robinson Library Special Collections, Newcastle University, GOT 123/75, H. J. Gladstone to G. O. Trevelyan, 1 June 1898. Used by permission of the Librarian, Robinson Library, Newcastle University.

46 FRO GG MSS 878, H. J. Gladstone to H. N. Gladstone, 8 September 1898.

47 *Ibid.*, H. J. Gladstone to H. N. Gladstone, 7 May 1899.

48 FRO GG MSS 957, Helen Gladstone to H. J. Gladstone, 12 April 1897.

49 FRO GG MSS 954, Catherine Gladstone to H. J. Gladstone, 28 April 1897 (dictated).

50 FRO GG MSS 957, Helen Gladstone to H. J. Gladstone, 4 September 1899.

under which he had been labouring for the last several years and his sister Agnes correctly observed that 'in a way perhaps the blank is a special one for you – she always showered such an unbounded wealth of love & pride upon you – the dear lucky baby!'[51]

Under the intense and prolonged stresses associated with the domestic situation, the unity of the Gladstone family, always much in evidence, began to show signs of fraying. Herbert had always been especially close to Harry, his senior by a couple of years. They had been schooled together and when Harry went to work in India Herbert looked after his affairs at home. On his return to England Harry more than returned the favour by providing significant and timely financial support for his brother. But the closeness of this relationship was tested when Harry married Maud Rendel in 1890. More than once Maud wrote to reassure Herbert that she had no wish to come between them. Harry similarly said he saw no reason why marriage should affect his relationship with Herbert. But inevitably there were frictions and disagreements, although by no means all of them involved Maud. Several of them centred on the handling of the family estate, where sometimes the brothers' aspirations and instructions seem to have clashed. Another bone of contention was Herbert's apparent obsession with golf. He had always been an enthusiastic games player and for many years had represented the House of Commons at cricket but in the 1890s he discovered golf, which, as he freely admitted, became something of a consuming passion. In July 1898, for instance, his total time on the golf course amounted to some seven and a half days. Harry expressed reservations at such a use of time, which, in his view, was drawing his brother away from more pressing and important matters, although it does not seem to have occurred to him that Herbert was under considerable strain and that, in the absence of alternatives, the game apparently afforded him some respite. Harry, of course, had the consolation of being married and his constant extolling of the marital state seems to have further irked his unmarried brother. Herbert confided in his best friend, Eddy Tennant, that Harry kept writing in varying states of ecstasy urging him to marry, and added, somewhat sourly, that 'we are not all Nabobs else we might'.[52] Things were probably not helped in this respect by the fact that Catherine, too, was constantly pressing marriage upon her favourite son, thereby emphasising the bachelorhood of which he needed little reminder. When Tennant asked him to be his best man in 1895

---

51 FRO GG MSS 976, Agnes Wickham to H. J. Gladstone, 24 June 1900, referring to the 'blank' left by Catherine Gladstone's death.

52 Tennant Papers, Scottish National Record Office, GD510/1/70, H. J. Gladstone to E. Tennant, 14 February 1890.

Herbert replied rather wistfully that 'I am getting to feel like an isolated rock in the wilderness – you are almost the last of my friends more or less contemporary to take the great & best step in life'.[53]

Throughout the 1890s, therefore, the familiar landmarks of Herbert Gladstone's life were shifting. His chief political mentor was gone, to be replaced initially by a leader with whom he had little empathy, either politically or personally, while the Liberal Party itself was disorganised and divided over tactics, imperial policy generally and Ireland in particular. At the same time, he was trying to cope with the needs of ageing parents, a task which he would never have dreamt of shirking but which entailed for him a particularly heavy emotional strain because of his especially close bonds with them. This manifested itself in more frequents spats with a brother with whom he had enjoyed the closest of relationships throughout his life and in a growing sensitivity to the absence from his own life of the domestic refuge which marriage could provide. His feelings surfaced with some passion in a very long and revealing letter to Harry, written in 1898, when the pain of his father's recent death must still have been rather raw. 'This year for me has been one of incessant movement, change anxiety & distraction.... Since Bournemouth I have felt incapacitated for politics & have no home life to fall back on.' Reproaching himself rather harshly for a lack of application to work, he claimed in justification that 'I have been hit far harder than my political colleagues.... I have had & still have no inclination or opportunity for political work & shall not resume it till Oct.' He similarly justified the time he was devoting to golf, by pointing out that he had given up on other favourite social activities, such as music, parties and theatre. He went on to appeal to Harry for some understanding. 'Now frankly I ask you to pitch into me whenever you think fit ... only don't rub it in just when we may fall out on ordinary matters. Another thing. You rightly say you do most of the Hn. [Hawarden] business. I have more than you know of perhaps for everyone seems to come to me about things wh are small but wh yet take time.' He was, he added, happy to take on anything Harry turned over to him but

> I cannot crawl in your wake when you mean to act.... Your ref to M[aud] is the first indication of that grievance. If my demeanour was bad I am unfeignedly sorry.... But look how these things work because of our saying either too little or too much to one another. M. naturally was conscious of your grievances against me. And she kept pinching me in tiny almost indefinite ways wh. I frankly own created in me a very unsatisfactory state of mind wh I daresay made me very irritable.... It seems we have all been

---

53 *Ibid.*, H. J. Gladstone to E. Tennant, 16 May 1895.

bottling ourselves up to bursting point & just fizzing out at the wrong time
… I know I owe you an apology…. Above all know that I look upon our
relations of forty years as a precious possession; & that even when hardest
pressed I have only wanted to do that wh. wd. retain it unimpaired.

Earlier in the same letter he complained with some feeling that 'the
curse of my life' was that he was not married. Now, Herbert Gladstone
was a highly eligible prospect and much admired in London society for his
good looks and social graces. His correspondence and the diary he briefly
kept in the 1880s provide ample evidence that he had a keen and apprecia-
tive eye for a pretty girl, while his family and friends certainly encouraged
matrimony. 'With every word said to me on that subject I agree', he told
his brother, but 'the difficulties lie deep. That they are not & cannot be
known is an added trouble & so long as this goes on I must put up with
the reproach of being a selfish bachelor & a bachelor for selfish purposes.'[54]
The difficulties to which he referred clearly meant his selfless prioritisation
of his parents' needs over his own. Once they had both gone, he was free
to follow his heart and it is significant that just over a year after Catherine's
death he announced his engagement to Dorothy Paget, a woman twenty
years his junior and whom he had got to know through their mutual enthusiasm for singing. The swift transformation in his personal demeanour
which followed was widely remarked upon in the family.

At the start of 1899 Herbert Gladstone was, like many Liberals, in
something of a political wilderness but in his case the frustrations of his
public life were compounded by the private emotional turbulence associated with his parents' declining years. The post of Chief Whip, even if it
implied a backward career step, offered not only an opportunity to help
restore Liberal fortunes but also something of a distraction from his own
inner turmoil. The state of the party and the added complication of the
Boer War made anything other than a Liberal defeat in the 1900 general
election unlikely. But whatever his precise contribution to the contrasting
outcome of the 1906 election, the vigour with which he embraced the
role of Chief Whip between the two contests owed much to the personal
rejuvenation he experienced as the circumstances of his domestic life
changed. He was to remark in later years that he had never been happier
than during his time in Parliament Street.[55]

---

54 FRO GG MSS 878, H. J. Gladstone to H. N. Gladstone, 28 July 1898, 'Most private'.
55 H. J. Gladstone Papers, BL Add MSS 46021, fol. 146, H. J. Gladstone to R. Hudson, 13
   October 1913.

3

A question of neutrality? The politics of co-operation in north-east England, 1881–1926

JOAN ALLEN

The British co-operative movement, which began as a small self-help group founded by the Rochdale Pioneers in 1844, had evolved by 1900 into a mass organisation of 1,439 registered societies with a loyal membership of 1,707,000 co-operators.[1] The independence of its retail stores was anchored by overarching institutions such as the Co-operative Wholesale Society, the Co-operative Union, the Co-operative Bank and the Co-operative Insurance Society, which collectively gave the movement its national identity and status. Early-twentieth-century Labour leaders such as Ramsay MacDonald and Keir Hardie sought to draw co-operators into the wider circle of trade unionists and activists. If their speeches and addresses were calculated to distinguish between their own socialist vision and that of Robert Owen's 'communitarian ideal', they were still at pains to acknowledge his commitment to working-class emancipation.[2] The co-operative movement's democratic structure and predominantly working-class membership have, quite naturally, been of interest to labour historians working on the understanding that party activists, trade unionists and co-operators shared a common world view, articulated most powerfully in slogans such as 'union is strength' and 'each for all

---

1 G. D. H. Cole, *A Century of Cooperation* (Manchester: Manchester University Press, 1944), p. 375.
2 Gregory Claeys, 'Robert Owen and some later socialists', in Noel Thompson and Chris Williams (eds), *Robert Owen and His Legacy* (Cardiff: University of Wales Press, 2011), pp. 3–53; Sidney Pollard, 'Nineteenth-century co-operation: from community building to shopkeeping', in Asa Briggs and John Saville (eds), *Essays in Labour History: In Memory of G. D. H. Cole* (London: Macmillan, 1960), p. 112.

and all for each'.[3] Yet, as Peter Gurney argued in his seminal study of co-operative culture, the belief that the lure of a quick dividend had fatally derailed the promise in Owen's idealistic, transformative vision unduly dominated early histories. The altogether gloomy assessment that the co-operative spirit lost its way in the later nineteenth century led many post-war labour historians to conclude that co-operators were passive consumers, not class warriors.[4]

Scholarly attention has concentrated on the movement's central function of providing working-class families with good-quality food, clothing, furnishings, insurance and funerals at affordable prices, and there is, even now, widespread ignorance of the Co-operative Party and its role in British political life.[5] Smaller parties have always struggled to make an impact on the British electoral system, but this does not adequately explain why the public know so little of the Co-operative Party, which was founded in 1917 and currently sponsors twenty-four Labour MPs and fifteen members of the House of Lords. As of February 2016 the party had seven members at Holyrood and eleven Welsh Assembly members.[6] Some party members, such as Alun Michael, Pauline Green and Ed Balls, have attained high office, while countless others have served on local councils or as MEPs.

---

3 For example, Bill Lancaster, *Radicalism, Co-operation and Socialism: Leicester Working Class Politics* (Leicester: Leicester University Press, 1987).

4 Peter Gurney, *Co-operative Culture and the Politics of Consumption in England, 1870–1930* (Manchester: Manchester University Press, 1996), pp. 2–5; Peter Gurney, 'The middle-class embrace: language, representation and the contest over co-operative forms in Britain, c. 1860–1914', *Victorian Studies*, 37(2) (1994), 253–86.

5 Beatrice Webb, *The Co-operative Movement in Britain* (London: Swann Sonnerschein, 1891); Arnold Bonner, *British Co-operation: A Survey of the History, Principles and Organisation of the Co-operative Movement in Great Britain and Ireland* (Manchester: Co-operative Union, 1961). Important recent works include Lawrence Black and Nicole Robertson (eds), *Consumerism and the Co-operative Movement in Modern British History: Taking Stock* (Manchester: Manchester University Press, 2009); Nicole Robertson, *The Co-operative Movement and Communities in Britain 1914–1960: Minding Their Own Business* (London: Routledge, 2010). See also Martin Purvis, 'Co-operative retailing in England, 1835–1850: developments beyond Rochdale', *Northern History*, 22 (1986), 198–215; Paul Johnson, *Saving and Spending: The Working Class Economy in Britain 1870–1939* (Oxford: Oxford University Press, 1985), chapter 5. For business history perspectives, see Tony Webster, 'Building the wholesale: the development of the English CWS and British co-operative business', *Business History*, 54(6) (2012), 883–904; Peter Gurney, 'Co-operation and the "new consumerism" in interwar England', *Business History*, 54(6) (2012), 905–24; John Wilson, Anthony Webster and Rachael Vorberg-Rugh, 'The co-operative movement in Britain: from crisis to "Renaissance", 1950–2010', *Enterprise and Society*, 14(2) (2013), 271–302.

6 Figures taken from the Co-operative Party's website, https://party.coop (accessed 10 January 2017).

Undoubtedly, the Co-operative Party's relative invisibility is a testimony to its seamless integration into labour politics, a measure of harmonious coexistence, which contrasts sharply with the combative and frequently irritable relationship between the Labour Party and the trade unions.

One explanation is that the Co-operative Party has never been identified with a separate, distinguishable political philosophy. At the 1832 Annual Co-operative Congress, Robert Owen observed that 'the Co-operative world contains persons of all religious sects and all political parties'.[7] For Owen, and successive leading co-operators, a balance had to be struck between the movement's progressive mission to create a 'co-operative commonwealth' and the guiding principles of political independence. But political neutrality was always open to interpretation. While some members believed this required complete disassociation from political affairs, others held that involvement was legitimate, provided alliance with any particular party was avoided. Even those members who preferred to distance themselves from political matters were drawn into the political arena over the vexed issue of tax liability. As mutual trading societies, co-operative stores had been able to claim exemption from tax on their profits, on the grounds that any surplus income was redistributed to the membership through the payment of the dividend. From the 1870s onwards there were repeated attempts to impose a liability to income tax. This led in 1892 to the establishment of a Joint Parliamentary Committee,[8] which acted as a sort of watchdog, monitoring legislation likely to have a detrimental effect, and lobbying sympathetic Members of the House of Commons for the protection of co-operative interests. Gradually, it became apparent that it lacked any real political muscle; members were entirely dependent upon the goodwill of others and they repeatedly urged the Co-operative Union to obtain direct political representation. Although the rhetoric of neutrality still had considerable purchase, the Joint Committee marked the movement's entry into politics.

The onset of war in 1914 brought the question of neutrality into sharper relief. The decision of the wartime Cabinet to impose excess profits duty is generally credited as a primary cause of the decision to obtain direct representation in Parliament and on local governing bodies. It was not, of course, the only immediate cause. Widespread anger and resentment had surfaced over the allocation of food supplies and the severe staffing

---

7 Quoted in T. F. Carbery, *Consumers in Politics: A History and General Review of the Co-operative Party* (Manchester: Manchester University Press, 1969), p. 3.

8 Paddy Maguire, 'Co-operation and crisis: government, co-operation, and politics, 1917–1922', in Stephen Yeo (ed.), *New Views of Co-operation* (London: Routledge, 1988), p. 188: Cole, *Century of Co-operation*, pp. 313–15.

shortages resulting from compulsory military service. With some justification, co-operative members believed that private traders were being given preferential treatment at their expense. Even the right to appeal seemed proscribed, since the members of military tribunals were predominantly drawn from the private sector. One co-operative society protested vehemently that of 102 male employees, 99 had been called to serve.[9] Moreover, the quantity and the quality of available food supplies to co-operatives were also subject to discriminatory practices.

The Annual Cooperative Congress which met at Swansea in May 1917 debated four resolutions calling for parliamentary representation and a show of hands declared the overwhelming support of delegates for the motion. An Emergency Conference, convened the following October at Central Hall, Westminster, dispelled any lingering doubts that support for political action had dissipated in the intervening months. The Conference, attended by 900 delegates representing over 500 societies, gave their resounding agreement to the formation of the Co-operative Party. The movement's official entry into national politics had begun.[10]

Until recently, this turbulent transition has occupied only a subsidiary place in historiography.[11] G. D. H. Cole's 1944 commemorative history rejected the possibility that there was 'any conscious will to unite on a common political programme', asserting instead that politicisation was a wholly defensive response.[12] This view found favour with many, including Tom Carbery, who concluded that politicisation should not be read as a bid to 'proselytise a basic social or political philosophy'.[13] Sidney Pollard thus represented something of a lone voice in 1971 when he claimed that historians had failed to factor in the steady growth of class consciousness and increased solidarity across working-class organisations. The natural corollary of this was to propose that long-term ideological change, 'not

---

9 Carbery, *Consumers in Politics*, p. 17.
10 Cole, *Century of Co-operation*, p. 316.
11 Greg Rosen, *Co-operative Party History from Fred Perry to Gordon Brown* (London: Co-operative Party, 2007). K. Manton, 'The Labour Party and the Co-op, 1918–58', *Historical Research*, 82(218) (2009), 756–778, focuses on the relationship between the two parties during the Attlee period. For official histories, see: Stan Newens, *Working Together: A Short History of the London Co-op Society Political Committee* (London: CRS London Political Committee, 1988); Jim Craigen, 'The Co-operative Party: out of labour's shadow', in Bill Lancaster and Paddy Maguire (eds), *Towards the Co-operative Commonwealth: 150 Years of Co-operation. Essays in the History of Co-operation* (Loughborough: Co-operative College, 1996), pp. 95–8.
12 Cole, *Century of Co-operation*, p. 269.
13 Carbery, *Consumers in Politics*, p. 257.

short term grievances', was the 'real basis' of politicisation.[14] Not everyone agreed. In the 1980s Tony Adams protested that Pollard's argument relied altogether too much upon 'impressions' – not least by failing to distinguish between the views of socialist activists and those of the ordinary rank and file – although he similarly stressed that the chief motivations were 'practical and short term'.[15] While there was broad agreement that the emergence of the Co-operative Party in 1917 was linked to wartime grievances, Pollard insisted that this hardly accounted for the abandonment of neutrality; class solidarities with other workers and their labour organisations had to be seen as 'part of the same process'.[16]

These studies thoroughly scrutinised the relevant national records: speeches and resolutions, correspondence and the political levy subscription lists. Yet this focus on the collective response has obscured as much as it has revealed. At the very least, the meta-narrative has masked the extent to which some branches opposed politicisation, or changed their minds after the initial levy was pledged. As both John Walton and Mary Hilson have argued since, historians must get to grips with the movement's 'intra-regional differences' if they are not to be misled by the chimera of uniformity.[17] Walton has long been an advocate of regional history.[18] In 2003, responding to an article by Barbara Blaszak on the 'gendered geography' of co-operation, he argued against her 'generalised' analysis, which could not capture the 'enormous variety of sub-regional

---

14 Sidney Pollard, 'The foundation of the Co-operative Party', in Asa Briggs and John Saville (eds), *Essays in Labour History 1886–1923* (London: Shoe Strings, revised edition 1971), vol. II, p. 209.

15 Tony Adams, 'Co-operators in politics – a rejoinder', *International Review of Social History*, 2 (1987), 178.

16 Sidney Pollard, 'The Co-operative Party – reflections on a reconsideration', *International Review of Social History*, 2 (1987), 168.

17 John K. Walton, 'Locality, gender and co-operation in England: a comment on Barbara J. Blaszak', *Women's History Review*, 12 (2003), 483; Mary Hilson, 'Consumers and politics: the co-operative movement in Plymouth 1890–1920', *Labour History Review*, 67(1) (2002), 7–28. For other studies which include regional and local perspectives, see Bill Lancaster and Paddy Maguire (eds), *Towards the Co-operative Commonwealth: 150 Years of Co-operation. Essays in the History of Co-operation* (Loughborough: Co-operative College, 1996); and *Co-operation – A Way of Life*, a special issue of *North West Labour History*, 19 (1994/95); special issue (untitled) of *North East History: The Journal of the North East Labour History Society*, 43 (2012), 18–57.

18 For example, see Luis Castells and John Walton, 'Contrasting identities: north-west England and the Basque country, 1840–1936', in Edward Royle (ed.), *Issues of Regional Identity: In Honour of John Marshall* (Manchester: Manchester University Press, 1998), pp. 44–81.

and local economies' of the north-west and the south.[19] Mary Hilson's study of Plymouth Co-operative Society's response to politicisation in 1917 specifically addresses this regional agenda, pointing out that the 'forms and meanings of co-operation differed from society to society and place to place', precisely at a time when regional and local concerns still exerted a powerful pull over political responses and affiliations.[20] Plymouth is an interesting case study, not just because of its size and strident politicisation, but because its membership was dominated by generations of dockyard workers whose espousal of self-help was so closely aligned with co-operative values. While it is clear that the Plymouth model cannot be used to 'extrapolate national trends', Hilson advances a persuasive case for further local studies to help to 'complete a fragmented national picture'.[21]

In this light, the present chapter explores the diverse responses of co-operators in the north-east of England and suggests that politicisation in 1917 was the culmination of a much longer transitional process, one which had as much to do with Pollard's class solidarities as with the fight for equitable treatment by the state. Co-operation took firm root in the region after 1858, particularly in the coalfields of Northumberland and Durham and in the Tyneside industrial belt, which has long been associated with precocious labour and trade union activism. Cole calculated that the membership of the Northern Section was 29 per cent of total population but in individual parishes such as Cramlington and Blaydon membership was virtually comprehensive.[22] By the 1870s the Section comprised seventy-four stores and had set up a number of producer co-operatives to further drive down household costs. These initiatives generated a large workforce of co-operative employees and, crucially, associational bonds that had meaning beyond the consumer imperative.

In the north-east, Chartism and Owenite socialism were parallel movements and, despite their ideological differences, Chartist meetings were frequently held in local co-operative stores and co-operatives benefited from the exclusive dealings practised by Chartist supporters. Co-operative enterprises, which emphasised the equal rights of all classes, came to be

---

19 Walton, 'Locality, gender and co-operation', p. 478; Barbara J. Blaszak, 'The gendered geography of the English co-operative movement at the turn of the nineteenth century', *Women's History Review*, 9 (2000), 559–84.

20 Hilson, 'Consumers and politics', p. 9. On the 'nationalisation' of popular politics before 1914, she cites Duncan Tanner, *Political Change and the Labour Party, 1900–1918* (Cambridge: Cambridge University Press, 1990).

21 Hilson, 'Consumers and politics', p. 10.

22 The Northern Section comprised the four counties of Durham, Northumberland, Cumberland and Westmoreland. Cole, *Century of Co-operation*, pp. 153, 158, 381–2, 391.

regarded as the practical application of Chartist principles.[23] It was not unusual for leading co-operators to be political reformers. On Tyneside, for example, the leading co-operators included Joseph Cowen MP, a renowned radical activist who established the first store at Blaydon, and John Rutherford, who campaigned for secondary education for working-class children.[24] Both were committed reformers and this shaped the Northern Section's adventurous programme of house building, education and welfare.

In 1900, the Newcastle (17,432 members) and Sunderland (14,362 members) societies ranked among the twelve largest in the country and in the following two decades north-east branches experienced the same unprecedented upsurge in membership experienced by trade unions, the Labour Party and other working-class organisations. Nor was this expansion confined to rising membership. Co-operative activity extended into new, diverse areas of economic activity, including banking, insurance, manufacturing, agriculture and printing. The establishment of the Co-operative Wholesale Society delivered greater control over costs and prices, and this bolstered the movement's enviably large share and loan capital (an estimated £44,935,713 in 1914).

Alarmed and resentful, private traders fought back, exerting their considerable influence in local and national political circles.[25] Equally, as hostilities deepened, demands grew apace for a more effective defence of co-operative principles. Between 1897 and 1917 the political question was repeatedly debated at annual congresses and several attempts were made to obtain a mandate for direct parliamentary representation. As early as 1892, the Co-operative Congress advised all societies to urgently consider fielding suitable candidates for election on local governing bodies. Progress proved to be slow and piecemeal. Despite unanimous support for political action at the Perth Congress in 1897 the response from the wider membership was disappointing. The Central Board was forced to admit that 'the time

---

23 Malcolm Chase, *The Chartists: Perspectives and Legacies* (London: Merlin, 2015), pp. 96, 167; Gurney, *Co-operative Culture*; Peter Gurney, 'Exclusive dealing in the Chartist movement', *Labour History Review*, 74(1) (2009), 90–110; Ray Challinor, 'Chartism and cooperation in the north east', *North East Labour History Society Bulletin*, 43 (2012), 18–24.

24 Joan Hugman, 'Joseph Cowen and the Blaydon Co-operative Society: a north east model', in Bill Lancaster and Paddy Maguire (eds), *Towards the Co-operative Commonwealth: 150 Years of Co-operation. Essays in the History of Co-operation* (Loughborough: Co-op College, 1996), pp. 63–74; Joan Allen, *Joseph Cowen and Tyneside Radicalism, 1829–1900* (London: Merlin, 2007); Joan Allen, *Rutherford's Ladder: A History of the University of Northumbria* (Newcastle upon Tyne: Northumbria University Press, 2005).

25 A. Bonner, *British Cooperation* (London: Co-operative Union, 1961).

is not ripe'.[26] A few years later, Mr T. Tweddell, a Hartlepool justice of the peace and a member of the Joint Parliamentary Committee, presented a paper on direct representation to the Paisley Congress (1905), which called on co-operators to give 'adequate consideration' to working-class interests, since both of the main political parties had 'for a generation or more ... divided between them as though it were a piece of inherited property, the political allegiance to the workingman'.[27] Working men, he claimed, were no longer prepared to exist in a state of 'helpless equilibrium' between the Tories and the Liberals and believed that they had an equal right to share in the government of the country. The motion was carried by 654 votes to 271, although it is notable that an additional motion proposing joint consultative action with the Labour Representation Committee was firmly rejected.[28] The Paisley motion met with the same apathetic response as the Perth resolution and, once again, further action was stalled.

To the onlooker, this seesaw rejection and support for political action seems puzzling and strangely contradictory. But several important considerations must be taken into account. First, the countless smaller branches, especially those in rural or mining areas, were often rather insular. Their abiding concern was the efficient management of the store and the interests of their own members. The autonomy and independence of each branch was often a greater priority than their connection to the wider movement. While branches in the major towns and cities normally sent several delegates to the annual Co-operative Congress, and vied with each other to act as host, smaller branches could not always afford the time or the cost of sending a delegate. Most often, an agreement would be brokered with adjacent societies to send a single representative from the district, thereby reducing the financial burden. Such arrangements required approval by a majority of members. As the votes at each branch meeting in the district were recorded and added together, this sometimes produced decisions at variance with those of individual branches. In essence, Congress decisions could often seem unimportant to those who were not regularly engaged in its deliberations and any mandate for action could be discounted more readily.

This is best understood by examining the processes of a typical Tyneside branch like Throckley, which sought such an arrangement with the Waltottle and Westerope branches. Representation at Congress does

---

26 Carbery, *Consumers in Politics*, p. 7.
27 National Co-operative Archive (NCA), Holyoake House, Manchester (HHM), T. Tweddell, 'Direct representation in Parliament', paper presented at the Paisley Co-operative Congress, 1905.
28 Carberry, *Consumers in Politics*, p. 9.

not seem to have been a regular arrangement, nor was there an established rota system such as the one that operated in Newcastle. Instead, the full membership of each branch was balloted at their three separate quarterly meetings. Only if a majority voted in favour was a single delegate selected to represent all three branches.[29] In contrast, a major branch such as the Newcastle Society engaged more in regional and national administrative affairs. It regularly sent three delegates to Congress, representing the board, the employees and the members. In 1906, when it sent four delegates, it was the membership who gained the additional voting advantage.[30]

There is little evidence here to support the contention that Congress delegates were socialist activists who did not accurately reflect the opinions of rank-and-file members.[31] The democratic method of selecting not just Congress delegates but committee members, too, ensured that members' views were fully articulated. They were hardly likely to elect as a delegate someone whose political stance was at odds with that of the majority. And it would be wrong to conclude that only activists attended meetings. Across the region, members enjoyed larger than average quarterly dividends. Three shillings in the pound was not at all unusual in the 1880s; in the Durham coalfield it could be as high as four shillings and setting the rate was a highly sensitive issue.[32] Members had a large stake in the judicious management of their branch and this translated into regular attendance at quarterly meetings, when policy matters, pricing and calibrating the next quarter's dividend were thrashed out.

Cole and others have made much of the 'close links between store and chapel' in the north, arguing that Methodists were instrumental in shoring up the strong Liberal loyalties of co-operators long after Liberalism had begun to decline.[33] Such arguments certainly have traction in Northumberland, where the influence of Thomas Burt and Charles Fenwick – both MPs sponsored by the Miners' Federation of Great Britain – exerted an almost unassailable hold over the mining communities which dominated the Wansbeck and Tyneside divisions and, by extension, the myriad of co-operative branches whose membership rolls were scarcely distinguishable

---

29 Northumberland Record Office (henceforth NRO) 1062/8, Quarterly meetings minutes (QMM), Throckley Co-operative Society, 24 November 1914, 18 January 1915, 22 November 1916.

30 Tyne and Wear Archives Service (TWAS) 1127/27, QMM, Newcastle Society, 31 January 1906.

31 Adams, 'Co-operators in politics', p. 176.

32 Hugman, 'Joseph Cowen and the Blaydon Co-operative Society', p. 70.

33 Cole, *Century of Co-operation*, p. 312.

from those of the lodges of the Northumberland Miners' Association.[34] Again, the Throckley committee in 1914 epitomised the unusually close associational networks across the northern coalfield: co-operative meetings were generally held at the Wesleyan Hall or in the adjacent school room and Thomas King, Society Chairman, was also Treasurer of the local Liberal Association; committee men Dick Browell, Dan Dawson, 'Henna' Brown and George Curwen were all miners, trade unionists and members of the Independent Labour Party (ILP), while Browell and Dawson were also committed Methodists.[35] Indeed, after Fenwick's death in 1918, Browell and Dawson used their seniority as officials of the Northumberland Miners' Association to persuade co-operators to support the establishment of Wansbeck District Labour Party.[36] The Liberals exercised an equally powerful influence over the Newcastle committee, at least until 1905, when the establishment of an ILP branch and a Labour Representation Committee in the city prefigured a breach in the status quo.[37] At the 1909 Co-operative Congress, in Newcastle, Alexander Wilkie MP led the call for greater collaboration between co-operators and trade unionists, reminding the assembled crowds that 'Co-operation has itself educated its members in the principles of the Movement and their minds have been further enlarged and broadened by their participation in Trade Unionism'.[38]

In 1912, a conference brought together representatives of the Co-operative Union, the Trades Union Congress and the Labour Party to discuss matters of mutual concern. The following year the Aberdeen Congress debated calls for 'closer union' between the movement and other working-class organisations, prompting some speakers, including the arch-Liberal Edward O. Greening, to reaffirm the importance of maintaining a neutral stance 'so that political dissension in our ranks be avoided'.[39] Despite such implacable resistance, the conference delegates found enough

---

34 Lowell J. Satre, *Thomas Burt, Miners' MP, 1837–1922: The Great Conciliator* (Leicester: Leicester University Press, 1999); A. W. Purdue, 'The Liberal and Labour Parties in north-east politics, 1900–1914', *International Review of Social History*, 26(1) (1981), 1–24; Celia Minoughan, 'The rise of Labour in Northumberland: Wansbeck Labour Party 1918–50', in M. Callcott and Ray Challinor (eds), *Working Class Politics in North East England* (Newcastle: Newcastle upon Tyne Polytechnic, 1983), pp. 79–95.

35 NRO, 1062/8, QMM, Throckley, 24 February 1915, 30 August 1915. See also Bill Williamson, *Class Culture and Community: A Biographical Study of Change in a Mining Community* (London: Routledge, 1982), pp. 58–60.

36 Minoughan, 'The rise of Labour in Northumberland', pp. 81, 83.

37 Tony Barrow, 'The Labour Representation Committee conference at Newcastle upon Tyne in 1903', in Callcott and Challinor, *Working Class Politics*, p. 40.

38 NCA, HHM, 1909 Co-operative Congress report, p. 13.

39 Carbery, *Consumers in Politics*, p. 13.

support to justify further meetings. While neutrality remained the official position at Congress in 1915, co-operators had made great progress in firming up their links with the Labour Party and trade unions.

The suggestion here is that formative political experiences and the decline of generational loyalties to Liberal politics were forces at work long before wartime grievances rendered neutrality untenable. A co-operative political voice had been making itself heard for some time, not least through the welfare reform campaigns of the Women's Co-operative Guild (WCG).[40] When the Women's League for the Spread of Co-operation (the forerunner of the WCG) emerged in 1883, north-east women were quick to seize the opportunity to carve out their own sphere of activity, and the first branch was formed at North Shields that same year.[41] Guild women had fewer qualms about setting a radical agenda for political and social reform, building links with trade unions and tackling difficult questions such as improved maternity and child care, the divorce laws, suffrage and employment conditions. For many, the WCG offered a springboard into other forms of activism, giving them the confidence to serve as Poor Law guardians and on school boards, and to join suffrage groups such as the Women's Freedom League.[42] They backed the campaign run by the Amalgamated Union of Co-operative Employees for a minimum wage and eventually secured a Congress ruling in 1909 to improve rates. However, the cost implications were stoutly resisted by many branches, including those in north-east England.[43] As with the establishment of the Sunderland Poor Store in 1902, in which they enlisted the assistance of the charismatic Margaret Llewelyn Davies, there was some resistance to admitting those who lived in the rougher districts, especially if the 'experiment' involved parting with any revenue which might reduce the dividend.[44] Despite such setbacks, women's role in north-east co-operation had shifted. No longer cast to the margins, women took on key management roles and

---

40 Jean Gaffin and David Thoms, *Caring and Sharing: The Centenary History of the Co-operative Women's Guild* (Nottingham: Co-operative Union, 1983), pp. 50–9, 85–90.
41 Gill Scott, "'Working out Their own Salvation": women's autonomy and divorce law reform in the co-operative movement, 1910–1920', in Yeo, *New Views of Co-operation*, pp. 128–51.
42 Hilary Frances, "'Dare to be free!" The Women's Freedom League and its legacy', in June Purvis and Sandra Holton (eds), *Votes for Women* (London: Routledge, 2000), p. 183; Steven King, *Women, Welfare and Local Politics 1880–1920* (Eastbourne: Sussex Academic Press, 2010), pp. 177–8; Mrs Yearn, 'A public-spirited rebel', in Margaret Llewelyn Davies (ed.), *Life As We Have Known It* (London: Virago, 1977), pp. 102–8.
43 Gurney, *Co-operative Culture*, p. 173; TWAS, 1127/27, QMM, Newcastle, 27 July 1910.
44 Kath Connolly, 'A new Rochdale? The Sunderland Poor Store', *North East History*, 43 (2012), 57–74.

were appointed to sub-committees, 'unanimously' backing politicisation at the annual congress of the WCG in June 1917.[45]

It could be argued that this gathering momentum in favour of closer association was, if anything, *stalled* by the outbreak of war. But this drag on progress was far from uniform. While leading co-operators were increasingly preoccupied by the day-to-day limitations on their business operations, the campaign for greater union continued apace in districts where support was already embedded in the local culture. At the national level, the impact of war was not wholly negative. The War Emergency Workers' National Committee (later the War Emergency Committee), set up in 1914 by the Labour Party, the TUC and the co-operative movement, was remarkable in that, for the first time, representatives of all branches of the labour movement were brought together as a united force 'to safeguard working class interests'.[46] The alacrity with which six co-operative representatives accepted an invitation to serve seems to contradict the supposedly entrenched position on political neutrality. Rather, it underpins the extent to which the joint conferences of the Labour Party and the co-operative movement in 1912 and 1913 had affirmed a sense of common enterprise. As Pollard asserts, by then an alliance with the Labour Party was implicitly understood.[47] Undoubtedly, co-operative members of the War Emergency Committee were being politicised by the experience of defending working-class interests; as food surpluses, rationing and profiteering assumed an ever greater priority, the movement was accorded a more respected and prestigious role within the broader labour movement.

Even the most cursory trawl of north-east co-operative minute books from the wartime years reveals widespread concern over food supplies, military conscription of key personnel and the threatened imposition of tax duties. The records of Hedgely, Felton, Hetton Downs and Fourstones co-operative societies are dominated by financial concerns and make no reference to the growing clamour for political action.[48] Other north-east branches were clearly exercised by the problems of securing adequate supplies of basic necessities such as meat, tea, sugar, margarine and milk; in rural societies such as Throckley the exorbitant cost of hay presented

45 *Daily Herald*, 30 June 1917.
46 Royden Harrison, 'The War Emergency Workers' National Committee, 1914–20', in Asa Briggs and John Saville (eds), *Essays in Labour History 1886–1923* (London: Shoe Strings, revised edition 1971), vol. II, p. 211.
47 Pollard, 'Foundation of the Co-operative Party', p. 189.
48 NRO, 1801, Minutes, Hedgeley Society, 17 June 1911–10 April 1918; NRO, 402/7, Minutes, Fourstones and Newbrough Co-operative Industrial Society, June 1915–December 1918; NRO, 362/1, Minutes, Felton and District, July 1903–November 1919; TWAS, 1066/3, Hetton Downs Amicable Industrial Society, April 1917–January 1927.

a particular difficulty.[49] The Newcastle Society attempted to introduce a fairer distribution scheme for everyday commodities but such moves were opposed by the Ministry of Food or local traders. Much of the difficulty stemmed from the adoption of a 'datum line' method of allocation, whereby levels of supplies were based on pre-war requirements. This took no account of the enormous increase in co-operative membership and allocations, and so fell far short of most societies' needs. In December 1916 a special meeting of the Newcastle Society resolved to lobby the government to 'control the price of the necessities of life, and thereby reduce the cost of living ... incidentally reducing the cost of the war', but to little avail.[50] At a conference of the Newcastle Society the following April, one delegate protested that the official allocation of sugar was supposed to be three-quarters of a pound per head per week; in practice, co-operative branches were being allocated just five ounces of sugar per head.[51] Efforts to improve the situation were frustrated because co-operators were invariably excluded from the Food Control Committees, which were packed out with private traders. The Newcastle and District Representation Committee (NDRC) took a keen interest in these prejudicial arrangements and launched a campaign to demand a more equitable distribution of food and fuel – an initiative which acted as a strategic bridge between co-operative and labour interest groups. Both Throckley and West Cramlington were represented at that Committee's meetings and contributed to the costs of sending a protest deputation to Westminster.[52]

In May 1917, the War Emergency Committee recommended that local labour, co-operative and industrial organisations form Special Food Vigilance Committees for the purpose of focusing attention on food supplies – a proposal swiftly adopted by several north-east societies. As an article in the *Daily Herald* highlighted, tensions were running so high by this stage that the government was pointedly reminded that 'although food shortage in Russia was not the cause of the overthrow of the Tsar's government, it at least was *the occasion*'.[53] The Parliamentary Committee, which had supported government food controls from the outset, tried to direct all enquiries about food supply through itself, but its interventions had little impact until the middle of 1917, when co-operatives were finally given proper representation on Food Control Committees.

---

49 NRO, 1062/8, Minutes, Throckley, 3 January 1916.
50 TWAS, 1069/1, QMM, Newcastle, 20 December 1916.
51 *Illustrated Newcastle Chronicle*, 16 April 1917.
52 NRO, 821/27, Minutes, West Cramlington, 24 May 1917; NRO, 1062/8, Throckley, 30 April 1917.
53 *Daily Herald*, 12 May 1917, original emphasis.

The inequities related to military recruitment were just as pressing. On countless occasions, the authorities recruited key personnel such as branch managers and administrative staff. Appeals to local tribunals were routinely dismissed, even where exemption would normally have been upheld on the grounds of age or protected occupation. Societies were obliged to appoint inexperienced female staff not only as clerical workers but in non-traditional areas such as butchery departments. At the beginning of the war, co-operatives had agreed to support the dependants of military recruits for its duration, and pledged that they would be re-employed afterwards. In the circumstances, they were aggrieved that they should be discriminated against by the Ministry of Defence and its local representatives. At a National Emergency Conference in October 1917, called by the Co-operative Union, Mr Allan of the Scottish Wholesale Society complained that co-operators were the butt of 'snubs, gibes and taunts', and accused administrators of trying 'to close some of our stores by the removal of salesmen'.[54]

Food and conscription were not the only or even the main source of conflict between co-operators and private traders. The imposition of excess profits duty in 1915 was regarded as a more serious threat, as it placed co-operators on the same footing as capitalists and profiteers; by equating members' dividends with profits, it attacked the core principles of the movement. The Newcastle Society called upon the Co-operative Union to make 'vigorous representations in the proper quarters' to secure an exemption. Meanwhile, societies were advised by the Union's solicitors to reduce dividends, adjust the price of basic commodities and avoid trading with non-members. This was expected to clarify their status as mutual trading associations and thereby reduce their liability to tax. The New-castle Society immediately reduced the dividend to two shillings in the pound and six months later reduced it to one shilling and six pence. This was a substantial reduction and board members were criticised for not taking protective measures sooner.[55] Across Northumberland, numerous deputations were made to Charles Fenwick, calling on him to appeal against the tax.[56] Although most societies managed to substantially reduce their surpluses and avoid paying large amounts of tax, the vastly reduced dividend rankled with individual members. It would be difficult to under-estimate the extent to which the dividend empowered and protected

54 NCA, HHM, National Emergency Conference, 1917, p. 17.

55 TWAS, 1127/27, QMM, Newcastle, 16 April 1916, 26 July 1916, 20 December 1916.

56 NRO, 361/8, Minutes, Amble, 2 July 1917; NRO, 821/27, Minutes, West Cramlington, 19 March 1917; NRO, 1794/16, Minutes, Ashington Industrial Society, 24 May 1917, 11 September 1917; NRO, 1062/8, QMM, Throckley, 30 April 1917.

working people – as savings against loss of earnings in a volatile industry, or as the means of purchasing major household items.

It was in this context that a large number of co-operators abandoned their commitment to political neutrality and sought direct representation. Increasingly they looked to the Labour Party for assistance. In the run-up to the 1917 Swansea Congress, societies received advance notice of a motion 'to secure direct representation in Parliament and on all administrative Bodies'. Strong views were expressed on both sides of the divide. The Secretary of the Scottish Section, J. Deans, argued powerfully that only 'political action' would suffice, but the opposition was equally vehement in rejecting change. As one Derby delegate cautioned, individuals were there to represent their own branch: they should 'stick to their instructions and not be swayed by any side issues. You are here at the bidding of your members, to do what they want.' Other delegates repeatedly referred to the great gulf between capitalists and working people. Working people, they said, should unite to secure the co-operative commonwealth.[57]

The resolution secured overwhelming backing from Congress (1,883 votes to 199) and the majority of Northern Section members appear to have supported it. Approval was given for a fighting fund to meet the costs and societies were asked to contribute £2 for every 1,000 members. Ashington, Newbiggin, Hexham, Throckley and Newcastle all immediately pledged their support but other societies, such as West Cramlington, Broomhill and West Wylam in the Tyne Valley, struggled initially to persuade their members to donate. Many societies were implacably opposed. Corbridge, Tweedside Industrial and Low Prudhoe all voted against the political levy at their meetings.[58] Overall, societies in mining areas were generally in favour of politicisation and this arguably reflected the particularly strong influence of the trade union leadership and the ILP in those areas.[59]

The Newcastle Society rapidly set up a selection committee comprising a balance of ordinary and board members to 'secure direct local and parliamentary representation', but they still struggled to reach agreement on payment of the political levy.[60] Official records of subscriptions received for the Parliamentary Representation Fund in June 1918 indicate that

57 NCA, HHM, Report, Proceedings of the Co-operative Congress, Swansea, 1917, p. 555.
58 NRO, 368/5, Minutes, Corbridge, 17 August 1917; NRO, 368/8, Minutes, Low Prudhoe, 4 March 1921; NRO, 1799/29, Minutes, Tweedside Industrial, 16 April 1917, 30 April 1918.
59 A.W. Purdue, 'The ILP in the North East of England' in David James, Tony Jowitt and Keith Laybourn (eds), *The Centennial History of the Independent Labour Party* (Halifax: Ryburn Press, 1992, pp.17– 42.
60 TWAS 1127/27/QMM, Newcastle, 24 April 1918.

the Northern Section donated just over £407 in all, with sizeable donations from Blaydon (£30), Middlesbrough (£52) and Newcastle (£80).[61] This constituted a fairly lukewarm response, with less than a third of the branches committing any monies to the fund. The Co-operative Union's accounts, moreover, conflict with some of the minute books. Neither the Newcastle nor the Newbiggin branches had reached agreement at that early stage. The only plausible explanation is that some branch secretaries took it upon themselves to send the donation in advance of the quarterly meeting and were unable to rescind the payment afterwards. At Newcastle, which had a healthy balance of over £166,000, the board was strongly in favour. However, after 'heated' debate at a quarterly meeting any payment to the fighting fund was roundly rejected amid concerns that the dividend would be reduced yet again.[62]

Most branch rules, in fact, had no provision for irregular payments and amendments to their constitutions could be made only with the agreement of two-thirds of the membership. At Newbiggin, for example, several motions to alter the rules were lost at successive meetings until in February 1920 they finally managed to persuade the majority to support it. Overturning opposition was a long-drawn-out process, not just because of the costs but because politicisation was regarded as a major step. The more progressive societies, notably West Cramlington, had anticipated the rule change and, in advance of the Swansea Congress, had leafleted their members and provided a series of lectures explaining the advantages of political representation.[63]

The WCG had taken a wholly positive view of the Swansea proposal, viewing it as an opportunity to strengthen working relations with other labour organisations.[64] It is not insignificant that Arthur Henderson, in his second term as leader of the Labour Party, was invited to address the Co-operative Union's National Emergency Conference in October 1917. He seized the opportunity to declare that, as the Trades Union Congress, the co-operative movement and the Labour Party 'were not separate forces, their ideals ought to be the same'.[65] The Northern Section was well represented at the conference, which also heard W. T. Allen assert that 'man

61 NCA, HHM, Co-operative Parliamentary Representation Fund, 5 June 1918, pp. 876–7.
62 TWAS, 1127/27, QMM, Newcastle, 30 July 1919 (motion lost by eight votes); 29 October 1919 (motion carried); 27 October 1920 (motion ratified); TWAS, 1069/1, Board minutes, Newcastle, 13 November 1917.
63 NRO, 821/27, Minutes, West Cramlington, 10 September 1917, 12 November 1917, 29 October 1917. Cramlington donated £10 in June 1918.
64 *Daily Herald*, 30 June 1917.
65 *Newcastle Illustrated Chronicle*, 19 October 1917. See also Chris Wrigley, *Arthur Henderson* (Cardiff: University of Wales/GPC, 1990).

has to be freed from the intolerable burden of being a profit for others ... every democratic force must march side by side ... there is no more peace for us until we have achieved the definite triumph of our principles'.[66] Nonetheless, the London correspondent of the *Daily Sketch* warned that there would be a serious crisis if the Co-operative Party was 'financed at the expense of members ... who are of all creeds and all political views'.[67]

It fell to the conference to agree a general policy for the new party. Mr Williams (Welwyn Garden City) spoke for many when he expressed his relief that there was no suggestion of a political alliance, for 'even if it had meant my own political party I would have been dead against it'.[68] Even Mr J. H. Thomas, the redoubtable Labour MP for Derby, who had actively defended the movement's interests in Parliament on questions of food supplies and excess profits duty, bluntly stated that it would be 'a very great mistake if you allied this movement to the Labour Party'.[69] There were some supportive voices, including that of Mr Gould, the delegate for Radstock, who saw discernible benefits in bringing together the forces of trade unionism and the Labour Party for the good of working people – but the clamour for a neutral position held sway.[70]

These developments coincided with the reorganisation of the Labour Party and its emergence as a serious contender for power. As Cole observes, there was certainly no scope for two working-class parties to compete at the national level.[71] In the event, the negotiations for a working relationship proved to be remarkably contentious and protracted. The fierce independence of the individual societies was a major obstacle, even in the Northern Section, where a degree of collaboration had already been in place for some time. As noted, the complex arrangements that saw votes from adjacent branches combined were once more the main stumbling block. For instance, votes cast in Ashington, a mining heartland, were cancelled out by those in the affluent county seat of Morpeth, where rural affairs, not mining concerns, defined the political affiliations of the members. Similarly, negative voting by Corbridge and Low Prudhoe prevented West Wylam and Hexham from driving through their desire for affiliation. In essence, while evidence suggests that the Northern Section

66 NCA, HHM, Report, National Emergency Conference, 1917, pp. 10–14.
67 As cited in the *Newcastle Illustrated Chronicle*, 20 October 1917.
68 Report, National Emergency Conference, 1917, p. 114;
69 *Ibid.*, p.118. For his speeches on Co-operative issues, see Hansard, *House of Commons Debates*, 12 March 1917, vol. 91: cc703–4 ['Sugar']; *House of Commons Debates*, 5 July 1917, vol. 95: cc1447–61 ['EPD'].
70 *Report*, National Emergency Conference, p. 117.
71 Cole, *Century of Cooperation*, p. 317; Wrigley, *Arthur Henderson*, pp. 112–43.

was officially opposed to affiliation, this masks the extent to which some were solidly in favour of an electoral agreement.[72]

Nationally, the Co-operative Party enjoyed its first taste of success. Although H. V. May failed to win the by-election at Prestwich, ten candidates were fielded in the general election in December 1918. There were plenty of plaudits when A. E. Waterson won the Kettering seat but his decision to join the Labour ranks in the House stirred up fresh controversy. The 1919 Congress recommended that a joint committee be set up to protect the interests of both sides, with the proviso that the final selection of candidates would be made by the Co-operative Political Council. The question of alliance became pressing but this seems to have hardened the resolve of those who were against politicisation and weakened the enthusiasm of those who had supported it. Younger men, returning from the war, were more willing to embrace the new politics but there was intense frustration on both sides of the divide: Labour supporters were impatient for radical change and unwilling to wait for an older generation of co-operators to be reconciled to what many still saw as a turn to extreme left-wing politics.[73] As Cole notes, the end of the war had mitigated some of the worst effects and as trading returned to near normal conditions the willingness of members to pay the political levy fell away.[74] Although some societies, mainly in London and the more affluent south-east, recruited well after the war, the new multiple retailers had begun to agitate for a further review of the excess profit duty, creating uncertainty and undermining the confidence of branches in the north-east, where the economy was stuttering towards a slump.[75]

Even so, efforts were still being made to bring the two sides together, not least through the initiatives taken by the WCG with Margaret Llewelyn Davies at the helm.[76] *Labour Woman* carried a report on the 1918 WCG annual congress, which applauded the fact that so many members of the Bradford branch of the WCG were Labour Party members and advocated a simple reciprocal arrangement whereby labour women should be co-operators and women co-operators members of their local Labour Party.[77] As Gillian Scott argues, WCG women played a leading role in

---

72 NRO, 1794/24, Minutes, Ashington, 21 June 1927, and Quarterly meeting (QMM), Morpeth, 2 September 1927.

73 Manton, 'The Labour Party and the co-op', pp. 756–7; Gurney, *Co-operative Culture*, pp. 226–7.

74 Cole, *Century of Co-operation*, pp. 319–20.

75 Gurney, 'Co-operation and the "new consumerism"', p. 907; Gurney, *Co-operative Culture*, p. 216.

76 Gurney, *Co-operative Culture*, p. 232.

77 *Labour Woman*, July 1918; Gaffin and Thoms, *Caring and Sharing*, p. 54.

politicising the movement and were committed to delivering the female vote at election times for Labour. Ironically, while they had freed themselves to be an independent voice as co-operators, they were thereafter shackled to the narrow conception of female activism articulated by the male-dominated Labour leadership.[78]

The attempt to debate the question of a Labour–Co-operative Party alliance was ruled out at the 1920 Co-operative Congress amid calls for an extended discussion to inform the decision. In the hiatus which followed, those opposed to an alliance seized the opportunity to rally their supporters. The Northern Section Committee convened a meeting at Newcastle in late January 1921 to reach agreement in preparation for the forthcoming Scarborough Congress but they had badly misjudged the mood of the majority: the alliance motion was soundly rejected by 253 to 84. 'Co-operation', insisted one speaker, 'was bigger than class; they looked to the interest of the whole community and not a section, and they ought to have time to develop their own policy not stultify themselves getting lost in another party'.[79] Mr Leach (Hartlepool) somewhat dramatically likened the whole issue to the story of Jonah and the whale: if the whale (Labour) was to swallow Jonah (the Co-operative Party), 'Jonah would never again recover his identity'. All humour aside, the point struck a strong chord. A rear-guard action in the form of an amendment was launched by delegates from Ashington, Blaydon, South Shields and Cleator Moor but this, too, was soundly rejected. The Society records reveal little other than the briefest of statements but some account must be taken of the scaremongering tactics of the by then Liberal-leaning *Newcastle Daily Chronicle*, which had a vast working-class readership across the region. The *Chronicle* repeatedly warned that an alliance with the Labour Party would 'result in disunion, loss of membership and the consequent withdrawal of share capital' – all matters of great concern to the region's co-operators.[80]

In the years which followed, both the Labour Party and the Co-operative Party forged an amicable working arrangement aimed at avoiding electoral clashes. By 1923, a Labour–Co-operative alliance was operational inside the House of Commons, and this culture of mutual

---

78 Gillian Scott, '"As a war horse to the beat of the drums": representations of working-class femininity in the Women's Co-operative Guild, 1880s to the Second World War', in Eileen Yeo (ed.), *Radical Femininity: Women's Self-Representation in the Public Sphere* (Manchester: Manchester University Press, 1998), p. 212.

79 *Newcastle Daily Chronicle*, 31 January 1921; NRO, 362/1, Minutes, Felton and District, Circular letter, A. Stoddart (Sec.), Co-operative Union, Northern Section, to the President and Committee, 15 March 1921.

80 *Newcastle Daily Chronicle*, 29 January 1921.

support was strengthened at the local level too. However, official Co-operative Union policy ruled out formal affiliation. Successive attempts to formalise agreements with the Labour Party were repeatedly defeated, albeit by small majorities. The years of depression, the General Strike of 1926 and the so-called 'Blacklegs Charter' (the 1927 Trade Union Bill) were the context in which the Cheltenham agreement was reached. Voting was very tight (1,960 to 1,843) but eventually those in favour carried the day.[81] The majority view was captured best by a Scottish speaker who reminded delegates that a 'working arrangement' had been in place since 1917: 'what we are asking is that agreement should be more definitely laid down'.[82]

Informal 'working arrangements' had been commonplace before the wartime crises and in the decade of wrangling which followed there was never any question where community loyalties lay when the need arose. When the Benevolent Committee of the Newcastle branch of the Amalgamated Engineering Union appealed for assistance in 1923 the Society supported its fund-raising activities and supplied free bread for several months; 3,000 loaves per week and food vouchers were distributed among striking miners in 1926; some societies, such as Ashington, abandoned their standing policy on credit by setting up instalment schemes.[83] This gave miners access to basic foodstuffs on the understanding that this would be repaid when the dispute ended.

For all its diversity, north-east co-operation displayed three distinct features that figured largely in the response to the call for politicisation: a long radical tradition that ran counter to the much-vaunted principle of neutrality; a highly successful regional movement that generated sufficient surplus to pay above-average dividends; and a strong independent guild movement that forged an additional interface between co-operators and labour activists. While none of this displaces the consensus that profiteering, inequitable access to basic foods and the threat of taxation forced the hands of unwilling traditionalists, it nonetheless points towards a longer transitional process. At the local, interpersonal level, working-class solidarities had always mattered and in the north-east it would be difficult to claim that war was the architect of an 'oppositional class consciousness' that radicalised the ideas and attitudes of co-operators – although it undoubtedly brought the class divide into sharper relief.[84]

---

81 Cole, *Century of Co-operation*, p. 323.
82 Carbery, *Consumers in Politics*, p. 32; Maguire, 'Co-operation and crisis', p. 190.
83 *Workers Chronicle*, 9 May 1926; TWAS, 120/44, Minutes, Newcastle, 14 August–31 December 1823, 15 and 29 June 1926; NRO, 1794/24, Minutes, Ashington Industrial Society, 21 June 1926.
84 Gurney, *Co-operative Culture*, p. 212.

4

Transforming the unemployed: trade union benefits and the advent of state policy

NOEL WHITESIDE

Introduction: defining unemployment

In his early work, Chris Wrigley wrote extensively on the relationship between the Liberal Party and the labour movement in general and on David Lloyd George and the trade unions in particular, notably during the years surrounding the First World War. The present chapter revisits this relationship – less to revise Chris's original contribution than to add to it, by reviewing the pre-war Liberal governments' well known welfare reforms and their impact on trade union organisation and work. In so doing, it seeks to reunite aspects of early-twentieth-century politics frequently studied separately, namely the history of twentieth-century industrial relations (to which Chris Wrigley contributed so extensively) and the early development of a British welfare state.

At the end of the nineteenth century, the concept of unemployment entered common parlance. Precisely how the 'unemployed' were to be identified, however, remained uncertain. Official and unofficial enquiries in the decades preceding the conflict of 1914–18 viewed unemployment from a dual perspective: one being the issue of poverty (and thus a cause of pauperism and industrial unrest) and the other the question of labour market disorganisation (a threat to Britain's economic and imperial pre-eminence). In policy-making circles, the latter tended to dominate. The introduction of labour exchanges in 1909 aimed to rationalise the distribution of work and to remove the least efficient elements, namely the infirm, the old and the pauperised casual 'residuum'. For reformers, the 'unemployed' formed a separate group from the general masses seeking work, distinguished by a past record of regular employment and their possession of skills and experience essential to future industrial prosperity. The classification of the labour market formed a necessary prelude to its reform. How to identify the 'real' unemployed became a practical problem that needed to be resolved for appropriate help to be offered to alleviate their plight.

The Board of Trade Labour Department, where reform was discussed, constructed statistical estimates of unemployment from returns made by trade unions that offered support to members who were out of work. These statistics principally covered skilled and better-paid elements of the labouring classes, excluded general workers and thus under-represented the extent to which job loss impacted on working-class lives.[1] However, not all workshops and trades observed conventions of dismissing staff during slack periods and the numbers covered by these union schemes represented a tiny fraction of the total workforce – and one biased considerably in favour of the construction, engineering, shipbuilding and metal-working industries. Here, shedding labour was the common response to industrial depression. Elsewhere, short-time working was more widespread. Many unions in other sectors negotiated work-sharing arrangements, either as an alternative to the provision of unemployment benefits or in conjunction with them.

Thus unemployment as negotiated by specific trade unions was far from identical to notions developed in official circles before 1914. These differences were in part anchored in how the problem was understood by different groups of participants. As indicated above, policy-making civil servants viewed the issue within a national framework, to separate the unemployed from the pauperised masses, and to remove impediments to the free movement of labour from declining to expanding sectors of the economy. Official views on an efficient labour market, however, were not reflected in trade union benefit systems, which sustained a network of controls to regulate access to a particular trade and the apportionment of work within it. State intervention in such delicate matters was not welcome: it threatened both organisational foundations and the destruction of bargaining power.[2] Changing economic conditions and the growth of less stable general labour unions came to modify the political complexion of the Trades Union Congress (TUC). In the 1900s, the union movement united behind demands for the development of state programmes in the areas of housing, education and public works for the

1 W. R. Garside, *The Measurement of Unemployment* (Oxford: Oxford University Press, 1980), chapter 1.
2 A. J. Reid, 'Old unionism reconsidered', in E. F. Biagini and A. J. Reid (eds), *Currents of Radicalism* (Cambridge: Cambridge University Press, 1991), pp. 214–44.

jobless. However, enthusiasm for state intervention remained limited, especially when it threatened to disrupt established trade agreements and negotiated working practices.

Different constructions of unemployment were rooted in different perceptions of how labour markets should be regulated, who should do the regulating and what the final objective of regulation should be. On the one hand, trade unions aimed to limit hours of work and raise wages to enhance the purchasing power of the working class and, with this, the demand for services and products, thereby expanding jobs in other sectors.[3] On the other hand, by removing the inefficient and incapable from the competition for work and by decasualising labour markets, state policy effectively sought to contain overall labour costs. Such objectives were hardly complementary. Their implicit opposition remained largely hidden in the years before 1914 as governments sought to win union support for their reforms. However, the introduction of national insurance forced a change in the construction of unemployment and the identification of the unemployed, eliminating variation by trade and region and removing all association with industrial bargaining. This transformation is analysed below. The first section examines diversity in union support for unemployed members, while the second reviews state intervention both as a new form of labour market regulation and as a project of trade union reform. The final section analyses the longer-term outcomes of this transformation and draws some conclusions.

Industrial bargaining and union benefits before 1914

The advantages of union membership in the early twentieth century rested in large part on the benefits that some offered to protect members against poverty and the disgrace of pauperism. Unemployment protection was less widespread than health insurance, which offered basic medical care and a low level of benefit to compensate for lost wages. Such help was offered by trade unions and also by friendly societies, which differed from unions principally in their universal coverage and more regulated commercial practices (being forbidden by law to raise levies to supplement scant funds, for example). About four million friendly society policies were extant in 1900. By contrast, union membership was lower (more than one million) but the protection that some offered was more complete – sometimes incorporating insurance of working tools and legal

---

3   *Ibid.*

protection as well as unemployment benefits of various types. Such protection was officially well regarded: it encouraged independence, regular working habits and thrift – all virtues that government wished to foster among the labouring classes. In 1892, the Royal Commission on Labour commented favourably on the independence, self-help and organisational capacities found among the established skilled sectors of the working classes, and noted how well developed unions in such trades offered protection against all types of risk.[4]

In an era of union expansion, the 682,000 trade unionists protected (in one way or another) against unemployment in 1891[5] grew to 1.46 million in 1906 and 1.84 million by 1908.[6] Total union membership stood at 2.4 million in 1907. Between 1905 and 1907, mutual benefits represented nearly 70 per cent of union expenditure, and the amount dispensed in strike pay was slightly over 8 per cent.[7] Union energies and funds were dedicated to providing health, accident and funeral benefits, with many also offering support to unemployed or retired members: not, as is often thought, to collective bargaining and industrial conflict. However, a twenty-first-century perspective cannot be imposed here: industrial bargaining and welfare support were integrated activities as unions aimed to protect their members in the widest sense. The regulation of wages and working conditions demanded control of work processes as each union developed idiosyncratic methods of coping with fluctuations in trade.

The most extensive unemployment benefits were to be found in engineering, shipbuilding, metallurgy, printing and building trades (albeit that, in some areas, the last retained the condition that unemployed members tramped in search of work). Similar systems were also run by boot and shoe operatives, cabinet-makers, carriage-makers and bookbinders – but the numbers covered here were relatively small. Such protection was hardly novel: the Friendly Society of Ironfounders (FSIF) had run an unemployment scheme for its members since the 1830s. In the early nineteenth century, the law forbade trade organisation for any purpose other than the provision of mutual benefits. From the 1840s, the Society of Brushmakers ran its own workshops – hiring out-of-work

---

4 Royal Commission on Labour *Fifth and Final Report*, C. 1421 (London: HMSO, 1894), pp. 24, 28.
5 Board of Trade Labour Department, *Report on Agencies and Methods for Dealing with the Unemployed*, C. 7812 (London: HMSO, 1893–94). p. 18.
6 During the same period, amalgamations and mergers caused the number of trade unions to contract from 749 to 679. The National Archive (TNA), LAB 2/14/LE22733/24/1911.
7 Board of Trade Labour Department, *Report on Trade Unions 1905–1907*, Cd 4651 (London: HMSO, 1909), pp. iii, xiii (Introduction by George Askwith).

members on a six-weekly rota and requiring the elderly to earn a pension by selling the brushes.[8] By the late nineteenth century, unemployment schemes were less ambitious, but equally essential. In the eyes of the wider public, social benefits transformed trade unions from agents of industrial conflict bent on destroying capitalist enterprise into mutual-aid societies that promoted thrift and working-class independence in a manner in keeping with middle-class values.

At first glance, the benefits offered by the unions of engineers, boiler-makers and iron-founders – which, together with those representing carpenters and joiners, ran the largest unemployment schemes – strongly resembled those introduced under Part II of the 1911 National Insurance Act. Benefit rights reflected the member's contribution record, a willing-ness to take work offered by the branch and acceptable reasons for leaving the previous job. The amount on offer and its duration commonly reflected length of membership and class of member. Most branches kept a vacancy book to be signed when a member lodged a claim. The branch acted as a placement agency; in this instance, local officials knew both the qualities of the applicants and the requirements of local firms in a manner that public officials were never able to replicate. Unemployed members were placed at the discretion of the branch, depending sometimes on specific abilities, sometimes on the duration of time 'on the books'. The printing and bookbinding trades offered the most extensive systems of support. The London Society of Compositors (LSC) provided unemployment benefits and operated a 'make up' wage for those earning less than a specified amount each week. The union was supported by voluntary clubs, which made donations in necessitous cases; casual work was allocated equally among applicants. In addition to the labour exchange service operated by the Society's houses, the LSC offered travel and emigration grants.[9]

Unions offering unemployment benefits grew from federations of local societies supplying help for their members. In cotton spinning and weaving, the right to union support was determined at district level; subsequent amalgamation did not transfer powers in this area to the national executive.[10] Even unions with centralised rulebooks kept benefit

---

8 The Society, at its zenith, had sixty-two branches; it provided sick, funeral, strike and unemployment pay and emigration grants. W. Kiddier, *The Old Trade Unions* (London: Allen & Unwin, 1931), chapter 11.

9 Board of Trade Labour Department, *Report on Agencies and Methods*, pp. 48–51.

10 Beveridge Papers, British Library of Political and Economic Science (BLPES), Coll. B, vol. XVII, Board of Trade Labour Department, 'Analysis of the rules of trade unions relating to unemployed, sick and accident benefits' (1906) (confidential print), pp. 102–36.

administration in local hands. All benefits (except strike pay) were usually locally funded, so prolonged local recession led to branches experiencing financial difficulties. Commenting on accounts submitted for a very poor year (1893), the FSIF secretary in Bristol wrote to his executive:

> I am sorry that we are in dept [*sic*] to start the new year. The cause of some of our members being in Arrears is that they have had to work short time. Trade will have to be good for Bristol to keep herself seeing that we have 7 superannuated Members on the funds it is a good number for a small branch, they are nearly all too Old to work at any time. I hope the time is not far distant when all our able bodied members will be at work.[11]

When finances deteriorated, branches raised a local levy or, in extreme cases, asked the national executive to negotiate a loan from another branch. Local responsibility for local funds gave members a vested interest in policing claims.[12] Help might be refused to members sacked for shoddy workmanship, poor timekeeping, drunkenness or unjustified insubordination. Frequently, branches ran additional benefit systems to supplement national rulebooks. Discretionary 'benevolent' or 'contingency' funds gave help in needy cases.[13] Union benefit systems thus formalised the 'whip round' in the workplace, long the common response to a colleague in misfortune. The rulebooks give an unnecessarily rigid impression of the way in which benefit systems actually worked. In practice, each claim was decided on its merits – and the operation of union welfare helped to reinforce branch autonomy in determining how trade practices might best be protected.

Unemployment benefits reflected the distribution of work within particular trades: a factor influenced in part by custom, in part by the production process. In shipbuilding and construction, skilled men moved from employer to employer as their services were required. Any slump in trade became reflected in longer gaps between jobs. Such experience

---

11 Modern Records Centre (MRC), University of Warwick, MSS 41/FSIF/1/5/1, Letter, 2 January 1894.

12 The Amalgamated Society of Engineers pooled funds on a district basis – and was accused of encouraging 'lax' administration as a result.

13 Royal Commission on Labour, *Minutes of Evidence: Group A*, Cd. 6894 (London: HMSO, 1893–94), pp. 168–9: Whittaker (ASE), 14 June 1892, on the use of such funds to supplement other benefits. FSIF minutes (1893) show that executive sanction was necessary for payments from the auxiliary, donation and dispute funds, but that branches administered their own benevolent grants. MRC, MSS 41/1/5/1 (1893–7). In the building trades, branches raised their own benevolent funds to supplement travel (not unemployment) benefit. Board of Trade Labour Department, *Report on Agencies and Methods*, p. 43.

of unemployment was far from universal. In textile manufacture and the coal-mining industry, slack demand was usually accommodated by short-time working. This allowed employers to retain the services of experienced hands in anticipation of economic recovery and to avoid the cost of closing – then reopening – the mill or the mine.[14] Unemployment benefits were correspondingly rare. The only coal-mining unions that provided them were found in the north-east. The Durham Miners' Association paid benefit to those out of work for a week or more and the Northumberland Miners' Mutual Confident Association subsidised the earnings of workers on fewer than four shifts a week.[15] In the general industrial unionism dominating coal-mining, workers could not afford the high dues required to maintain effective systems of unemployment relief. For similar reasons, textile trade unions ran very circumscribed systems. The Cotton Spinners and the Bradford Overlookers' Society offered unemployment benefits.[16] Elsewhere, help was confined to unemployment resulting from flood, fire or breakdown in machinery – not slack trade. Short-time working was found in textile engineering as well as textile manufacture and mining in Yorkshire and Lancashire: in boots and shoes, hosiery, clothing trades and small metal working in the Midlands and in both tinplate works and mines in South Wales. Low and irregular earnings also precluded the development of any benefits other than strike pay among general labour unions. The sole exception was the Workers' Union, founded in 1898, which managed to offer unemployment pay – and which expanded rapidly as a result.[17]

The provision of mutual benefits offered organisational advantages and created stability while reinforcing trade practices. Lapsed members forfeited all benefit rights. There were strong incentives for the union member to pay the dues, especially if the amount that could be claimed – or the period over which it could be claimed – rose with length of membership. Superannuation, offered by the Amalgamated Society of Engineers (ASE) and the FSIF, was particularly influential in this respect. Furthermore, benefits protected trade agreements:

> It is obvious that if a workman is unemployed, and has no means of subsistence, he is much more likely to accept work under unfavourable conditions than the man who has a sufficient income to be in no fear of

14 Board of Trade Labour Department, *Report on Agencies and Methods*, p. 83.
15 Royal Commission on Labour, *Group A: Precis of Evidence*, C. 6708–1 (London: HMSO, 1892), p. 144.
16 Board of Trade Labour Department, *Report on Agencies and Methods*, p. 69. Royal Commission on Labour, *Group C: Precis of Evidence*, C. 6708-III (London: HMSO, 1892), p. 267.
17 Workers' Union, *Annual Report* (1905), p. 1.

actual starvation. Thus the unemployment benefit of the trade union acts as a regulator of the labour market. Practically, the trade union of this class is in a position to minimise the competition of the individuals composing it, by using the benefit for the purpose of lessening pressure upon the labour market, while the same fund is also available for withholding or withdrawing the members from work for the purposes of organisation.[18]

Aside from slackness in trade, union workers were expected to leave employers who ignored trade practices – by cutting wages, raising hours or taking on too many apprentices. 'Donation' or 'contingency' or 'victim' benefit might be paid to those who lost work in such circumstances. Branch accounts show that local secretaries were not very fussy about how cases were categorised. Unions aimed to place 'legal' workers in 'legal' shops. Members who violated union rules, by (for example) failing to notify the branch of a vacancy or by allowing a non-unionist to take the place of a union worker, were fined. Unpaid fines had the same status as membership arrears; all rights to benefit were forfeit until they were paid. The sums involved could be substantial. The Leeds branch of the FSIF, for example, operated a bye-law which dictated that any member who helped a non-union member get work while there were union members unemployed was liable to a fine of twenty shillings.[19] The boilermakers' union (the United Society of Boilermakers and Iron and Steel Shipbuilders) fined members for defective workmanship (to repay the employer) and expelled any who refused to comply with union directives. On Clydeside, which (the union claimed in the 1890s) was 95 per cent organised, this was serious, as a man without a union card was unlikely to be hired.[20] The arrangement enabled the union to provide the competent worker with a decent job and guaranteed the workmanship of members to employers who respected trade practices. Such a system of mutual reliance was unusual, but many skilled unions strove to emulate it – and the operation of unemployment benefits represented a key factor in its establishment.

Thus union benefits reinforced collective bargaining, being available only to members who observed trade agreements (insofar as a branch was able to enforce them). They reinforced strategies to regulate the distribution of work through rules about the proportion of journeymen to apprentices, job demarcation, manning levels, hours of work and overtime. Those who paid their dues and observed regulations received support when in need. As union organisation was not uniform and as even

---

18 Board of Trade Labour Department, *Report on Agencies and Methods*, p. 21.
19 MRC, MSS/41/1/5/1, FSIF minute book, 4 July 1894.
20 Royal Commission on Labour, *Minutes of Evidence: Group A*, pp. 41–2: Evidence of Knight, 18 May 1892.

advanced industries like engineering remained technologically diffuse right up to the war, local working practices remained heterogeneous. Some rules (notably on apprenticeship regulation) were strictly enforced in some areas while being ignored (because unenforceable) in others. Hence definitions of unemployment varied not only between trades but also from area to area, according to the ability of the local branch to protect trade practices.

Trade union constructions of unemployment were neither uniform nor consistent, varying by trade, and between geographical areas according to the strength of local organisation, the state of industrial relations and the politics of the branch. Moreover, distinctions between unemployment and strike action were not self-evident. The print unions, for example, drew up price lists and rules and then looked to the branches to enforce them by supporting members who refused 'black' work.[21] The difference between the 'unemployed' union member and one on strike depended on whether the executive decided to 'close' the shop. In hard times, sanctioning an official strike might spell financial ruin – but it was possible to use out-of-work benefits to secure the same ends. This quote is taken from a letter from the FSIF executive to a branch seeking a minimum wage of thirty shillings from a local employer in the summer of 1884:

> Now in order to act the EC [executive committee] desire that by mutual agreement among yourselves let one man in a shop ask for the 30/– ... of course give a week's notice (or the usual notice) then in the event of being refused the Member can leave and have the Benefit of the Auxiliary allowance [strike pay]. After that let another man try who will be allowed the same benefit if unable to get the money and so on. Do it gradually without any noise or talk.... Observe if our members are faithful to each other and quietly carry out the plan indicated; you are bound ultimately to get the money. It must be distinctly understood that the Auxiliary will only be allowed to the men who have to start the movement; those who may start in their places, if not getting the money, will only have ... such benefit as they may be entitled to from entry.... As to striking the shops, the Executive cannot sanction that: it would be simply madness to attempt it.[22]

Dispute pay, in this union as in others, supplemented unemployment benefit, was centrally funded and was available only if sanctioned by the executive. However, a union branch could fight covertly for a wage rise, or against a wage cut, outside the context of a formal strike. A decade later, as trade improved, the FSIF minutes noted numerous cases of members

---

21 J. Zeitlin, 'Craft regulation and the division of labour', unpublished PhD thesis, University of Warwick, 1981, pp. 75–6.
22 MRC, MSS 41/FSIF/1/3, Letter, 19 June 1884, fol. 3.

being granted dispute pay – not mere unemplcyment benefit – for resisting 'unreasonable' overtime, for refusing a job where apprentices undertook 'struck' work, for refusing to take on labouring work and so on.[23] The prevailing climate in terms of industrial relations thus determined how 'unemployment' was understood, as the following comparison between British trade unions and their German counterparts demonstrates:

> [German trade union] members … are by no means so scrupulous about accepting work on conditions inferior to those approved of by their unions as is the case with British Trade Unionists, whose unemployment is no doubt in a considerable number of cases traceable to their rejection of work, which they could easily secure, if they were willing to take it on non-union terms.[24]

No distinction existed between claimants whose unemployment was due to their support of union policy from those out of work for other reasons. This distinction, developed during the twentieth century, did not then exist. Employer organisations also recognised that the classification required by the 1911 National Insurance Act was, in practical terms, unrealistic:

> How do you know it [unemployment benefit] is not being paid to men who should not be paid it? The question comes up then – what is a strike? What is a trade dispute? Do you know? I do not know. I maintain that a man is out on a trade dispute and the union say he is not, but he is out of employment and you will use my money to help him.[25]

This preoccupation with trade agreements led some organisations to pay benefits, if at lower rates, to people who managed to get work of some kind. This was not the case for all unions: the ASE and the Associated Society of Shipwrights (from 1908 the Ship Constructive and Shipwrights Association) insisted on a 'waiting period' before a member could claim – a regulation subsequently adopted by the national scheme. Elsewhere, things were different. The Amalgamated Association of Operative Cotton Spinners paid a lower rate of benefit for longer periods to unemployed members who took work temporarily as piecers or general labourers. The ironfounders' union and the LSC granted out-of-work pay for odd days not worked. In the building trades, where benefit was commonly

---

23 MRC, MSS 41/FSIF EC/1/5/1, FSIF minutes, 8 November and 20 December 1893, 7 March and 23 May 1894.

24 TNA, LAB 2/1564/CL&SL 1216/05, Schloss memo, October 1905, p. 14.

25 MRC, MSS 237/B/1/144, Henderson, Shipbuilding Employers Federation, Deputation to the Board of Trade, 14 June 1911, p. 56.

conditional on the tramp for work, regulations stipulated the distance to be covered and the maximum number of days' benefit that could be claimed, but the plumbers', stonemasons', plasterers' and bricklayers' unions expected members to pick up the odd casual labouring job as long as it was not 'in the trade'.[26] There were limits: the United Operative Plumbers Association formally refused travel benefit to members getting more than three days' work a week and the Operative Ship and House Painters means-tested claimants to unemployment pay.[27] Formal regulations, however, could not dictate local practices; branches continued to determine access on the merits of the individual case, using contingency funds where necessary. The purpose of union schemes was to protect the trade rate and unemployment benefit was not sufficient to maintain a family for months on end. Members did not want to resort to labouring but, if they were forced to, this was not in itself a reason for withdrawing union support. It was better that they take such casual jobs than be forced to take 'blacked' work. 'Unemployment' therefore meant, essentially, unemployment in the trade.

Finally, unemployment benefits were only one of a range of payments made by unions of skilled workers to members in need; the categorisation of claimants was very fluid. In periods of recession, older and more infirm workers were the first to lose work. In the shipyards, the foundries, the engineering workshops and the coalmines, physical strength was at a premium and its impairment made the worker less productive. Divisions between the 'sick', the 'unemployed' and the 'retired' (for the few unions providing superannuation payments) were not rigid. In recessions, the age at which an employee might be regarded as 'too old' tended to fall. In evidence to the Royal Commission on Labour in June 1892, the Engineers reported that, in the current recession, members aged over forty years were commonly regarded as 'too old' and that Belfast firms were dismissing, as 'infirm', men who wore spectacles.[28] Industrial recession imposed burdens on union funds over and above simple unemployment benefits. Fluctuations in trade in the 1890s and early 1900s threatened the viability of local finances and were instrumental in changing union attitudes towards the prospect of state intervention in the years before 1914.

In reviewing unemployment in pre-war Britain, the short conclusion is that this was not a homogeneous category. This short review has paid most attention to the major unions. Large numbers still belonged to tiny societies, all operating under their own rules. In 1894, some 149,000 union

---

26 Board of Trade Labour Department, *Report on Trade Unions*, pp. 102–14.
27 Board of Trade Labour Department, *Report on Agencies and Methods*, pp. 46–7.
28 Royal Commission on Labour, *Minutes of Evidence: Group A*, pp. 184–5.

members were organised in 118 societies in the building trades alone.[29] As socialist sympathisers noted, such societies were renowned for their sectional politics; there was little interest in promoting organisation outside 'the trade' or in encouraging state intervention in what their leaders defined as 'industrial' affairs. It was only as repeated slumps in trade bit deep into union reserves that these attitudes changed and trade unionists developed more interest in state subventions to their funds, as found in continental Europe, where the Ghent system encouraged local municipalities to supplement union benefits. However, partnership in a state-run scheme in Britain required the unions to conform to official definitions of unemployment – and this implied changes in the ways in which they identified their unemployed and managed their finances.

Redefining unemployment: the reform of union benefits

The union movement welcomed legislative action to solve the unemployment problem in the early twentieth century, although not necessarily the insurance scheme proposed by the government. Political debate over how unemployment should be tackled (and the union contribution to that debate) has been extensively documented elsewhere.[30] It is not proposed to rehearse that analysis here. Rather, this section will demonstrate how Part II of the National Insurance Act 1911 reconstructed unemployment while acting as an instrument of trade union reform, changing the division between political and industrial affairs. This legislation covered employers and employed in five industrial sectors, who were required to pay joint weekly contributions to a central Unemployment Fund. Insured workers could receive benefit for up to fifteen weeks a year if unemployed for at least six days, due to slack trade. Unemployment became legally defined as a uniform category, quite separate from trade bargaining. Trade unionists came to adapt their understanding of unemployment to suit these new circumstances, but not without some difficulty.

Union leaders were open to the merits of state help because of the consequences of economic fluctuations for branch funds. In the depressed years of 1906–8, contributory income slumped as claims to benefit soared. In the absence of any government support for legislation endorsing the 'right to work', union leaders began to take an active interest in the proposed national scheme of unemployment insurance – with the view to

---

29 Board of Trade Labour Department, *Report on Agencies and Methods*, p. 49.
30 See, particularly, J. Harris, *Unemployment and Politics, 1886–1914* (Oxford: Oxford University Press, 1972).

getting its administration vested in union hands to the maximum possible extent.[31] As was widely acknowledged, trade union branches were in a very advantageous position for undertaking such work, thanks to extensive contacts with local markets, their experience in detecting fraudulent claims and the trust they enjoyed from the organised working class. By contrast, state-run labour exchanges (introduced in 1908) were shunned by respectable workers as potential sources of blackleg labour. Although unity of opinion was not the hallmark of TUC debates on the issue, the majority favoured official unemployment benefits being amalgamated with existing union schemes, thereby (the more optimistic claimed) allowing unions to reinforce their organisation at public expense.[32] In general, union leaders recognised that refusing to have anything to do with official unemployment insurance could be suicidal. Their members would be obliged to subscribe to the state scheme and might allow union dues to lapse rather than pay for insurance against unemployment twice over.[33]

Support existed in official circles for involving unions under the new Act. Opposition to contributory insurance had to be contained and already general labour leaders were objecting vociferously to labour exchanges, decasualisation proposals and the levying of flat-rate contributions on the poorly paid. Further, the voluntary provision of social benefits should be encouraged, to protect the respectable worker from destitution and the Poor Law. The reform of trade union financial management formed a hidden aspect of this official agenda: to allow the provision of 'friendly' benefits, which the state wanted to encourage, to be separated from 'trade' activities, which it wished to contain.

The problem was that unions did not run separate funds for separate benefits.[34] All branch activities were financed from the same resources. Craft unions had long eschewed collective action liable to damage financial reserves, as this might force cuts in benefit and undermine organisation. Hence the engineering dispute of 1897 in support of the eight-hour day had taken the form of rolling regional action, to enable areas at work to subsidise those on strike. As indicated above, the methods used by societies of skilled workers commonly obviated the need for lengthy and expensive mass action. Official support for trade unions inside the Board of Trade was founded on their provision of mutual benefits. The legislation of 1875, which ostensibly secured trade union immunity from prosecution,

---

31 TUC, *Quarterly Report*, March 1910, p. 41.
32 TUC, *Annual Report, 1909*, pp.55–7; also *Quarterly Report*, December 1910, pp. 11–15.
33 TUC, *Annual Report, 1911*, pp. 204–8.
34 Royal Commission on Labour, *Final Report*, C. 1421 (London: HMSO, 1894), p. 28.

aimed to promote voluntary insurance against misfortune.[35] Following the appearance of militant 'new' labour unions in the 1890s, which had more of the vices and none of the virtues of their counterparts representing skilled workers, public officials began to regard trade unions with a more jaundiced eye. Protection for union activities began to be eroded: a development culminating in the Taff Vale judgement of 1901.

Following a railway strike in South Wales in 1900, the Taff Vale Railway Company sued the Amalgamated Society of Railway Servants for damages, arguing that union officials had been responsible for causing railwaymen to break their contracts of employment. The action was successful and the union was fined a very substantial sum of money. This resulted in consternation in the TUC. Although the judgement aimed to discourage militancy, it posed a fundamental threat because unions became liable for the actions of their officials, whether operating with executive sanction or not. Fines threatened the viability of union benefits and thus the basis of craft organisation. Following the case, the TUC gave political and financial support to the new Labour Representation Committee, renamed the Labour Party in 1906. Following the general election that year, the Trade Disputes Bill – drafted to restore trade union immunity to prosecution – topped the list of private members' bills sponsored by Labour MPs.

The ensuing Act gave the unions everything that they wanted: unconditional legal protection for all financial resources. This triumph was not, however, won without a fight. Official pressure had long encouraged unions to distinguish funds used for 'friendly' benefits from those designated for trade purposes – a strategy resisted by the majority of unions.[36] During discussion of the Trade Disputes Bill, the proposal was revived as a compromise that would allow protection for friendly benefits while retaining legal sanctions against strikes.[37] The Act, by restoring the status quo ante, disappointed those seeking the reform of trade union practices. National unemployment insurance, however, promoted this agenda more successfully.

The definition of unemployment embodied in the 1911 National Insurance Act was highly normative. The 'unemployed' were those deemed

---

35 C. G. Hanson, 'Craft unions, welfare benefits and the case for trade union law reform, 1867–1875', *Economic History Review*, 26 (1975), 243–59, describes debates addressing the reform of trade union financial management, while misunderstanding the benefit systems involved.

36 Unions registered under the 1872 Friendly Societies Act made the distinction – but not all unions were so registered.

37 *The Times*, 29 March 1906, report on the House of Commons debate on the Trade Dispute Bill; also *The Times*, 24 April 1906, reporting the arguments of the Cotton Employers' Parliamentary Association.

surplus to industrial requirements for up to fifteen weeks a year, who were not in dispute with their employer and whose unemployment could not be attributed to dismissal or to any voluntary decision to quit work. Under this definition 'long term' unemployment was impossible. Those out of work for any length of time simply lost their right to benefit and – if all else failed – rejoined the pauper class. Similarly, regulations governing the scheme excluded irregular workers. Right to benefit depended on contributions paid and the requirement that six days' idleness be proved before any claim was lodged effectively disqualified casual workers. The regulations were loosely based on the schemes already operating among unions of skilled workers in the 'insured trades'.

Trade unions were permitted to register to administer both health and unemployment benefits under the Act on behalf of their members. A small subsidy was also available to unions organising workers outside the 'insured trades', to encourage the voluntary provision of unemployment benefits, in a similar fashion to the Ghent system.[38] However, differences between official regulations identifying the unemployed and prevailing trade union practices swiftly became evident. Despite initial appearances to the contrary, the state subsidies did not allow trade union officials to proceed as they had done before. State benefits were repaid to unions retrospectively, following official audit of their accounts. Any irregularities meant no reimbursement of monies already spent: an outcome which gave some general secretaries a severe shock.[39] Compensation for odd days of unemployment was not allowed; similarly, 'unemployment' now came to mean total idleness – any casual labouring job taken on to help make ends meet meant the loss of a week's benefit.

Unsurprisingly, the 'trade dispute' disqualification clause emerged as the main issue at stake, as this required new classifications from trade unions long accustomed to use unemployment pay in defence of trade agreements. While both union and state schemes disqualified claims from those who refused work or were sacked for 'misconduct', the official scheme gave the employer (not the union official) the right to decide whether 'misconduct' had occurred. Further, union branches and labour exchanges took opposing views in the case of the worker sacked or walking out in defence of trade practices. The exchanges would send unemployed

---

38 National Insurance Act 1911, Part II, section 106. The subsidy of one-sixth of benefit paid was much smaller than anything found elsewhere in Europe.

39 For its impact on the FSIF, see H. J. Fyrth and A. Collins, *The Foundry Workers* (Manchester: Manchester University Press, 1959), pp. 134–5.

non-union workers to vacancies no union member would touch.[40] In short, the state scheme introduced a new and rigid distinction between unemployment due to personal misfortune (sickness or redundancy) and loss of work consequent on disagreement between worker and employer.[41] Priorities underpinning financial compensation for unemployed union members underwent a subtle change. Before the 1911 Act, those involved in a dispute (thanks to the supplement of dispute benefit) received higher rates of support from their union. After the Act was passed, members defending working agreements were financially penalised because they could not claim the state benefits available to those unemployed for less controversial reasons.

Thanks to the Treasury's auditing requirements, the Act pushed through an internal reform of union financial management: payments of unemployment benefits were vetted centrally; accounts had to be submitted from each individual branch; and benefit funds had to be distinguished from other financial resources. The initial result was a great degree of confusion; the response of the Treasury was to tighten up auditing procedures to foster greater uniformity.[42] Central union executive authority over local benefit administration expanded, to ensure that official regulations were respected and state subsidies could be claimed. This increased authority ended local powers to assess the rights of local claimants. Finally, in order to register under the scheme, unions were persuaded to change their benefit regulations to conform to those of the state. Although there was no law to prevent an organisation running the two schemes side by side, to do so was administratively confusing and expensive. The alternative (refusing to have anything to do with the new system) was equally dangerous, as the provision of national unemployment benefit might discourage members from maintaining their dues. Caught between a rock and a hard place, most unions conformed and amended their rulebooks.

This reopened conflicts about unemployment and its association with trade regulation: as the central union executive was responsible for enforcing the new rules, so tension mounted between branches and executive, a tension more famously exacerbated during the war. Problems focused less on state insurance as such than on the labour exchanges, where claims to benefit were lodged. As placement agencies, these rivalled

---

40 TNA, LAB 2/ 1482/ED 937915, Deputation of Building Trades, 13 March 1913, minutes on file.

41 TNA, LAB 2/1483/LE 9169, Letter from H. Llewellyn Smith to Ramsay MacDonald, 13 October 1911.

42 TNA, T 1/11856/27866. By 1914, 6,000 union branch accounts were centrally audited each quarter year.

the union branch. Although ostensibly refusing to supply labour to break strikes or to work at less than the 'established rate', exchanges could not and did not acknowledge sectional agreements and the lists of 'fair firms' that determined local union placements.[43] Resented as potential sources of blackleg labour before the war, exchanges became even more unpopular during it, as they were charged with official dilution, conscription and general manpower policies. The reaction to centralised manpower policies from both sides of industry following the armistice saw policy swing abruptly into reverse, with civil servants and ministers alike committed to restoring 'home rule for industry'. As far as unemployment was concerned, however, a national, uniform definition was to become a permanent feature (and the national scheme was extended to all workers in 1920, in spite of union wartime opposition).

Conclusion

By examining the birth of state-sponsored unemployment insurance less in terms of welfare state history and more in terms of its impact on trade union organisation and practices, this chapter re-establishes links between social welfare and industrial relations that have generally been studied as separate spheres of labour politics. Here we address aspects of labour policy that enabled trade unionists to protect their trades and sustain membership. This change of focus offers a slightly different perspective on the significance of the Taff Vale judgement and the Trades Dispute Act of 1906, while linking both to the National Insurance Act, the reform of trade union financial management and the recalibration of spheres of union activity.

The question remains: why did not a more powerful union movement (membership virtually doubling between 1914 and 1920) not manage to repudiate state control over unemployment relief after the armistice?[44] There are certainly signs that it tried to do so. Lloyd George's post-war administration sought to accommodate union demands for autonomy in this area. The 1920 Unemployment Act allowed industries to 'contract out' of the state scheme, on condition that they created equivalent support

---

43 Beveridge Papers, BLPES, Coll. B XVI/10, Beveridge: 'Memo on employment exchanges and trade unions', 17 December 1906.

44 See Noel Whiteside, 'Industrial relations and social welfare, 1945–1979', in C. J. Wrigley (ed.), *A History of British Industrial Relations, Volume III: 1939–1979* (Cheltenham: Elgar, 1996), pp. 107–28; Noel Whiteside, 'Who were the "unemployed"?' *Historical Social Research/Historische Sozialforschung*, 40(1) (2015), 150–70.

of their own. However, this opportunity fell foul of the Treasury, whose officials argued that trades were not industries and that new schemes would be admitted only if they covered skilled and unskilled alike in specified industrial sectors – a stipulation that outlawed most union proposals. In the event, only banking and insurance broke free. Subsequently, the advent of mass unemployment undermined further efforts and, in time, the ability of many trade unions to sustain the levels of support they had offered before 1914. Better-organised employers seized the opportunity to weaken union organisation: in 1922, the Engineering Employers forced a national lock-out, effectively bankrupting the ASE. Finally, we should note that the uniformity created by benefit rules under the state scheme became, over time, more apparent than real. Relaxation of contribution regulations, careful negotiation of short-time working and the provision of allowances to accommodate families – all won public support while forcing the official state Unemployment Fund into deficit. Union members came to recognise that the depth of state resources offered better protection than their own funds. In consequence, those out of work who once would have turned to their union for support now turned to the state and this explains the unequivocal support for the Beveridge report (1942) when it promised state-sponsored protection 'from the cradle to the grave'.

In contrast to continental Europe, where union representation was central to benefit administration, the post-1945 settlement sustained a peculiarly British compromise that vested benefit rights in the hands of a central bureaucracy totally under state control. In the immediate post-war years, this left trade unions free to negotiate manning levels, hours of work and job demarcation as the main safeguards against unemployment, leaving the state to rescue market casualties, but completely external to the management of manpower resources. The consequences laid the foundations for Britain's poor productivity record, both at the time and since. Central administration also helped to divorce national insurance contributions from benefit rights (bar the state pension), transforming those contributions into just another tax while simultaneously destroying the link between the identification of the 'unemployed' and any association with previous working life.

As help for the unemployed has become increasingly associated with testing both means and willingness to work in recent years, so their identification becomes increasingly reminiscent of the undeserving poor and their treatment reminiscent of the Victorian Poor Laws – not an identity either trade unions or Beveridge himself would have recognised. Viewed from this angle, we can observe how classifications fluctuate in response to changing circumstances. This leads to the conclusion that unemployment is not a singular object and nor can the 'unemployed' be reduced to an objective number, in spite of every effort by economists and economic historians to render it so. Rather, as reflected in its earliest conception, unemployment is a product of negotiated compromise that varies across occupation, place and time.

Even so, official intervention in all cases represented an attempt to adapt particular types of self-help to broader client groups. In so doing, government entered into complex problems of deciding which claimants merited public help and which did not. This demanded the real definition of the problem that was being tackled and, in the process, the imposition of uniform regulations on very diverse local labour market practices. When seen from this angle, the political discussions determining how the unemployed were to be identified become as significant in our appraisal of the unemployment question as its economic causes, with which its measurement is more commonly associated.

5

The trade union contribution to the British Labour Party

ANDREW THORPE

The debate about the relationship between the trade unions and Labour politics in Britain is older than the Labour Party itself. It has been the stuff of great controversy, arousing considerable comment as well as important academic work. Lewis Minkin, in particular, has offered a series of detailed analyses of the relationship.[1] Essay and article-length works look at various aspects the relationship, particularly for the period since 1945.[2] The fifteen years or so after the Second World War were the subject of a number of what are now extremely superannuated books.[3] This chapter attempts to identify the benefits and problems that the union link has brought to the Labour Party. Overall, it argues that more good than harm has come from the relationship, and that Labour and the trade union movement have been stronger together than they would have been apart.

The relationship between Labour and the unions has been seen in a number of ways. It has been described as an 'alliance', albeit sometimes a

1 Lewis Minkin, *The Labour Party Conference: A Study in the Politics of Intra-Party Democracy* (London: Viking, 1978); Lewis Minkin, *The Contentious Alliance: Trade Unions and the Labour Party* (Edinburgh: Edinburgh University Press, 1991); Lewis Minkin, *The Blair Supremacy: A Study in the Politics of Labour's Party Management* (Manchester: Manchester University Press, 2014).

2 See particularly Alan Campbell, Nina Fishman and John McIlroy (eds), *British Trade Unions and Industrial Politics* (2 vols) (Aldershot: Ashgate, 1999).

3 See for instance V. L. Allen, *Trade Union Leadership: Based on a Study of Arthur Deakin* (London: Longman, Green & Co., 1957); Leslie Hunter, *The Road to Brighton Pier* (London: Barker, 1959); Martin Harrison, *Trade Unions and the Labour Party Since 1945* (London: Allen & Unwin, 1960).

'contentious' one.[4] Metaphors of 'marriage' abound, and talk of 'divorce'
characterised much of the 'New Labour' period.[5] Another metaphor came
from Ernest Bevin, the founder of the Transport and General Workers'
Union (TGWU) and one of the key figures in the labour movement's
history, when in 1935 he stated that the party 'grew out of the bowels of the
Trades Union Congress'.[6] This comment has usually been read as showing
simply that there was an organic relationship between unions and party.
But, in a context where Bevin was far from happy with the leadership
of the party, it could be read as a much cruder message about Labour.[7]
Indeed, the picture is more complicated than any of these models will
allow. Relations between the party and the unions have been complex and
have always been subject to change.

The Labour Party and the unions: change over time

It is worth noting at the outset that we are not dealing with constant,
unchanging entities. The party has changed very considerably since its
formation as the Labour Representation Committee (LRC) in 1900. In
the years before the First World War, it was expanding, and consolidating
its organisation and status, but it struggled at times to escape the image
of being an appendage to the Liberal Party. It was the war that gave it its
great opportunity, giving its arguments credibility, dividing and weakening the Liberals, and recasting electoral politics in ways favourable to the
new type of labour politics represented by the party's 1918 constitution.
From 1922 onwards, it could compete for office with the Conservatives,
and Ramsay MacDonald was able to lead minority Labour governments in
1924 and 1929–31. The party finally came to compete with the Conservatives on equal terms in and after the Second World War, first in Winston
Churchill's coalition and then in office under Clement Attlee in the great
reforming government of 1945–51. It spent thirteen years in opposition
after 1951, leading some people to worry that it might be fated never
to govern Britain again; but it returned to power under Harold Wilson
in 1964. It remained in office for most of the period between then and

---

4 Minkin, *Contentious Alliance*.
5 Michael White, 'Unions warned against "divorce"', *Guardian*, 10 July 2002; Peter Hain,
   'Divorce? Never', *New Statesman*, 22 September 2011.
6 *Labour Party Annual Conference Report, 1935* (London: Labour Party, 1935), p. 180.
7 For more on this, see Andrew Thorpe, 'George Lansbury', in Kevin Jefferys (ed.),
   Leading Labour: From Keir Hardie to Tony Blair (London: I. B. Tauris, 1999), pp. 61–79,
   at pp. 73–4.

1979, and looked briefly, in Wilson's phrase, like 'the natural party of government'; but it lost the 1979 election and then remained in opposition for eighteen years. That lengthy period was succeed by thirteen years in government under Tony Blair and Gordon Brown, before the election defeats of 2010 and 2015 led to the election as leader of first Ed Miliband and then Jeremy Corbyn.

Over that same period, the unions changed almost beyond recognition. In 1900, union membership stood at 2,022,000, and was especially concentrated in the industries of the Industrial Revolution, such as cotton, coal, heavy engineering and railways.[8] Membership rose from 1910 (2,565,000) onwards, and then soared in and immediately after the First World War (peaking at 8,348,000 in 1920), but economic depression between the wars saw it virtually halve (to a trough of 4,392,000 in 1933). Steady increase in the 1930s (to 6,298,000 in 1939), and the increasing complexity of a modern 'warfare state' preparing for international conflict, brought the Trades Union Congress (TUC) closer to government than ever before, even under the ostensibly anti-union government of Neville Chamberlain from 1937 to 1940.[9] This was cemented in 1940 when Bevin, the General Secretary of the largest union (the TGWU), became Minister of Labour and National Service in Churchill's wartime coalition. Full employment during the war served the unions well, with membership reaching 7,875,000 in 1945; after the war it served them even better, and membership rose steadily even into the late 1970s, to peak at 13,212,000 in 1979, well after the post-war 'golden age' had come to an end. Trade union leaders came to enjoy increasing prestige within, and knowledge and inside understanding of, the state, through membership of the National Economic Development Council (which first met in 1962).[10] From the late 1960s, however, there was increasing pressure to 'deal' with 'union power' and after a number of ultimately abortive efforts – Wilson's *In Place of Strife* (1969), Heath's Industrial Relations Act 1971, and the Labour government's Social Contract in the mid-1970s – a series of new laws,

---

8 The figures in this paragraph are taken from the Department for Innovation, Business and Skills, *Trade Union Membership 2014: Statistical Bulletin* (2015), as well as accompanying tables, at https://www.gov.uk/government/statistics/trade-union-statistics-2014 (accessed 22 December 2015).

9 David Edgerton, *Warfare State: Britain, 1920–1970* (Cambridge: Cambridge University Press, 2006); see also Keith Middlemas, *Politics in Industrial Society: The Experience of the British System Since 1911* (London: Harper Collins, 1979), especially pp. 256–8.

10 Astrid Ringe and Neil Rollings, 'Responding to relative decline: the creation of the National Economic Development Council', *Economic History Review*, 53(2) (2000), 31–53; Keith Middlemas, *Power, Competition and the State, Volume II: Threats to the Post-War Settlement, 1961–74* (Basingstoke: Palgrave, 1990), pp. 39–40, 50–4, 99–100.

and the defeat of high-profile steel and miners' strikes, under the 1980s
Conservative government restricted unions' rights, with membership
falling to 8,231,000 in 1997. Under Blair from 1997 onwards, there was
no wholesale repeal of this legislation, but new rights were granted, and a
national minimum wage was established. Union membership fell overall
between 1997 and 2010, but at a much slower rate than in 1979–97, and it
still stood at 7,086,000 in 2012–13.

Brief overviews are helpful, but they need nuance. In particular, any
sense of 'the unions' as a homogeneous block has to be challenged. The
term is a convenience for historians and, still more, for journalists and
(often hostile) politicians. But it is also very problematic. Although on
some issues unions could take a broadly common view, there was no single
block with a single view and a single set of interests. Six points of fissure
should be noted.

Early in the period of Labour Party history there was a distinction to be
made between national unions and regional, or even local, ones. In 1919,
the first full year of operation of its new constitution, 126 unions with a
total membership of 3,464,020 were affiliated to the Labour Party. They
included UK-wide organisations such as the Amalgamated Society of Engineers (171,000 members), the National Union of Railwaymen (169,100),
the Amalgamated Society of Carpenters, Cabinetmakers and Joiners
(89,524) and the Dock, Wharf, Riverside and General Workers' Union
(75,402). But they also included unions that covered only part of the UK.
For example, the Friendly Society of Ironfounders (20,900) – the union
of the architect of the 1918 constitution, Arthur Henderson – covered
England, Ireland and Wales, but not Scotland, where the Central Iron-
moulders' Association (5,000) held sway. Furthermore, two of the largest
organisations were, in reality, federations of smaller unions. The Miners'
Federation of Great Britain (MFGB), the largest union affiliated to the
Labour Party in 1919, with 600,000 members, in fact comprised fourteen
county, regional or national bodies, whose interests did not always coincide
very closely. The United Textile Factory Workers' Association (296,765)
was a federal body which, in 1919, brought together forty-seven separate
organisations, many of them local to a particular town or district. And
then there were the small local unions, such as the Cardiff, Penarth and
Barry Coal Trimmers' Union (1,899), the Greenock and District Transport
Workers' Union (1,000), the Leeds Willeyers and Fettlers' Union (330),
and the Bolton Enginemen and Firemen's Union (120).[11] The decline of
local unions through amalgamation was a feature of the inter-war period,

---

11 *Labour Party Annual Conference Report, 1920* (London: Labour Party, 1920), pp. 58–90.

but their continued presence did demonstrate something about the variations within the movement, and of course local distinctiveness remained even once the number of local unions had diminished.[12]

Secondly, there was a distinction to be made between craft unions, industrial unions and general unions. In the United States, the distinction between the craft unions and the rest was often seen as being between the American Federation of Labor and the Congress of Industrial Organizations. The British trade union movement was never divided in that way, with the TUC continuing to act as the umbrella for pretty much all trade unions, including the smaller number that were actually affiliated to the Labour Party. Even so, there were distinctions of form and there could be differences of interest.

Thirdly, there were often distinctions within unions. Those unions that catered for a whole industry, for example, could have starkly different terms and membership rates depending on levels of skill and, partly related to that, of gender. This was certainly the case in the textile unions, and in the National Union of Boot and Shoe Operatives.[13] The merger of the National Union of Women Workers with the National Union of General and Municipal Workers in the aftermath of the First World War might have saved the former from collapse, but it certainly contributed to a diminution in the number of women delegates at Labour Party conferences throughout the inter-war period.[14] The Amalgamated Engineering Union (AEU) barred women from membership altogether until industrial dilution in the Second World War made it more politic to allow them to join; but, even then, they were very much second-class members, were treated, at least initially, as a temporary phenomenon, and often found that male attitudes were reactionary in the extreme.[15]

Fourthly, the overall gender balance of trade unionism changed. In 1900, union membership was overwhelmingly, although far from solely, male. In 2010, women made up almost 55 per cent of union members. This reflected a series of changes in the industrial base over the whole period, as well as significant changes in the nature and extent of female employment. But it also followed from deliberate union initiative towards the end of the

---

12 See for instance Hugh Armstrong Clegg, *A History of British Trade Unions Since 1889, Volume II: 1911–1933* (Oxford: Oxford University Press, 1985), pp. 304–5.

13 See for instance Alan Fox, *A History of the National Union of Boot and Shoe Operatives, 1874–1957* (Oxford: Blackwell, 1958), pp. 308–13.

14 Sarah Boston, *Women Workers and the Trade Union Movement* (London: Lawrence & Wishart, 1980), pp. 149–50.

15 *Ibid.*, pp. 213–16; James Hinton, *Shop Floor Citizens: Engineering Democracy in 1940s Britain* (Aldershot: Edward Elgar, 1994), pp. 118–20.

twentieth century, and here the efforts of both the unions and the party to move towards concrete affirmative action were important.[16]

Fifthly, and partly related to those gender factors, the class nature of trade union membership also changed over the period, from being predominantly blue collar to becoming increasingly white collar. This phenomenon was already under way during the inter-war period, and in some industries, such as the railways, the 'black-coated worker' was already a factor.[17] The Railway Clerks' Association was a relatively early affiliate to Labour: in an industry so dependent on safety legislation and a sympathetic state, it was not surprising that, by 1939, the Association was affiliating 50,000 members to the party, or that its ten delegates to the 1940 Labour Party conference included four MPs.[18] The trend intensified after the Second World War: full employment made employers unwilling to challenge white-collar trade union expansion, while the growth of the state, both directly and indirectly (through nationalisation and the establishment of the National Health Service), provided an environment within which union membership could grow.

Finally, there was the question of public sector, as against private sector, employment. On the whole, the public sector was more tolerant of union membership and activities. As the size of the public sector grew after the Second World War, membership grew also; as the sector shrank somewhat from the later twentieth century onwards, membership overall came under increasing pressure. Even so, it is important to note that in the National Health Service, as well as in local authorities, trade unionism remained well embedded, and that the relevant unions could make significant contributions to Labour's wider policy debates that extended well beyond the confines of wages and conditions.[19]

There was, therefore, great complexity about union membership, and about what 'the unions' meant. The shorthand term hid a range of issues and questions which were often deeply significant.

---

16 Meg Russell, *Building New Labour: The Politics of Party Organisation* (Basingstoke: Palgrave Macmillan, 2005), pp. 101–9; Helen Bewley and Sue Fernie, 'What do unions do for women?', in Howard Gospel and Stephen Wood (eds), *Representing Workers: Trade Union Recognition and Membership in Britain* (London: Routledge, 2003), pp. 92–118.

17 David Lockwood, *The Blackcoated Worker: A Study in Class Consciousness* (London: George Allen & Unwin, 1st edition, 1958).

18 *Labour Party Annual Conference Report, 1940* (London: Labour Party, 1940), p. 96; David Howell, *Respectable Radicals: Studies in the Politics of Railway Trade Unionism* (Aldershot: Ashgate, 1999), pp. 7–8.

19 See for instance Stephen Bach and Rebecca Kolins Givan, 'Union responses to public–private partnerships in the National Health Service', in Sue Fernie and David Metcalf (eds), *Trade Unions: Resurgence or Demise* (London: Routledge, 2005), pp. 118–37.

What did the unions do for the Labour Party?

There are, therefore, all sorts of reasons to be cautious about taking an overly deterministic view of 'the unions'. But even with all the appropriate caveats entered, it is still possible to talk in broad terms about a trade union contribution to the Labour Party. And, indeed, a series of significant impacts can be identified.

A number of unions contributed to the creation and establishment of the party in the first place. It is true that the LRC was a coming-together of socialists and trade unionists. Keir Hardie of the Independent Labour Party (ILP) and others had long advocated such a 'labour alliance' and had opposed the alternative of a 'big' socialist party which would have united the ILP with the Marxist-inclined Social Democratic Federation. It was felt that the reach of the 'alliance' would be greater, in that it would offer a way into working-class communities and so offer the prospect of a ready audience of workers who could be converted to socialism.[20] This approach was beginning to bear fruit in the 1890s. But changing union attitudes were primarily responsible for the timing of the LRC's foundation in 1900. It was as a result of increasing interest in the possibilities of state intervention on issues such as hours and conditions, along with increasing concern about the legal position of trade unions, that the TUC in 1899 agreed to convene the conference of February 1900 which would in turn agree to set up the LRC.[21] The Amalgamated Society of Railway Servants was the key mover on the day: significantly, it had a particular concern to seek state intervention to secure better safety and other regulations, and had had a long struggle against companies that were reluctant to recognise unions.[22]

Some unions stayed aloof for a time. But among the larger unions, the MFGB was looking anomalous in its non-affiliation as early as 1906, when the LRC became the Labour Party. In part, this was a question of momentum: once it was formed, and the longer it survived, the LRC began to look like a serious proposition. Unions such as the Ironfounders, initially sceptical, were converted to such an extent that by 1903 they were encouraging the erstwhile Liberal, Henderson, to fight the Barnard Castle

---

20 David Howell, *British Workers and the Independent Labour Party, 1888–1906* (Manchester: Manchester University Press, 1983), especially pp. 389–99.
21 For these changing attitudes, see for example Alastair J. Reid, *The Tide of Democracy: Shipyard Workers and Social Relations in Britain, 1870–1950* (Manchester: Manchester University Press, 2010), especially pp. 149–78, 264–71.
22 Philip S. Bagwell, *The Railwaymen: The History of the National Union of Railwaymen* (London: Allen & Unwin, 1963), pp. 199, 204, 206.

by-election as a Labour candidate, despite his residual doubts.[23] Here, the Taff Vale case provided a ready recruiter for the LRC. It took the skill of Ramsay MacDonald, as LRC Secretary, to maximise points of contact between moderate socialists like himself and sometimes wary trade union leaders; but the result was a major change as numerous unions affiliated. By the time of the 1906 general election, helped by a limited electoral pact with the Liberals, Labour was able to win twenty-nine seats in Parliament, a position from which it would never look back. The accession of the MFGB in 1909, and its determination, finally established by 1914, to ensure that the parliamentary candidates brought forward by its county associations were Labour, rather than Lib–Lab, in orientation, confirmed a very solid trade union basis for the party.[24] Calls for a trade-union-only party, shorn of socialists, got short shrift.[25]

Union membership and finance continued to play a key role in the party's development. The early establishment of the principle of affiliated membership, whereby a union would pay a set fee per member per annum, was crucial. Importantly, it offered the party the prospect of a relatively assured income, year on year. Too much can be made of this: it did not produce a bottomless pit of money, and it could fluctuate, according to trade conditions and other factors. The affiliation fee was low (and always lower than the party's organisers and officials would have liked), and unions were usually very reluctant to increase it.[26] It was also subject to legal challenge. The 1909 Osborne judgement saw union donations to the party ruled *ultra vires*. The 1913 Trade Union Act regularised the position by enabling unions to create a political fund, derived from a political levy out of which members could opt, should they so wish. Conservative hard-line pressure in the aftermath of the 1926 General Strike led to this changing, so that between 1927, with the Trade Disputes and Trade Union Act, and 1946 (when the Attlee government restored the 1913 position), members had to opt into paying the levy. By placing inertia on the side of non-payment, the 1927 Act cut Labour Party income by about a third:

---

23 Friendly Society of Ironfounders Papers, Modern Records Centre, MSS 41/FSIF/1/7, Executive council, 30 April, 3 June, 1 July 1903; Labour Party Papers, Labour History Archive and Study Centre (henceforth LHASC), LB 2/247, Ramsay MacDonald to Arthur Henderson, 1 July 1903.

24 Roy Gregory, *The Miners and British Politics, 1906–1914* (Oxford: Oxford University Press, 1968), especially p. 191.

25 R. I. McKibbin, *The Evolution of the Labour Party, 1910–1924* (Oxford: Oxford University Press, 1974), pp. 102–3.

26 See for instance *Report of the Third Annual Conference of the Labour Representation Committee, 1903* (London: LRC, 1903), pp. 34–5; *Labour Party Annual Conference Report, 1929* (London: Labour Party, 1929), p. 244.

trade union affiliation fees were the largest part of the party's income, and fell from around £40,000 to £25,000 per annum between 1927 and 1928.[27] That said, the 1913 Act established, and the 1927 Act did not remove, a political fund which unions were, at least to some extent, forced to spend on political ends, and particularly on Labour politics. In 1984, the Thatcher government introduced legislation which compelled unions to hold membership ballots regarding the continuation of political funds, but if this had been intended to damage the Labour–union relationship it backfired, since all thirty-eight unions that held ballots voted overwhelmingly in favour. Indeed, some unions not affiliated to Labour, and which had not previously had political funds, opened such funds for the first time. The ten-yearly ballots that followed saw similar levels of support for the principle.[28] These legislative restrictions could be irritating, but they did offer a degree of democratic credibility to Labour Party finances that could not be claimed for either the Conservatives or the Liberals. The affiliation fee was periodically increased, which meant that the party's real income was more or less sustained. While the failure of Labour to develop a mass membership can certainly be overdrawn,[29] the presence of union funding was a major relief to the party.

There were also times when at least some unions came forward to help the party with special contributions, such as for general elections or in periods of real financial difficulty. In both 1931 and 1939, the party was in such straitened circumstances that some feared bankruptcy, and in both cases unions ultimately came forward to offer immediate relief, which allowed things to be restored to a more even keel.[30] The modernisation and professionalisation of the party's organisation in the 1940s rested very

---

27 Labour Party, *Report of the 30th Annual Conference* (London: Labour Party, 1930), p. 36.
28 Doug Pyper, *Trade Union Political Funds and Levy*, House of Commons Library Briefing Paper 00593, 8 August 2013, pp. 5–6.
29 For an overly pessimistic view, see Christopher Howard, 'Expectations born to death: local Labour Party expansion in the 1920s', in J. M. Winter (ed.), *The Working Class in Modern British History* (Cambridge: Cambridge University Press, 1983), pp. 65–81. An important corrective comes from Matthew Worley, 'The fruits on the tree: Labour's constituency parties between the wars', in M. Worley (ed.), *The Foundations of the British Labour Party: Identities, Cultures and Perspectives, 1900–39* (Aldershot: Ashgate, 2009), pp. 193–212.
30 Richard Shackleton, 'Trade unions and the slump', in Ben Pimlott and Chris Cook (eds), *Trade Unions in British Politics* (London: Longman Higher Education, 2nd edition, 1991), pp. 109–36, at pp. 111–13; Clare V. J. Griffiths, *Labour and the Countryside: The Politics of Rural Britain, 1918–1939* (Oxford: Oxford University Press, 2007), p. 124; Labour Party Papers, LHASC, Finance and General Purposes Committee minutes, 26 September and 16 November 1939.

much on the back of continued generous union funding in the conditions
of full employment in wartime and afterwards, and the party remained
well endowed financially for many years thereafter, even if the money was
not always terribly well spent.[31] The Blair years saw a lot of talk about
income diversification, but although gifts from wealthy benefactors and
business did diminish the significance of union funding for a time, it
never went away.[32] And when those other sources began to dry up for
various reasons after 2000, the unions once again came to centre stage:
as Andrew Rawnsley put it, '[a]s rich men abandoned the party, Labour
ended up almost entirely dependent on the unions' for money.[33] Ed
Miliband's reforms of the party–union relationship after 2010 were much
debated. Some saw them as a very positive development; but others felt
that their main effect might well be to leave the party in financial trouble,
by reducing its funding 'take' from its union affiliates.[34]

At local level, too, union money was often crucial. The willingness of
a union to sponsor a parliamentary candidate, or to fund a parliamentary
agent, was often vital in terms of ensuring electoral success for Labour.
Understandably, of course, the unions wanted to back winners: there was
usually no incentive for them to spend a lot of money on a candidate who
would not be able to get into Parliament to defend and advance union
rights and progressive legislation. But even where sponsorship, or the
funding of an agent, was out of the question, local union branches could
still play an important role in terms of more modest funding and general
support. In a context where local parties often found it beyond their abilities to recruit and retain individual members in significant numbers, such
contributions could be extremely significant. And pockets of unionised
workers – such as railway workers in areas like rural Devon and Dorset –
could often play a part in sustaining Labour activity in even the most
unlikely locations.[35]

---

31 For more on the start of this period, see Andrew Thorpe, *Parties at War: Political Or-
    ganization in Second World War Britain* (Oxford: Oxford University Press, 2009), pp.
    256–68.
32 Russell, *Building New Labour*, p. 221; Andrew Rawnsley, *Servants of the People: The
    Inside Story of New Labour* (London: Penguin, revised edition, 2001), pp. 89–95.
33 Andrew Rawnsley, *The End of the Party: The Rise and Fall of New Labour* (London:
    Penguin, 2010), pp. 373–4.
34 For a very positive view, see John Rentoul, 'Ed Miliband's Labour Party reforms are
    good news for all', *Independent*, 2 March 2014, at http://www.independent.co.uk/voices/
    comment/ed-miliband-s-labour-party-reforms-are-good-news-for-all-9162681.html
    (accessed 22 December 2015).
35 Howell, *Respectable Radicals*, p. 21.

It followed from this that unions also played a significant role in organising the party at all levels. This might not always have been consistent, or even welcome. There were always those who rather resented what they saw as union interference, or the packing of candidate selection meetings by members who were otherwise rarely seen at party gatherings (a particular complaint in some coalfield areas). But such images carry an element of caricature. It is clear that many local Labour organisers were trained in the trade union field, and that this was an asset when it came to establishing and running local Labour parties. The skills required of a union organiser were readily transferrable into much Labour Party work: the South Wales coalfield was just one area that was replete with people who transferred with some ease from one to the other.[36] At national level, the party organisation owed much to the traditions of management and administration established by trade unions and the TUC during the latter part of the nineteenth century: the annual conference, the election of an executive to oversee business between conferences, careful control of finances, a branch structure and a weather eye on the leadership were all derived, in part, from those practices.

Unions, either singly or collectively, also played a significant role in the making of Labour Party policy. This was often the case in relation to particular industries. The MFGB emerged from the First World War with a clear view as to the merits of state control of coal mining, and spent much of the immediate post-war period trying to resist decontrol.[37] Once it had come in 1921, it was very clear that it wanted it reversed through the nationalisation of the industry; and even at the 1929 general election, when Labour was desperately trying to play down its radicalism in order to appeal to voters in the political centre ground, the one industry whose nationalisation they still felt they had to propose was coal mining.[38] This pressure continued, and because of the size and importance of the mining union, Labour kept closely focused on it until it could be delivered in 1946. Similarly, there were major strategic reasons for the Attlee government to nationalise the railways, but one very clear incentive was provided by the fact that the industry's three unions were all very significant components of the Labour Party.

---

36 See for instance James Griffiths, *Pages from Memory* (London: Littlehampton Books, 1969); Cliff Prothero, *Recount* (Ormskirk: G. W. & A. Hesketh, 1982).

37 See Chris Wrigley, *Lloyd George and the Challenge of Labour: The Post-War Coalition, 1918–22* (Hemel Hempstead: Prentice Hall, 1990), especially pp. 233–90.

38 'Labour's appeal to the nation' (1929), in F. W. S. Craig (ed.), *British General Election Manifestos, 1900–1974* (Chichester: Political Reference Publishers, 1975), pp. 81–6, at p. 83.

Policy was also influenced by the unions more generally. The basic principle of 'work or maintenance', which went right back to the early years of the party, was fundamental to unions; the sense of a right to work, and a right to a degree of security in the event of unemployment, was a key theme.[39] It became a major factor in the conduct of the TUC and its constituent unions in the 1931 crisis, when MacDonald's Labour government was proposing benefit cuts as a way of balancing the budget in the light of a major financial crisis.[40] Welfare policy more generally became an increasing concern, too. Pensions were one area of considerable interest, where there was a good deal of consensus.[41] Family allowances were regarded with a good deal more scepticism before the Second World War, with some seeing them as state aid to capitalism whose introduction would subsidise employers who were paying low wages.[42] The trade union establishment saw the foundation of the welfare state by the Attlee government in the later 1940s as being, in large part, its own achievement: in the lavishly illustrated volume published to commemorate the TUC's centenary in 1968, the section on the later 1940s was headed 'The welfare state is born and the TUC is named as godfather'.[43] Unions were in the forefront of attempts to prevent Margaret Thatcher's 1980s government making cuts to public expenditure: this resistance derived in one sense narrowly, from a concern with the likely impact on their members' jobs and status, but also because of wider concerns about working people more generally. And it is hard to see how the Blair government would ever have introduced a national minimum wage, or guaranteed unions the statutory right of recognition in the workplace, without the careful and focused pressure applied by trade unions and their leaders.

Union leaders often played a key role in moments of crisis for Labour. In the crisis of August 1931, immediately following MacDonald's formation of a National government with the Conservatives and Liberals to drive through spending cuts to balance the budget, Bevin told a meeting of key Labour figures: 'This is like the General Strike. I'm prepared to put

---

39 Jose Harris, *Unemployment and Politics: A Study in English Social Policy, 1886–1914* (Oxford: Oxford University Press, 1984).

40 Ben Jackson, *Equality and the British Left: A Study in Progressive Political Thought, 1900–64* (Manchester: Manchester University Press, 2007), p. 80.

41 John Macnicol, *The Politics of Retirement in Britain, 1878–1948* (Cambridge: Cambridge University Press, 1998), especially pp. 227–43.

42 John Macnicol, *The Movement for Family Allowances, 1918–1945: A Study in Social Policy Development* (London: Heinemann, 1980; Aldershot: Ashgate, 1984), pp. 3, 141–4, 172–6.

43 J. Bingham, *The History of the TUC 1868–1968: A Pictorial Survey of a Social Revolution* (London: TUC, 1968), pp. 126–7.

everything in.'[44] During the Second World War, he and other leading figures were instrumental in getting Labour to work with the Chamberlain government to a limited extent, and then to enter the Churchill coalition in May 1940; they were also instrumental in keeping Labour in that coalition, when some people on the left were contemplating rebellion or even schism.[45] Bevin was also crucial in 1947, refusing to move against Attlee when many of the premier's other leading lieutenants were looking for a change.[46] In the mid-1970s, Jack Jones of the TGWU was instrumental in ensuring the success of the Social Contract, until his position was rendered untenable by the Callaghan government's insistence on ever tighter pay restraint.[47] Dianne Hayter has argued that '[t]he trade unions ... took fright in 1981 when they glimpsed the possibility of Labour becoming unelectable', and shown how a group of leading trade unionists played a significant role in the St Ermin's Group, which sought to move the party away from the left.[48] The leader of the GMB (formerly the General, Municipal, Boilermakers and Allied Trades Union), John Edmonds, was one of the key figures on the union side in the early years of New Labour, ensuring that the party was not divided in the run-up to the 1997 general election which saw Blair win a landslide. Key union figures really could keep Labour together and bring it back from the brink on occasions. That the Conservatives did not have such a force after their heavy defeat in 1997 was arguably one of the main reasons why they took so long to recover.

The unions also provided a training ground for many Labour leaders. It is true that the majority of the leaders who achieved the greatest prominence did not come from a union background: out of the six Labour premiers so far, MacDonald, Attlee, Wilson, Blair and Brown had little experience of, and in at least some cases, affection for, the trade union movement; they were all more likely to see themselves as, in one way or another, products of the party's socialist wing. But this was not true of Callaghan, who had been Douglas Houghton's deputy at the Inland

44 Hugh Dalton, *Call Back Yesterday: Memoirs, 1887–1931* (London: Muller, 1953), p. 274.

45 Thorpe, *Parties at War*, p. 196.

46 Hugh Dalton, *High Tide and After: Memoirs, 1945–1960* (London: Muller, 1962), pp. 239–47.

47 Robert Taylor, 'The rise and fall of the Social Contract', in Anthony Seldon and Kevin Hickson (eds), *New Labour, Old Labour: The Wilson and Callaghan Governments, 1974–79* (London: Routledge, 2004), pp. 70–104, especially pp. 91–2.

48 Dianne Hayter, *Fightback! Labour's Traditional Right in the 1970s and 1980s* (Manchester: Manchester University Press, 2005), p, 191; see also Stephen Meredith, *Labours Old and New: The Parliamentary Right of the British Labour Party and the Roots of New Labour* (Manchester: Manchester University Press, 2008).

Revenue Staff Federation from 1936 to 1942.[49] Henderson (who also led the party in 1908–10, 1914–17 and 1931–32) and Bevin were Labour's first two Foreign Secretaries; George Brown, of the TGWU, its fifth (1966–68). Other prominent trade unionists to become Cabinet ministers have included J. H. Thomas of the National Union of Railwaymen (NUR), Margaret Bondfield and J. R. Clynes of the National Union of General and Municipal Workers (NUGMW), James Griffiths of the National Union of Mineworkers (NUM) and Frank Cousins of the TGWU. More recently, Eric Varley and Roy Mason were miners who served as Cabinet ministers in the 1970s, while John Prescott, deputy leader under Blair, had once been an official of the National Union of Seamen. It would be true to say that the union connection has been somewhat under-represented at the higher levels of the party – Wilson's 1960s Cabinet contained at least as many graduates of a single university as it did trade unionists – but they did, nonetheless, have a part to play. That said, the party will need to consider in future how to bring more trade unionists, and particularly women trade unionists, into its higher echelons. Of course, it was not all about the highest reaches of government: trade unions also provided training for many of the people who staffed the Labour Party in Parliament, as officials at party headquarters, in the constituencies and also in local government. The life of Henderson shows the value that a key Labour figure derived from being trained both as a local trade union official and as a Wesleyan Methodist local preacher. It is a moot point as to where Labour's future working-class leaders will get a training that will provide for them as effectively in Labour politics in the round. This is not to say that they will necessarily have to be trade unionists or, still less, Methodists, in order to succeed, but there does need to be some way in which working-class people can have a realistic prospect of getting into senior positions in politics.

Finally, the trade unions also helped to determine the ethos of the party. The language of solidarity was something that seeped from the unions into the party. It was often inimical to the interests of some of the less conventional or acquiescent party members, a difference from the old Liberal Party, which had seemed to be more forgiving of diversity. At its worst, it could be expressed crudely. One example is when Sir William Lawther (President of the NUM) shouted 'Shut your gob!' at left-wing hecklers at the 1952 party conference.[50] Another is when in 2010 Len McCluskey

---

49 Kenneth O. Morgan, *Callaghan: A Life* (Oxford: Oxford University Press, 1997), pp. 20–40.

50 *Labour Party Annual Conference Report, 1952* (London: Labour Party, 1952), p. 79; David Howell, 'Shut your gob! Trade unions and the Labour Party, 1945–64', in Alan

of Unite shouted 'Rubbish!' from the conference floor in response to Ed Miliband's criticism of 'irresponsible' strikes in his first speech as Labour leader.[51] This kind of thing could come across as an 'aggressive and intolerant proletarianism', in the words of that most unproletarian figure, Roy Jenkins.[52] But in essence it was a way of ensuring that democracy counted: that numbers mattered. A Labour Party that was undisciplined, and which did not pay heed to loyalty to majority decisions, would face trouble against a Conservative opponent that was, for the most part, kept in line by its fear of losing property, privilege and rank. The unions gave the party, in addition, both a set of traditions, around certain events in the year – of which congress/conference was only one of many – and also a keen sense, through the system of reporting back on the expenditure of subscriptions, of accountability of the leadership and the management of the party to the rank and file. A whole calendar of events such as the Durham Miners' Gala, or the Tolpuddle celebrations – never more in evidence than in the centenary year of 1934[53] – attested to Labour's celebration of its trade union roots.

None of this, of course, is intended to imply that the unions had a monopoly in any of these areas: leaders, policies and even money came from other areas of the movement as well. But without the union contribution, it is hard to see how Labour's history could have been anywhere near as successful as it has been.

Yet it was not all positive. Indeed, at some points when the unions took a very prominent role in Labour politics, the results could be quite negative. In 1931, for example, Bevin and the unions' putting 'everything in' – to the extent of a significant financial contribution, a major effort in terms of speeches at the election by the likes of Walter Citrine (General Secretary of the TUC for twenty years from 1926 onwards) and C. T. Cramp (NUR), and Bevin himself standing unsuccessfully for election at Gateshead – was followed by a massive electoral defeat.[54] This was not the case in 1945, when the union link was also emphasised, but it

Campbell, Nina Fishman and John McIlroy (eds), *British Trade Unions and Industrial Politics, Volume 1: The Post-War Compromise, 1945–64* (Aldershot: Ashgate, 1999), pp. 117–44.

51 *Guardian*, 28 September 2010.

52 Roy Jenkins, 'Home thoughts from abroad: the 1979 Dimbleby Lecture', in Wayland Kennet (ed.), *The Rebirth of Britain* (London: TUC, 1982), pp. 7–29, at p. 29.

53 See for instance the high-quality illustrated volume published by the TUC General Council: *The Book of the Martyrs of Tolpuddle, 1834–1934* (London: TUC, 1934).

54 Andrew Thorpe, *The British General Election of 1931* (Oxford: Clarendon Press, 1991), p. 189; Archie Potts, 'Bevin to beat the bankers: Ernest Bevin's Gateshead campaign of 1931', *Bulletin of the North East Group for the Study of Labour History*, 11 (1977), 28–38.

seems likely that a broadly positive view of the role of unions in wartime, itself assisted by wartime censorship of news about strikes, was a significant factor.[55] Conservative strategists at various points clearly thought that they could make hay with the image of Labour leaders being pushed around by trade union leaders. The image of cosy conspiracy conjured up by the regular attendance of union leaders at 10 Downing Street, especially at the time of the controversy over *In Place of Strife* in 1969, was potentially damaging, implying as it did a world in which leading trade unionists enjoyed privileged access to senior Labour ministers, who were portrayed as running the country in favour of a vested interest – precisely the kind of charge that Labour had traditionally found so powerful against the Conservatives. Finally, Ed Miliband's leadership of the party got off to a bad start in 2010 when it became clear that he had won only because of the trade union votes that he had received in the electoral college. The fact that it was only there that he had defeated David Miliband, whereas the latter had won among party members, MPs and MEPs, was something from which he arguably never quite recovered. It certainly made it easier for Labour's opponents, and a hostile media, to construct an image of 'Red Ed' that was far from flattering.[56]

Strikes could pose particular problems. They were easy for Labour's opponents to portray as being disruptive to 'the public'. This, in turn, allowed the unions to be presented as an unrepresentative minority, and as 'other' and oppositional to the national or public interest. Ross McKibbin has demonstrated how this 'othering' of that part of the working class most associated with trade unions took place during the inter-war period, and also the extent to which it was at least suspended as a result of the events of 1940 and immediately afterwards.[57] It was not just a matter of the more spectacular set-tos of, say, 1926 (the General Strike), 1978–79 (the 'Winter of Discontent') or 1984–85 (the miners' strike). Bob Crow, General Secretary of the National Union of Rail, Maritime and Transport

---

55 R. B. McCallum and Alison Readman, *The British General Election of* 1945 (London: 1947; Basingstoke: Palgrave Macmillan, 2003), pp. 236–7.

56 Matt Chorley and John Rentoul, 'Union votes crucial in narrowest of votes for Ed Miliband', *Independent*, 26 September 2010, at http://www.independent.co.uk/news/uk/politics/union-votes-crucial-in-narrowest-of-wins-for-ed-miliband-2089968.html (accessed 22 December 2015); Richard Jobson and Mark Wickham-Jones, 'Reinventing the block vote? Trade unions and the 2010 Labour Party leadership election', *British Politics*, 6(3) (2011), 317–44; Hugh R. Pemberton and Mark Wickham-Jones, 'Brothers all? The operation of the electoral college in the 2010 Labour leadership contest', *Parliamentary Affairs*, 66(4) (2012), 708–31.

57 Ross McKibbin, 'Class and conventional wisdom', in Ross McKibbin, *Ideologies of Class: Social Relations in Britain, 1880–1950* (Oxford: Clarendon Press, 1990).

Workers (RMT) between 2002 and 2014, polarised opinion: he led the RMT in a series of successful disputes on the London Underground, but at the same time those disputes were seen as inconveniencing large numbers of people who relied on the Tube to go about their normal business.[58] The fact that New Labour and the RMT distanced themselves from each other during the period meant that Labour did not suffer as much collateral damage as it might have done; but in earlier periods Labour often caught the backlash of public irritation with, and concern about, strikes, as was certainly the case with Callaghan in 1979 and Neil Kinnock in 1984–85. In 1926, MacDonald was so desperate to see an end to the General Strike that he secretly took Sir Allen Smith – who, as Chairman of the Engineering Employers' Federation had in 1922 all but smashed the AEU in a lockout – to Downing Street to meet the Conservative Prime Minister, Stanley Baldwin, and propose a settlement that would not have been at all lenient towards the strikers or the TUC.[59]

All of this fed into broader perceptions of unions as an over-mighty 'interest' within the state, particularly in the 1960s and 1970s. In the early 1950s, Churchill's peacetime government had adopted a relatively benign attitude towards the trade union movement, but attitudes hardened from the middle of the decade onwards.[60] In 1958 the publication of the Society of Conservative Lawyers' pamphlet *A Giant's Strength* was symbolic of a new mood among younger Conservatives: its authors included Geoffrey Howe, who would go on to be Thatcher's Chancellor from 1979 to 1983.[61] When, in 1969, Wilson told Hugh Scanlon of the AEU that he was 'not going to surrender to your tanks, Hughie', he was to some extent subscribing to the view that the unions had taken too much power and needed to be reined in.[62] This violent imagery was to find ample repetition and development from the 1970s onwards, whether during the coal and power disputes that seemed to characterise much of the Heath government between 1970 and

---

58 Christian Wolmar, 'Bob Crow obituary', *Guardian*, 11 March 2014.
59 Thomas Jones, *Whitehall Diary, Volume II: 1926–1930*, ed. Keith Middlemas (Oxford: Oxford University Press, 1969), pp. 39–40.
60 Henry Pelling, *Churchill's Peacetime Ministry, 1951–55* (London: Palgrave Macmillan, 1997), p. 14; John Ramsden, *The Winds of Change: Macmillan to Heath, 1957–1975* (London: Macmillan, 1996), pp. 10–11.
61 Margaret Thatcher, *The Path to Power* (London: HarperCollins, 1995), pp. 109–10; E. H. H. Green, *Ideologies of Conservatism: Conservative Political Ideas in the Twentieth Century* (Oxford: Oxford University Press, 2002), pp. 225–7.
62 Barbara Castle, *The Castle Diaries, 1964–70* (London: Weidenfeld & Nicolson, 1984), p. 662, 1 June 1969. The allusion was to the previous year's events in Czechoslovakia, where the liberalising leader Alexander Dubček had been overthrown with the help of Soviet tanks.

1974 (with special mention of the Yorkshire miners' flying pickets' victory at 'the battle of Saltley Gate' in 1972)[63] or in terms of Thatcher's 'enemy within' references at the time of the 1984–85 miners' strike.[64]

One particular complaint was that the union presence stymied what might have been wider and more productive debate within the party. The block vote at conference, whereby the votes of hundreds of thousands of affiliated members could be cast by the union's delegation (and sometimes, in effect at least, its leader) was often seen by party activists, some of whom were of course themselves trade unionists, as a particular obstacle to open discussion. David Marquand and others lamented the fact that the Labour Party had not kept up a supposedly high level of debate from the Edwardian Liberal Party that it had replaced, but had instead allowed itself to be bound by loyalty to majority decisions, often based around the lowest common denominator (represented especially by the party conference 'composite motion').[65] As Duncan Tanner and others have shown, this probably underestimates the quality of intellectual debate within the Labour Party as it matured,[66] and it is certainly possible, on the other side of the equation, to overstate the sophistication of the Edwardian Liberal Party, one of whose favourite binaries was 'the big loaf of free trade or the little loaf of protection', and which was able to play host to Lloyd George's class rhetoric against the House of Lords with some ease. It was also the case that much of inter-war Labour's inferiority complex in relation to the German Social Democratic Party as a much richer cultural and intellectual organisation was rather overdone.[67] Additionally, some leading trade unionists were intellectually powerful in their own right. Bevin had left school in Devon at the age of eleven and worked as a farm boy and a carter before becoming a full-time trade unionist; but he had a sharp mind, took his chances to learn more around his work, and learnt a considerable amount from Keynes on the Macmillan Committee on Finance and

---

63 R. Taylor, 'The Heath government and industrial relations: myth and reality', in Stuart Ball and Anthony Seldon (eds), *The Heath Government, 1970–74* (London: Longman, 1996), p. 177.

64 Robin Harris, *Not for Turning: The Life of Margaret Thatcher* (London: Bantam, 2013), p. 234.

65 David Marquand, *The Progressive Dilemma: From Lloyd George to Kinnock* (London: William Heinemann, revised edition, 1992), pp. 18–25.

66 Duncan Tanner, 'The development of British socialism, 1900–1918', *Parliamentary History*, 16(1) (1997), 48–66.

67 Stefan Berger, 'The formation of party milieux: branch life in the British Labour Party and the German Social Democratic Party in the interwar period', in Matthew Worley (ed.), *Labour's Grass Roots: Essays on the Activities of Local Labour Parties and Members, 1918–45* (Aldershot: Ashgate, 2005), pp. 240–59.

Industry between 1929 and 1931.[68] Citrine was a powerful force for rethink-
ing the relationship between the unions and the party.[69] Clive Jenkins,
General Secretary of the Association of Supervisory Staffs, Executives and
Technicians (ASSET) and then the Association of Scientific, Technical
and Managerial Staffs (ASTMS) (1961–88), was intellectually capable, if
often seen as opportunistic.[70] They might not have been Oxford-educated
barristers along the lines of Edwardian Liberals such as H. H. Asquith,
but they were serious contributors to the development of modern British
industrial relations and politics.

Overall, the majority of the unions tended to support the centre right
of the party, but their support was conditional and could be withdrawn;
and, at various points, the balance shifted to the left. Most unions were
pretty solidly behind the MacDonald–Henderson project to make the
party electable, at any rate until the problems of 1930–31 forced them into
a more critical position.[71] But although there was a leftward movement
in the early 1930s, the critical mass of the unions was soon back in the
business of pulling the party towards more immediately practicable
politics, working hard with Labour centrists like Dalton, Attlee and
Morrison to make the party more electable.[72] In the 1950s, the short-lived
leftward swing after the general election defeat of 1951 was largely contained and negated as the 'Big Three' – Lawther, Arthur Deakin (TGWU),
and Tom Williamson (NUGMW) – worked hard with the party leadership to manage the key votes at conference and in Parliament, in a process
that would culminate in the election of Hugh Gaitskell as party leader in

68 Alan Bullock, *The Life and Times of Ernest Bevin, Volume I: Trade Union Leader, 1881–1940* (London: William Heinemann, 1960), pp. 4–5, 9–13; Peter Clarke, *The Keynesian Revolution in the Making, 1924–1936* (Oxford: Clarendon, 1988), pp. 120–4, 216.

69 Neil Riddell, 'Walter Citrine and the British labour movement, 1925–1935', *History*, 85(273) (2000), 285–306.

70 Robert Taylor, *The Fifth Estate: Britain's Unions in the Modern World* (London: Rout-ledge, revised edition, 1980), p. 376; Joseph Melling, 'Red under the collar? Clive Jenkins, white collar unionism and the politics of the British left, 1947–65', *Twentieth Century British History*, 13(4) (2002), 412–48; Joseph Melling, 'Leading the white-collar union: Clive Jenkins, the management of trade union officers, and the politics of the British labour movement, c. 1968–1979', *International Review of Social History*, 49 (2004), 71–102.

71 Neil Riddell, *Labour in Crisis: The Second Labour Government, 1929–31* (Manchester: Manchester University Press, 1999), especially pp. 87–90.

72 Ben Pimlott, *Labour and the Left in the 1930s* (Cambridge: Cambridge University Press, 1977); John Swift, *Labour in Crisis: Clement Attlee and the Labour Party in Opposition, 1931–40* (Basingstoke: Palgrave Macmillan, 2001).

1955.[73] Rebellions from some union quarters against Gaitskell (over nuclear disarmament in 1960) and Wilson (over *In Place of Strife* in 1969) were ultimately overcome with union help. The leftward swing of the 1970s was not so easily managed, and a number of unions passed into more left-wing control.[74] In particular, the performance of the Wilson and Callaghan governments in the 1970s was such as to antagonise a number of unions and their leaders, with the result that the arguments of the left found ready adherents among trade unionists at all levels. Even so, their patience began to fail as further electoral defeat by the Conservative Party began to loom from 1982 onwards, when the Thatcher government turned its attention to the unions. Labour's heavy defeat at the 1983 general election, the failure of the 1984–85 miners' strike, and an increasing aversion towards the far left more generally, all helped to bring a critical mass of unions firmly behind Neil Kinnock's plans for modernisation.[75] That set the tone for a decade and a half of broadly amicable relations with Kinnock, Smith and, more cautiously, Blair: even though the last was clearly not an enthusiast for unions, his first period in office did deliver the gains that most unions had wanted, as stated above.[76]

After 2001, however, relations soured. Although the majority of unions continued to affiliate to the party, in 2004 the expulsion of the RMT (for funding rivals to Labour) and the departure of the Fire Brigades Union signified a change of mood.[77] As seen above, by the time of the 2010 leadership election, the majority of unions were declaring for Ed Miliband rather than the more centrist David Miliband. In the campaign to replace Ed Miliband in 2015, more unions – including two of the largest, Unite and Unison – supported the left candidate, Jeremy Corbyn, than anyone else. Such union support was of less numerical significance following Miliband's reforms to the party, but it was far from unimportant.[78] It said a lot about

73 Minkin, *Labour Party Conference*, pp. 68, 85, 254, 269, 322; Eric Shaw, *Discipline and Discord in the Labour Party: The Politics of Managerial Control in the Labour Party, 1951–1987* (Manchester: Manchester University Press, 1988), pp. 45–50; Brian Brivati, *Hugh Gaitskell* (London: Richard Cohen Books, 1996), p. 227.
74 Shaw, *Discipline and Discord*, pp. 182, 296; Patrick Seyd, *The Rise and Fall of the Labour Left* (Basingstoke: Palgrave Macmillan, 1987), pp. 20–1.
75 See Hayter, *Fightback, passim*; Martin Westlake, *Kinnock: The Biography* (London: Little Brown, 2001), pp. 359–60.
76 Robert Taylor, 'Employment relations policy', in Anthony Seldon (ed.), *The Blair Effect: The Blair Government, 1997–2001* (London: Little Brown, 2001), pp. 245–69.
77 Minkin, *Blair Supremacy*, p. 590.
78 In winning the leadership, Corbyn took votes as follows: party members 121,751 (49.6 per cent); registered supporters 88,449 (83.8 per cent); and affiliated supporters 41,217 (57.6 per cent), to emerge with 59.5 per cent of the votes overall.

the extent to which union leaders and, to some extent, members had been alienated by the perceived disappointments of New Labour in office and the failure of Miliband's party in opposition. Corbyn's ability and willingness to offer an unapologetic case for trade unionism was a significant factor in his victory; and those Labour MPs who reacted in horror to the result might have reflected on the extent to which they had failed to realise the unions' continuing importance. It is noteworthy that the periods of Labour's previously most pronounced swings to the left – the early 1930s, the early 1970s and the early 1980s – were all when the leaders of many of the biggest trade unions were most antagonised by the behaviour of the parliamentary leadership of the Labour Party. By and large, those were quite transient periods. At the time of writing, it remained to be seen whether history would, in that sense at least, repeat itself.

Conclusion

The trade union movement did not support Labour solely out of the goodness of its heart. This was a practical relationship based as much on value for money as it was on abstract ideology. There were, in reality, many positives for the unions from the Labour link. Labour pressed in opposition, and worked in government, on a number of key areas of union concern. These included: defence and enhancement of the unions' legal position; defence of workers' rights; and the implementation of various social and economic policies by Labour governments, in areas relating both to the narrow interests of the unions and the broader concerns of union members. We should also remember the contribution that Labour local authorities often made, for example by building up large direct works departments which were heavily unionised and which could in turn set a benchmark of wages and conditions for certain trades within a particular town or city. This is not to say that unions have always been happy with what they have had from Labour governments. There was particular disappointment in 1929–31, and considerable alienation by the end of the governments of the 1960s and the 1970s. Where the possibilities were greater – as in 1945–51 – or the demands more modest – as in 1997–2010 – then it was possible for unions to come out of periods of Labour government with more of a feeling of satisfaction.

The period since the mid-1990s has seen considerable amounts of conjecture about the future of the party–union relationship. The early years of New Labour were flooded with it. At one point, scarcely a week seemed to pass without some true-believer New Labour MP such as Stephen Byers being reported as making on-the-record off-the-cuff remarks to journalists in some bar or restaurant to the effect that the unions were about to be jettisoned.[79] Leader writers competed with each other to invent the most ludicrous marriage–divorce metaphors possible. After all, it seemed, New Labour was awash with money and, after 1997, credibility. Unions were a thing of the past, in any case: membership was falling inexorably. Soon New Labour would become the 'progressive party' some had wanted all along – and without all that working-class baggage. It would be, after all, a party safe for Social Democrats of a 1981 vintage. It was with this future very much in mind that Blair had stated as early as 1995 that Labour 'must value the contribution of Lloyd George, Beveridge and Keynes and not just Attlee, Bevan or Crosland'.[80] Writing in 1999, one academic argued that, given New Labour's dislike of the unions, a 'final removal of the institutional link between the industrial and political wings of the labour movement [was] now almost inevitable'.[81] But, as stated above, it did not happen. The Blair government did deliver some key union demands and the unions, for their part, knew that this was better than the alternative of a Conservative government. The Blair government did not deliver everything that every trade union wanted. But it could not have done so, any more than its predecessors could, especially given the point, made above, that 'the unions' were and are not one homogeneous mass but, instead, often had and have diverse interests. And, of course, unions were not a thing of the past – a point proven as, after many years of decline, membership began to stabilise.

The link between Labour and the unions has been fundamental and enduring. It has also proved to be of very considerable value to both sides. It continues to be a significant asset to a Labour Party, which is, arguably, in rather short supply of assets. It remains to be seen how the relationship will develop as the party moves further into its second century, but those

---

79 For an early example of this kind of thing, see the reaction to Byers' comments made in 'a fish restaurant' about a possible severing of links between Labour and the unions in 1996: Colin Brown and Barrie Clement, 'Blair scorns furious union leaders', *The Independent*, 13 September 1996, at http://www.independent.co.uk/news/blair-scorns-furious-union-leaders-1363136.html (accessed 22 December 2015). See also Minkin, *Blair Supremacy*, pp. 283, 285; and, for evidence that Byers later began to shift his position as he saw the need for strong unions as a lobbying counterweight to business, see *ibid.*, pp. 456, 724.

80 Tony Blair, 'The radical coalition', speech to the Fabian Society, 5 July 1995, in Tony Blair, *New Britain: My Vision of a Young Country* (London: Basic Books edition, 1996), pp. 4–21, at p. 7.

81 Chris Howell, 'Unforgiven: British trade unionism in crisis', in Andrew Martin and George Ross (eds), *The Brave New World of European Labour: European Trade Unions at the Millennium* (New York: Bergahn, 1999), pp. 26–74, at p. 67.

who wish to see it come to an end will have to work very hard, and very imaginatively, to find an alternative that will even begin to rival its achievement and potential.

Acknowledgements

Andrew Thorpe would like to thank John Edmonds, Billy Hayes and the other speakers and attendees for their comments on an earlier version of this paper at the History and Policy Trade Union Forum meeting on 'The Labour Party and the Trade Unions' at King's College London in March 2012.

6

The disaffiliation crisis of 1932: the Labour Party, the Independent Labour Party (ILP) and the opinion of ILP members

KEITH LAYBOURN

On 9 and 10 June 1928, the National Administrative Council (NAC) of the Independent Labour Party (ILP) held a closed meeting to discuss its future relations with the Labour Party. Manny Shinwell, a Clydeside MP, reflected that:

> In his view the ILP couldn't get a distinctive policy. There was no hope of the ILP setting itself up in opposition to the Labour Party either politically or in organisation. This led him to ask what was the function of the ILP. Was it to become a definitely socialist propaganda body having few if any responsibilities?

Answering this question, he favoured a new party organisation:

> [one] which had a relatively small effective membership of Socialist missionaries, locally and nationally affiliated to the Labour Party ... becoming a Socialist missionary body cutting loose from its present political entanglements. He realised that this raised some difficult questions with regard to continued affiliation of the ILP with the Labour Party.[1]

Others at this meeting offered their visions of the ILP's future, ones that largely saw it as remaining within the Labour Party. Oswald Mosley, the future fascist leader and author of the Mosley Memorandum while in the Labour government, felt that the ILP had to be built up into an active,

---

1 British Library of Political and Economic Science (BLPES), ILP Archives, Section 10, Summary of discussion on present position of the party which took place at the NAC meeting 9 and 10 June 1928 (copy).

rather than academic, body of socialist missionaries within the Labour Party. Fred Jowett, a founder member of the ILP, believed that there was a need to clarify 'the relationship between the Labour Party and the ILP'. E. F. Wise, an economist, felt that the ILP lacked a group in the House of Commons and doubted its future as a distinctive party, while John Paton, the Secretary, opposed the abandonment of political activity as he felt that the ILP had a distinctive policy that lay in 'the root idea of the Living Income Programme'.

This meeting vitally captured the feeling of the ILP that it had lost its way following the introduction of the Labour Party's socialist constitution in 1918. It had posed a basic question – was the ILP to continue as a socialist organisation affiliated to the Labour Party, with its MPs subject to the control of the Parliamentary Labour Party (PLP), or should it consider becoming a small independent propaganda group inside or outside the Labour Party? Discussions of this type were common in the early 1920s, when ILP membership rose to 55,000 under Clifford Allen's chairmanship. They reached their zenith during the years of the second Labour government (1929–31) and finally led to the momentous decision to disaffiliate from the Labour Party in July 1932. They further re-emerged in 1939 when the ILP, having seen its membership plummet to fewer than 2,500, considered re-affiliating to the Labour Party.

Discussions were fuelled by the failure to secure socialism. In 1928, James Maxton, Chairman of the ILP, warned the Labour Party conference at Birmingham that socialism could be no longer approached by a 'long, slow process of gradualist, peaceful, Parliamentary change', for under the parliamentary system socialism would still be as far away as ever. He also criticised the failure of the first minority Labour government of 1924, and he ended with the cry, 'Let your slogan be, Socialism is the only remedy'.[2] During the next four years the ILP moved to a new revolutionary stance, abandoning the 'Socialism in Our Time' programme and the introduction of the living wage, and looking to trade union action, rather than parliamentary democracy, to create a socialist workers' commonwealth. Consequently, the Labour Party and the ILP were moving apart because their visions of how to secure socialism were different. While many ILP activists felt that parliamentary democracy prevented significant change, the Labour Party's vision, perhaps because of its protean nature, was based upon the essentially progressive and liberal conceptions of winning broad support across all social classes for gradualist moves towards the state control of industry.

---

2 W. Knox, *James Maxton* (Manchester: Manchester University Press, 1987), pp. 79–80.

This debate has been placed into its wider context by Ross McKibbin, who suggests that the major British political parties accepted a form of parliamentary democracy, based on universal male and partial female suffrage, in 1918. This had been by no means certain at the end of the Great War and was possibly anathema to the ILP with its vision of a working-class state, because it involved general elections that could return different parties with different objectives.[3] Jon Lawrence's work on the transformation of British public politics after the First World War offers a further clue to the divergence of the Labour Party and the ILP. He observed that the Labour Party championed the more peaceable, rational and unassertive policies that emerged in the inter-war years, with less interaction between the politicians and the people, than the exuberant 'rowdyism' that was favoured by the ILP.[4] Lawrence, indeed, reflects that after the criticism of Labour 'rowdyism' at the general elections of 1924, particularly in the ILP strongholds of Glasgow and London, there was an increasing tendency for Labour Party leaders to promote discipline. This contrasts with Jimmy Maxton's penchant for 'applauding disorder as evidence of working class "self-expression"', and his disruptive behaviour and that of other ILP MPs in 1922 that led to their suspension from the House of Commons.[5] The Labour Party's Standing Orders of 1929, the pretext for the ILP's disaffiliation from the Labour Party, were part of that process of imposing discipline and restricting individual freedom of expression in the parliamentary context which was rejected by much of the ILP's membership.

The main argument of this chapter is that the Labour Party and ILP disaffiliation debate was a continuing theme throughout the inter-war years and not just confined to the years 1929–32. It was part of the birth pangs of a newly extended progressive parliamentary democracy that emerged in Britain from 1918. Labour adopted the new parliamentary democracy and the discipline it required. However, this brought with it a slowness of change, dictated by swings resulting from general elections. The ILP could not accept this and the conflict between the two parties reached a new intensity with the launching of the part reformist and part revolutionary 'Socialism in Our Time' programme in 1926. The debate grew more fractious during the second Labour government (1929–31), as some ILP MPs, critical of Labour's lack of socialist policy, often voted against the MacDonald administration.

---

3 R. McKibbin, *Parties and the People: England 1914–1951* (Oxford: Oxford University Press, 2010).
4 J. Lawrence, 'The transformation of British public politics after the First World War', *Past and Present*, 190(1) (2006), 185–216.
5 Lawrence, 'Transformation', 200, 211–12.

Nevertheless, the enforcement of the new 1929 Standing Orders to maintain PLP unity became the pressing issue, by restricting the freedom of action of ILP-sponsored MPs. Fundamental differences were also revealed between the ILP and the Labour Party over the speed and means by which socialism would be secured by adopting the parliamentary route to Westminster. These concerns became major milestones to disaffiliation in 1932 as a prominent minority of the active and rowdier element of the ILP became frustrated with Labour politics.

Disaffiliation: historical analysis

The ILP's decision to leave the Labour Party in July 1932 is one of the watersheds in British political history. The breaking of the ILP's link with Labour, which had existed since February 1900, led to the further collapse of ILP membership and the complete reshaping of Scottish Labour politics, in which the ILP had been the powerful player.[6] ILP strongholds such as Bradford were decimated, although there were temporary rises in ILP membership in Norwich, Glasgow, Nottingham and Derby from the mid-1930s when the ILP was facing rapidly declining membership figures.[7]

The rapidly falling membership figures indicate that disaffiliation was unpopular with the majority of members. There was a brief period in 1932 when it seemed as though the ILP National Affiliation Committee would unite sufficient support to reverse the decision. Such hopes were quickly dashed as the ILP disintegrated and many members opted to leave it to rejoin the Labour Party, often through the newly created Socialist League.[8] Within a few years, some of those who had supported disaffiliation recognised their mistake. Jennie Lee viewed disaffiliation 'as the silliest decision of all made by the ILP' because it meant self-imposed exile, while even Fenner Brockway, General Secretary of the ILP and sometime Chairman in the 1930s, concluded that it was a 'stupid and disastrous error' and that 'My support of disaffiliation was the greatest political mistake of my life'.[9]

Analysing the disaffiliation crisis, historians are broadly in agreement that the decision was a product of long-term conflict between the Labour

---

6 W. W. Knox and A. MacKinley, 'The re-making of Scottish Labour in the 1930s', *Twentieth Century British History*, 6(2) (1995), 174–93.

7 R. Stevens, '"Rapid demise or slow death?" The Independent Labour Party in Derby, 1932–1945', *Midland History*, 22 (1997), 113–30.

8 B. Pimlott, *Labour and the Left in the 1930s* (Cambridge: Cambridge University Press, 1977).

9 J. Lee, *My Life with Nye* (London: Jonathan Cape, 1980), pp. 80–1; A. F. Brockway, *Towards Tomorrow: The Autobiography of Fenner Brockway* (London: Hart-Davis, 1977), p. 107.

Party and the ILP and that the decision probably did not reflect the views of the majority of the ILP membership. However, considerable academic skirmishing has occurred over conflicting interpretations of whether or not it was a 'deliberate and sensible policy', as Gidon Cohen has suggested, or 'suicide during a fit of insanity', the product of vaunted ambition and political petulance, as argued by both Keith Middlemas and R. E. Dowse.[10]

Party tensions and 'Socialism in Our Time', 1916–29

The first strains in the relationship between the ILP and the Labour Party had emerged during the First World War: the ILP officially opposed war, but allowed individual conscience in the face of patriotic Labour. This meant that in Bradford, for instance, twenty-two conscientious objectors, mainly ILP members and Quakers, refused army conscription from 1916 onwards, while over 500 ILP members had already attested their willingness to fight under the pre-conscription Derby scheme, the government's voluntary system for those attesting their willingness to join the army.[11] The strain increased in 1918 when the Labour Party introduced its new constitution with the socialist clause 4 (3d) and individual membership, which may well been partly responsible for the increase in the number of constituency Labour parties as rivals to ILP branches.[12] In one fell swoop,

---

10 R. K. Middlemas, *The Clydesiders: A Left-Wing Struggle for Parliamentary Power* (London: Hutchinson, 1965), pp. 295–71; R. E. Dowse, *Left in the Centre: The Independent Labour Party 1893–1940* (London: Longman, 1966), pp. 152–84; G. Cohen, 'The Independent Labour Party, disaffiliation, revolution and standing orders', *History*, 86 (282),180–99; K. Laybourn, '"Suicide during a fit of insanity" or the defence of socialism? The secession of the Independent Labour Party at the special conference at Bradford, July 1932', *Bradford Antiquary*, 3 (1990), 41–53. See also D. Howell, 'Traditions, myths and legacies: the ILP and the Labour left', in A. McKinley and R. J. Morris (eds), *The ILP on Clydeside 1893–1932: From Foundation to Disintegration* (Manchester: Manchester University Press, 1991), pp. 204–32; A. Marwick, *Clifford Allen: The Open Conspirator* (London: Oliver & Boyd, 1964). For the Labour perspective on relations between the Labour Party and the ILP, see P. Riddell, *Labour in Crisis: The Second Labour Government, 1929–1931* (Manchester: Manchester University Press, 1999). See also G. Cohen, *The Failure of a Dream: The Independent Labour Party from Disaffiliation to World War* (London: I. B. Tauris, 2007) and D. Howell, *MacDonald's Party: Labour Identities and Crisis 1922–1932* (Oxford: Oxford University Press, 2001).

11 T. Jowitt and K. Laybourn, 'War and socialism: the experience of the Independent Labour Party 1914–1918', *Journal of Regional and Local Studie*, 4(2) (autumn 1984); paper reissued in D. James, T. Jowitt and K. Laybourn (eds), *The Centennial History of the Independent Labour Party* (Halifax: Ryburn, 1992), pp. 163–78.

12 Arthur Marwick, 'The Independent Labour Party in the nineteen-twenties', *Bulletin of the Institute of Historical Research*, 35 (1962), 62–74.

the two main distinctions between the ILP and the Labour Party were removed. It now seemed that there was no longer any point in being a member of the ILP and both Philip Snowden and Ramsay MacDonald, two of its main pre-war leaders, had drifted away by 1930.

The ILP was struggling to find a role and it was not until it introduced a new constitution 1922 that it declared its intent to continue. Although Clifford Allen, Chairman of the ILP in the early 1920s, revived the ILP with his middle-class friends and their money, the dominating force was the Clydeside group of ILP MPs. After the 1922 general election this included fifteen MPs from Glasgow and another five from West Scotland. Famously, David Kirkwood exclaimed to cheering crowds at Glasgow's St Enoch railway station, in their send-off to Westminster, that 'When we come back, this station, this railway, will belong to the people!'[13] Such optimism, based on working-class commitment to improving domestic conditions, contrasted sharply with the more international pacific approach of the ILP leadership, under Allen. In fact, it should be recognised that the ILP still held a local and municipal approach to politics in Scotland and in the West Riding of Yorkshire, which contrasted with the much less democratic policy of state socialism, with industries and services run by impartial administrators, favoured by Labour.

Further tensions emerged between Labour and the ILP, and within the ranks of ILP membership, with the advent of the Labour government in January 1924. On the one hand, at the launch of the *New Leader*, which MacDonald attended, H. N. Brailsford, its editor, announced that MacDonald was 'the only possible leader. His personal distinction, his intellectual power, his stature as a man and a thinker rank him amongst our great assets.'[14] While Allen announced to the ILP conference at York in April 1924 that the Labour government was preparing the way for future developments in socialism,[15] he later admitted that a minority government was restricted in what it could do, adding that the electorate 'have not accepted socialism' and warning 'of an excess of Parliamentary strategy'.[16] Such ardent support for MacDonald contrasted sharply with the views of Maxton and the Clydesiders, who criticised MacDonald for his lethargy as

---

13 A. J. P. Taylor, *English History 1914–1945* (Oxford: Oxford University Press, 1975), pp. 198–9.

14 F. M. Leventhal, *The Last Dissenter: H. N. Brailsford and His World* (Oxford: Oxford University Press, 1985), pp. 180–1. Brailsford had previously been a critic of MacDonald: see the diary entry by A. Ponsonby for 11 December 1923. Bodleian Library, A. Ponsonby diary.

15 *Forward*, 26 April 1924.

16 C. Allen, *Putting Socialism into Politics* (London: ILP, 1924), pp. 6, 9.

Prime Minister and the first Labour government as a whole for its failure
to achieve anything other than housing reform.[17]

Divided over the Labour administration's performance, the ILP
nevertheless agreed to hold a joint meeting of the National Executive
Committee of the Labour Party and the NAC of the ILP, in May 1925, to
consider its role. Allen was at pains to stress the educational, intellectual
and propaganda work of the ILP: 'It is claimed that it is the special duty
of the ILP to develop in detail the Socialist objectives of the Movement
and supplement its general propaganda with the advocacy of fundamental
Socialist principles.'[18] Arthur Henderson, for the Labour Party, mini-
malised this view, warning that 'So long as the two bodies present their
individual policies without regard to each other, it is obvious that overlapping and friction will continue'.[19] Unproductive discussions continued
through a sub-committee.

Labour and the ILP tensions intensified when Allen and his supporters
developed a reformist package of policies – including a minimum living
wage, child allowances and other measures to stimulate consumption –
to deliver 'Socialism in Our Time'.[20] Allen, prompted by the impressive
speech of Dr Salter in the House of Commons debate on the 'living wage',
declared in his presidential address to the 1924 ILP Easter conference that
'a living wage must be enforced as a national policy'.[21] In the ensuing
months, ideas on how to achieve this were developed and policy statements were drawn up by a number of the Inquiry Commissions into the
living wage that had been set up by Allen. The most important of these,
whose members included H. N. Brailsford, J. A. Hobson, Frank Wise
and Arthur Creech Jones, Research Officer of the Transport and General
Workers' Union, in 1926 produced a full report, *The Living Wage*.

The economic theory driving the programme was Hobson's view 'that
higher production is in the long run unattainable or at best can be spas-
modic and temporary, unless there was a parallel increase in the purchasing
power of the mass consumers'.[22] The aim was to increase purchasing power
by redistributing wealth and introducing a scheme of family allowances,

17 *The Report of the Independent Labour Party Annual Conference Held at York 1924*
(London: ILP, 1924), p. 9.
18 Labour Party Archive, People's History Museum, Manchester, NEC minutes of the
Labour Party, 23 May 1925, Joint meeting of the NEC of the Labour Party and the NAC
of the Labour Party.
19 BLPES, ILP Archives, NAC minutes, 23 May 1925.
20 Dr A. Salter, *A Living Wage for All* (London: ILP, 1924), based on his parliamentary
speech of 8 March 1923.
21 Marwick, *Clifford Allen*, p. 102.
22 ILP, *The Living Wage* (London: ILP, 1926), p. 8.

to be paid out of taxation. Further purchasing power would be injected by imposing statutory wage minimums throughout industry, to be paid for by printing money. Though this was inflationary the added purchasing power of the workers would soon absorb industrial output and force a rise in output, thus stimulating industry and reducing unemployment. These actions were to be supported by socialist controls such as the nationalisation of the Bank of England, industries and services. There would be public ownership of land, the re-organisation and development of agriculture, and a raft of measures to control imports and exports, to end militaristic and imperial wars and to establish friendly relations with Russia.[23]

This ameliorative programme was accepted by the Clydesiders when Allen resigned as Chairman of the ILP, in September 1925, in favour of Jowett and then Maxton. However, the mood of the party changed quickly to the more revolutionary one of bringing about the speedy end of capitalism while accepting and adapting Allen's palliatives and reforms. This, as David Howell has rightly argued, proved to be 'a balancing point between the old methods of negotiation and compromise, and a new more confrontational politics'.[24]

The NAC of the ILP issued an interim report, through the *New Leader* in January 1926, stating that 'The Independent Labour Party sets before itself the object of winning Socialism for this generation' and projecting the need for a 'direct attack on poverty'.[25] It was known as the 'Socialism in Our Time' programme. Accepted at the ILP's 1926 Easter conference at Whitley Bay as the *Living Wage*, which set out 'the object of winning Socialism for this generation', it was published in September 1926.[26] It was clear to all that the new policy represented a symbolic break with MacDonald and Labour, for the ILP wanted 'Socialism in Our Time' while the Labour Party accepted the more serpentine parliamentary decisions of the electorate, by seeking a harmony of class interests. Reflecting this, John McNair wrote later that 'The ILP's duty is to keep the ultimate ideal clearly before the working-class movement of the country'.[27]

'Socialism in Our Time', with its reformist and revolutionary policies, caused confusion within both the Labour Party and the ILP.[28] While

---

23 *The Times*, 22 February 1926.
24 Howell, *MacDonald's Party*, p. 274.
25 *New Leader* quoted in the *Bradford Pioneer*, 1 January 1926.
26 *The Times*, 22 February 1926.
27 J. McNair, *James Maxton: The Beloved Rebel* (London: 1955), pp. 153–4; G. Brown, *Maxton* (Edinburgh: Mainstream, 1986).
28 D. Howell, 'Beyond the stereotypes: the Independent Labour Party 1922–1932', *Scottish Labour History Society Journal*, 29 (1994), 16–49.

offering palliatives for unemployment, the major problem of capitalist society, the preamble to the policy, pushed forward by the Clydesiders, presented the view that it had become clear that the 'old order is breaking down'.[29] Apart from being a contradictory programme, it contained inflationary policies to stimulate industry and cure unemployment which were alien to Philip Snowden (MP for Colne Valley and Labour's Chancellor of the Exchequer in 1924) whose liberal economic approach was based upon deflationary policies to strengthen the pound, support for the gold standard and the revival of international free trade as a solution for economic growth and unemployment. Moreover, MacDonald's antipathy to the ILP ensured that its new campaign would receive short shrift. He wrote in the *Socialist Review* of March 1926 that the ILP's measures would be a 'millstone' around the parliamentary party's neck and later attacked it as 'a programme of flashy futilities'.[30]

Although broadly supported by ILP members in Scotland and London, 'Socialism in Our Time' proved contentious. The Bradford branch of the ILP, for instance, first discussed the living wage policy in February 1926, before its official adoption, and voted in its favour after raising a wide range of criticisms. Councillor Brooke was 'anxious lest trade union powers should be undermined',[31] while others felt that the whole programme would 'bolster up the whole capitalist system'. One critic felt that the policy was 'too previous', 'fathered by Impatience and mothered in Piety'.[32] Indeed, when Brailsford lectured on the policy at St George's Hall, Bradford, in September 1926, explaining that it should be seen as a transition stage from capitalism to socialism, necessary because unemployment and poverty would persist during the period of redistribution of property and income, he was heckled by a small group who dubbed him a Liberal. Harold Child, an old Bradford stalwart, emphatically demanded the 'immediate nationalization of everything'.[33] There also appears to have been sufficient doubt about the policy for it to require a very large supportive campaign throughout West Yorkshire in 1926 and 1927. Percy Hamer lectured on 'Socialism in Our Time' to the Armley ILP branch, in Leeds, in April 1927, and Jowett felt compelled to explain the policy in four articles for the *Bradford Pioneer* as late in September 1927.

The contentious programme was faltering by January 1927, when Maxton sought to develop an alternative policy which involved building

29 *Bradford Pioneer*, 1 January 1926.
30 Quoted in D. Marquand, *Ramsay MacDonald* (London: Jonathan Cape, 1977), p. 454.
31 *Bradford Pioneer*, 5 February 1926.
32 *Bradford Pioneer*, 9 April 1926.
33 *Bradford Pioneer*, 1 October 1926.

up the industrial power of the trade unions and increasing the economic influence of the co-operative movement in a form of guild socialism arrangement (where the individual was both a producer and a consumer), which would strengthen the political actions of the ILP.[34] This became the 'revolutionary policy' he later pressed forward, which Brockway added might involve something like a Russian five-year plan in which key industries would emerge based upon socialist principles and the control of foreign imports, alongside a dramatic reform of the parliamentary system. Impetus later was given to Maxton's future policy when the 1927 Labour Party conference debated the 'living wage' policy and referred it to the executive, where MacDonald condemned it to political oblivion.[35]

Relations between the ILP and the Labour Party, as well as within the ILP membership, worsened with the Cook–Maxton manifesto of June 1928, which criticised Labour and threatened to raise the possibility of establishing a new alliance of the Labour left between trade unions and the ILP.[36] Maxton made the agreement with A. J. Cook, Secretary of the Miners' Federation of Great Britain, without previously announcing it to the ILP. Even Paton, his faithful supporter, considered it wrong. The divisions produced by that manifesto appeared strongly at a mass meeting at Cumnock, where Kirkwood supported it and Dollan, Wise and Shinwell condemned it.[37] Maxton's action was criticised at an NAC meeting on 30 June 1928 but, by a vote of seven to five, the ILP endorsed it.[38] However, the hostility of the Communist Party, the Labour Party and the trade unions ensured that the Cook–Maxton manifesto was stillborn. At the end of 1928 a meeting of forty-eight ILP MPs (including those whose election expenses were paid by the ILP and ILP/Labour Party members whose expenses were paid by Labour) condemned Maxton's 'reckless leadership'. Dr Alfred Salter wrote to the *New Leader* that they did not want to see the ILP 'driven to the rocks by the pirate chief who has run the Jolly Roger to the masthead, and who is co-operating with his fellow buccaneer who has already done his best to wreck and shatter another great vessel, the MFGB'.[39]

By 1929 the ILP was fragmenting into three main groups. The first, led by Maxton, Wheatley and the Clydesiders, was moving towards

---

34 *The Times*, 7 January 1927.
35 Marquand, *MacDonald*, pp. 474–5.
36 Taylor, *English History 1914–1945*, pp. 198–9; *The Times*, 8 July 1928, referred to it as a campaign for the rebirth of the Socialist Labour Party.
37 *The Times*, 24 June 1928.
38 Cohen, 'The Independent Labour Party', p. 206.
39 *The Times*, 7 December 1928.

disaffiliation; it had support from some London, Glasgow and Midland branches. A. W. Pugh, of the Bilston branch, supported disaffiliation at the Birmingham ILP Federation meeting on 4 December 1929 and his branch wrote to Maxton and the *New Leader* supporting the policy of encouraging ILP MPs to vote against the second Labour government on the Unemployment Bill.[40] On 5 October 1930 the Bilston branch further debated disaffiliation from the Labour Party when J. W. Pugh put forward a motion for disaffiliation, raised again in the Birmingham Federation of the ILP, and stated that he felt that the Labour government's policy on India was deficient and its failure to apply socialist measures was enough to justify a decision 'to part with a Labour Capitalist and Imperialist Party'.[41] A. W. Pugh, Secretary of this branch, and A. Pugh, the Chair, supported the motion, which was passed by a vote of four to one. The branch was concerned about the unwillingness of the Labour government to consider a Living Wage Bill.

The Birmingham Federation's disaffiliation debate of 4 December 1929 was supported by the West Bromwich ILP branch on 8 January 1930 and put to the Midlands conference at Leicester on 28 and 29 January 1930, in the form of a motion 'That the Labour Party having now become in theory and in practice both Capitalist and Imperialist it is now necessary for the Independent Labour Party to cease affiliation to it.'[42]

A second group, led by Dr Carl Cullen of the Poplar ILP and Jack Gaster of Marleybone ILP, and based in London, favoured Marxism and a closer link with the Communist Party. As a result, the Revolutionary Party Committee (RPC) was formed within the ILP in 1930. Its influence was limited and its supporters eventually left the ILP for the Communist Party in 1934.

The third, much more important group was led by Dr Salter of London and Willie Leach of Bradford, and many members of the ILP in Lancashire, Yorkshire and Scotland. This was a pro-affiliation 'Unity' group. The *Bradford Pioneer* summarised the Unity group's position by stating that 'The ILP is a spiritual endeavour. It must sow and leave others to reap. ILP members should be attracted to all Labour Groups.... Their function and duties are not competitive, but complementary to the functions of the Labour Group.'[43] Angus Cook Livingstone, of Bo'ness ILP branch in Scotland, particularly endorsed this view at the ILP Easter conference

---

40 BLPES, ILP Archives, Bilston branch minutes, 9 December 1929.
41 *Ibid.*, 5 October 1920.
42 BLPES, ILP Archives, West Bromwich ILP minute books 1925–1932, General meeting, 3 September 1929, General meeting, 8 January 1930.
43 *Bradford Pioneer*, 12 March 1926.

held at Carlisle in 1929, stating that 'The ILP should not compete with the Labour Party. It should remain a critical Socialist Party rather than an electoral body.'[44]

The disaffiliation debate, 1929–32

The policies of the second Labour government further soured relations with the ILP, whose MPs voted against the Unemployment Bill, the Anomalies Bill, as well as other measures they considered increased working-class poverty. The ILP had sponsored thirty-seven of the MPs returned in the general election of 1929 (including seventeen from Scotland), although another 123 non-sponsored card-carrying members of the ILP were returned, who were primarily Labour MPs. There was support from the ILP-sponsored MPs for Maxton's policy of voting against unemployment measures but when all the 160 sponsored and unsponsored ILP MPs gathered together there was a different result. Indeed, Maxton was unable to gain a majority of the ILP group meeting on 21 October 1929 to support his opposition to the Labour government's unemployment measures. When a group of eighty ILP MPs met on 28 October his opposition to the Labour government was once again rejected, by forty-one votes to fourteen. However, Maxton was not constrained by this vote, claimed the sovereignty of the ILP conference and continued his opposition of the Unemployment Bill. In response, sixty-six ILP MPs, mainly unsponsored by the ILP, supported MacDonald in an overt condemnation of Maxton's actions.[45]

The PLP responded to the ILP voting by invoking the Standing Orders of 1929, which insisted that no Labour MP could vote in Parliament against a PLP decision, although abstention on a matter of conscience was allowed. It was this move that became a sensitive issue for the ILP and one to which Jowett, Maxton, Brockway were vociferous opponents. Jowett argued that MPs owed allegiance to their electors and to party conference decisions and should not have their views interfered with by the Standing Orders of their party.[46] This was clearly hypocritical, since the ILP imposed its own Standing Orders on ILP MPs in 1929 and 1930,

---

44 *The Report of the Annual Conference Held at Carlisle, March and April 1929* (London: ILP, 1929), p. 62.

45 Cohen, 'The Independent Labour Party', p. 209.

46 F. Jowett, *The ILP Says No to the Standing Orders of the Labour Party* (London: ILP, 1932).

although only eighteen of its thirty-seven sponsored MPs agreed to them at the ILP conference of April 1930.[47]

The ILP and the Labour Party corresponded in order to resolve their differences well before the collapse of the Labour government in August 1931. Maxton wrote to Henderson on 30 December 1930, accepting the Labour Party constitution but complaining of the restrictive nature of the present rules.[48] On 6 July 1931 Paton's letter to Henderson complained that Standing Orders might prevent ILP MPs honouring the decisions of the Labour Party and might prevent him from introducing the 'Socialist principles he professes'.[49] This ongoing conflict led to the divided ILP and the Labour Party squabbling over the seats that they would contest. In the general election of October 1931, partly as a result of this conflict and partly as a result of the national political situation, the ILP was reduced to five sponsored MPs (four from Clydeside) and Labour to forty-six MPs.[50]

Following the collapse of the second Labour government, the NAC of the ILP raised the issue of its continuing affiliation to Labour in nine divisional conferences in early 1932. Six of the nine, representing about 80 per cent of the party's membership, decided that they wished to remain with Labour. The largest support for continued affiliation was found within the Scottish division, with its 250 branches, which feared that disaffiliation would undermine the structure of Scottish Labour politics. Dollan and Kirkwood, from Glasgow, along with Tom Johnson, supported continued affiliation and the Scottish divisional conference voted in favour by eighty-eight votes to forty-nine. Support for affiliation was further endorsed in the Lancashire, the North-East, Yorkshire and Wales divisions, although many ILPs members were dissatisfied with the Labour Party.[51]

The main support for disaffiliation came from the large ILP division of London and Southern Counties. Here the RPC hoped to push ILP members towards an alliance with the Communist Party. The two small South-West and East Anglia divisions also supported disaffiliation, though for different reasons. In 1931 the South-West had twenty-two branches and East Anglia had merely ten. In the South-West there was a narrow victory

---

47 M. Pugh, *Speak for Britain* (London: Bodley Head, 2010), p. 212.

48 *Report of the Annual Conference Held at Blackpool, March 1932* (London: ILP, 1929), appendix 6, pp. 44–52, gives all the correspondence on Standing Orders between the ILP and A. Henderson between December 1930 and July 1931. His letter is on p. 44.

49 Pugh, *Speak for Britain*, refers to T. Irwin unsuccessfully contesting the Tory seat at East Renfrewshire while being unwilling to sign the PLP declaration and selection disputes at Clapham, Kemingrove and Camborne.

50 The ILP contingent comprised four Clydeside MPs, J. Maxton, J. McGovern, G. Buchanan and D. Kirkwood, plus R. C. Wallhead, who represented Merthyr.

51 *New Leader*, 5 February and 29 January 1932.

for disaffiliation encouraged by the RPC supporter Robert Rawlings of Taunton, and the conference favoured ILP affiliation to the Comintern.[52] The problem in East Anglia was that the Norwich branch of the ILP, with more than half the divisional membership, came into conflict with the Labour Party because its candidate, Dorothy Jewson, had not been endorsed as parliamentary candidate by the Labour Party and met with great hostility from W. R. Smith, the endorsed Labour candidate, in the 1931 general election. In the end, the division voted twelve to eight for disaffiliation, eight of the votes in favour coming from the Norwich branch and some from the Yarmouth branch.[53]

By the beginning of 1932 there was clearly rising ILP frustration at the slow pace of moves towards socialism in Britain, the failure of the second Labour government to introduce socialism, and the imposition of Labour's Standing Orders. The Bilston and West Bromwich ILP branches, the Birmingham ILP Federation and the Midlands Federation were moving to support disaffiliation. The Poplar branch of the ILP, controlled by Dr Carl Knight Cullen and the RPC, produced its *Memorandum on the Present Political and Economic Situation*. It asked whether or not 'democracy can be won over to Socialism' since it was weighted in favour capitalism.[54] It called for the sweeping away of the capitalist state for a socialist one, ranted against the obvious 'failure of the [second] Labour Government to patch up capitalism' and asserted that 'Industrial upheaval or war must be made the opportunity for smashing capitalism. Dictatorship will be necessary until the stabilisation of the power of the workers.'[55] It argued that the revolutionary situation was 'more likely to come in the form of an industrial upheaval resulting from waning economic conditions or a general strike'.[56] These views were supported by the Marylebone ILP, where Jack Gaster of the RPC was active. Brockway and Maxton were also attracted to them, although, as Gidon Cohen rightly suggests, Brockway's meaning of revolutionary socialism proved different and more ephemeral than that of the RPC.[57]

---

52 *New Leader*, 22 January 1932.
53 BLPES, ILP Archives, Coll. Misc. 496, Division Five Minute book, Minutes, 10 January 1932.
54 Poplar Branch of the ILP, *Memorandum on the Present Political and Economic Situation* (London: Poplar ILP, 1932), p. 4.
55 *Ibid.*, p. 5.
56 *Ibid.*, p. 7.
57 Cohen, 'The Independent Labour Party', p. 203. See also F. Brockway in The National Archives, KV1, KV2, which suggest that Brockway, despite his courting of the Communist Party of Great Britain, was never likely to agree with it on the nature of revolutionary action.

The divisional votes often hid deeper local and personal divisions. In Bradford, the birthplace of the ILP, there were painful differences between Jowett and his one-time acolyte Willie Leach, both of whom had been ILP MPs. Jowett believed that the ILP must be free to defend socialist policies, and emphasised the need to fulfil pledges that 'are in conformity with the Labour Party Conference decisions and, or with, the Labour Party's own election programme.'[58] Rejecting Standing Orders, he stated that 'The answer to those who demand that it must surrender the freedom of its MPs' pledges honestly made in accordance with the principles advocated officially for the Labour Party for election purposes is – NO, NO, NEVER.'[59] In contrast, Leach blamed the ILP for weakening the whole Labour movement by its criticism of the second Labour government and by 'its continuous assertion of Labour untrustworthiness, and yapping at the heels of the present leaders'.[60] He felt that there was now more need than ever for unity and that the Standing Orders were flexible. The Bradford ILP clearly suffered divided loyalties but, persuaded by Jowett, favoured disaffiliation, by 112 votes to 86. Leach accepted that the local branch would vote against him but felt that only a small part of the branch membership would remain with it and 'It will be regarded as a freak party'.[61] Throughout the rest of the Yorkshire district there was a mood of general opposition to disaffiliation. In Leeds, for instance, John Arnott called for the Labour Party to avoid it; the *Leeds Citizen* agreed and felt that the ILP could be 'committing suicide in a passion of indignation'.[62]

Disaffiliation conferences

The ILP's 1932 Easter conference discussed disaffiliation but delayed making a decision.[63] Cullen and Paton, supported by Poplar and thirteen other ILP branches, argued for disaffiliation, Jim Garton of Rugby and the Midlands division spoke in favour of conditional affiliation, and Dollan, Kirkwood and Wise for unconditional affiliation.[64] Wise prophetically reflected that 'Disaffiliation meant inevitable conflict and they would be out

---

58 *Bradford Pioneer*, 17 June 1932.
59 F. Brockway, *Socialism Over Sixty Years* (London: Allen & Unwin, 1946).
60 *Bradford Pioneer*, 8 January 1932.
61 *Bradford Pioneer*, 19 February 1932.
62 *Leeds Citizen*, 11 December 1931, 29 January and 1 April 1932.
63 *The Report of the Annual Conference Held at Blackpool, March 1932* (London: ILP, 1932), p. 48.
64 J. Paton, *Left Turn: The Autobiography of John Paton* (London: Secker & Warburg, 1936), p. 387.

of contact with the mass of trade unions and Labour Party', adding that 'They and the whole Labour movement were going to spend their years in futile conflict'.[65] Dollan disparagingly suggested that it was not the industrial areas but the 'deserts of the far South-West' that favoured dis-affiliation.[66] Nevertheless, voting saw the two extremes of unconditional affiliation rejected by 98 votes to 214 and disaffiliation defeated by 183 to 144 votes. The conference opted for the compromise of conditional af-filiation, the 'Rugby resolution', by 250 votes to 53, and the reopening of negotiations with Labour.[67] These negotiations proved futile, however, and attention switched to Bradford, where a special conference of the ILP was held at Jowett Hall, at the end of July 1932.

The Bradford special national conference opened at 3 p.m. on Saturday 30 July 1932, the day after the *Bradford Pioneer*, edited by Frank Betts (father of Barbara Castle) and Willie Leach, had published an open letter imploring delegates not to vote for disaffiliation and stating that 'The ILP was born in Bradford, Have you come to bury it'.[68] The conference moved immediately to the issue of disaffiliation. Dollan challenged the legitimacy of any vote by pointing out that there should be 700 delegates with 1,000 votes present, instead of 300 delegate with 400 votes (there had been only 250 delegates and 327 votes at Blackpool) and that 'It was therefore altogether impossible to get a representative judgement which so vitally affected the whole future'.[69] The major debate took place on the evening of that Saturday, when Kirkwood, John Beckett and Dollan advocated continued affiliation, although Dollan feared that there was a generational impact within the ILP: 'The young people seemed to have a disposition towards disaffiliation due, he thought, to the lack of ex-perience and knowledge'. He believed that the vote would represent only 25 per cent of the party, although another estimate suggested 37 per cent.[70] George Buchanan's riposte for the disaffiliationists was that 'They [the ILP] had no right to be affiliated to a Party neither working-class nor Socialist.[71] In advocating disaffiliation, Maxton did not see himself taking the ILP into political oblivion: 'There was no wilderness where there were 3,000,000 unemployed and where there were millions in poverty'.[72]

65 *Ibid.*, p. 46.
66 *Ibid.*, p. 48; *The Times*, 29 March 1932.
67 *The Times*, 29 March 1932.
68 *Bradford Pioneer*, 29 July 1931.
69 *Report of the Special National Conference Held at Bradford July 30th–31st* (London: ILP, 1932), pp. 4–5.
70 *Ibid.*, p. 18; *The Times*, 1 August 1932.
71 *Report of the Special National Conference*, p. 18.
72 *Ibid.*, p. 18.

Shortly afterwards the historic vote for disaffiliation was passed by 241 votes to 142.[73] At 9.30 p.m. the delegates rose spontaneously and sang 'The Internationale' in unison, although one account suggests that 'the singing had more solemnity about it than enthusiasm as the figures of the vote imposed a severe restraint on jubilation'.[74]

The following day, 31 July, the Special National Conference reflected upon its rebellion against Standing Orders, its nebulous revolutionary policy and the new revolutionary spirit. It particularly focused on the practical implications of ILP members not paying the trade union levy and withdrawing from membership of the Co-operative Party and on its own constitution, which, it was argued, now stood for the 'complete over-throw of the economic, political and social organisation of the Capitalist State and its replacement by a Socialist Commonwealth'.[75]

Shortly after the conference, Brockway wrote *The Coming Revolution. Socialism at the Cross-Roads: Why the ILP Left the Labour Party* and justified the disaffiliation through the failures of Labour: 'We have come to the conclusion that the leadership, policy and organization of the Labour Party are unequal to the needs of the working-class, and that the freedom neces-sary to transform it into an effective socialist instrument for the present period is now denied to Socialists within the Party'.[76] He maintained that the second Labour government had been worse than the first and that it had adopted non-socialist and even anti-socialist policy and that the ILP, in the assertion of its socialist convictions, inevitably came into conflict with the Labour Party's Standing Orders.[77] He concluded, that 'We have heard much of loyalty. It was not the ILP which was guilty of disloyalty. It was the Labour Government.'[78] Jowett echoed these sentiments and also blamed disaffiliation on the unwillingness of the Labour Party to leave a 'bridge however narrow' and that 'the jealousy (if that is the right word) of the Trade Union Leaders, against a Socialist organization convinced of the need for a definite Socialist Party made the break inevitable'.[79]

In contrast, the *Bradford Pioneer* now reflected upon the 'total sterility of a once great and influential party'.[80] The Leeds Constituency Labour

---

73 *Ibid.*, p. 21.
74 *The Times*, 1 August 1932.
75 *Report of the Special National Conference*, pp. 33–5.
76 A. F. Brockway, *The Coming Revolution. Socialism at the Cross-Roads: Why the ILP Left the Labour Party* (London: ILP, 1932), p. 1.
77 *Ibid.*, p. 3.
78 *Ibid.*, p. 5.
79 F. Johnson Collection, BLPES, ILP Archives, 1933/31, Letter from F. W. Jowett to J. H. Bell of Fife, 12 January 1933.
80 *Bradford Pioneer*, 5 August 1932.

Party agreed: 'a small section of the ILP will now re-organise itself on the basis of "the Marxian philosophy of the Class Struggle" to fight the Labour and Trade Union Movement with semi-Communist thunder'.[81] Wise felt that disaffiliation was 'an act of treachery to the Labour Party and suicide for the ILP'.[82]

Post-disaffiliation division and decline

Disaffiliation proved divisive, although there was significant support for it in all regions. Councillor George R. Smith of the Wakefield branch of the ILP wrote to Councillor T. Crowe, Secretary of the Labour group in Wakefield, on 1 August, indicating that he believed in the ILP 'fight against the policies of compromise' and promptly resigned from the Labour Party,[83] as did G. E. Smith, Honorary Secretary of the Wakefield ILP branch.[84] Seven members of the Labour group in Glasgow Town Hall followed suit.[85] Bradford ILP-ers withdrew from Labour. On the broader front the *New Leader* optimistically claimed that, as a result of disaffiliation, the ILP 'will gain in membership and branches far more than it will lose'.[86] About seventy of the ninety London branches were reported to be in favour of disaffiliation.[87] There was some support for disaffiliation in the Bilston branch, in the Midlands, where A. W. Pugh and J. W. Pugh led a revolt against the prevailing affiliationist position. The ILP branches in Nottingham and Derby also left the Labour Party, but continued to be active and indeed had an increased membership for a number of years.[88]

Yet there remained an overwhelming groundswell of ILP opinion against disaffiliation. The Yorkshire branches were clearly divided, many eventually leaving the ILP to stay within the Labour Party, and in Lancashire a number of the large branches, including Platting, Farnworth, Nelson and Colne, declared themselves to be anti-disaffiliationists.[89] The Labour correspondent of *The Times* remarked upon 'the intention of its

---

81 *Leeds Citizen*, 5 August 1932.
82 *The Times*, 3 October 1932.
83 Working Class Movement Library, Salford, Letter collection, Letter from G. R. Smith to Councillor Crowe, 1 August 1932, 22 July 1927.
84 Working-Class Movement Library, Salford, Letter from E. Smith to Mr J. P. Butterworth, Secretary, Wakefield Labour Party, 9 August 1932.
85 *The Times*, 6 August 1932.
86 *The Times*, 5 August 1932, quoting the *New Leader*.
87 *The Times*, 29 August 1932.
88 Stevens, 'Rapid demise or slow death?'
89 *The Times*, 29 August 1932.

[disaffiliationist] leaders to organise the dissenting branches [in]to a new association maintaining affiliation with the Labour Party and the probability also of a legal battle over the ownership of party property, combined with the spirits of the victors in the debate'.[90] The Bradford branch of the ILP lost thirty-one of its thirty-two councillors to Labour in August 1932, and more than half of its membership of 750 in 1932.[91]

In August and September 1932 attempts were made to reverse disaffiliation. A group opposed to disaffiliation met at the end of the Bradford Special National Conference to form the National Provisional Affiliation Committee and convened in London on 20 August. There were ninety-five delegates present, more than a third of the number who attended the conference,[92] including Wise, Dollan, Brailsford, Dan Griffiths, Creech Jones, Kirkwood, Leach, A. Pickles, Ben Riley and F. Wynne Davies. They were largely from Yorkshire, London and Scotland.[93]

Many divisional meetings were held by the anti-disaffiliationists. In the Yorkshire division, county councillor Hyman, alderman A. Pickles and councillors J. J. Wilson and A. W. Brown, all from Bradford, convened a meeting at Jowett Hall on 8 August to help organise support for the re-affiliation campaign and also arranged a Yorkshire conference of affiliated ILP-ers on Saturday, 24 September, at which Leach was present.[94]

There were also deep divisions in Scotland, where, within a few months of disaffiliation, 128 of the 275 ILP branches had reverted to Labour.[95] The main forces of disaffiliation seem to have been around Glasgow, where three ILP MPs had their seats.[96] Shettleston, Govanhill, Hutchenstown and Queens Cross were among the Glasgow branches that favoured disaffiliation, along with Corluke and Lanark.[97] Nevertheless, of the forty-three Labour Party representatives on the city council, thirty-three of the forty who identified with the ILP had formed their own group against disaffiliation by 16 August 1932.[98] In the wake of this, Dollan held an affiliation conference at Glasgow on 21 August 1932, which attracted 500 ILP-ers from all over Scotland, and Dollan defamed Maxton as the 'Robinson Crusoe of working-class politics', resulting in his expulsion

90 *The Times*, 1 August 1932.
91 *Bradford Pioneer*, 5, 12, 26 August and 9 September 1932.
92 *The Times*, 2 August 1932.
93 *The Times*, 3 October 1932.
94 *Bradford Pioneer*, 12 August 1930, 30 September 1932.
95 Knox and MacKinley, 'The re-making of Scottish Labour', p. 193.
96 *The Times*, 29 August 1932.
97 Knox and MacKinley, 'The re-making of Scottish Labour', p. 176.
98 *The Times*, 17 August 1932. The report indicates also that the disaffiliationists intended to stand eighteen candidates for the November city council elections.

from the ILP, along with fourteen other prominent Scottish figures.[99] Subsequently, many ILP branches, such as Bo'ness, fought off attempts at disaffiliation, had their members expelled from the ILP and, in Glasgow on 11 September 1932, formed the Provisional Committee of the Scottish Socialist Party, which remained affiliated to the Labour Party and officially formed on 5 October 1932.[100] The party was led by Dollan, Kirkwood and others, and by the end of 1932 had 100 branches and over 1,000 members.

The anti-disaffiliationist movement reached the climax of its brief existence on 2 October 1932, when, at a meeting held as a prologue to the Labour Party conference in Leicester, the Socialist League was formed and linked itself with the Scottish Socialist Society, the Society for Socialist Inquiry and Propaganda, and other socialist bodies, and affiliated to the Labour Party.[101] Wise chaired the meeting which drew up a draft constitution forming a provisional committee, which included many former members of the ILP. Apart from Wise as Chairman, those present included Brailsford, G. D. H. Cole, Stafford Cripps, J. F. Horrabin, Kirkwood, William Mellor, Arthur Pugh, Dr Salter, Sir Charles P. Trevelyan and Mrs E. Pethwick-Lawrence.[102] The formation of the Socialist League offered alternative membership for many ex-members of the ILP.

Inevitably, the ILP's membership declined rapidly in the 1930s (see Table 6.1). Of the 653 ILP branches in February 1932, only 288 had given definite support for disaffiliation, some by very small majorities.[103] By the end of 1932 the ILP was down to 450 branches and there were only 284 in 1935. These figures contrast sharply with the pre-war total of 887 in 1909 and an inter-war peak of 1,028 in 1925.[104]

In the six of the nine ILP divisions that opposed disaffiliation, there was a greater fall in branch and membership numbers than in London, the Eastern Counties, and the South-Western Counties divisions, where disaffiliation was supported – although membership declined everywhere. The membership of the ILP dropped from 16,773 at the beginning of 1932 to 11,092 in 1933, 7,166 in 1934, 4,392 in 1935 and to a low of 2,441 in 1939.[105] This suggests that initially about a third of ILP members were prepared to leave the ILP because of disaffiliation. Most of the remainder

---

99 *Glasgow Herald*, 20 August 1932; *The Times*, 16 August 1932.

100 BLPES, ILP Archives, Minutes of the Bo'ness ILP, 26 August, 11 September 1932.

101 Pimlott, *Labour and the Left in the 1930s*.

102 *The Times*, 3 October 1932.

103 J. Jupp, *Radical Left in Britain 1931–1941* (London: Routledge, 1982), p. 39.

104 *The Report of the Annual Conference Held at Gloucester, April 1925* (London: ILP, 1925), p. 7.

105 Cohen, *The Failure of a Dream*, pp. 31, 33.

Table 6.1 Divisional branch numbers for the Independent Labour Party, selected years 1922–35

Division	1922	1929	1930	1931	1932	1932	1935
Scotland (and Ireland)	158	262	275	273	250	122	91
North-eastern counties	58	64	59	54	49	36	21
Yorkshire	76	65	69	63	63	40	24
Midland counties	57	58	57	56	45	37	22
Eastern counties (East Anglia)	11	13	12	10	8	8	5
London and southern counties	74	100	107	98	89	88	56
South-western counties	23	23	23	21	23	19	15
Wales and Monmouth	60	71	53	45	40	28	21
Lancashire	97	90	93	92	86	72	24
Total	614	746	748	712	653	450	279

Sources: *Report of the NAC, 1922*, p. 3; *Report of the NAC, 1929*, p. 4; *Report of the NAC*, 1931, p. 9; *Report of the NAC, 1932*, p. 18 (copies of the NAC reports are to be found in both the BLPES archives and the archives held at the Working Class Movement Library, Salford); G. Cohen, *The Failure of a Dream: The Independent Labour Party from Disaffiliation to World War* (London: I. B. Tauris, 2007), p. 33.

fell away after the failure of the Unity group to reverse the decision and as the ILP fragmented into warring factions.

The Scottish Socialist Society and the Labour Party took on left-wing policies in Scotland. In Lancashire many ILP members moved back into the Labour Party and many members joined the newly formed Independent Socialist Party – established to counter the RPC, which was drawing support from London, East Anglia and Lancashire – and followed it into the Labour Party in 1934. In London many ILP activists joined the RCP and formed a Third International Group but left for the Communist Party in 1934. In the textile district of the West Riding of Yorkshire the ILP collapsed. Even Jowett failed to win Bradford East in the 1935 general election. At the municipal level the ILP achieved only patchy success, in Nottingham, Derby, Norwich Keighley and Bradford.

Initially, the disaffilitionists were optimistic about their prospects for success. Brockway's Chairman's speech at the 1932 Blackpool conference, published as *The Coming Revolution*, explained the inevitability of disaffiliation and promoted the new, if amorphous, 'revolutionary spirit' to bring about socialism.[106] At the 1933 ILP Derby conference, Maxton pointed to

---

106 Brockway, *The Coming Revolution*.

industrial and class organisation, and thus industrial action, as the way to overthrow capitalism but advocated working through Parliament, 'the instrument of government of the Capitalist state', until class change was achieved.[107] But these views were bullish optimism and even the NAC of the ILP had to admit to failure in its 'Draft Statement of Policy', which suggested 'The results are the reverse of satisfactory'.[108] With declining membership, few lasting results from the *ad hoc* committees and 'very bad' election results, 'the prestige of the ILP is now at a lower level amongst the workers than ever before'. Evidently, the reason for this failure was that the Labour Party was recovering its vote, 'despite its past', and 'the Labour Party today is the immediate expression of the masses'. It reflected:

> All the ILP can claim are isolated individual successes, some dwindling support based upon sentimental regard for our past, occasional large meetings and a weekly paper whose struggle for existence absorbs the major part of the energy of the membership. This is all the past two years 'independent' policy associated with the CP [Communist Party] has left us....
>   Our weaknesses are a lack of programme and of policy, immediate and long-term.[109]

The small rump of the ILP which survived into the late 1930s, shorn of its contending factions, discussed the possibility of re-affiliating to the Labour Party at a meeting of the NAC of 5 August 1939, where a vote of eight to six committed the ILP to holding a special conference to discuss it.[110] A special conference called for 17 September 1939 had to be cancelled because of the outbreak of war.

Conclusion

Historians have generally agreed that the ILP's disaffiliation in 1932 was a product of the tensions that had been developing since the end of the First World War. The 1918 Labour Party constitution committing Labour to socialism, 'Socialism in Our Time' and *The Living Wage*, as well as personal conflict, conspired to ensure that the ILP pushed forward to disaffiliation

---

107 *Report of the Annual Conference* (London: ILP, 1933), p. 18.
108 Working Class Movement Library, Salford, Letters, 'Draft Statement of Policy' (H. L. Gearing).
109 *Ibid.*
110 BLPES, ILP Archives, NAC, Minutes, 5 August 1929. See also McKibbin, *Parties and the People.*.

in its attempt to speed up the move to socialism. Disaffiliation was a bold move but it failed, largely because many of its members did not wish to leave the Labour Party for the amorphous policy of a 'workers' revolution' and the ILP did not provide the effective missionary leadership Shinwell hoped for. Even if disaffiliation had created a significant socialist propagandist party, it is highly unlikely that the creation of a permanent socialist state was ever possible in parliamentary Britain – something which Brockway suggested in his demands for revolutionary change in 1932 and 1933.[111] In *The Next Step* Brockway asked, 'Is there any Socialist today who believes in the policy of administering capitalism and seeking to reform it?' In his view, the only policy 'is to pull down its ruins and rebuild upon its foundations'. The purpose of socialism became nothing less than 'revolution'.[112]

Yet this was not a view held by most in the Labour Party, or possibly the majority of ILP membership in 1932, who were ready to accept conventional and disciplined politics. In the end, petulance, rather than sensible decision-making, drove the ILP out of the Labour Party.

Acknowledgements

I would like to thank both Chris Wrigley and John Shepherd for their close friendship, help and advice over more than a quarter of a century.

---

111 Brockway, *The Coming Revolution*; A. F. Brockway, *The Next Step: Towards Working-Class Unity* (London: ILP, 1933).
112 Brockway, *The Next Step*, p. 4.

7

Voices in the wilderness? The Progressive League and the quest for sexual reform in British politics, 1932–59

JANET SHEPHERD

9.30 a.m., August 1954. The notes of 'Dashing White Sergeant' float across the grounds of Frensham Heights School. Progressive League (PL) members gather on the lawn for country dancing – an integral part of their annual summer conference.[1] Two months later, in the PL's monthly bulletin *PLAN*, founder member Jack Coates complained that the PL's original aims had been superceded by such cultural pursuits. He reminded the League of the original ideals, most notably, anti-fascism, world government and progressive humanism on which the PL, initially the Federation of Progressive Societies and Individuals (FPSI), had been founded in 1932.[2] Like-minded activists from the South Place Ethical Society at Conway Hall, Hampstead Ethical Institute, the Rationalist Press Association, the World League for Sexual Reform and other small progressive groups had united to form a new federation.[3] From 1940 it became the Progressive League, and it was to last until 2005.

The FPSI soon became known for its radical aims, and for the fame of its founder, the redoubtable philosopher Cyril Joad.[4] Joad, by then

---

1 Author's recollection.
2 Jack Coates, 'A word to the Progressive League', *PLAN*, October 1954, p. 115.
3 Other small groups that initially affiliated included the Woodcraft Folk, the Fabian Nursery, Youth House, the Promethean League, the Artists' International Association, the Federation of Sun Folk, the Modern Cultural Institute, the National Sun and Air Association and the National Society for the Prevention of Venereal Disease. PL Papers, British Library of Political and Economic Science (BLPES), PL 1/1, PL Executive Committee minutes, 1936–1947, final page, n.d.; Tony Judge, *Radio Philosopher: The Radical Life of Cyril Joad* (London: Create Space, 2012), p. 545.
4 C. E. M. Joad (1891–1953) was a progressive philosopher, public intellectual and BBC radio personality.

a notable radio personality and prolific writer of popular radical books on politics, philosophy and education, was able to command considerable public attention.[5] Writing in the *Manchester Guardian*, Joad invited groups of 'advanced thinkers' to combine to represent 'all lines of progressive thought ... a crystallisation of advanced opinion ... relating to human welfare'.[6] Coates had convened the first meeting at Joad's house, aimed at creating a 'unified progressive movement capable of exercising political influence'.[7]

The FPSI programme was set out in *Manifesto* (1934), edited by Joad, which had an introduction by the renowned writer and outspoken socialist H. G. Wells and contained essays on fascism, pacifism, education, town and country planning, secularisation, reform of the criminal law and, the subject of this essay, sexual reform.[8] The FPSI's journal, *PLAN*, had several name changes, reflecting alterations in emphasis over the years: *Plan: For World Order and Progress* (April 1934–September 1939), *Plan Bulletin* (October 1939–December 1941), *Plan* (January 1942–June 1948), *Plan: For Freedom and Progress* (July 1948–1990), *Plan* (1990–2002) and *Progressive League Newsletter* (2002–05).[9]

Sexual liberation, mostly seen as 'taboo' by the general public, gradually became of paramount importance – with the FPSI ironically nicknamed the 'Federation for the Promotion of Sexual Intercourse'.[10] However, this nomenclature trivialised the informed and serious part the organisation played in the evolution of mid-twentieth-century sexual reform. Whereas the organisation's early political views, especially 1930s anti-fascist agitation, have been discussed in some detail by R. A. Wilford, there has been no study of the organisation's long-lasting involvement in twentieth-century social issues, including sexual reform.[11]

---

5 Judge, *Radio Philosopher*, p. xi.

6 C. E. M. Joad, *Manchester Guardian*, Letters page, 4 October 1932; *PLAN*, April 1934.

7 Coates, 'A word to the Progressive League'.

8 H. G. Wells, 'A common creed for left parties throughout the world', in C. E. M. Joad (ed.), *Manifesto: The Book of the Federation of Progressive Societies and Individuals* (London: Allen & Unwin, 1934), pp. 12–19; Philip Coupland, 'H. G. Wells's "liberal fascism"', *Journal of Contemporary History*, 35(4) (October 2000), 545.

9 The title *PLAN* will be used throughout this chapter.

10 David Tribe, *A Hundred Years of Free Thought* (London: Elek Scientific Books, 1967), pp. 149–50.

11 R. A. Wilford, 'The Federation of Progressive Societies and Individuals', *Journal of Contemporary History*, 11 (1976), 49–82. Throughout its long existence, the organisation also ran a full programme of cultural activities – most notably music, poetry, theatre trips, painting, country dancing and rambling.

This chapter will examine the role of the little-known PL in the progress of sexual reform in the mid-twentieth century, including birth control, eugenics, abortion law reform, marriage reform, the legalisation of homosexuality and reform of the obscenity laws.

Lesley Hoggart has argued that 'visions of sexual liberation' may have seemed remote during the rise of fascism in the 1930s.[12] Undoubtedly, fascism dominated most political agendas, including within the FPSI – an organisation founded at a time of factionalism in the labour movement following the Labour Party's catastrophic 1931 defeat.[13] In the 'greatest landslide of British democratic history', Labour was reduced to fifty-two seats and only septuagenarian George Lansbury from the old Labour Cabinet remained to become leader of a decimated party.[14] Emasculated, Labour made little impact on such critical issues as mass unemployment and the infamous means test. By the time of the 1935 election, although Joad actively campaigned for Labour, most FPSI members remained sceptical.

The FPSI was spawned, not as a rival or mouthpiece for the Labour Party, but in a manner more typical of extra-parliamentary left-wing groupings full of idealistic individuals bent on applying rational and scientific measures to solve a range of social and economic problems at home and exceedingly fearful of the rise of fascism abroad.[15] The FPSI's core belief in reason, rationality and humanism, popular among contemporary intellectuals, was summarised by an early member, Ernest Seeley: 'Reason is the still voice that never dies. Drive it out as you can, it always comes back for it alone can lead to enduring solutions of all the problems set by our desires.'[16]

---

12 Lesley Hoggart, *Feminist Campaigns for Birth Control and Abortion Rights in Britain* (Lampeter: Edwin Mellen Press, 2013), p. 141.

13 James Jupp, *The Radical Left in Britain 1931–1941* (London: Routledge, 1982), p. 67.

14 Ben Pimlott, *Labour and the Left in the 1930s* (Cambridge: Cambridge University Press, 1986), p. 15; John Shepherd, *George Lansbury: At the Heart of Old Labour* (Oxford: Oxford University Press, 2002), pp. 282–3.

15 Judge, *Radio Philosopher*, pp. 81–2.

16 *PLAN*, September 1939. See also Wilford, 'The Federation', p. 80; Ernest Seeley, 'The humanist approach to social problems', *The Ethical Record*, 71(2) (February 1966), 6–7. Dr Ernest Seeley (1900–89), the author's father, was a scientist and a prominent member of the FPSI/PL from 1936 to his death in 1989, a member of the Burnham Committee that reported on teachers' salaries in 1950 and President of the Association of Teachers in Technical Institutions (ATTI), forerunner of NATFE, 1955–60. 'Editorial', *PLAN*, June 1944, p. 2. Other prominent long-term members included Geoffrey Elphick, Leslie Minchin, Joan and Tom Miller, Philip Soper, also the notable crime writer Celia Fremlin, and Fanny Cockerell, writer and mother of the celebrated documentary filmmaker Michael Cockerell.

The initial line-up of FPSI protagonists was impressive. In addition to Joad and Wells, an array of renowned radical names from science, philosophy, education and literature became Vice-Presidents, among them biologist Julian Huxley, psychologists Cyril Burt and J. C. Flugel, sexologist Norman Haire, actor Miles Malleson, journalist Kingsley Martin, philosophical thinkers and writers Harold Nicolson, Vera Brittain, Aldous Huxley, Beverley Nichols, Rebecca West, Leonard Woolf, A. S. Neill and Bertrand Russell. Joad was the first President, followed by scientist and philosopher Gerald Heard, then sociologist and criminologist Barbara Wootton, attracted by the Federation's 'humanist socialism'.[17]

The new organisation soon reflected its members' diverse interests by creating a series of groups: Peace, Political and Economic, Education, Civil Liberties, Law, Philosophy and Sex Reform.[18] Many were long lasting and some were so successful that they became independent, for example the Marriage Law Reform Committee (MLRC), directly generated from the FPSI.[19] Members Janet Chance, Stella Browne and Dora Russell were all also notable founders of the Abortion Law Reform Association (ALRA) in 1936.[20] Chance publically acknowledged the progressive sexual aims of the FPSI, writing the chapter in *Manifesto* on sex reform.[21] Eugenics was also advocated as a means of control and optimal distribution of the world's population. [22]

'Under Mr Wells's inspiration', the FPSI programme, as set out in *Manifesto*, initially emphasised Wells's ambitious aims for world government.[23] However, the adoption of Wells's 'world order' was tentative,

---

17 Joad (ed.), *Manifesto*, p. 21. Other Vice-Presidents were Oliver Baldwin, Lionel Britton, David Low, Olaf Stapledon and Geoffrey West. For Barbara Wootton (1897–1988) see Ann Oakley, *A Critical Woman: Barbara Wootton, Social Science and Public Policy in the Twentieth Century* (London: Bloomsbury Academic, 2011). Wootton spoke on FPSI platforms and wrote articles in *PLAN*. Wootton differed from the FPSI/PL over abortion, believing in the right of the foetus.

18 'Group discussion meetings', *PLAN*, 1937, pp. 40–3.

19 The MLRC began as a PL sub-group but later became an autonomous committee. Haldane Papers, Wellcome Institute, 4/26/41, MLRC statement of policy, Progressive League, 1946; 'The Marriage Law Reform Society', *PLAN*, January 1947, p. 4, and March 1953, p. 4; Tribe, *A Hundred Years*, p. 221.

20 Janet Chance (1885–1953), notable birth control and abortion law reformer; Stella Browne (1880–1955), militant suffragette, socialist and birth control campaigner; Dora Russell (1894–1986), feminist author and social campaigner.

21 Janet Chance, 'The Reform of the Sex Laws', in Joad, *Manifesto*, pp. 165–182.

22 Joad, (ed,), *Manifesto*; Wilford, 'The Federation'.

23 Bill Cooke, *The Blasphemy Depot: A Hundred Years of the Rationalist Press Association* (London: Rationalist Press Association, 2004), p. 100.

secured by only one vote, and with Joad himself voting against.[24] Despite nominally remaining a Vice-President, Wells abjured the FPSI's lack of commitment to global unity, referring to members as 'extremely woolly vegetarians', 'barely cryptic nudists' and 'flimsy people' lacking the backbone for revolution. Wells eventually left the organisation in 1943.[25] Kingsley Martin was also critical, if less harsh: 'intelligent and enthusiastic persons who disinterestedly want to promote peace, sanity and a progressive attitude towards social problems.... But ...will not their influence necessarily be of a very limited kind?'[26] Although membership never exceeded 600, with Hampstead as its 'natural habitat', the organisation initially thrived, keen to heed Joad's warning not to become 'just another little society'.[27] By October 1936, there were branches in Manchester, Bournemouth and Poole, Southampton and Reading.[28]

The heady early days, amidst disillusion with Labour, brought some affinity with the better-known Socialist League (SL), also founded in 1932 and evolving from another small left-wing grouping, the Society for Socialist Inquiry and Propaganda.[29] Notable members, like Chance, joined both societies.[30] They mutually viewed the economic crisis of 1931 as a self-evident 'Bankers' Ramp' – when bankers set out deliberately to destroy MacDonald's second Labour government by demanding cuts in unemployment benefit. With notable politicians Stafford Cripps, Aneurin Bevan and Harold Laski in the SL, and Wells and Joad in the FPSI, each possessed a talented core but was numerically small, with limited influence. A. J. P. Taylor's caustic description of the SL as 'intellectuals and nothing else, all leaders and no followers', could equally well have

---

24 Coupland, 'H. G. Wells's "liberal fascism"', p. 546.

25 H. G. Wells, 'The new world society', in *The Holy Terror* (London: 1939; House of Stratus edition, 2002), pp. 73, 82; Coupland, 'H. G. Wells's "liberal fascism"', p. 546.

26 Kingsley Martin, 'Mr Wells and Sir Oswald Mosley', *New Statesman and the Nation*, 29 October 1932, p. 518.

27 PL Papers, BLPES, PL M262, Box 1, Undated cutting, PL scrapbook 1937–39.

28 Judge, *Radio Philosopher.*, p. 83; *PLAN*, October 1936. The subscription was ten shillings per annum (students five shillings), to include *PLAN* and half-price admission to all FPSI meetings.

29 Wilford, 'The Federation', pp. 66–7.

30 The founding of the SL, an amalgamation of the Society for Socialist Inquiry and Propaganda and the Independent Labour Party (ILP), was announced in the *Manchester Guardian* the same day as Joad's FPSI letter, *Manchester Guardian*, 4 October, 1932; Shepherd, *Lansbury*, p. 292. David Tribe sees a similarity between the FPSI and Humanist Group Action, founded in 1961, when a liaison sought between likeminded groups was never achieved. Tribe, *A Hundred Years*, p. 54; Janet Chance, *PLAN*, February 1954, p. 23; *PLAN*, March 1954, p. 27.

described members of the FPSI.[31] Like the SL, the FPSI feared communist infiltration and the impending rise of European fascism, although there was some sympathy with the industrial and social advances of the Soviet Union.[32] Wilford regards the early FPSI organisation as 'obsessed with fascism' in its support of Stafford Cripps's call for a Popular Front – a view not held by mainstream Labour.[33] Both societies were London-centric, attracting a radical progressive intellectual elite with research and propaganda lectures, weekend schools and conferences. However, while the SL was overtly political, and committed to the Labour Party, the FPSI gradually began to involve itself in wider issues.[34] By 1937, while the SL had disbanded rather than be forced to disaffiliate from the Labour Party, the FPSI continued.

Nonetheless, it soon became clear that the organisation's original unification plans, as a federation of societies, were proving impractical. Each constituent group held to its own agenda, unwilling to compromise for the good of a larger whole. Some groups left; others did not join.[35] While retaining its progressive beliefs, in 1940 the FPSI became a society of *individuals,* under a new name – the Progressive League.[36] Dora Russell recalled: 'each small society clung to its individual status and the plan for federation did not succeed. But there were a great many progressively minded individuals who wanted a forum for wide-ranging discussion. Thus the Progressive League came into being.'[37] A *PLAN* editorial in 1948 eloquently encapsulated the PL's progressive *raison d'être*:

> The progressive postulates that we must pursue the happiness of all mankind, present and future…. Politically, he is somewhere on the Left, a Liberal or Socialist. He may be sympathetic with the Communists but will rarely be a Party member. He gives no 100% submission to any party. He himself is the final judge of the rightness of a policy and he is not afraid to say that on some particular issue his own Party is wrong.[38]

---

31 A. J. P. Taylor *English History 1914–45* (Oxford: Clarendon Press, 1965), p. 349.

32 Wilford, 'The Federation', p. 59.

33 *Ibid.,* pp. 52, 57.

34 Ben Pimlott, 'The Socialist League: intellectuals and the labour left', *Journal of Contemporary History,* 6(3) (1971), 12–38.

35 The resignation of the H. G. Wells society, Cosmopolis, was a fatal blow, 'The merger with Cosmopolis', *PLAN,* November 1937, p. 38; Tribe, *A Hundred Years,* p. 150.

36 Tribe, *A Hundred Years,* pp. 149–50.

37 Dora Russell, *The Tamarisk Tree, Vol. 2: My School and the Years of War* (London: Virago, 1981), p. 65.

38 Editorial, 'What is a progressive?', *PLAN,* 16(12) (December 1948), 1–2; PL Papers, BLPES, LSE 3262, PL scrapbook 1932–47, Vol. II, Introduction.

When Coates criticised the PL's lack of political direction in 1954, it was part of an ongoing debate that had been running in *PLAN* for ten years. Some members, like Coates, urged a return to the FPSI's original aims.[39] However, reduced emphasis on political issues after 1945 was justified by post-war weariness, plus the fact that 'other more specialised bodies have left little scope for a separate political initiative by the League'.[40] Membership had fallen during the war and paper shortages reduced *PLAN* to a few stapled sheets.[41] Other members saw the strength of the PL primarily in its fellowship, unconventional lifestyle and, importantly, its zeal for social and sexual change.[42]

Marie Stopes had brought sexual issues to public prominence with *Married Love* (1918), heralding much public discussion.[43] The short-lived World League for Sexual Reform attracted prominent FPSI activists Russell, Brittain, Chance and Browne.[44] However, while retaining a late-nineteenth-century utopian vision of sex, many on the left recognised this was a difficult arena. Sex was generally regarded as a private matter, to be walled inside the domestic sphere. Despite some liberalisation, after the First World War Britain remained sexually conservative.[45] By the 1930s, the late-nineteenth-century 'ethical socialism' associated with Edward Carpenter arguably became secondary to the more dominant politics of fair wages and the reduction of male unemployment, especially among Labour Party men. Carpenter had argued for more equality between the sexes. It was Labour *women*, both middle and working class, who took up the cause of sexual reform, together with groups such as the FPSI, outside the Labour Party, who wished to progress an earlier, utopian vision.[46]

---

39 Jack Coates, 'Is the Progressive League redundant?', *PLAN*, June 1945, p. 3.

40 PL Papers, BLPES, LSE PL 1/1, Report of PL Executive Committee, 1 October 1946.

41 *PLAN*, 1(1), October 1939.

42 Ralph Thacker, 'The role of the Progressive League', *PLAN*, October 1946, pp. 1–3.

43 Marie Stopes, *Married Love* (London: Putnam, 1918). While lauded for her birth control stance, Stopes has been heavily criticised over eugenics. Recently, her views were termed 'slightly to the right of Hitler's': Zoe Williams, 'Marie Stopes: a turbo-Darwinist ranter, but right about birth control', *The Guardian*, 2 September 2011. See also Victoria Brignell, 'The eugenics movement Britain wants to forget', *New Statesman*, 9 December 2010; G. R. Searle, 'Eugenics and politics in Britain in the 1930s', *Annals of Science*, 36(2) (1979), 159.

44 The World League for Sexual Reform, 1921–32, held conferences in Copenhagen, London, Vienna and Brno.

45 Stephen Brooke, *Sexual Politics: Sexuality, Family Planning and the British Left from the 1880s to the Present Day* (Oxford: Oxford University Press, 2011), p. 40.

46 Lesley A. Hall, '"Arrows of desire": British sexual utopians of the late nineteenth and early twentieth century and the politics of health', 'Socialism and Sexuality' Workshop, International Institute of Social History, Amsterdam, 6 October 2000; Lesley A. Hall,

Feminist and sexual reformer Stella Browne, influenced by Havelock Ellis, recognised the 'beautiful and inspiring aspects of sex', courageously advocating that a woman be 'mistress of her own body'.[47] Browne recognised the urgent need for birth control and espoused the eugenicist views held by many FPSI members.[48] Their radical views were decades ahead of the national norm. In *Manifesto,* Chance called for relaxation of the divorce laws, legalisation of abortion, voluntary sterilisation and birth control.[49] Sexual issues were dominant in *PLAN* throughout the whole period under discussion here, but particularly during and after the Second World War. The wide and controversial range of articles covered venereal disease in wartime, universal access to birth control, eugenics, abortion and sex education.[50] In addition to Browne and Chance, a leading PL voice was the prolific sexual reform writer Alec Craig:

> Sex reform has played a considerable part in the work of the Progressive League – some people have thought it too considerable a part. The reason is that the League has tended to do what other reformist bodies were not doing, and sex reform is the Cinderella of progressive causes.[51]

During the 1930s and on into the 1950s, there was considerable public sexual ignorance. Schools tended to avoid sex education, citing large class

---

"No sex please, we're socialists": the British Labour Party closes its eyes and thinks of the electorate', in Jesse Battan, Thomas Bouchet and Tania Regin (eds), *Meetings and Alcoves: The Left and Sexuality in Europe and the United States since 1850* (Dijon: University of Dijon, 2005), p. 66; Martin Francis, 'Labour and gender', in Duncan Tanner, Pat Thane and Nick Tiratsoo (eds), *Labour's First Century* (Cambridge: Cambridge University Press, 2000), p. 192.

47 Sheila Rowbotham, *A New World for Women. Stella Browne: Socialist Feminist* (London: Pluto, 1977), p. 13; A. A. Burall, 'Obituary for Stella Browne', *PLAN*, July 1955, p. 81; Beryl Henderson, 'Obituary for Stella Browne', *PLAN*, August 1955, p. 94; Alec Craig, 'Stella Browne's writings', *PLAN*, July 1955, p. 101.

48 F. W. Stella Browne, 'Birth control in Taff Vale', *New Generation*, 2 (October 1923), 117.

49 Janet Chance, 'The reform of the sex laws', in Joad (ed.), *Manifesto*, p. 165.

50 *PLAN*, May, July, September 1940.

51 Alec Craig, 'Sex in war time: an abridgement of the inaugural lecture to the series being given under the auspices of the Sex Education Group', *PLAN*, March 1943, p. 2. Alexander George Craig (1897–1973) was a prominent sexual reformer and author of many books, notably *Sex and Revolution* (1934), *The Banned Books of England* (London: George Allen & Unwin, 1937), *Above All Liberties* (1942) and *The Prometheans* (London: George Allen & Unwin, 1955). The University of London Senate House Library holds Craig's collection of 543 volumes. See also Coates, 'Is the Progressive League redundant?', *PLAN*, June 1945, p. 2. Earlier, Craig complained about the 'unhappy juxtaposition' of sexology being shelved next to pornography in many bookshops: Craig, *The Banned Books of England*, p. 169.

sizes and likely parental objections.[52] In 1954, PL member Eda Collins complained that official history textbooks still 'almost entirely ignored the subject'.[53] The PL urged more open, unprejudiced discussion and criticised the conventional sexual morality which condemned any form of extra-marital sex. Fear and misunderstanding of the PL's attitude towards sexual reform was evident. In 1942, Craig castigated the 'alarming' juxtaposition of 'homosexuality, incest and abortion' in a written parliamentary question concerning the morals of the PL put by Conservative MP Sir Waldron Smithers.[54] While some PL opinions reflected more generally held progressive sexual attitudes, such as 'the study of sex is the study of life', other views were far more controversial.[55] Monogamous sexual partnerships were under discussion in 1945, with PL member Michael Bullock deriding 'the idiocy of lifelong monogamy'. This was undoubtedly a predominant PL attitude.[56] The sexual views of the League exceeded societal norms, arguing that young people should feel safe to experiment without fear of unwanted pregnancies or the 'calamity of a precipitate marriage'. Most radically, adolescents were encouraged to practise 'a carefully nurtured promiscuity, under the shelter of enlightened parental approval'.[57] Such an approach could still be considered outside societal norms in 2017.

Health and fitness agendas became more widespread from the 1920s and naturism became an integral part of the FPSI programme.[58] In *Manifesto*, among its practical aims, J. C. Flugel listed the 'abolition of restriction relating to dress'.[59] This was associated with the view that the absence

---

52 Lesley A. Hall, 'Birds, bees and general embarrassment: sex education in Britain, from social purity to Section 28', in Richard Aldrich (ed), *Public or Private Education? Lessons from History* (London: Routledge, Woburn Series, 2004), p. 103.

53 Basil Bonner, 'The dangers of biased education: sex education or propaganda?', *PLAN*, July 1944, pp. 10–12; Eda Collins, 'The garden of love', *PLAN*, April 1954, p. 42.

54 Alec Craig, 'Abortion, homosexuality and incest', *PLAN*, 9(2); Sir W. Smithers, Written answers, *Parliamentary Debates*, 5th Series, 376, p. 499.

55 *PLAN*, April 1955, pp. 46–7; Robert Wood, 'Sexual relations in marriage', *PLAN*, June 1955, pp. 67–8.

56 Michael Bullock, 'Sex education: its limitations and potentialities', *PLAN*, June 1945, p. 5; J. Conrad Fuller, 'Sex reform: is there a goal?', *PLAN*, August 1945, p. 5; Author conversation with Ernest Seeley, c. 1970s.

57 'Wheatear', 'Sex rebel or sex reform?, *PLAN,* October 1945, p. 8.

58 Naturism was increasingly popular. Even the austere politician Stafford Cripps was reportedly a devotee: see Andrew Rawnsley, 'The creepy Mr Cripps', review of Peter Clarke, *The Cripps Version* (Harmondsworth: Penguin, 2002), *The Guardian*, 28 April 2002.

59 R. S. Koppen, *Virginia Woolf: Fashion and Literary Modernity* (Edinburgh: Edinburgh University Press, 2009), p. 117; J. C. Flügel, *The Psychology of Clothes* (London: Hogarth Press, 1930); Joad, *Manifesto,* p. 24.

of clothing had an equalising effect. However, the dichotomy remained
between whether discarding clothes was 'freeing' or sexual.[60] Naturism
was arguably closely associated with sexual freedom. In 1937, 'nude sun-
bathing' was a listed activity of the FPSI's Sexual Reform Group – with
'competent and sparkling' Joad reportedly on one occasion demanding
to lecture naked.[61] Many members thought naturism should offer opportunities for 'experimental …sex reform' so adolescents could grow up
sexually happy.[62] This was totally at odds with public norms; around
this time, women's two-piece costumes were banned at London County
Council's Parliament Hill Fields lido.[63] Throughout its long existence,
the PL included naturism as an integral part of its regularly well attended
summer conferences, which were an essential and important component
of the annual programme.[64]

With individual freedom a central core belief, FPSI members were
active in both the birth control and the abortion law reform movements.[65]
Birth control gave women choice, control and sexual freedom without fear
of unwanted pregnancy – whether within marriage or *without*. This was
critically important; many FPSI, and later PL, members were in sexual
liaisons of choice, outside formal marriage and societal norms. In 1936,
Craig derided public attitudes: 'birth control means sexual freedom for
the unmarried as well as the married, for the poor as well as the rich, and
is therefore anathema to most of the older generation, to the sex repressed,
to the sex obsessed and the bourgeois'.[66] Only in progressive feminist and
left-wing circles was birth control linked to women's emancipation and
utopian visions of sexuality. Both Browne and Dora Russell propounded
these views, initially campaigning through the Workers' Birth Control
Group in the 1920s for the advancement of birth control and the eradica-
tion of differences of access between the middle and working classes.[67]

---

60 E.H., 'Nudery – prudery', *PLAN,* November 1945, p. 10.
61 'Sex Reform Group, 1937 activities', *PLAN,* November 1937, p. 42; PL Papers, BLPES,
   M3262, Undated, unsigned reminiscence, Scrapbook 5; Ernest Seeley, 'The unrepentant
   rationalist', *PLAN,* May 1949.
62 'Wheatear', 'Nudists are such prudists', *PLAN,* July 1945, p. 10.
63 *PLAN,* September 1940.
64 A PL conference photograph (author's possession) taken at Frensham Heights School
   in August 1950 shows that over 100 people attended the summer conference that year;
   Russell, *The Tamarisk Tree,* p. 66.
65 Alice Jenkins, *Law for the Rich* (London: Gollancz, 1960), p. 81. A Birth Control Association was established in July 1930.
66 Alec Craig, 'Books on birth control', *PLAN,* October 1936, p. 23.
67 Brooke, *Sexual Politics,* pp. 46–9.

Dora Russell, Browne and other FPSI members differed from the Labour Party over birth control – seen by Labour as primarily a *woman's* concern. The 'separate spheres' ideology, which saw women as equal but different, with a wife's primary role as home-maker, persisted.[68] Concerned about male unemployment, the Labour Party feared that the legalisation of birth control would lead to more women usurping men in the workplace. Unemployment insurance was extended in 1930, favouring men and further disadvantaging women.[69] Women's opinions and influence in the Party remained secondary. Overwhelming mandates from women's sections over birth control and women's unemployment, among other issues, were regularly ignored.[70] Additionally, there was fear that persistent opposition from religious bodies, notably the Roman Catholic Church, would have a detrimental effect on the Labour vote.[71] Change was gradual. 1930s Labour Party leader George Lansbury, with twelve children, originally adopted a Victorian attitude towards sex and birth control. By the 1920s, influenced by the burgeoning women's movement and birth control activists, including his daughter Dorothy Thurtle, Lansbury's views fundamentally changed.[72] The establishment of the National Birth Control Association in 1930 highlighted 'the large amount of work waiting to be done'.[73] Over many years, the FPSI/PL participated in the push for change but in 1948 birth control remained conspicuously absent from the Labour Party's National Health Service legislation.[74]

Closely linked to birth control campaigns came a resurgence of interest in eugenics. *Eugenics Review* had a wide appeal in the 1930s and 1940s, with many contributors from across Europe concerned about population trends and fertility. From its early days, the Eugenics Society attracted left-wing thinkers and its membership peaked in 1932/33. 'Socially responsible' eugenics appealed to progressive scientists, who argued that only in an equal-opportunities society could a eugenics programme be

---

68 *Ibid.*, pp. 43–4. There were many articles on birth control and abortion in the *New Generation* journal in the 1930s.

69 Pat Thane, 'Labour and welfare', in Duncan Tanner, Pat Thane, Nick Tiratsoo (eds), *Labour's First Century* (Cambridge: Cambridge University Press, 2000), p. 94.

70 Hall, 'Arrows of desire', p. 192.

71 Hoggart, *Feminist Campaigns for Birth Control*, pp. 56–8.

72 Shepherd, *George Lansbury*, pp. 349–50; see also John Shepherd's contribution to the present volume, 'We never trained our children to be socialists' (Chapter 10). Dorothy Thurtle wrote most of the minority report of the Inter-Departmental Report on Abortion: see 'Abortion: right or wrong', *Eugenics Review*, 32(1) (1940), 10–16.

73 The inaugural meeting of the National Birth Control Association (NBCA) was held on 17 July 1930. Wellcome, DD/CPB/C3/1.

74 Hall, 'Arrows of desire', p. 6.

defensible; in a class-based society it was impossible to compare intrinsic individual worth.[75] The FPSI supported the birth control movement over individual freedom and women's rights but also as a means to reduce the fertility of the unemployed and unemployable, especially during the 1930s depression. Both birth control and abortion were seen as critical to global population issues.[76] Notable FPSI members Julian Huxley, Bertrand Russell and H. G. Wells advocated the use of selective breeding to create better versions of humanity, a view promoted by Aldous Huxley in *Brave New World* but attacked by theologians like C. S. Lewis, who regarded humans' attempts to improve themselves as contrary to God's will.[77]

Once the full horror of the Nazis' aims for genocide of the Jewish race became known, few eugenicists favoured the extreme line emanating from Germany.[78] Nonetheless, the more moderate view adopted by left-wing geneticists, recognising a link between biological and social progress, persisted. Sterilisation, especially of the 'feebleminded', had long been discussed by the FPSI and other radical groups.[79] Members such as Seeley went further, calling for the sterilisation of disabled women.[80] Even in 1954 the PL was still supporting the Eugenics Society.[81]

Alongside 1920s birth control campaign came demands for reform of abortion law. The 1929 Infant Life Preservation Act permitted abortion only under certain conditions, resulting in a ratcheting up of abortion campaigns in the 1930s. This was a key issue for many progressives. In June 1934, *PLAN* published Browne's argument for abortion reform.[82] National coverage came with the creation of the ALRA, with Chance as Chairman.

---

75 Diane B. Paul, 'Eugenics and the left', *Journal of the History of Ideas*, 45 (October–December 1984), 589.

76 Ernest Seeley, 'The population problem', *PLAN*, October 1936, pp. 3–7.

77 Aldous Huxley, *Brave New World* (London: 1931, and numerous editions); C. S. Lewis, *The Abolition of Man* (1943); John Gray, 'Point of view', Radio 4, 4 September 2015.

78 B. W. Hart, 'Watching the "eugenic experiment" unfold: the mixed views of British eugenicists toward Nazi Germany in the early 1930s', *Journal of Historical Biology*, 45(1) (spring 2012), 33–63.

79 L. J. Ray, 'Eugenics, mental deficiency and Fabian socialism between the wars', *Oxford Review of Education*, 9(3) (1983), 213–22; Diane B. Paul 'Eugenics and the left', *Journal of the History of Ideas*, 45 (October–December 1984), p. 590.

80 Even by the late 1970s, Seeley argued that disabled children should not be kept alive through medical intervention. In 1978, Seeley's grand-daughter, twelve-year-old Karen Livingstone, gave an impassioned speech supporting the right of disabled children to the same quality of life as able-bodied people. Seeley fundamentally disagreed but, in a typically rational PL response, applauded his grand-daughter's right to differ. Author's knowledge.

81 C. O. Carter, 'The Eugenics Society', *PLAN*, July 1954, pp. 78–80.

82 Stella Browne, 'The constructive case for abortion law reform', *PLAN*, September 1943.

Chance, Dora Russell and Browne all promoted the FPSI's core belief in individual freedom. Ostensibly non-political, the ALRA nonetheless found a natural affinity with the Labour Party's women's sections and the Women's Co-operative Guild, but had little impact on official Labour policy. Even the Socialist Medical Association fought shy of the issue and never discussed abortion in the 1930s.[83] Nonetheless, increasing concern from the British Medical Association (BMA) over medical aspects led to the 1938 report from the Interdepartmental Committee on Abortion (the Birkett report), which concluded that abortion should be legalised only to preserve the physical or mental welfare of the mother following an assault – or if the baby was likely to be 'abnormal'.[84] This resonated with FPSI eugenicists. However, the start of hostilities in 1939 meant the Birkett report was shelved.

The FPSI reached national headlines in 1938 with the acquittal of its Vice-President, obstetrical gynaecologist Aleck Bourne, who had performed an abortion on a fourteen-year-old girl following a rape. The girl was referred by Bourne by physician Dr Joan Malleson, a prominent advocate of the legalisation of abortion, who gave evidence in court on Bourne's behalf. Malleson was also the wife of one of the first Vice-Presidents of the FPSI, the comedy actor Miles Malleson. This judgement 'greatly liberated English abortion law' but was based solely on medical arguments.[85] The ALRA sought a wider, social and economic, remit. Although unwanted pregnancies affected the poor more than the rich, therapeutic abortions remained unavailable for working-class women. Unable to afford private health care, they had access almost solely to back-street abortionists.[86] In 1944, Chance argued that planned parenthood should be an integral part of post-war social reconstruction. Women desiring abortion should be *entitled* to medical advice.[87] The PL urged abortion on demand. Bourne himself, however, took a more conservative approach. In 1943 he urged caution, arguing it was 'libertine' to claim that

---

83 Hoggart, *Feminist Campaigns for Birth Control*, p. 139; 'Report of the Council of the FPSI for the year 1935/36', *PLAN*, October 1936; Brooke, *Sexual Politics*, p. 100. Browne, Chance and Alice Jenkins (1886–1967) were the leading early ALRA protagonists.

84 Hoggart, *Feminist Campaigns for Birth Control*, p. 140. A leading member of the Birkett Committee was Dorothy Thurtle, daughter of George Lansbury and founder member of the ALRA. See also Shepherd, 'We never trained our children to be socialists'.

85 ALRA, *The Bourne Case and After* (London: ALRA, 1938), cited in Brooke, *Sexual Politics*, p. 104.

86 Middle- and working-class attitudes to abortion were highlighted by Alice Jenkins, notable ALRA campaigner, in *Law for the Rich* (London: Gollancz, 1960).

87 Janet Chance, 'Letter from the Abortion Law Reform Association', *PLAN*, February 1944, p. 9.

a woman should be mistress of her own body. Unsurprisingly, this put him at odds with many other PL members.[88]

After the war, although abortion did not figure so prominently in *PLAN*, the PL continued to support the ALRA. A 1952 booklet contained over sixty impassioned letters sent to the ALRA from desperate women fearing unwanted pregnancies. By then the emphasis was less on poverty and more on health and unsuitable living conditions.[89] There was acute disappointment over the failure of the 1954 Abortion Bill. *PLAN* urged members to write to the press to keep the issue alive, especially a woman's right to consult a doctor if she felt unable to continue her pregnancy.[90] By the late 1950s, abortion issues gradually moved centre-stage through novels and films such as Alan Sillitoe's *Saturday Night and Sunday Morning* (book, 1958; film, 1960).

During the 1950s, the PL's views on sexual reform gained public prominence with its evidence to three national social investigations, namely the Royal Commission on Marriage and Divorce, 1951–56; the Wolfenden Departmental Committee on Homosexual Offences and Prostitution, 1954–57; and the Select Committee on Obscene Publications, 1958.[91] This coincided with the evolving left-wing argument that socialism should show more awareness of the rights of the individual, a stance welcomed by the PL.[92]

In the post-war reconstruction years, public concern grew over the increasing number of broken marriages. The Royal Commission on Marriage and Divorce, convened in 1951, noted a 'tendency to take the duties and responsibilities of marriage less seriously than formerly'.[93] Much public debate over the divorce laws had ensued in the 1930s, highlighted in contemporary works by Chance and Craig and most notably

---

88 Jenkins, *Law for the Rich*, p. 83; Brooke, *Sexual Politics*, p. 94; B.H., 'Abortion – the social evil', *PLAN*, May 1943, pp. 3–5.

89 *'In Desperation': Letters Sent to the Abortion Law Reform Association* (London: Burlington Press, n.d.). Ernest Seeley, 'In desperation', *PLAN*, August 1952, pp. 4–5.

90 'The Abortion Law Reform Association', *PLAN*, August 1954, p. 95.

91 Presenting detailed worthwhile evidence incurred considerable expense. Members were asked to contribute towards the cost. 'Homosexuality and prostitution', *PLAN*, May 1955, p. 59. By 1959, evidence to government bodies was listed as one of the PL's main activities. 'What is the Progressive League?', *PLAN*, August 1959, p. 8.

92 See Anthony Crosland, *The Future of Socialism* (London: Constable, 1956), and, later, *New Left Review* from 1960.

93 Carol Smart, 'Divorce in England 1950–2000: a moral tale', CAVA Workshop Paper 2, Workshop One, 'Frameworks for Understanding Policy Change and Culture', 29 October 1999, p. 3; *Report of the Royal Commission on Marriage and Divorce* (London: HMSO, 1956), p. 8.

in *Holy Deadlock*, a satirical novel castigating the current state of the law, by writer, MP and law reform activist A. P. Herbert.[94] Herbert's subsequent successful Private Member's Bill led to the 1937 Matrimonial Causes Act, which, in broad terms, extended divorce laws to include cruelty, incurable insanity and desertion – but only after three years of separation. The Divorce Law Reform Union, formed in 1908, to which the PL was affiliated, provided much of Herbert's information.[95] Herbert's clause stipulating a three-year separation was nowhere near the progressives' goal of 'divorce by consent' and almost nullified the Act's benefits. Disappointed but undaunted, the PL continued to support the campaign for change.[96] The Royal Commission presented a unique opportunity for the PL to promote its long-held views. The FPSI/PL had always strongly favoured 'no fault' divorce along the lines proposed by the Woman's Cooperative Guild as early as 1909, and wanted to abolish many aspects of the current law.[97] Although seeking a total sexual revolution, the MLRC was pragmatic, recognising the need for well argued smaller steps. Public Brains Trust meetings were organised to garner publicity, proclaiming: 'Public opinion … is not only ripe but eager [for change] … the times are propitious. The most progressive House of Commons since 1906 has recently been elected.'[98]

In its evidence to the Commission, the PL cited the many prominent people who had been associated with the organisation since its inception as the FPSI. The PL continued to adhere to 'the application of liberal and enlightened principles to the sphere of sexual law'.[99] Seeley succinctly summarised the PL's stance, emphasising 'marriage and divorce are man-made institutions to be handled in a rational manner'. He described 'no fault' divorce by mutual consent as 'dispassionate social engineering' and 'eminently reasonable' – a radical departure from the current law. All children should be seen as 'legitimate', whether born within marriage or without. Furthermore, the separation period for non-mutual divorce should be

---

94 Janet Chance, *The Cost of English Morals* (London: Douglas, 1931); Craig, *Sex and Revolution*; A. P. Herbert, *Holy Deadlock* (London, 1934; London: Methuen edition, 1971).

95 Edith M. Watson, 'The world does move', *PLAN*, February 1954, p. 21.

96 'How has Herbert's divorce law worked?', Report of a lecture to the Progressive League Sex Education Group, 21 May 1943, by Robert S. W. Pollard, *PLAN*, July 1943, p. 6.

97 'The Marriage Law Reform Society', *PLAN*, March 1953, p. 4. This 'no fault' proposal was not legalised until 1970. Hall, 'No sex please, we're socialists', pp. 66–7; 'Marriage Law Reform Committee. Public meeting', *PLAN*, January 1947, p. 4.

98 'Marriage Law Reform Committee. Public meeting', *PLAN*, January 1947, p. 4.

99 Haldane Papers, Wellcome Institute, 4/26/41, Statement of policy, MLRC, Progressive League, 1946, 'Marriage Law Reform Committee. Public meeting', *PLAN*, January 1947, p. 4.

drastically reduced, from seven years to two.[100] Among Seeley's list of reasons for divorce (e.g. adultery without consent; drunkenness; refusal of 'reasonable sex relations') was a *wife's* 'persistent failure to maintain a home with the money her husband provided' – an extraordinary statement from an individual member whose society advocated gender equality. This was not an isolated case of PL sexism. In 1947, sexual writer and psychiatrist Eustace Chesser, frequently featured in *PLAN*, strongly opposed female sexual freedom, arguing that a woman's sexual needs were different.[101]

The PL's views on 'no fault divorce' accorded with those of other progressive groups, but were a radical departure from the current law and sharply contrasted wtih the Royal Commission's 1956 report.[102] The League regretted that letters from members of the public, in the report's appendix A, were not printed, especially as the PL was 'the only organisation to submit such direct and incontrovertible evidence'.[103] After four years, all the commissioners, bar one, insisted that 'fault' be retained as the prime basis for divorce. Their findings firmly adhered to the status quo, with the Church of England commissioners seen as particularly 'harsh and unyielding' on this point.[104] Divorce continued to be permissible solely on the grounds of matrimonial fault, necessitating evidence of adultery, cruelty and/or desertion for three or more years. Stagnation ensued for more than a decade but the PL had played a significant role in the pressure for reform.

Homosexuality was also prominent among the many sexual issues highlighted by the PL, as an integral part of the general reform agenda. In 1925, Bertrand Russell had encapsulated views later espoused by the PL: 'certain forms of sex which do not lead to children are at present punished by criminal law; this is purely superstitious, since the matter is one that affects no-one except the parties directly involved'.[105] Homosexuality was on the extreme edge of public acceptability. After the Second World War,

---

100 Ernest Seeley, 'Divorce law reform', *PLAN*, March 1951, p. 4. At this point, Seeley was separating from his second wife, although they did not get divorced until much later, as 'divorce had been unnecessary'. Seeley later married for a third time.

101 'Evidence submitted by the Progressive League for the consideration of the Royal Commission on Marriage and Divorce, 1951', eight-page typed pamphlet in the author's possession, p. 8; Ernest Seeley, 'Divorce law reform', *PLAN*, March 1951, p. 4. Seeley's view may be linked to his background: unlike most PL members, his family was working class, with a breadwinner father and mother at home. Eda Collins, 'Review: *Marriage and Freedom*. Dr Eustace Chesser', *PLAN*, February 1947, p. 10.

102 Hall, 'No sex please, we're socialists', p. 67.

103 Edith M. Watson, 'The world does move', *PLAN*, February 1954, p. 18.

104 Smart, 'Divorce in England', p. 6.

105 Bertrand Russell, *What I Believe* (London: Routledge, 1925), p. 57.

the tabloid press assiduously reported rumours of homosexuality among high-profile figures and the number of successful convictions increased. However, public pressure to decriminalise homosexuality also grew. In 1954, the privacy and 'personal choice' aspect of homosexuality was highlighted in the public Montagu–Wildeblood trial.[106] The same year, the Wolfenden Departmental Committee on Homosexual Offences and Prostitution began taking evidence, with the PL one of the first organisations submitting evidence:

> We ... respectfully submit the considered views of our organisation, which throughout the 21 years of its existence has endeavoured to maintain the liberal tradition in its approach to social problems ... while recognising the need to protect minors ... [the PL] nevertheless calls for an amendment to the law so that homosexual practices between freely consenting adults shall not constitute a legal offence....[107]

Three PL members appeared before the Committee on 29 April 1955 – solicitor and justice of the peace Robert Pollard, author and sexual rights campaigner Alec Craig, and scientist and PL Honorary Secretary Ernest Seeley.[108] They were congratulated on the detailed factual evidence they gave to the twenty-strong enquiry (which contained only three women), particularly concerning prevailing attitudes abroad. The PL especially urged the Committee to examine evidence from France, where private homosexual acts were not considered to have 'any repercussions on the life of the nation'.[109] The PL also addressed the question of possible harm to persons under eighteen years of age, using various statistics to support its conclusion: 'In general ... the chance of direct harm is slight if both persons are under 18, but appreciably greater for the person under 18 if the other person is over 18'.[110] The Ethical Union submitted broadly similar evidence. Both societies spent less time considering prostitution because other groups, particularly the Association for Social and Moral

---

106 Brooke, *Sexual Politics*, p. 155.
107 'League notes. Homosexuality and prostitution', *PLAN*, June 1955, p. 71. The PL's evidence to Wolfenden was oral as well as written and therefore available for public scrutiny. Its evidence to the Marriage and Divorce Commission and Obscene Publications Select Committee (1958) was *written* only, and thus not included in the Committee's final report.
108 'Homosexuality and prostitution', *PLAN*, May 1955, p. 59. Probably for greater impact, Ernest Seeley was referred to as 'Dr', a title he rarely used.
109 'League notes. Homosexuality and prostitution'. *PLAN*, June 1955, p. 71.
110 'Home Office Committee on Homosexuality and Prostitution', *PLAN*, August 1955, pp. 92–3; Robert Wood, 'Homosexual offences and prostitution', *PLAN*, September 1955, pp. 102–3.

Hygiene, had exhaustively covered the subject. Both agreed the category of 'common prostitute' should be abolished.[111] Wolfenden (1957) concluded that homosexual acts between consenting adults in private should no longer be an offence. The PL members felt vindicated – for once their views accorded with informed official opinion. From 1958, increased pressure came from the newly formed Homosexual Law Reform Society but Wolfenden's proposals were not implemented until 1967.[112]

The PL had always urged reform of the obscenity laws, in operation since 1857.[113] Notable bans on literary works, for example *The Well of Loneliness, Ulysses* and *Lady Chatterley's Lover*, were current when the FPSI was formed in 1932.[114] Seeley recalled the claustrophobic gagging effect in the 1930s when 'a single four-letter word could get a book refused by publishers, whatever its literary merit'.[115] The Society of Authors and individual prominent writers, including H. G. Wells, argued that good literature was educative, releasing readers from repression.[116] Regular articles appeared in *PLAN,* particularly by Craig and Eustace Chesser – who was arrested for obscenity after the publication of his explicit sex manual, *Love Without Fear* (1940). In 1943, Craig castigated the imprisonment of a mail-order lending librarian who had been arrested under the current obscenity law.[117]

The Select Committee on Obscenity began sitting in 1957, and focused on works of literary or artistic merit. In 1958, the PL submitted a written memorandum ot it. As any written evidence presented to the Committee was not to be included in its eventual report, the PL separately published not only its own memorandum but two more items – an individual view from Craig and one from the Society of Labour Lawyers. Each highlighted aspects of the current law considered to be in need of reform. Craig's evidence was wide ranging, emphasising the importance of literary freedom. The Society of Labour Lawyers urged concentration

---

111 'Annual report of Progressive League Council for 1954–5', *PLAN*, October 1955, p. 6.

112 Sexual Offences Bill, 1967.

113 Obscene Publications Act 1857 (Campbell's Act).

114 James Joyce, *Ulysses* (London, 1922); Radclyffe Hall, *The Well of Loneliness* (London, 1928; London: Scriber first edition, 1976); D. H. Lawrence, *Lady Chatterley's Lover* (London: Bantam Books, 1928).

115 Seeley Papers, Ernest Seeley, 'Choosing a wife', in 'The Hunting Park and Other Stories', n.d., p. 19.

116 Rachel Potter, 'Introduction', in David Bradshaw and Rachel Potter (eds), *Prudes on the Prowl* (Oxford: Oxford University Press, 2013), p. 1.

117 'Love without fear: a summary of the second of the Sex Education Group's lectures, delivered by Dr Eustace Chesser', *PLAN,* April 1943, pp. 2–4; Alec Craig, 'Prison for lending books', *PLAN,* December 1943, pp. 3–5.

on the 'dominant effect' of the whole, rather than specific parts. The PL memorandum centred on: the rights of minorities to full 'literary and artistic freedom compatible with public order'; the prevention of excessive legal interference into individuals' lives; the freedom of scientific enquiry; the negative effect of excessive prohibitions; plus the need for enlightened sexual education. The League wanted a new clause inserted that no drawings/photographs should be deemed obscene solely because they depicted the naked human form.[118]

For once, the prevailing climate accorded with the PL's long-held views and the Obscene Publications Act 1959 brought a new definition of obscenity, focusing on whole publications rather than discrete words or passages. 'Publication for the public good' became an acceptable defence. The most famous case to test the new Act's veracity came quickly with Penguin's acquittal in the famous 1960 *Lady Chatterley's Lover* trial. Two million copies of D. H. Lawrence's 'infamous' book were sold before the year was out.[119] However, as Craig observed, the Act 'obviated neither the need for present vigilance nor the urgency for further reform'.[120] As late as 1970, Barbara Wootton was still calling for the complete abolition of all censorship, declaring 'the right to openly purchase Lady Chatterley is not enough'.[121]

In 1959, the PL took part in the Aldermaston march organised by the Campaign for Nuclear Disarmament. Solicitor and PL member Edward Moeran commented: 'It was good to see the [PL's] distinctive and distinguished banner ... carried high all the way from Aldermaston field to Trafalgar Square'.[122]

In the 1960s, under a radical Home Secretary Roy Jenkins, a Labour government at last passed some of the pioneering measures so long campaigned for by the FPSI/PL. The League was no longer crying in the wilderness. In 1967, Seeley proudly listed some of the successful sexual reforms in which the PL had played a part, notably the availability of birth control, decriminalisation of homosexuality between consenting adults, abortion on request, relaxation of the obscenity laws and film and theatre

---

118 The Progressive League, *Memoranda of Evidence Submitted to the Select Committee of the House of Commons on Obscene Publications by the Progressive League, 1958*, p. 11.

119 Lesley A. Hall, *Sex, Gender and Social Change in Britain Since 1880* (Basingstoke: Palgrave Macmillan, 2013), p. 150.

120 Craig, *The Banned Books of England*, p. 129.

121 Wootton Papers, Girton College Archive, Cambridge, 3/1/8, Barbara Wootton, 'The state of the nation', Tawney House Lecture, 15 May 1970, pp. 14–15.

122 Edward Moeran, 'We marched on London', *PLAN*, May 1959, pp. 3–4; Fanny Cockerell, 'The dinosaur failed to adapt', *PLAN*, May 1959, pp. 2–3.

censorship.[123] The PL continued campaigning on social issues for a further forty years.

Marcus Collins described the FPSI as a 'thirties curio'.[124] It is true that tge organisation was spawned in a decade of disparate and short-lived left-wing groups. However, as others fell by the wayside, the Federation of Progressive Societies and Individuals developed into the long-running Progressive League, which did not finally fold until 2005, seventy-three years after Joad's initial letter to the *Manchester Guardian*. Throughout its existence, its progressive ideals were frequently at odds with the zeitgeist. A verse from 'Dare To Be a Daniel', quoted by Seeley in 1948, aptly describes the courageous stance taken by members over the years in support of their principles.

> Dare to be a Daniel
> Dare to stand alone!
> Dare to have a purpose firm!
> Dare to make it known.[125]

Acknowledgements

I would like to express my appreciation to Karen Livingstone and Vivien Mathieson for sharing their recollections of the Progressive League. I am also most grateful to the British Library of Political and Economic Science (the Progressive League Papers), the Wellcome Institute (Haldane Papers); Girton College Archive, Cambridge (Barbara Wootton Papers) for permission to quote from material for which they hold the copyright. Every effort has been made to trace copyright holders and to avoid infringement. I apologise unreservedly to any copyright holders who have been inadvertently overlooked.

---

123 Seeley also listed the abolition of capital and corporal punishment (for adults), landlord and tenant reforms and reform of the blasphemy laws, in which the League had played a part. Ernest Seeley, 'In six years', *PLAN*, October 1967, p. 3.

124 Marcus Collins, *Modern Love: An Intimate History of Men and Women in Twentieth Century Britain* (London: Atlantic Books, 2003), p. 39.

125 Ernest Seeley, 'Freedom of thought', *PLAN*, November 1948, p. 1. The hymn 'Dare To Be a Daniel' was written by American composer and hymn writer Philip P. Bliss in 1873. *Dare To Be a Daniel: Then and Now* (London: Hutchinson, 2004) was also the title of Labour left-winger Tony Benn's autobiography.

8

Working-class culture in Britain and Germany, 1870–1914: a comparison

DICK GEARY

Britain

After 1860 there began to develop in Britain a working-class culture, which, according to Gareth Stedman Jones, was unlike the earlier work-based and radical artisan culture of the Chartist period. This later culture Richard Hoggart famously described in the 1950s as 'traditional working-class culture'.[1] In Stedman Jones's account, this culture was indeed specific to the working class but did not threaten the existing social and political order. Rather, it was a commercialised culture of leisure and entertainment and was characterised by a split between the workplace and the home. As far as skilled workers were concerned, the union might dominate the former but leisuretime became characterised by a multifaceted consumerism. Elements of this can be found in the emergence of fish and chip shops (the first 'fast food'), of which there were 25,000 in the working-class districts of Britain's cities by 1913. A survey in Southwark in 1914

---

1 Gareth Stedman Jones, 'Class struggle in the Industrial Revolution', *New Left Review*, 90 (1975), 35–69; Gareth Stedman Jones, *Outcast London* (Oxford: Oxford University Press, 1971); Gareth Stedman Jones, *The Languages of Class* (Cambridge: Cambridge University Press, 1983); Richard Hoggart, *The Uses of Literacy* (Harmondsworth: Penguin, 1957). Other works of relevance to the study of British working-class culture, of which there are a huge number, include Ross McKibbin, *The Ideologies of Class* (Oxford: Oxford University Press, 1990); Eric Hobsbawm, *Worlds of Labour* (London: Littlehampton Books, 1984), especially pp. 176–53; Peter Bailey, *Leisure and Class in Victorian England* (London: Routledge, 1975); Joanna Bourke, *Working-Class Cultures in Britain 1890–1960* (London: Routledge, 1994); James Walvin, *Leisure and Society 1830–1950* (London: Pearson, 1978).

found that 58 per cent of those from worker families had purchased fish and chips from such shops within the previous week.

Around 1890, high-street shopping became increasingly important for working-class families as they went out to buy cheap, factory-manufactured clothes and shoes. They were also able to buy a wide range of products from co-operative retail stores; and by 1913 those connected with the Co-operative Wholesale Society had a turnover of £88,000,000 a year and controlled 10 per cent of the British retail trade; the Society itself had over 3,000,000 members. The same period saw the emergence of chain stores such as Liptons, in which an exceptional range of foodstuffs from around the British Empire (including – after 1900 – bananas) were purchased by worker families. There was also a spectacular growth in the consumption of butter, margarine and meats; and consumption of all kinds was enhanced by the emergence of hire-purchase agreements, of which there were already one million in 1891. The emergence of cheap railway travel and the progressive shortening of the working week, combined with wage increases, also saw a huge expansion in the number of workers enjoying trips from industrial centres, such as Manchester, to rapidly expanding seaside resorts, such as Blackpool, where commercial entrepreneurs seized the opportunity to increase various forms of entertainment aimed precisely at this new clientele. Amusements and funfairs proliferated in the resort towns, as did pubs and music halls.[2]

Another characteristic of this culture was the appearance of cheap, mass-circulation newspapers aimed at workers, in particular the *News of the World*, which appeared on Sundays and was dedicated to entertainment, reporting scandals and sporting events.[3] Visitors to Britain often commented on the nation's obsession with the playing and watching of sports, which, together with betting, took off massively in the years before the First World War. Despite the fact that the mass of supporters were working class (and usually wore their distinctive flat caps), the English

---

2 Hobsbawm, *Worlds*, pp. 186–7; John Walton, *Fish and Chips and the British Working Class* (Leicester: Leicester University Press, 1992); Paul Johnson, *Saving and Spending: The Working-Class Economy in Britain 1870–1979* (Oxford: Clarendon Press, 1985); John Benson and Gareth Shaw (eds), *The Evolution of Retail Systems, c. 1860–1914* (Leicester: Leicester University Press, 1992); Bill Lancaster and Paddy Maguire, *Towards a Co-operative Commonwealth* (Manchester: Manchester University Press, 1996); Johnston Birchall, *Co-op: The People's Business* (Manchester: Manchester University Press, 1994).

3 Hobsbawn, *Worlds*, p. 186; Stedman Jones, *Languages*, p. 203; Asa Briggs, *Mass Entertainment* (Adelaide: Griffin, 1960); James Walvin, *Beside the Seaside* (London: Viking, 978); John Walton, *The English Seaside Resort* (Leicester: Leicester University Press, 1983); John Walton and James Walvin (eds), *Leisure in Britain 1780–1939* (Manchester: Manchester University Press, 1983).

Football League was already becoming professionalised and was organised by bourgeois entrepreneurs before the turn of the century. The rewards for them were massive. The Cup Final of 1900, for example, was watched by no fewer than 50,000 paying working-class (and almost exclusively male) workers. At the same time there developed, especially in the mining districts of northern England, a professional variant of rugby, known to this day as Rugby League, played and watched by working-class males. Despite the fact that British workers were only just playing cricket at this point in time, there is plenty of evidence that they displayed a keen interest in the game, not least because they bet upon the results of both cricket and football matches, as well as horse racing. According to Ross McKibbin, betting constituted the 'most successful form of working-class self-help'.[4]

British workers, mainly young and for once also female, further came to frequent in increasing numbers the music halls, which had begun in London's larger public houses and in which songs and jokes celebrated the joys of British proletarian existence: eating beef, drinking beer and travelling to the seaside. Work, on the other hand, was portrayed as something to be avoided, and marriage as a disaster. The cinema, which was to become the greatest symbol of the modern leisure industry, had also appeared in the working-class districts of the country's large cities before the First World War. (There were 3,000 by 1914.) Its working-class clientele, which was also predominantly young and included both sexes, tended to frequent not the grand cinema palaces of the city high street but local 'fleapits'. However, it was only in the inter-war period that the cinema came to dominate working-class leisure, together with the radio and dance halls.[5]

There is no doubt that the consumerist culture described above was further developed in Britain (and in England in particular) than in most European countries, because the country was both more uniformly and more maturely industrial than other countries in Europe and because English workers enjoyed a standard of living much higher than their continental counterparts. In terms of the country's economic and social structure, by 1901 some 85 per cent of the active population were wage workers and 75 per cent were manual workers (whether skilled or

---

4 Hobsbawm, *Worlds*, p. 185–6; A. Paterson, *Across the Bridges* (London: Edward Arnold, 1911); A. Freeman, *Boy's Life and Leisure* (London, 1914), pp. 151–2; James Walvin, *The People's Game* (London: Allen Lane, 1975); Tony Mason, *Association Football and English Society* (Brighton: Harvester, 1980); Richard Holt, *Sport and the British* (Oxford: Clarendon Press, 1989); Neil Tranter, *Sport, Economy and Society in Britain* (Cambridge: Cambridge University Press, 1998); McKibbin, *Ideologies*, p. 9.
5 Stedman Jones, *Languages*, pp. 205–6, 218–20, 223–9; Peter Bailey (ed.), *Music Hall* (London: Open University Press, 1986); McKibbin, *Ideologies*; Walvin, *Leisure*, pp. 97–112.

unskilled). Fewer than 12 per cent were employed in agriculture and the number of artisans in craft shops had dropped dramatically. In contrast, in Germany in 1913 almost 30 per cent of the population still worked in agriculture and over 50 per cent of those registered as 'workers' in the 1907 census lived in small towns and villages (of under 10,000 inhabitants). Almost one-third of all those employed in 'industry and crafts' at the same time worked in firms employing five or fewer people; and as late as 1914 over 500,000 German industrial workers came from non-industrial backgrounds. A comparison of working-class incomes is also telling in terms of the development of consumption. In 1904, for example, German money wages were only three-quarters and French only two-thirds of the English level, despite the fact that rent, fuel and food were on average 20 per cent more expensive in these continental countries. At the same time, the combination of free trade (the comparative absence of import duties and state levies) with the provision of foodstuffs from the Empire increased the well-being of British workers. One real-wage index charts a rise from 100 in 1850 to 190 by 1914. The period also saw an almost continuous fall in the number of weekly working hours from 1860. By the 1880s there came into existence a pattern of work described by continental contemporaries as the 'English week' (*semaine anglaise*), in which most trades enjoyed a work-free Saturday afternoon, which was precisely when soccer and rugby league matches were played. The average working week of sixty hours or more in the 1860s had been reduced to around forty-eight hours by the First World War, which may explain why Belgian and German visitors to England commented that English workers displayed no great interest in their work and that their employers did not seem to care about the state of affairs![6]

According to Eric Hobsbawm, the appearance of this class-specific culture was also a consequence of the increasing segregation of the British working class into distinct residential areas and a decline in socially mixed communities. It was further related to the emergence of a larger new middle class of white-collar workers, which had previously been much smaller in number. This now created a barrier between the middle class and the so-called labour aristocracy, which – again according to Hobsbawm – was characterised by a powerful sense of class solidarity and by a multiplicity of forms of mutual support.[7]

---

6 John Benson, *The Working Class in England* (London: Routledge, 1989); Hobsbawm, *Worlds*, p. 186; Bourke, *Working-Class Cultures*, pp. 5–12; Ernst Dückershoff, *How the English Workman Lives* (London: P. S. King, 1899; Andesite edition, 2015), p. 19; R. H. Best *et al.*, *Brassworkers of Berlin and Birmingham* (London: P. S. King, 1907), pp. 23, 139.

7 Hobsbawm, *Worlds*, pp. 176–93.

This said, the fact that the consumerist culture described above was a consequence of the relative prosperity of the British working class also reveals its limits. This was a culture of better-off workers with some disposable income and stability of employment. Contemporary reports pointed out that the poor were not to be seen in the theatre, dance and music halls, or around cricket matches and horse races.[8] This was also, with the exception of attendance at the music hall and cinema, an overwhelmingly male culture, in which the public house and alcohol played a prominent role and in which women were not welcome. While men participated in or watched sporting events outside the home, for the great majority of working-class women, especially the married and less young, it was the home (and sometimes the churches) which formed the centre of sociability.[9] The consumerist culture described above, however, was not only constrained by disposable income and gender but was also predominantly a product of the metropolis and other large urban centres. It was only weakly developed in the provinces and the countryside, where more traditional festivals and forms of recreation remained important.[10] It has also been pointed out that British working-class culture was not as passive as Stedman Jones suggests.

Many workers were involved in more active forms of recreation, such as playing (not just watching) football, as well as in boxing, pigeon-breeding, choral singing, performing in brass bands, breeding canaries, stamp collecting and cycling. In some small mono-occupational towns, as in the coal-mining communities of South Wales and County Durham, there was a close interaction between the Miners' Institute, miners' festivals, choirs, brass bands and the trade unions.[11] Furthermore, British workers developed working men's clubs and mechanics' institutes, which sought to educate and improve their members and not simply to entertain them. The co-operative movement also played a role in developing worker education, providing grants for part-time students, as well as material aid to the Dublin transport workers' strike in 1913. Through the Co-operative

8 M. Loane, *The Englishman's Castle* (London: Edward Arnold, 1907; Bibliolife Classics reprint, 2009), p. 35.

9 Jennie Calder, *The Victorian Home* (London: Batsford, 1977); M. J. Daunton, *House and Home in the Victorian City* (London: Hodder & Arnold, 1983); Bourke, *Working-Class Cultures*, pp. 62–97; Walvin, *Leisure*, pp. 47–53.

10 McKibbin, *Ideologies*, pp. 13–16, 141.

11 *Ibid.*, pp. 13–16. For coalfield culture in South Wales see Kenneth O. Morgan, *Rebirth of a Nation: Wales, 1880–1980* (Oxford: Oxford University Press, 1981), pp. 59–90. More generally see Stefan Berger, *et al.*, *Comparative History of Coalfield Societies* (Aldershot: Ashgate, 2005) and especially Dick Geary's chapter therein, 'The myth of the radical miner', pp. 43–64.

Women's Guild, established in 1883, it also prepared women for a role in national and local government and agitated for the reform of maternity provision and the divorce laws.[12]

The extent to which this culture helped further a solidaristic working-class identity is, however, hotly disputed. This is not to say that skilled and better-off workers, who enjoyed the benefits described above, were necessarily debarred from class identity by increasing consumption. On the contrary, it went hand in hand with the growth of both trade-union membership and, after 1900, a marked increase in support for the Labour Party. Moreover, some working-class sporting heroes, such as Arthur Henderson and Will Thorne, were political activists as well as boxers! However, what is questionable is whether this culture of skilled and relatively well paid workers embraced all sections of the British working class. There were, for example, marked regional differences. In the mining communities of the Welsh valleys in the years before the First World War there did develop a fusion between leisure activities, trade-union struggle and political radicalism. (Subsequently, the South Wales Miners' Federation wrote 'The Destruction of Capitalism' into a statement of its aims!) On the other hand, the coal miners of north-east England still supported political liberalism and returned Liberal Party MPs at elections before the First World War.[13] Equally, we have already pointed out the differences in male and female experiences within the British working class, while generational difference may have been important too.

What is quite clear, however, as already noted, is that there was a divide between those workers with income and time to enjoy the culture of consumption and poorer workers. In particular, there remained a gulf between the 'rough' and the 'respectable' workers of Britain. It is true that this gap was to some extent diminishing after the mid-Victorian age; but it remained important until 1914. Before the First World War it was predominantly skilled and better-off workers who joined both the trade unions and political organisations of labour, while poorer ('rougher') workers existed in a culture of poverty, of which more will be said in subsequent comments on internal class divisions within Germany. Before 1914 it was overwhelmingly skilled workers who dominated labour organisations, whether economic, social or political.[14] Moreover, in the case

12 Hobsbawm, *Worlds*, pp. 186–7; Lancaster and Maguire, *Co-operative Commonwealth*, pp. 6, 94–107, 109, 131; Johnston Birchall, *Co-op*, pp. 109–10.
13 See note 11.
14 On the dominance of skill in labour movements see Dick Geary, *European Labour Protest* (London: Palgrave, 1981). On respectability see Geoffrey Crossick, 'The labour aristocracy and its values: a study of mid-Victorian Kentish London', *Victorian Studies*,

of trade unions, what is revealed is a strong occupational loyalty on the part of workers, especially craftsmen, but this often led to sectionalism (division between skilled and unskilled and between different skill levels) rather than solidarity.[15] In terms of politics, voting returns in the general elections in the last decade before the First World War clearly indicate that those male workers with the franchise (which was restricted by residential conditions) were more likely to vote Liberal than Labour, although in some areas of strong Irish immigration Irish nationalists had some success, as did the Conservatives in certain areas of north-west England populated by (often Catholic) 'working-class Tories'.

Although various social organisations did become more class specific in their membership and a former mix of classes disappeared after 1870, as in the case of the Volunteers' Associations in Edinburgh, working-class and middle-class club and society members continued to participate in one and the same religious and church activities in many parts of Britain.[16] What struck on-looking German contemporaries who lived and worked in Britain before 1914 was precisely the relative harmony across classes, which they compared with a much more conflictual society in their homeland. As the miner Ernst Dückershoff remarked when living and working in northern England, 'the middle and working classes are on very friendly terms. This is because they are brought together in clubs and religious associations....'[17] Another German visitor of a different class background commented: 'Nowhere do we meet the social passion so familiar in Germany, nowhere the belief among the lower classes that salvation can only come through the overthrow and destruction of the existing order ... the deepseated mistrust, which makes the German worker regard every man in a good coat as an enemy, if not a spy.'[18]

19(3) (1976), 301–28; Caroline Reid, 'Middle-class values and working-class culture in nineteenth century Sheffield', in Sidney Pollard and Colin Holmes (eds), *Essays in the Economic and Social History of South Yorkshire* (Sheffield: South Yorkshire County Council, 1976), pp. 275–82.

15 See Dick Geary, 'Germany', in Dick Geary (ed.), *Labour and Socialist Movements in Europe Before the First World War* (Oxford: Berg Reprint, 1989), pp. 8, 22, 53. Also Dick Geary, 'The industrial bourgeoisie and labour relations in imperial Germany', in David Blackbourn and Richard J Evans (eds), *The German Bourgeoisie* (London: Routledge, 1991; new edition, 1993), pp. 140–61. Both articles contain British as well as German material.

16 Walvin, *Leisure*, pp. 47–57.

17 Dückershoff, *English Workman*, pp. 25, 55.

18 G. Schulze-Gaevernitz, *Social Peace. A Study of the Trade Union Movement in England* (London, 1983).

It was virtually impossible to find in Britain before 1914 any national mass social-democratic or labour cultural organisations of the kind that existed in imperial Germany, although the Clarion cycling club, based on a leftist newspaper, did have a national membership of 20,000 by the outbreak of war. Even this, however, was by German standards relatively small.

Germany

By 1914 the German Social Democratic Party (Sozialdemokratische Partei Deutschlands, SPD) had over one million fee-paying members and was not only the largest party in the Second Reich but the largest socialist organisation in the world. It also had a relevance to the lives of ordinary workers which extended well beyond the realm of politics: through a huge number of cultural and leisure associations, it influenced the daily lives and attitudes of working-class culture in the country's large Protestant industrial centres such as Berlin, Hamburg and Leipzig. There were social-democratic chess, drama, skittles, sports and gymnastic clubs, which held competitions, as well as smoking clubs. These were accompanied by choral societies, ramblers' clubs (the *Naturfreunde*) and educational associations. The clubs, usually with 'Workers' (*Arbeiter*) in their title, developed on a massive and national scale. The Workers' Cycling Club (Solidarity) had 150,000 members, the Workers' Gymnastic and Sports Association 187,000, and the Workers' Choral League 165,000 members by 1914. In total over 660,000 German workers belonged to social-democratic cultural and leisure organisations, many of which had their own specialist newspapers, published by SPD print houses, which also produced alternative children's comics (*King Mammon*) and fairy tales written from a socialist perspective.[19]

There has been a debate over the precise function of such organisations among contemporary SPD members and subsequent historians. In the official literature of the party, the cultural and leisure associations were

19 There is a massive literature on German social democracy. For a detailed survey of this and a reference to the specific evidence in this text see Dick Geary, 'Beer and skittles? Workers and culture in early twentieth-century Germany', *Australian Journal of Politics and History*, 46(3) (2000), 388–402; for the specific references here on the scale of the movement see pp. 388–9. See also Horst Groschopp, *Zwischen Bierabend und Bildungsverein* (Berlin: Dietz, 1987), p. 45; W. L. Guttsman, *The German Social Democratic Party* (London: HarperCollins, 1981); Vernon L. Lidtke, *The Alternative Culture* (Oxford: Oxford University Press, 1985); and a special issue of *Journal of Contemporary History*, 13(2) (1978).

the 'third pillar' of the movement, serving to foster class consciousness in the same way as did the other 'pillars': the socialist unions and the political party itself. For others, such organisations actually served to integrate workers into existing society and largely reproduced 'high' and 'bourgeois' culture. It is true that the workers' drama societies performed classical plays by Goethe and Schiller, while the choral associations sang traditional folk songs and often carried names devoid of socialist content (Edelweiss, Forest Green, Harmony). Moreover social-democratic bands and orchestras at party events and cultural evenings performed a classical repertoire of works by Beethoven, Mendelssohn, Verdi, Lehár, Strauss and Wagner. Perhaps even more telling in terms of the workers themselves are the lending library figures of the 'Workers' Libraries', which show firstly that few party members used them but of those who did most preferred works of historical fiction to the Marxist classics, with Dumas's *Count of Monte Cristo* clear favourite. Equally, the entertainment magazine *Neue Welt* and the satirical magazine *Wahrer Jakob* enjoyed much higher subscription numbers than the theoretical magazines of the party. Not surprisingly, therefore, some commentators have argued that far from radicalising German workers the SPD's cultural and leisure organisations served to integrate them into the prevailing system; and it is true that the party (and even Rosa Luxemburg) were proud of the fact that areas dominated by the SPD had remarkably low crime rates. Indeed, the SPD saw part of its function as an agency for the 'improvement' of the working class and denounced criminality and violence as the behaviour of the 'uneducated' and 'unorganised', of *Lumpen*.[20]

This picture of social-democratic harmlessness, of *embourgeoisement*, however, was not shared by Germany's imperial authorities, is partial and ignores a mass of more complex evidence. First of all, workers' reading habits differed from those of their middle-class contemporaries, not least in their preference for historical fiction and radical history. Their song books included Audorf's radical *Arbeitermarseillaise* and their choirs parodied Christian anthems. For example, Bach's Reformation hymn (*Eine feste Burg ist unser Gott*) became *Eine feste Burg ist unser Bund, wie ihn Lassalle geschaffen* – 'Our league is a fortress, as Lassalle made it') (Lassalle being seen as the founding father of the German labour movement). In

---

20 The integrationist case is made by Guenther Roth, *Social Democrats in Imperial Germany* (Totowa, NJ: Bedminster Press, 1963). For detailed references and literature supporting this case see Geary, 'Beer and skittles?', pp. 389–91. See also Mary Nolan, *Social Democracy and Society* (Cambridge: Cambridge University Press, 1985) and Michael Grüttner, 'Working-class crime and the labour movement' in Richard J Evans (ed.), *The German Working Class* (London: Barren & Noble Imprint, 1982), pp. 54–79.

fact, there was something of a Lassalle cult in the party, whose choirs also transformed the Christmas carol 'Silent Night' into a fight against oppression and poverty. Moreover, the works of high culture most popular with workers' choirs, orchestras and drama societies were not chosen at random from the bourgeois repertoire. The final movement of Beethoven's Ninth Symphony (Schiller's *Ode to Joy*) and Schiller's *Wilhelm Tell*, for example, owed their popularity, at least in part, to their celebration of fraternity and liberty. Further, the workers' choirs often had names which did carry a political message: Lassalle, Lassalliana, Vorwärts, Brüderlichkeit (Brotherhood), Liberté, Einigkeit (Unity) and Union. Such activities did not take away from the party's essential political message, as many found their way into the SPD from the choral societies, including the party leader, August Bebel.

Although it is true that social-democratic festivals were moved to Sundays and often included a variety of side-shows, they also usually involved a march or demonstration and were accompanied by placards with radical slogans such as demands for a shorter working week or 'international solidarity'. Such events helped bring the previously unorganised into the party.[21]

Most important of all, the workers' organisations and activities described above were socially and organisationally separate from those of the German middle class. In 1905 not one but two Schiller festivals were held in Germany: one by the SPD and one by middle-class dramatists. When Social Democrats played bowls or skittles in places as far apart as Hamborn in the Ruhr and Göppingen near Stuttgart they did so in what were specifically workers' bowling clubs. In Bremen in 1908 workers deserted the local Goethe Society to form their own alternative after hearing a lecture from the academic Werner Sombart! The Workers' Gymnastics and Sports League was established expressly in opposition to nationalist gym clubs and remained hostile to militaristic values throughout its existence. The very fact that German workers belonged to specifically workers' cultural and leisure associations testifies to the centrality of class to their lives, as did their language (*Genosse* – comrade) and their icons (red flag, clenched fist). They further celebrated different festivals from those of the German bourgeoisie: not Sedan Day but the day of the 'March Fallen' (those who lost their lives in the Revolution of 1848), not the Kaiser's but Lassalle's birthday, and above all May Day.[22]

---

21 The counter-case is made by Geary, 'Beer and Skittles', pp. 391–4. For further detailed references and evidence see *ibid.*, pp. 391–4.

22 Geary stresses the separation of social-democratic from bourgeois culture in 'Beer and skittles', pp. 393–5, which again contains multiple references to further literature and

In imperial Germany, to belong to a workers' association was not to belong to a Christian, nationalist or company club. It was a statement of identity feared by the Wilhelmine authorities, not least as there was a huge overlap between the membership of these organisations and membership of both the Free Trade Unions (SPD-affiliated) and the SPD itself. For example, in Leipzig in 1910 over 90 per cent of the Worker Singers were members of the Free Unions and 88 per cent subscribed to the local social-democratic newspaper. Fourteen years earlier in Hamburg, 75 per cent of the members of the Workers' Choir were members of the SPD.[23] Belonging to these cultural organisations in Germany before the First World War was thus a statement of identity, as was demonstrated by the behaviour of the imperial authorities, which frequently closed them down. The workers' leisure associations were proscribed not only during the overt repression of the Anti-Socialist Law (1878–90) but much later too (nullifying certain views on the increasing liberalism of the regime). In 1901, for example, the Wetsphalian Workers' Choral League was banned by the Prussian police, as had been the workers' choir in the Ruhr town of Bochum three years earlier. As late as 1912 there was a rash of such bans, all of which served to radicalise and further politicise the membership of these organisations. That membership of leisure clubs did not detract from the SPD's political message was further demonstrated by the Worker Cyclists' self-description as 'the cavalry of the revolution' (they rode round town putting up and distributing political messages) and by the 10,000 members of the Berlin sports club Fichte, who gave their support to the radical left and the councils' movement during the revolution of 1918–19.[24]

Further aspects of social-democratic culture before the First World War were its irreligion and the absence of a culture of domesticity. The large Protestant cities of imperial Germany saw a general decline in religious observance in the late nineteenth and early twentieth century; and, though many German liberals were often staunchly anti-clerical, nowhere was the process of secularisation more advanced than in the working-class districts of Germany's large industrial cities, where they were Protestant. In 1900, 14 per cent of Protestant Berliners took communion but the

---

evidence. See also Dieter Langewiesche and Klaus Schönhoven, 'Arbeiterbibliotheken', *Archiv für Sozialgeschichte*, 16 (1976), 135–207.

23 Geary, 'Beer and skittles', pp. 394–5.

24 On persecution and discrimination in imperial Germany see Dick Geary, 'The Prussian labour movement, 1871–1914', in Philip G. Dwyer (ed.), *Modern Prussian History 1830–1947* (Harlow: Routledge, 2001), pp. 131–35; Dick Geary, 'Radical culture and local identity: Berlin, 1871–1920', in Krista Cowman and Ian Packer (eds), *Radical Cultures and Local Identities* (Newcastle upon Tyne: Cambridge Scholars, 2010), pp. 15–26.

figure was much lower in proletarian districts (only 5 per cent in Wedding, for example). According to some conservatives, such places had become 'spiritual cemeteries'. Although the official line of the SPD (primarily for electoral reasons) maintained that religion was a 'private matter', in fact many party members taunted church-goers among their colleagues.[25]

One absolutely clear line dividing bourgeois from working-class culture in Germany before the First World War, however, was the absence of a culture of domesticity in the latter. The ideal of providing a decent home, in which domestic virtues could be protected from intrusion and interference, where wife and family could be safe and which was filled with precious objects, was beyond even the skilled and most affluent sections of the German working class. The massive and incredibly rapid expansion of Germany's industrial cities after 1870 led to spectacular levels of urban overcrowding. Even in the Ruhr, where the large companies such as Krupp provided more spacious accommodation for some of their employees, 11 per cent of households in Essen had six or more lodgers, 15 per cent took in three and 26 per cent two. Yet the situation in older cities was much more dire. In 1905 there were over thirty-six occupants to every building in Breslau and Munich, almost thirty-seven in Hamburg and just over seventy-seven in Berlin. This density was housed in high-rise tenement blocks, with four or more storeys. Moreover, these tenements stretched back to as many as six, badly lit interior courtyards (*Hinterhöfe*).

Within such buildings the smallest flats, with only a single heated room, would often have to accommodate families of six or more people. Toilet and bathing facilities were communal. In such circumstances privacy was impossible and socialisation took place in the corridors, on the staircases, in the yards and on the streets of the working-class neighbourhood. Solidarity was built not only by shared experience in the workplace but by the bricks and mortar of the tenement. A further consequence was that the menfolk, especially the younger, spent time outside the home, often in pubs and bars. As the party theorist Karl Kautsky wrote, 'the solitary bulwark of the proletarian's freedom, which cannot be taken from him easily is the public house…. Without the pub the German worker is not only deprived of social but also political life.' It is important to note the reference to the association of the pub and politics in this quotation. In most industrial cities the authorities barred the SPD and its members from the use of municipal buildings. As a result, and not only because of

---

25 On irreligion and the SPD see Hugh Mcleod, 'Protestantism and the working class in imperial Germany', *European Studies Review*, 12 (1982), 323–43; Richard J. Evans, 'Religion and society in Germany', *European Studies Review*, 12 (1982), 281; Geary, 'Beer and skittles', p. 395.

a proletarian predilection for beer, it was precisely in the neighbourhood pubs that the SPD and its ancillary organisations held their meetings and recruited their members.[26]

So far we have seen the huge numerical support mobilised by the cultural organisations of the SPD, which had few counterparts in Britain. It is important to recognise, however, this movement had to compete with other working-class cultures in Germany. An organised culture of Catholic workers, strong in the Rhineland and southern Germany, and quite strong among the Catholics of the Ruhr, blocked SPD advances, which were always much more successful in Protestant Germany, and especially its large industrial cities such as Berlin, Hamburg and Leipzig, where rates of secularisation were higher. There even existed an Evangelical movement of clubs in the Ruhr, fostered by the Lutheran Church in competition with Catholic organisations, although it was very small and is still awaiting its historian.[27] Social-democratic organisations were virtually non-existent in the German countryside among agricultural workers;[28] and the large number of Polish workers in some eastern territories of the Reich and among Ruhr miners developed their own – often quite radical – cultural organisations, but they were not enticed by either social democracy or by German Catholicism.[29] Another group of incomers into industrial areas from Germany's rural east were the Masurians. They not only stayed away from the SPD and its ancillary organisations but were also hostile to the Poles, being Protestant and loyal to the Kaiser.[30] At the same time, the cultural, trade-union and party organisations of the SPD remained weak in areas with high labour turnover and an ethnically mixed workforce. Such was the case in the Ruhr, where large and extremely powerful employers developed a series of strategies to attract especially skilled workers and tie them to the firm. Nationally the bosses' unions (the 'Yellow' Unions) had 279,000 members in 1914, when the membership of Catholic unions

---

26 Geary, 'The Prussian labour movement', pp. 130–1. For the Kautsky quote see *Neue Zeit*, 9 (1891), 107–8. See also Gesine Amus, *Hinterhof, Keller, Mansarde* (Reinbek: Akademie Verlag, 1982); and Gerhard A. Ritter and Klaus Tenfelde, *Arbeiter im deutschen Kaiserreich* (Bonn: Dietz, 1992), pp. 582–617.

27 Geary, 'The Prussian labour movement', pp. 131, 136–40; Michael Schneider, *Die Christlichen Gewerkschaften* (Bonn: New Gesellschaft, 1982); Eric Dorn Brose, *Christian Labour* (Washington, DC: Catholic University of America Press, 1982).

28 Geary, 'The Prussian labour movement', pp. 140–1.

29 Geary, 'The Prussian labour movement', p. 139; also Christoph Klessmann, *Polnische Bergarbeiter im Ruhrgebiet* (Göttingen: Vandenhoek & Ruprecht, 1978); John H. Kulcycki, *The Foreign Worker and German Labour* (Oxford: Berg, 1994).

30 Geary, 'The Prussian labour movement', p. 139; Franz Brüggemeier, *Leben vor Ort* (Munich: C. H. Beck, 1983), p. 34.

numbered 343,000 and the SPD-related 'Free' Trade Unions had over two million members. Some of the workers at Krupp and other paternalist firms were provided with company housing and were bound to their employers by company insurance and welfare schemes. They celebrated festivals specific to their firm, played in company sports clubs, sang in company choirs, went on works outings and proclaimed their loyalty on the birthday of their employer.[31] At the same time, Germany's extremely large white-collar working class in both the private and the public sector stayed away from the SPD and its ancillary organisations in a country where the *Kragenlinie* (collar line) was of huge importance in terms of social standing.[32]

The cultural and leisure organisations were restricted in their social bases in further ways too. As with membership of the SPD itself (and in fact as with the great majority of labour movements in Europe at the time), they mobilised predominantly skilled male workers in regular employment and had far less success with less skilled workers, who also had less disposable income, less spare time and were intermittently unemployed. Some of the latter existed in a 'culture of poverty' (in Oscar Lewis's phrase), in which the settled, future-oriented vision of the social-democratic organisations with their ideal of 'improvement' made little sense. For the casually employed and desperately poor it made little sense to invest in organisations which promised returns in the future and they inhabited a world of direct action, physical force and criminality, which the socialist movement looked down on and criticised.[33]

The mobilisation of women also proved relatively difficult for the party, union and leisure organisations of the SPD. Although the party leader, August Bebel, had advocated gender equality in his famous *Die Frau und der Sozialismus* (1879) and the party's women's organisation had no fewer than 170,000 members on the eve of the First World War, women stayed away from the heart of the party (the public house) and felt ill at ease with

---

31 Geary, 'The Prussian labour movement', pp. 138–9. See also Dick Geary, 'The industrial bourgeoisie and labour relations in imperial Germany', in David Blackbourn and Richard J. Evans (eds), *The German Bourgeoisie* (London: Routledge, 1991), pp. 140–61; Peter Ullman, *Tarifverträge und Tarifpolitik in Deutschland* (Frankfurt am Main: Lang, 1977).

32 Jürgen Kocka, *Unternehmerverwaltung und Angestelltenschaft* (Göttingen: Vandenhoek & Ruprecht, 1975); Jürgen Kocka, *Die Angestellte in der deutschen Geschichte* (Göttingen: Vandenhoek & Ruprecht, 1981); Iris Hamel, *Völkischer Verband und nationale Gewerkschaft* (Frankfurt am Main: M. Europaische Verlagsantalt, 1967); Klaus Mattheier, *Die Gelben* (Düsseldorf: Schwann, 1973).

33 Michael Grüttner, 'Arbeiterkultur versus Arbeiterbewegungskultur', in Albrecht Lehmann (ed.), *Studien zur Arbeiterkultur* (Münster: LIT-Verlag, 1984), pp. 244–82.

the masculine values of its clubmen (physical strength and the ability to down large quantities of ale). For many working-class women, though not all, it was the home, the family and sometimes the church which was the focus of their attention. The problem of recruiting women related firstly to the fact that they were concentrated in unskilled and poorly paid jobs: non-residential domestic service (1.5 million in 1907); residential domestic service (1.25 million) and agriculture (4.5 million). Women's wages were even lower than those of unskilled males and their hours longer (compounded by domestic chores). Moreover, women working outside the home were usually single and under twenty-four years of age, suggesting that such work preceded marriage and childbirth and ceased thereafter. A further problem for the social-democratic organisations was that the process of secularisation was much less marked among German women than among men; and areas of high labour organisation were most commonly found where religion had lost its hold.

Of course, working-class wives and daughters played an important role in supporting striking husbands and brothers by caring for offspring, providing sustenance on picket lines and taking in washing, sewing and lodgers. Though few females joined unions, many unorganised women did go on strike. Moreover, in some trades (cobbling, textiles and tobacco) unorganised women were more likely to strike than their organised colleagues. Kathleen Canning has also identified a group of female textile workers who did develop a work-based culture, who returned to factory work after childbirth and who turned to the Free Textile Workers' Union in increasing numbers. In fact, women constituted 37 per cent of that SPD-linked trade union by 1907. Yet the fact remains that the German labour movement remained overwhelmingly male on the eve of the First World War, with women constituting only 16.09 per cent of the SPD's total membership. Moreover, most of these were not working outside the home but were the wives of SPD members.[34]

Another potential rival to the SPD's dominance of working-class culture among ostensibly Protestant males in the large industrial cities emerged in the years before the First World War. This came in the shape of

---

34 For a survey of the massive literature see Geary, 'Prussian labour movement', pp. 141–3. See also Richard J Evans, *Sozialdemokratie und Frauenemanzipation* (Bonn: Dietz, 1979); Jean Quartaert, *Reluctant Feminists in German Social Democracy* (Princeton, NJ: Princeton University Press, 1979); Heinz Niggemann, *Emanzipation zwischen Sozialismus und Feminismus* (Wuppertal: Peter Hammer, 1981); Kathleen Canning, *Languages of Labour and Gender: Female Factory Work in Germany* (Ithaca, NY: Cornell University Press, 1996); Stefan Bajohr, *Die Hälfte der Fabrik* (Marburg: Verlag Arbeiterbewegung und Gesellschaftswissenschaft, 1979); Rosemarie Beier, *Frauenarbeit und Frauenalltag im Kaiserreich* (Frankfurt am Main: Peter Lang, 1983).

the profit-making leisure industries of commercial entrepreneurs and mass entertainment. It manifested itself in the publication of the *Groschenheft* (penny dreadful), dance and music halls, pub-restaurants and popular theatres. At the same time, serials like *Nick Carter* and *Buffalo Bill* sold 80,000 copies a week; and above all the cinema arrived. By 1914 there were 2,446 cinemas in the Reich, many in working-class districts of the large cities, which, as in Britain, attracted the young of both sexes. Yet the growth of the leisure industry in Germany before the First World War should not be exaggerated and mass spectator sports were nothing like as developed as their British counterparts.[35]

Differences between Britain and Germany

So far we have seen that there were some similarities between working-class culture in Germany and Britain in this period. In both countries males dominated and skilled workers constituted the backbone of labour organisations, whether political, trade union or social. Moreover, working-class cultures varied from area to area within each country and were faced with various competitors. The different loyalties of Catholic Poles and Protestant Masurians might be likened, for example, to sectarian Irish politics in the UK. However, there were also salient differences between Germany and Britain. Firstly, the early emergence of a mass socialist movement in Germany, which had already come into existence in the 1860s, lacked any British counterpart. Moreover, the separation of the German movement from the cultural organisations of the bourgeoisie was much more marked and cross-class collaboration was much less marked where German Social Democracy was powerful than it seems to have been in some parts of Britain. Explanations of difference fall into two principal parts, one political and the other essentially related to different living standards, which will be examined first.

We have already seen that disposable income was significantly higher and working hours were significantly shorter in Britain than in Germany in this period, which manifestly constitutes an explanation for the greater size and cultural dominance of a commercialised leisure industry in the former. Moreover, the relative absence of such a culture in Germany also

---

35 Geary, 'Beer and skittles', pp. 400–2; Wolfgang Kaschuba, '1900: Kaiserreich, Arbeiterkultur und Moderne', in Jürgen Kocka *et al.*, *Von der Arbeiterbewegung zum modernen Sozialstaat* (Munich: Beck Verlag, 1994), pp. 74–8, 85–6; Viktor Noak, *Der Kino* (Münster: Gautzsch, 1913); Robin Lenman, 'Mass culture and the state in Germany, 1900–1926', in R. J. Bullen *et al.*, *Ideas into Politics* (London: Croom Helm, 1984), pp. 51–9.

helps to explain (and created a space for) the massive development of the cultural organisations of social democracy. It is also important to realise that German workers did not benefit from a huge global decline in food prices, on account of the tax and tariff policies of Reich governments. The absence of a national system of income tax as state spending escalated in the arms race before the First World War meant that taxes on items of consumption rose as the Reich avoided higher taxes for the wealthy and even subsidised Junker grain producers in the east. As SPD electoral pamphlets pointed out, the price of bread and beer in Germany was thus a political issue in a way it was not in free-market Britain. You did not need to have read Marx to realise that the state benefited some at the expense of others.[36]

Different residential structures also had different consequences for workers in the two countries. It has already been pointed out that solidarity in Germany was partly a consequence of incredibly high housing density, which pushed some workers into the spaces where the leisure and political organisations of the SPD were most active. In Britain it is also true of course that housing conditions were appalling for many workers. There were significant improvements in the living conditions of the labour aristocracy from the 1870s, however, which enabled the development of a family and domestic leisure culture largely lacking among even better-off workers in imperial Germany. These workers in Britain lived in single-family terraced housing of the kind one can still see to this day, for instance in Nottingham and Leicester. By 1914 four-fifths of all English families of three or more members occupied at least four rooms, who were thus able to enjoy what Ross McKibbin has described as a 'modest domesticity'. Tenement blocks (*Mietskasernen*) so typical of working-class districts in Germany's cities were extremely rare outside London, Liverpool and Glasgow. This culture of domesticity in single-family working-class homes saw the purchase of all kinds of furniture for the home and a concern with household appearance, deemed to reflect their *respectability* (though this had little to do with thrift, abstinence or church attendance). The gap between *rough* workers, who often changed accommodation to avoid paying rent, and their *respectable* compatriots was of central importance to Victorian society and did not disappear before 1914. In the homes of skilled workers new rituals such as family festivals and the 'workers' Christmas' became important. The public house also remained important to working-class males but the home was the realm of the working-class wife.[37]

---

36 Geary, 'The Prussian labour movement', pp. 131–2.
37 *Ibid.*

The turn of German workers to the workers' leisure and cultural organisations, closely linked to membership of the Free (socialist) Trade Unions and the SPD itself, which also denoted a break with middle-class and mixed sociability, was in turn a consequence of the relative lack of success of German labour in industrial disputes, with German employers proving far less willing to negotiate than their British counterparts. For example, in 1913 there were in Britain 230,000 metalworkers, 460,000 textile workers and 900,000 miners covered by collective wage agreements. The respective figures for Germany were 1,376 metalworkers, 16,000 workers in textiles and a staggeringly paltry 83 miners! Moreover, strikers in Germany had less success in the outcome of their actions and German employers more success with lockouts than their British counterparts.[38]

Independent working-class politics and culture in Germany also stemmed from the general hostility of bourgeois parties to the labour movement. It is true that there were signs of a resurgent liberalism in the empire in the years immediately before the First World War but as far as labour was concerned they turned out to be relatively inconsequential. The isolation of the SPD and its cultural organisations was partly brought on itself by its ostensibly Marxist ideology but this was not the whole story. In the run-offs in the second round of elections, other parties usually did deals to prevent the election of socialist candidates, while in the elections to the Prussian Landtag of 1908 the left-liberals did not back SPD candidates in the second round of voting. There was an electoral agreement between Social Democrats and Progressives in the 1912 national elections; but this was observed more by SPD members than the liberals in actual practice. Moreover, the SPD was the only party in Prussia to campaign actively against the discriminatory 'three-class franchise', in a series of massive demonstrations between 1905 and 1914, which often led to conflict with the police.[39] Of course it is true that in some other states (Baden, Bavaria and Hesse-Darmstadt) with liberal traditions, especially in southern Germany, the prospects of collaboration were much better; but some of the largest industrial cities, such as Hamburg and the industrial state of Saxony, were actually thinking of making their franchises even more restrictive in the pre-war period.[40]

The emergence of a separate socialist movement and its cultural organisations in imperial Germany was above all a consequence of the discriminatory nature of the regime, which I have described at some length

---

38 Calder, *The Victorian Home*; Daunton, *House and Home*; John Burnett, *A Social History of Housing 1815–1970* (London: David & Charles, 1978).
39 Geary, 'The industrial bourgeoise', pp. 140–61.
40 Geary, 'Radical culture and local identity', pp. 16–18.

elsewhere. To summarise briefly here, firstly the imperial and state authorities interfered with the daily lives of their citizens in a way unimaginable in Britain before the First World War. The police sometimes intervened to separate unmarried but cohabiting couples and police permission was required for marriage. In Berlin in 1912 the length of your hatpin and the colour of your car were determined by police ordinances. In the words of Richard Evans, 'the laws were formulated in such a way that they meant a massive interference not only in the activities of the labour movement but in the everyday life of the working class'. However, crucially there were also frequent prosecutions of SPD cultural, as well as political, organisations not only in the period of the so-called Anti-Socialist Law (1878–90) but throughout the regime's existence, including as late as 1912. Discriminatory economic policies, described earlier, combined with the closure of leisure associations, made it clear to the German worker that the regime favoured some at the expense of others in a way that clearly differed from the more liberal state, the more liberal middle class and the more liberal working class in Britain.[41]

41 Geary, 'The Prussian labour movement', pp.131–34; Richard J. Evans, 'Introduction' to *The German Working Class: The Politics of Everyday Life* (London: Barnes & Noble Imports, 1982), p. 27; Raymond B. Fosdick, *The European Police System* (New York: Century Press, 1916; Andesite edition, 2015).

9

Women at work: activism, feminism and the rise of the female office worker during the First World War and its immediate aftermath

NICOLE ROBERTSON

One of the most dramatic changes to working lives in twentieth-century Britain was the exponential growth of the non-manual labour force. Clerical work was one of the fastest-growing categories within this sector, as the expansion of modern corporations and government administration caused a flood of paperwork, necessitating a dramatic increase in office staff.[1] Prominent changes in this sector are often associated with the late nineteenth century, when feminisation of the office began, a process which has been well documented.[2] Major changes are also associated with two decades in the mid-twentieth century: it was during the 1950s that female clerks began to outnumber their male colleagues; and in the 1960s there was a rapid growth in trade unionism among non-manual workers. However, as this chapter argues, the First World War and its immediate aftermath was also a particularly important period when complex changes took place both in female occupational identity and in work-based activism among clerical workers. This chapter draws on fresh

1   D. Gallie, 'The labour force', in A. H. Halsey and Josephine Webb (eds), *Twentieth Century British Social Trends* (London: Palgrave Macmillan, 2000), p. 287.
2   Michael Heller, *London Clerical Workers, 1880–1914* (London: Pickering & Chatto, 2010); R. Guerriero Wilson, *Disillusionment or New Opportunities? The Changing Nature of Work in Offices, Glasgow 1880–1914* (Aldershot: Ashgate, 1998); Meta Zimmeck, 'Jobs for the girls: the expansion of clerical work for women, 1850–1914', in Angela V. John (ed.), *Unequal Opportunities: Women's Employment in England 1800–1918* (London: Basil Blackwell, 1986); Gregory Anderson, *Victorian Clerks* (Manchester: Manchester University Press, 1975); Lee Holcombe, *Victorian Ladies at Work: Middle-Class Working Women in England and Wales 1850–1914* (Devon: David & Charles, 1973).

evidence from the Association of Women Clerks and Secretaries (AWCS), the only single-sex organisation representing female office workers in both private business and state administration. Many non-manual workers have traditionally been considered predisposed to individualism rather than collectivism. However, examining attempts by female clerical workers to shape, resist and challenge prevailing working conditions can inform important debates concerning women's participation in collective action. This can also reflect wider shifts and factions in the campaign for women's rights in early-twentieth-century Britain.

Although it was not until the 1950s that there were more female than male office clerks, 'the writing was very much on the wall by the First World War, and briefly during the war women predominated'.[3] Yet there is little recognition of these women in the historiography of women's war work. As Deborah Thom has noted, the predominant 'image of women workers in wartime, then and now, is of a frail girl wrestling alone with a machine, working heroically and against her nature for the duration of the war only'.[4] By examining clerical workers through the prism of the little-studied AWCS, it is possible to add fresh perspective to the well established debate on women and work during the First World War. Moreover, such research can help to shed light on the changing shape of Britain's non-manual workforce. This chapter examines mechanisms used to cope with unemployment, an issue seldom associated with these workers prior to the 1920s, and the war's impact on the complex gender terrain within what became known as the white-collar sector.

What, then, was the AWCS? Originally founded as the Association of Shorthand Writers and Typists in 1903, its objectives were: to raise the level of proficiency and encourage a higher standard of training in clerical work; to secure 'a just remuneration' for its members; to assist with employment opportunities; and to provide legal aid and advice.[5] Although the original Association was established to represent female clerks, men were not excluded. However, in 1912 the Association of Shorthand Writers and Typists changed its name to the Association of Women Clerks and Secretaries, and revised its rules to confine membership exclusively to

---

3   Jane E. Lewis, 'Women clerical workers in the late nineteenth and early twentieth centuries', in Gregory Anderson (ed.), *The White-Blouse Revolution: Female Office Workers Since 1870* (Manchester: Manchester University Press, 1988), p. 34.

4   Deborah Thom, *Nice Girls and Rude Girls: Women Workers in World War I* (London: I. B. Tauris, 1998), p. 89.

5   AWCS, *The Association of Women Clerks and Secretaries: What It Is and What It Has Done* (leaflet, n.d.), p. 1. The records of the AWCS used in this chapter are located at the Working Class Movement Library, Salford, and the Trades Union Congress Library at London Metropolitan University.

women. Marsh and Ryan suggest that this was because male clerks were
primarily served by another organisation, the National Union of Clerks,
and because women already formed the most active members within the
Association.[6] The AWCS recruited nationally, but in practice the majority
of its membership was based in London. Its rules included minimum
salary and qualification restrictions,[7] leading to it being referred to as an
'elitist' organisation.[8] Admittedly, its membership was relatively small –
even after a period of growth, its membership stood at only 7,500 in 1920.
However, many of its campaigns were designed to improve conditions for
trained and skilled clerks and secretaries generally, regardless of whether
or not they were members. By the end of the First World War, the AWCS
considered itself 'within the Front ranks of the women's organisations'.[9]

Recent research shows that levels of female involvement in labour
relations were higher than traditionally thought; however, the main focus
of work to date has been on women in manual occupations.[10] Given the
common assumption that the experience of work for non-manual workers
centred on individualism, this is perhaps understandable. This is all the
more so given that in Britain the lower middle class has been considered
particularly weak, compared with the greater cohesion of the group in,
for example, France and Germany. This has in part been attributed to
particular patterns of women's employment in white-collar work.[11] This

---

6 Arthur Marsh and Victoria Ryan, *The Clerks: A History of Apex 1890–1989* (Oxford:
 Malthouse Publishing, 1997), p. 22.

7 AWCS, Rulebook, 1916.

8 Arthur Marsh and Victoria Ryan, *Historical Directory of Trade Unions, Volume 1: Non-
 manual Union* (Farnborough: Gower, 1980), p. 46. Working conditions within offices
 varied enormously; however, certain features are evident. Working-class female clerks
 tended to undertake routine clerical work and lower-middle-class women dominated
 the secretarial grades. For lower-middle-class women, clerical work was considered
 respectable and attractive, as it was clean and required a certain level of specialised
 education and training. This work had the appeal of being a viable alternative to other
 work considered suitable for lower-middle-class women, for example as a governess or
 shop-keeping. See Teresa Davy, '"A cissy job for men; a nice job for girls": women shorthand typists in London, 1900–1939', in Leonore Davidoff and Belinda Westover (eds),
 Our Work, Our Lives, Our Words (London: Macmillan Education, 1986), pp. 126–7;
 Arthur J. McIvor, *A History of Work in Britain 1880–1950* (Basingstoke: Palgrave, 2001),
 pp. 189–90).

9 AWCS, Annual report, 1919, p. 1.

10 Cathy Hunt, *The National Federation of Women Workers, 1906–1921* (Basingstoke:
 Palgrave Macmillan, 2014); Angela Woollacott, *On Her Their Lives Depend: Munitions
 Workers in the Great War* (London: University of California Press, 1995).

11 Michael Savage, 'Career mobility and class formation: British banking workers and the
 lower middle classes', in Andrew Miles and David Vincent (eds), *Building European
 Society: Occupational Change and Social Mobility in Europe 1840–1940* (Manchester:

chapter adds a British context to this research. Thus, with regard to the members of the AWCS, both class and gender have played a role in clerical workers being overlooked. This chapter addresses this neglected area, one that lies between the sub-disciplines of women's history and labour history. By locating the AWCS at the intersection of histories of women workers during the First World War and accounts of trade unionism among non-manual workers, this chapter will contribute to the growing literature on the history of work in Britain. It will reveal how a separatist, feminist presence developed, constructed around career opportunities for trained women clerks (clerks being the most numerous of the non-manual workforce). It examines the conflict that this caused in a male-dominated labour movement and explores how this was shaped by gender-based hostility in the aftermath of the war.

The First World War and the rise of the business girl

The Great War's initial impact on women's employment has traditionally been assessed by focusing on the dramatic increase in unemployment among women workers in domestic service and 'luxury' trades (such as jewellery, millinery and dressmaking). In these areas expenditure was cut as people turned 'their minds and pockets to the serious business of war'.[12] High levels of unemployment within these manual occupations are often compared to an increase in employment opportunities for the non-manual work undertaken by the 'business girl' (opportunities which ranged from executive secretaries to shorthand typists). As one proponent of this view argued, 'the war which, in creating simultaneously a prolifera-tion of Government committees and departments and a shortage of men, brought a sudden and irreversible advance in the economic and social power' of this group of women.[13] The case of the AWCS, however, throws

---

Manchester University Press, 1993); J. F. McMillan, *Housewife or Harlot: The Place of Women in French Society 1870–1940* (London: Palgrave Macmillan, 1984); H. Boak, 'The state as an employer of women in the Weimar Republic', in W. R. Lee and Eve Rosen-haft (eds), *The State and Social Change in Germany 1880–1980* (London: Berg, 1990); Helen Boak, *Women in the Weimar Republic* (Manchester: Manchester University Press, 2013).

12 Gail Braybon, *Women Workers in the First World War* (London: Croom Helm, 1981), p. 44.

13 Arthur Marwick, *Women at War 1914–1918* (London: Croom Helm, 1977), p. 74; see also Deborah Thom, 'Women and work in wartime Britain', in Richard Wall and Jay Winter (eds), *The Upheaval of War: Family, Work and Welfare in Europe 1914–1918* (Cambridge: Cambridge University Press, 2005), pp. 297–326.

into sharp relief the experience of these 'business girls' at the outbreak of war, contributing to a greater understanding of unemployment among non-manual workers more generally. It is clear from the AWCS's records that these workers were affected by unemployment at the outbreak of war and that they did not experience a sudden rise in employment opportunities. In its annual report for 1914–15, the AWCS described the 'rude lesson taught by the war' that 'efficient workers, who have never been out of employment, may lose that employment through no fault whatever of their own'.[14] The closing down of the Stock Exchange, the dismissal of staff from German shipping companies and the loss of jobs from firms with continental connections resulted in a period of difficulty. In an attempt to mitigate these circumstances, the AWCS established a War Emergency Fund to provide assistance to female clerks – including those who were not members of the Association – thrown out of work due to the disruption caused by the outbreak of war. During the first few months almost £1,000 was raised, necessitating the appointment of a full-time secretary. The Fund remained in place until March 1916, when employment conditions improved to the extent that it was closed.[15] Assistance to unemployed clerks was also provided via training, maintenance grants and use of an employment bureau.[16]

This provides a valuable insight into the economic distress suffered by white-collar workers. Unemployment within this group is seldom associated with the period prior to the inter-war years. Lockwood's pioneering study highlighted that it was generally assumed that office workers could rely on being permanently employed prior to the 1920s.[17] Subsequent studies have disputed the extent of unemployment among clerks before 1914; however, the experience of unemployment among female clerks during the war years has remained largely hidden within these debates.[18]

---

14 AWCS, Annual report, 1914–15.

15 Dorothy Evans, *The AWCS* (unpublished notes, 1927), p. 1; AWCS, Annual report, 1915–16.

16 Evans, *The AWCS*, p. 1.

17 David Lockwood, *The Blackcoated Worker* (London: Unwin University Books, 2nd edition, 1966), pp. 55–6.

18 Anderson argued that although clerks did not figure prominently among the unemployed in Victorian society they 'were not immune from the seasonal distress and changes in the trade cycle which affected other workers', citing the example of the trade depression in 1878–79. Anderson, *Victorian Clerks*, pp. 65–6. By comparison, Heller's more recent study concludes that there is no strong evidence to support the view that clerks were increasingly vulnerable to unemployment prior to 1914, although he notes that one group that did suffer was older clerical workers. Heller, *London Clerical Workers*, pp. 104–6.

By locating the experience of this group of white-collar workers within the broader context of female unemployment in the early war years, the case of the AWCS sheds further light on the impact of the outbreak of war on women's job security and unemployment.

By 1915, with increasing numbers of men joining the army, it was reported that women were 'urged by the Government, by public bodies and by employers to come forward and take the places of men withdrawn from office work'.[19] For the AWCS, however, this surge in work posed a new problem: how to protect their members' work as a skilled occupation. Historiography on labour relations during the First World War has drawn attention to the suspicion of male workers, their trade unions and employers to the introduction of women into manual work and industrial production as they sought to ensure future working conditions were protected for skilled men.[20] There is a tendency to perceive this as an issue associated only with the trade unions representing male, manual workers. The case of the AWCS, however, illustrates wider concerns regarding women war workers undermining working conditions, as skilled women also vented distrust of untrained or semi-skilled female workers. The AWCS was concerned that a 'flood' of these office workers on a low rate of pay would result in employers using this as a basis for their ideas 'of the capacity of the woman worker'. It feared this would lead to the long-term 'lowering of the whole status of the clerical profession', making it 'impossible for even the well qualified worker to command an adequate salary'.[21] The AWCS considered it a duty to protect clerical work as a skilled occupation. It used a variety of measures to preserve work for those who were qualified. For example, its War Emergency Fund Committee did not just assist unemployed skilled clerks to find work but also acted as a 'means of directing away from clerical work to other openings many women who were entirely unadapted for such work'.[22] Its Information and Intelligence Bureau not only gave advice regarding clerical training and opportunities, but also provided information regarding other jobs, to place some 'girls in work other than clerical and for which they were far more suitable'.[23]

19 'The need for combination among women clerical workers', reprinted from the *Liberal Women's Review*, July 1915.

20 Gerard J. DeGroot, *Blighty: British Society in the Era of the Great War* (London: Longman, 1996), pp. 130–2; Cathy Hunt, 'Sex versus class in two British trade unions in the early twentieth century', *Journal of Women's History*, 24(1) (2012), 97.

21 AWCS, *Special Organising Campaign Among Women Clerical Workers* (no date).

22 AWCS, Annual report, 1915–16.

23 AWCS, Annual report, 1916.

Recent scholarship on women's experience of the First World War has moved away from 'watershed' interpretations. Instead, new perspectives seek to uncover a more complex gender terrain that was navigated during the war, with, for example, research focusing on aspects of motherhood, citizenship and propaganda.[24] The AWCS's campaigns for equal opportunities for skilled female clerks provide an insight into how this terrain was negotiated in the non-manual sector. The organisation's wartime campaigns were complex and at times contradictory, illustrating how new forms of feminist presence aimed at shifting assumptions about women's role in the workplace existed alongside traditional assumptions about the position of men. On the one hand, the AWCS confidently protested against female clerks employed in government departments being restricted to the lowest-paid posts, arguing that it was in the best interests of the country, as well as the women themselves, to utilise the expertise of skilled female workers.[25] The AWCS considered equal working conditions, hours and pay between skilled female and male clerks to be essential. For example, much indignation was aroused within the AWCS when female staff working on temporary government contracts received half the bonus awarded to their male colleagues, and the AWCS was successful in getting the issue raised in Parliament.[26] On the other hand, however, the AWCS admitted that it was difficult to 'arouse the sympathies of the general public' to the cause of the skilled woman clerk during wartime.[27] Facing hostility to arguments around equal opportunities, it is clear that the AWCS was not convinced that there had been any change in the wartime gender terrain within white-collar work.

Perhaps this goes some way to explaining why an organisation committed to furthering the interests of women clerical workers at one point argued the case for equal pay on the basis that it would be beneficial to men rather than women. It was stated that it would be 'most unfair' to the men returning from military service to office work if the employment of women during the war had 'lowered the standard of remuneration in the banks, insurance offices and public departments where they are now

---

24 Susan R. Grayzel, *Women's Identities at War: Gender, Motherhood and Politics in Britain and France During the First World War* (London: Longman, 1999); Nicolette F. Gullace, *'The Blood of Our Sons': Men, Women and the Renegotiation of British Citizenship During the Great War* (London: Palgrave Macmillan, 2002); David Monger, 'Nothing special? Propaganda and women's roles in late First World War Britain', *Women's History Review*, 23(4) (2014), 518–42.

25 AWCS, Minutes of the Executive Committee, 7 September 1915.

26 AWCS, Annual report, 1916; *House of Commons Debates*, 26 June 1916, vol. 83, cc. 537–8, and 4 July 1916, vol. 83, c. 1362.

27 AWCS, Annual report, 1914–15.

employed'.[28] Rather than promoting career opportunities for women, in this instance the AWCS was at risk of being seen to do this only to protect working conditions for men. This illustrates how far, even in an occupation such as clerical work, where women had been present from the late nineteenth century, questions of women's employment continued to be shaped by the priorities of male workers. However, the work of the AWCS also signals growing attempts to rework this tradition by canvassing support for a discourse of equality within the workplace. Although campaigns for equal pay had been part of the women's movement since the nineteenth century, the renewed vigour of such campaigns – and the re-focus on equality in opportunities within the workplace – is often associated with equality feminists of the inter-war years. Yet the case of the AWCS demonstrates that a heightened awareness of this discourse of equality did form part of the feminist movement during the war years, thus providing an important platform for the construction of feminist activism in the inter-war decades.

Feminism and the AWCS

The history of inter-war feminism remains controversial. Some historians claim that conflicting priorities weakened the women's movement and fractured feminist goals, thus signifying the movement that advocated women's rights was in retreat.[29] One of the ways such accounts have been challenged is by questioning what constitutes 'achievement' and being wary of placing unrealistic expectations and demands on the movement.[30] For some, a key reason why the women's movement of the 1920s is considered weak is because it is juxtaposed with an image of a unified movement in previous years.[31] Scrutinising the interactions between the AWCS and

---

28 AWCS, *Special Organising Campaign Among Women Clerical Workers*.
29 Susan Kingsley Kent, 'The politics of sexual difference: World War I and the demise of British feminism', *Journal of British Studies*, 27(3) (1988), 232–53; Hilda Kean, 'Searching for the past in present defeat: the construction of historical and political identity in British feminism in the 1920s and 1930s', *Women's History Review*, 3(1) (1994), 57–80.
30 Maria DiCenzo, '"Our freedom and its results": measuring progress in the aftermath of suffrage', *Women's History Review*, 23(3) (2014), 421–40; Gail Braybon, 'Winners or losers: women's symbolic role in the war story', in Gail Braybon (ed.), *Evidence, History and the Great War: Historians and the Impact of 1914–18* (Oxford: Berghahn Books, 2003); Pat Thane, 'What difference did the vote make? Women in public and private life in Britain since 1918', *Historical Research*, 76(192) (2003), 268–86.
31 As noted by Joanne Workman, 'Wading through the mire: an historiographical study of the British women's movement between the wars', *University of Sussex Journal of Contemporary History*, 2 (2001), 1–12.

other organisations concerned with women's rights during the war years and the war's immediate aftermath provides an insight into connections and ruptures within the movement immediately before the 1920s. Tracing some of these divisions challenges perceptions of a unified movement, providing another means by which narratives of a 1920s 'demise' (in part based on a preconception of a previous unity) are somewhat undermined when placed into a broader chronological perspective.

As Martin Pugh puts it, 'in one sense the events of August 1914 proved to be decisive: in a matter of days the "sex war" had been swamped by the Great War'.[32] Although the outbreak of war brought a hiatus in campaigns for women's right to vote, other aspects of this 'sex war' continued as women's trade union leaders persisted with campaigns on women's pay and workplace injustices. The AWCS was engaged in these campaigns and supported organisations providing women with a voice in the workplace, not only those in non-manual occupations but also those that represented female workers more widely. It paid subscription fees to the National Union of Women Workers and the Women's Trade Union League, distributed literature from the Fabian Women's Group and sent representatives to meetings of the Women's Industrial Council.[33] Addressing an AWCS meeting in 1916, Margaret Bondfield (already well established in the trade union and feminist movement) commended the AWCS for engaging with the wider women's rights movement:

> the professional women will recognise their happiness and content are bound up in that of those now described as sweated women workers.... If I had felt you were going to build up an organisation ... to get more opportunities for those who had already great opportunities, I am afraid I should not have been in the least interested in you.[34]

It is tempting to suggest a shift in the AWCS's policy during the war to one more engaged with the wider women's rights movement. This would fit with an image of various women's groups, including trade unions, working in unity during the war. As Deborah Thom has argued, women trade unionists were closely linked with a variety of causes, including the network of campaigners seeking to improve conditions for women

---

32 Martin Pugh, *Women and the Women's Movement in Britain 1914–2000* (Basingstoke: Macmillan, 2nd edition, 2000), p. 7.
33 AWCS, Annual report, 1915–16; Annual report, 1917; Minutes of the Executive Committee, 27 April 1915; Minutes of the Executive Committee, 4 February 1918.
34 AWCS, 'Address given by Miss Margaret Bondfield at a meeting held by the Association of Women Clerks and Secretaries at Essex Hall, Strand, on 1 March 1916', pp. 1–2.

in the 'sweated trades' as well suffrage organisations.[35] Such a line of argument, however, ignores the fact that these groups were not necessarily supportive of causes central to the women's movement. This can be seen in relation to the AWCS. For example, in 1917 the executive committee was invited by the National Union of Women's Suffrage Societies to participate in a deputation to the Prime Minister to discuss the extension of the franchise to women. Although a fierce campaigner for women's rights, the AWCS declined, on the basis that suffrage did not form part of its official remit.[36] Likewise, the Women's International League for Peace and Freedom requested that the AWCS send a representative to its conference to draft resolutions affecting women for consideration at the Peace conference.[37] The AWCS declined, citing 'pressure of work'.[38] Although it may be tempting to view a period of international military conflict as one which witnessed greater unity within the women's movement (because aspects of the 'sex war' were scaled back), as the example of the AWCS illustrates, conflicting priorities within the movement remained. It is clear that discrepancies within the women's movement concerning how to move the cause of women's rights forward did not pertain solely to the 1920s; nor was this necessarily indicative of irreconcilable differences between different groups. Rather, the relationship of the AWCS with other women's organisations is suggestive of a movement responsive to the needs of a wide variety of women, where various components prioritised different causes at different times as they reacted to broader political and economic agendas.

The value to women at the beginning of the twentieth century of maintaining organisations solely for female workers was reappraised in the aftermath of the First World War. Most notably, the National Federation of Women Workers (NFWW) – a female-only trade union – chose not to maintain its sex barrier and merged with the National Union of General Workers (a mixed-sex organisation) in 1921. Cathy Hunt argues that the alliance between men and women workers was welcomed by the NFWW; its earlier single-sex policy, though it might appear at first glance to be a separatist, feminist politics, was in fact a necessity of circumstance 'to ensure that women were able to take their place within the trade union movement'.[39] The AWCS, however, continued to operate as a single-sex

35 Thom, *Nice Girls and Rude Girls*, p. 27.
36 AWCS, Minutes of the Executive Committee, 5 February 1917.
37 On the history of the British section of the Women's International League for Peace and Freedom, see Sarah Hellawell's forthcoming PhD thesis.
38 AWCS, Minutes of the Executive Committee, 10 March 1919.
39 Hunt, *The National Federation of Women Workers*, p. 22.

organisation, avoiding amalgamation with the National Union of Clerks (NUC), which, although male dominated, was a mixed-sex union.[40] Working relations between women-only and mixed-sex organisations inform debates concerning the importance of how a distinctly female identity could be construed, and also sheds light on dissident voices who felt mixed-sex groups were unable to represent women's rights sufficiently.

As a trade union representing both men and women, the NUC felt it had 'always stood for equal pay' and that a separate women's organisation was therefore unnecessary.[41] Amalgamation was driven by concerns that increased numbers of women in the clerical occupation during the war would be used by employers to 'depress the conditions of service'; unified workers would combat this.[42] The AWCS, although concerned with issues of pay and conditions, ultimately considered it was not in the interests of the Association 'to sink their identity by joining the NUC'.[43] For the AWCS, maintaining a separate identity for female clerks remained a key priority as a means to represent women's interests satisfactorily. During amalgamation discussions in February 1919, the AWCS was adamant that any working arrangements needed to provide a clear identity for women. Its demands included a special women's department, a proportion of seats on the executive reserved for women, and female representatives in all delegations to the Trades Union Congress (TUC).[44] Negotiations between the two organisations ultimately broke down. This was somewhat unsurprising, given that relations between the AWCS and NUC in this period were often strained – for example, in 1916 the AWCS accused the NUC of publicly misrepresenting its policies on pay in *The Clerk* (the NUC's monthly periodical).[45] Their relationship continued to be strained following failed attempts at amalgamation, most notably in late 1919, when the NUC tried to block the AWCS's affiliation to the TUC. It did so partly because it claimed that the AWCS was not a 'real trade union', based on its low subscriptions, its preference to avoid strike action and its recent change from an association to a trade union – and also, partly,

---

40 The AWCS remained a separate, single-sex organisation until the Second World War, when it amalgamated with the NUC (known as the National Union of Clerks and Administrative Workers after 1920), creating the Clerical and Administrative Workers Union in March 1941.

41 NUC, Twenty-eighth annual report and balance sheet, 1919, p. 8. The papers of the NUC used in this chapter are located at the Working Class Movement Library.

42 NUC, Twenty-sixth annual report and balance sheet, 1917, p. 19; NUC, Twenty-fifth annual report and balance sheet, 1916, p. 11.

43 AWCS, Minutes of the Executive Committee, 7 February 1916.

44 *Ibid.*, 3 February 1919.

45 *Ibid.*, 6 November 1916.

because it was a women-only organisation.[46] Herbert Elvin, General Secretary of the NUC, stated that it was against the principle of the TUC to affiliate any body that was organised on sex lines. The retort from the AWCS's representative drew attention to the inequality inherent in this line of argument, stating: 'Mr Elvin surely did not mean to suggest that the Amalgamated Society of Engineers should be ejected from Congress because it did not open its ranks to women'.[47] The AWCS affiliated to the TUC, with just one voice of opposition, namely that of the NUC.

Although operating in a dramatically changed international environment as a result of the war, as far as the AWCS was concerned campaigning for women's rights meant maintaining a gender-based organisation, as it had done prior to 1914. This was at odds with policies adopted by some other groups that continued to believe that improvements in the conditions and status of women workers would be best achieved through their membership of mixed-sex trade unions. Yet, in the context of these campaigns for women's rights in the workplace, it can be seen that these approaches – though different – were not necessarily indicative of inherent weaknesses within the wider women's movement. This largely concurs with revisionists' accounts which criticise those who imply that feminism before and after the war was constructed around one dominant view of social and sexual relationships.

Activism in the immediate aftermath of the First World War

The NUC was highly sceptical of the activism practised (or, more specifically, not practised) by the AWCS, particularly its desire to avoid strike action. In 1919, *The Clerk* published a copy of a letter, allegedly signed by the Assistant Secretary of the AWCS, detailing that: 'this Association is not of a militant character, though we have a Sustentation Fund, *but there is no probability of using it*, and hope it may never be necessary, for we believe that strikes are very much to be avoided.' In response, *The Clerk* quipped that the AWCS was 'evidently an Association for Perfect Ladies',[48] alluding to its lower-middle-class membership base. Although it was not prepared to use, or even threaten, strike action as a means to

---

46 AWCS, Minutes of the Executive Committee, 29 September 1919; TUC, *Annual Congress Report, 1919* (London: TUC, 1919), p. 206. The AWCS became a trade union in 1916. The NUC had affiliated to the TUC in 1908.

47 AWCS, Minutes of the Executive Committee, 29 September 1919; see also TUC, *Annual Congress Report, 1919*, p. 207.

48 *The Clerk*, October 1919, p. 114 (italics in original).

advance the interests of its members, the AWCS actively responded to the
challenges it faced in the immediate aftermath of the war. By exploring
this, it is possible to obtain an insight into women's work-based activism.
Although much has been written on the 'backlash' against women in the
war's aftermath, the resistance to this by lower-middle-class women has
received relatively little attention. Crossick's seminal 1978 study of the
lower middle class in Britain prior to 1914 highlighted that associations of
any kind among this group 'were the exception. The lower middle class in
this period was expanding yet, at the same time, frustrated and lonely.'[49]
Subsequent work sought to challenge and explain this apparent lack of
collective identity, which has been considered particularly weak compared
with the levels of cohesion found in France and Germany. For example,
Savage demonstrated how patterns of male career mobility among bank
workers in Britain prevented a distinct lower-middle-class identity from
forming (as men's careers progressed from clerical to managerial roles,
made possible by routine clerical work being 'hived off' to women). The
position women occupied in organisations for clerical workers prior to
1914 has been explored in subsequent studies.[50] Where there is less research
is in organised responses to challenges faced by this group of non-manual
workers in the immediate aftermath of the war.

Towards the end of the conflict thousands of women from a range of
occupations (including munitions workers, tram conductors and farm
workers) lost their jobs. Protests by women factory workers against being
laid off had little effect.[51] What of women who had occupied non-manual
posts during the war? In 1917, an article in *Gregg Shorthand Magazine*
was optimistic about the future employment prospects for female office
clerks. Airing concerns that 'when the boys come home again it will be
a case of "Sorry, girls, but we don't want you anymore. Close the door
as you go out, please"', the article concluded with the author stating:
'When the war is at an end there will be work and to spare for us all'.[52]
The AWCS did not share this optimism and was more apprehensive about
the impact of post-war reconstruction. In creating a land fit for (male)

49 Geoffrey Crossick, 'The emergence of the lower middle class in Britain: a discussion',
   in G. Crossick (ed.), *The Lower Middle Class in Britain* (London: Croom Helm, 1978),
   p. 27.
50 Savage, 'Career mobility and class formation'; Susan D. Pennybacker, *A Vision for
   London 1889–1914: Labour, Everyday Life and the LCC experiment* (London: Routledge, 1995); R. Guerriero-Wilson, 'Women and the Scottish Clerks' Association: from
   contempt to collegiality', *Scottish Economic and Social History*, 23(1) (2003), 26–42.
51 Susan R. Grayzel, *Women and the First World War* (London: Routledge, 2002), p. 106.
52 *Gregg Shorthand Magazine*, August 1917, p. 208.

war heroes, women workers suffered, and female clerks were among these. *The Woman Clerk* attributed this to employers' perception that 'all women clerks arrived with the war, and must, therefore, go with the peace'.[53] This became evident in the shifting attitudes following the hostilities towards female clerks on temporary contracts in the Civil Service. The campaigns initiated by the AWCS to protect these workers did not include strike action; however, that is not to say they were not active in challenging hostile working conditions. In March 1919, representatives from the AWCS went to Downing Street to meet with Bonar Law as part of a deputation of women workers.[54] The AWCS submitted various suggestions aimed at preventing further unemployment among these female clerks, including transferring temporary clerical workers to the permanent Civil Service and a training scheme for those suitable for other professions.[55] The AWCS took up individual cases where members had been dismissed from government service with very limited notice (normally only one week) and took collective action by sending a deputation to meet with the Prime Minister, Lloyd George, to campaign for one month's notice or a month's pay in lieu of notice.[56] In this it had some success, and a full month's notice (with a month's warning where possible) was given to temporary government clerks, which the AWCS claimed benefited some 10,000 women.[57] The campaign brought the AWCS greater recognition among temporary clerks in the Civil Service. Membership increased more than threefold in the aftermath of the war, which the AWCS attributed to the influx of large numbers of temporary women clerks.[58]

Much of the historiography exploring public anxiety about women in the workplace at the end of the war focuses on the position of women in manual work and in jobs which, prior to the war, were undertaken mainly by men.[59] Through the prism of the AWCS it is possible to gain an insight into attitudes towards women in non-manual occupations in which they had participated prior to the war, as in the case of clerks, and thus to highlight the complex positions women in paid employment occupied in the minds of public at this time. This is perhaps most clearly demonstrated

---

53 *The Woman Clerk*, spring 1923, p. 9. *The Woman Clerk* was the journal of the AWCS.
54 Bonar Law had been Chancellor of the Exchequer until two months prior to this meeting. At the point the deputation met with him, however, he still had political influence as leader of the Conservative Party and Leader of the House of Commons.
55 *The Times*, 29 March 1919, p. 8.
56 AWCS, Annual report, 1920; *The Times*, 31 January 1920, p. 9.
57 AWCS, Annual report, 1920.
58 AWCS, Annual report, 1919.
59 Braybon, *Women Workers in the First World War*; Thom, *Nice Girls and Rude Girls*; DeGroot, *Blighty*.

by the tension and anxiety caused by an AWCS campaign to support female bank clerks in 1919. It was reported that the Bank Officers' Guild 'intended to press for the expulsion of women clerks from banks'.[60] Male bank workers claimed that there was a tendency for women employed temporarily during the war to be made permanent, 'to the detriment of Service men seeking re-employment', and in some cases long-serving male clerks returning from the army were placed in an 'impossible' position subordinate to women, leading to their resignation.[61] Other reports in the press were more threatening, including one from a bank clerk which simply said 'discharge the women and put them back into domestic life, or there will be trouble'.[62] In the face of these challenges, members of the AWCS's Executive Committee, authorised by women bank clerks, held a number of mass meetings before presenting a programme to the directors of the London banks. This included demands for the retention of as large a number as possible of the temporary women clerks on terms fair to them and their permanent colleagues, along with equal conditions of entry, pay and opportunities, regardless of sex.[63]

The AWCS, however, carefully tried to ensure that its arguments for equality did not run counter to the wave of public sympathy for the ex-serviceman. The reworking of the AWCS's central campaign message on equal opportunities for women, from one of equality between the sexes to one emphasising that this would not be detrimental to the ex-servicemen, reflected political shifts of the period concerning the position of war heroes in post-war Britain. Its shift in focus can be understood in the context of the Pre-War Practices Act and the re-assimilation of servicemen into civilian life. The Secretary of the AWCS, Dorothy Evans, clarified to the press that 'none of the women complained when called upon to give up their posts to discharged Service men'.[64] Instead, the AWCS's campaign was aimed at drawing attention to the fact that trained women were losing their jobs to men who had not been service personnel or who had not previously worked in offices. In situations where women were taking jobs previously held by men who had joined the forces it was emphasised that these jobs belonged to those who had perished in the war and would not be returning.[65] This campaign was also constructed around the proposition that trade unionism provided essential protection for both sexes. For

---

60 *Manchester Guardian*, 7 November 1919, p. 7.
61 *Daily Mail*, 31 October 1919, p. 5.
62 *Daily Mail*, 7 November 1919, p. 5.
63 *Daily Express*, 7 November 1919, p. 7.
64 *Daily Herald*, 7 November 1919, p. 6.
65 *The Woman Clerk*, December 1919, p. 2.

the AWCS, it was specifically the 'non-union' ex-servicemen who played a role in undermining working conditions and who 'certainly help[ed] the more reactionary employers to bring down wages'.[66]

Yet this is not to suggest that the AWCS was fully supportive of the trade union movement or the wider labour movement. During its campaign to support female bank clerks, the AWCS reiterated that it would not be using strikes as a 'weapon' to advance the interests of its members, a stance which, as previously mentioned, was criticised. This raises questions more broadly about the AWCS's ambivalent attitude towards some aspects of the labour movement and the political left. The AWCS lost members from at least one of its branches when it applied for registration as a trade union (in 1916), and although some AWCS members felt that the Labour Party was the only party representing and uniting workers 'by hand or by brain', no decision on the motion to affiliate to the Labour Party was taken when it was raised at the AWCS annual delegates' conference.[67] Perhaps its position as an organisation representing lower-middle-class women made it uncomfortable with certain aspects and policies of a labour movement largely dominated by working-class men. In a period noted for industrial militancy within the labour movement,[68] for the AWCS an emphasis on training, deputations to MPs and mass meetings represented a more attractive means of framing its discourse on activism.

Keeping up appearances: clothing and the construction of the female worker

Research into the backlash against working women following the end of the war has drawn attention to the 'venom' aimed at those in uniforms, as public opinion shifted rapidly from approval of their work to the expectation that it would be given up to make way for returning war heroes.[69] Uniforms made these women a particularly identifiable group and the object of public anger and hostility. For these women, including

---

66 *The Woman Clerk*, January 1921, p. 13.
67 AWCS, Minutes of the Executive Committee, July 1916; *The Woman Clerk*, May 1922, p. 5.
68 Chris Wrigley, 'The state and the challenge of labour in Britain 1917–20', in Chris Wrigley (ed.), *Challenges of Labour: Central and Western Europe 1917–1920* (London: Routledge, 1993), pp. 262–88.
69 Lucy Noakes, 'Demobilising the military woman: constructions of class and gender in Britain after the First World War', *Gender and History*, 19(1) (2007), 143–62; Gullace, '*The Blood of Our Sons*', p. 158.

munitions workers, members of the auxiliary services and bus conductors, clothing was easily linked with a specific wartime job. The armies of
clerical workers were not uniformed workers in the same sense; however,
their clothing and appearance did attract attention both during and after
the war. Their dress exemplified wider currents concerning the creation of
a distinctly feminine identity for lower-middle-class women and one that
provided new ways of discussing their suitability for work.

In the late nineteenth century, clerical work was considered a suitable
occupation for middle-class women as it did not cause the loss 'of those
feminine graces, of dignity, of delicacy, of reserve'.[70] Zimmeck emphasises
this, explaining that '[i]t was clean. It was dainty.' Moreover, she notes
that 'it allowed women to dress nicely'.[71] During the First World War,
certain expectations about appearance were not confined to a discourse of
'feminine graces', but could also be linked to the ability to carry out work
efficiently. For example, *Gregg Shorthand Magazine* advised how particular
items could affect work rate. It claimed that 'office managers have discovered that of two typists of equal ability the girl with loose sleeves or
bare wrists will do from ten to twenty-five per cent. more work than the
one whose wrists are hampered by tight sleeves or stiffly starched cuffs'.[72]
For lower-middle-class women seeking clerical work, appearance and dress
were linked not just to the ability to work effectively, but to their ability
to work at all. Commenting on the period of unemployment during the
economic depression following the war, *The Woman Clerk* noted that 'the
lot of the unemployed woman clerk is indeed pitible' (*sic*) and advised
these women to hide their poverty and 'keep up appearances', noting that
as soon as a woman 'begins to do otherwise her chances of getting employment begin to decrease'.[73]

Female munitions workers were often criticised in the press for re-
ceiving what was considered an exceptionally high wage (and therefore
they were often accused of benefiting from the war) and, what is more,
spending this frivolously on expensive and unnecessary items of clothing.[74] Although this tends to be primarily associated with factory workers,
the case of female clerks demonstrates how anger manifested in discourses

---

70 Lady John Manners, *Employment of Women in the Public Service* (1882), pp. 50–1, quoted
   in Meta Zimmeck, 'Jobs for the girls: the expansion of clerical work for women, 1850–
   1914', in A. V. John (ed.), *Unequal Opportunities. Women's Employment in England
   1800–1918* (1986), p. 158.
71 Zimmeck, 'Jobs for the girls', p. 158.
72 *Gregg Shorthand Magazine*, July 1916, p. 194.
73 *The Woman Clerk*, spring 1923, p. 9.
74 Braybon, *Women Workers in the First World War*, p. 166.

on appearance was also directed towards these non-manual workers. Press reports concerning the role of these women in post-war society drew attention to their appearance to express growing concerns regarding gender boundaries in the workplace. For example, during the AWCS's campaign in 1919 to demand the retention of female bank clerks taken on during the war, newspapers provided descriptions of the way they dressed. They described 'the almost-flapper bankers, in their woolly jumpers and jaunty tam-o'-shanters' and those with 'the most unmathematical bobbed heads'.[75] These were images depicting fashionable young women; their appearance was symbolic of a perceived frivolous attitude towards 'pin money' employment. This ultimately resulted in resentment of them by some male bank clerks. There was a perception that they had profited from the war (in terms of both financial reward and career opportunities), and were unwilling to give back jobs to men returning from the Front. As one male bank clerk reported to the press, these were 'Chocolate dollies who are now beginning to cry have been earning £7 to £10 a week during the war'.[76] Within this context, clothing and appearance became closely entwined with wider unease regarding women's role in post-war society.

The AWCS was keen to highlight that not all clerks worked for 'pin money'. In campaigning for higher salaries for its members, the AWCS was clear that it was not doing so 'in order that members who live at home and do not pay their way may have more money to spend on powder and chocolates (as has been suggested)',[77] but so that women could earn a wage. Sometimes this was expressed using language of equal opportunities, for example a 'woman's right to live by clerical work' or a right to contribute her 'full share towards the public service'.[78] On other occasions it was expressed as a necessity for women lacking other means of support (i.e. a father or husband). Although the war strongly influenced the development of women's rights, the barriers women continued to face were all too apparent in the legislation passed in its immediate aftermath. The introduction of the Representation of the People Act (1918) failed to enfranchise women on the same terms as men and the Sex Disqualification (Removal) Act (1919) applied only to certain occupations and in practice did nothing to address marriage bars. Unlike the middle-class voluntary associations which, as Helen McCarthy has shown, only half-heartedly shaped an awareness of gender inequalities into political consciousness

---

75 *Daily Express*, 7 November 1919, p. 7.
76 *Daily Mail*, 7 November 1919, p. 5.
77 *The Woman Clerk*, December 1920, p. 66.
78 *The Woman Clerk*, February 1921, p. 26, December 1920, p. 66.

among its members,[79] the AWCS drew attention to what it considered the double standards of the period. Acknowledging that at least some women had been enfranchised, it objected to the continuing 'unsurmountable restrictions' women were subjected to, which were made all the more difficult in a period when 'many thousands of women ha[d] to earn their own living' and many supported dependants, a fact the AWCS felt 'never seems to trouble the powers that be'.[80]

Dress formed part of the discourse through which the AWCS articulated one campaign for greater equality: that concerning unequal pay between men and women. A strategy used by the AWCS was to highlight the expense incurred in obtaining the business attire expected of women in this work. Although not a uniform *per se*, there were certain expectations around what was considered suitable business-wear for clerks and secretaries and this formed an essential part of their working identity. In their research on English travelling salesmen, Andrew Popp and Michael French refer to a style or code of dress these men voluntarily adopted and how their dress spoke to a masculinity linked with occupational autonomy and independence. Katrina Honeyman, too, highlights how the popular practice of suit-wearing among men helped to create a masculine identity, in this case one that symbolised values of hard work and sobriety.[81] For female clerks and secretaries, certain items of clothing, including the business frock, white blouse, serge frock and wool cardigan, were felt by the AWCS to be essential wear for the workplace. These signified a feminine working identity that spoke of respectability and professionalisation, and they were one of the visible markers that distinguished these women from manual workers. The cost of such a uniform – specifically the relatively higher costs for a woman, given the pay differences between men and women – also highlighted inequalities between the sexes. To draw attention to this, the AWCS's campaign on the cost of living listed the outgoings faced by female clerks, which included items of essential business dress – 'to provide appearance and health expected by City Employers'[82] – alongside other essential costs (for example lodgings, transport

---

79 Helen McCarthy, 'Service clubs, citizenship and equality: gender relations and middle-class associations in Britain between the wars', *Historical Research*, 81(213) (2008), 545.

80 *The Woman Clerk*, February 1921, p. 25.

81 Andrew Popp and Michael French, '"Practically the uniform of the tribe": dress codes among commercial travelers', *Enterprise and Society*, 11(3) (2010), 437–67; Katrina Honeyman, 'Following suit: men, masculinity and gendered practices in the clothing trades in Leeds, England, 1890–1940', *Gender and History*, 14(3) (2002), 426–46.

82 AWCS, *The Cost of Living for Women Clerical Workers: Some Facts and Figures* (London: AWCS, 1922), p. 11.

to the office and food). The AWCS published *The Cost of Living for Women Clerical Workers* in 1922, in which it concluded that the pay given to many women was insufficient to maintain healthy living and that large numbers of women clerks were 'underfed, underclothed and ha[d] inadequate recreation', although 'the single man working beside [his female colleague] on similar work shews a very much higher average personal balance owing to differential on the grounds of sex'.[83] Seen from this angle, clothing formed an integral part of debates regarding the working lives of lower-middle-class women in post-war Britain.

Conclusion

How does the case of the AWCS inform our understanding of the First World War's impact on women's employment and of work-based activism? The immediate effect of the war on women workers is often discussed with reference to the initial unemployment suffered in trades that traditionally employed large numbers of women (for example domestic service, jewellery, millinery and dressmaking). Shifting the focus to the impact of the outbreak of war on non-manual, clerical workers can help to shed light on women's experiences of war and the support mechanisms utilised during periods of economic hardship. This group of non-manual workers also faced job insecurity and unemployment. By examining the AWCS, this chapter has illustrated how women addressed this situation with practical measures, and also how the focus of campaigning shifted as the war progressed, moving from women's pay and conditions to defending women's right to work.

Consideration of the campaigns organised by the AWCS can also help to inform research on the impact of the First World War on the women's movement more widely. Revisionist work has challenged 'pessimistic' perspectives which suggested that the onset of the war gradually resulted in many feminists embracing an ideology that foregrounded women's separate sphere, claiming that, in doing so, the women's movement lost some of its ability to advocate equality and justice. In turn, revisionist discourses explore how campaigns around citizenship, women's industrial welfare and feminist peace activism formed a means of engaging women in debates on gender relations and women's roles during the war and in post-war society. The work-based activism of the AWCS provides an opportunity to reappraise these accounts in light of women's paid employment in the

---

83 *Ibid.*, p. 1.

non-manual sector, thus providing a case study through which to explore the capacity to challenge and shape the gender terrain in this important sector of the labour market. The chapter illustrates how the AWCS sought equality in training, pay and conditions, and in this sense sought to shift assumptions about women's career opportunities. Yet, at the same time, it also failed to challenge traditional gender roles. For example, although often viewing clerical work as a career opportunity for women, the AWCS did not challenge well established discrimination against the employment of married women. The organisation provided a platform for feminist ideology that was reformist rather than revolutionary.

The work of the AWCS challenges perceptions of an apparent absence of a collective identity among the lower middle classes in Britain. Representing lower-middle-class clerks and secretaries (although the AWCS argued that some of its campaigns for equality were of benefit to female clerical workers beyond the membership base), the capacity for collective action was structured around an occupational identity. The AWCS tried to carve out a position for itself as an organisation for professional women. It compared itself to other professional organisations, such as those for schoolmistresses and nurses,[84] and, in encouraging female clerks and secretaries to join the organisation, asserted that 'it is no more below her to unite with other shorthand-typists in self-defence than it is for their chief to join his Employers' Union, a solicitor to join the Law Society, or a doctor the British Medical Association'.[85] This was, however, an identity that was challenged as the war drew to a close. The backlash against female industrial workers who had occupied jobs previously undertaken by men has received much attention within the historiography on the impact of the First World War on gender relations. Whereas female clerks and secretaries took on additional responsibilities and roles during the war, women had been present in clerical work since the late nineteenth century. When viewed in this context, the gender-based hostility faced by the AWCS in the immediate aftermath of the war sheds light on ways this 'backlash' was encountered and navigated in an occupation that had seen female participation for some forty years.

Acknowledgements

I would like to thank Daniel Laqua, Keith Laybourn, John Shepherd and the reviewers for their valuable comments and suggestions, and the staff at the Working Class Movement

---

84 *The Woman Clerk*, December 1919, p. 10.
85 *The Woman Clerk*, December 1920, p. 16.

Library and the Trade Union Congress Library Collections, London Metropolitan University, for their assistance. Thanks are also due to the Arts and Humanities Research Council for financial support for this research. Chris Wrigley's enthusiasm and passion for modern British history have been hugely influential in shaping the direction of my own research. My interest in twentieth-century clerical workers originated from discussions with him some years ago and I would like to thank him for his invaluable support and guidance over the years.

10

'We never trained our children to be socialists': the next Lansbury generation and Labour politics, 1881–1951[1]

JOHN SHEPHERD

The Christian socialist, pacifist, feminist, anti-imperialist and republican, George Lansbury MP – at the helm of the Labour Party from 1932 to 1935 – was imprisoned twice for his political beliefs.[2] He recalled that in 1913 at least six children from his large family were in prison or in danger of going to jail for their political activities during the struggle for 'votes for women'.[3] The eldest, Annie and William, served one and two months respectively in Holloway and Pentonville for window breaking during Sylvia Pankhurst's East London suffrage campaign. William's release was celebrated in his father's fledgling newspaper, the *Daily Herald*, including pictures of William's suffragette wife, Jessie, and their baby daughter, Esme.[4] Edgar Lansbury and his wife Minnie were discharged by the magistrates with a caution after a peace demonstration at the East India Dock gates addressed by Tom Attlee, a member of the Independent Labour Party (ILP) and brother of Clem Attlee, later Labour leader and Prime Minister. Sylvia Pankhurst observed that 'Edgar Lansbury was arrested for no particular reason, and Minnie for running beside him'.[5]

---

1 The quote in the chapter title is taken from George Lansbury, *My Life* (London: Constable, 1928), p. 77. The date range spans the birth of George's first child, Bessie, to the opening of the Festival of Britain exhibition, which featured the celebrated Lansbury housing estate in Poplar as a 'Living Architecture' project.

2 John Shepherd, 'George Lansbury', in Charles Clarke and Toby S. James (eds), *British Labour Leaders* (London: Biteback Publishing, 2015), pp. 145–66.

3 George Lansbury, *Looking Backwards – And Forwards* (London: Blackie, 1935), p. 110.

4 *Daily Herald*, 19 February 1913; see also Barbara Wimslow, *Sylvia Pankhurst: Sexual Politics and Political Activism* (London: UCL Press, 1996), pp. 42–4.

5 E. Sylvia Pankhurst, *The Home Front: A Mirror to Life in England During the World War* (London: Hutchinson, 1932), pp. 431–2.

The police arrested Edgar's sister, Daisy, disguised as Sylvia Pankhurst in a bizarre escapade to help the suffragette leader evade the police and address a rally elsewhere.[6] Afterwards, ever conscious of the value of publicity, the Lansburys sought legal counsel's advice on a civil prosecution of the police for false arrest.[7]

During a time of fervent political dissent the Lansbury family was always highly visible in East End radical politics, particularly in support of women's suffrage and in the peace movement during the Great War. In 1912 when Speaker Lowther dismissed their father from Parliament after his angry confrontation with Prime Minister H. H. Asquith over the forcible feeding of suffragette prisoners. Lansbury finally surrendered his Bow and Bromley parliamentary seat to force a by-election in 1912, mainly over votes for women – the only case in British politics of a MP resigning from Parliament over women's rights. Suffrage and anti-suffrage societies poured into the working-class constituency. Despite an ardent campaign conducted by his family and political allies, defeat to the Conservative and anti-suffragist Reginald Blair kept Lansbury out of Parliament until 1922.[8]

After returning from a traumatic emigration to Queensland, Australia, in 1884–85, Bessie and George Lansbury and their growing family had finally settled in Bow – first at 105 St Stephen's Road and then at 39 Bow Road, a stone's throw from their family-owned sawmill and timber yard. Their children were brought up close to the East End locations of the major industrial struggles of the late nineteenth century and early twentieth century, such as the strikes of the Bryant & May match women, the London dockers and the pre-war years of 'Labour unrest'. Situated in the heart of the Bow and Bromley constituency, the family home became an important centre of political campaigning, as well as a pioneering 'citizens' advice bureau' for all and sundry.[9]

From an early age, Bessie and George Lansbury's children were caught up in their father's turbulent political life. Edgar later recalled early family memories of GL – as he was often affectionately known – as an itinerant propagandist for socialism waving his unfurled red flag from the Great Eastern express as it thundered close by their Bow home on his journeys

---

6 Lansbury, *My Life*, pp. 125–6. See also John Postgate and Mary Postgate, *A Stomach for Dissent: The Life of Raymond Postgate* (Keele: Keele University Press, 1994), p. 102.

7 *Daily Herald*, 6 September 1913; George Lansbury Papers (LP), British Library of Political and Economic Science, Volume 7, fols 139–40, E. C. Rawlings (solicitor) to George Lansbury, 15 November 1913.

8 John Shepherd, 'George Lansbury and the Bow and Bromley by-election of 1912', *East End Record*, no. 19 (1998), 2–8.

9 Raymond Postgate, *The Life of George Lansbury* (London: Longman, 1951), p. 104.

to preach the new religion.[10] They witnessed a political odyssey that took him from Gladstonian Liberalism through the ranks of the Marxist Social Democratic Federation and eventually to the ILP and the British Labour Party, where he spent most of his political life. Raised in a socialist family, the Lansbury children saw at first hand many of the defining moments that brought new recruits to the fledgling Labour Party.[11] Also Bessie played a crucial role in providing a stable home base while her husband was away. In one way or another, the majority of this Lansbury generation was destined to play a part always on the left in British politics, often in association with married partners and with others in the wider family circle. Yet, in his 1928 autobiography, George Lansbury boldly claimed: 'We never trained our children to be socialists'.

This chapter explores the predominant influences of family, social class and community that shaped the career paths, and the political and social activism, of Bessie and George Lansbury's family in British politics. With merger through marriage, particularly of the Lansbury and Postgate families, the next generation achieved recognition not only in politics but also in many other fields in public life, particularly journalism, business and entertainment, in Britain and abroad. While the focus is primarily on the members of the Lansbury family in the history of the Labour Party, attention is also given (in some brief case studies) to the contributions of marriage partners, their descendants and associates in their extended family networks.

The family of Bessie and George Lansbury

Bessie (Elizabeth) (1860–1933) and George Lansbury (1859–1940) were married on 29 May 1880. Their happy marriage lasted over fifty years and produced twelve children, born between 1881 and 1905 – eight girls and four boys – with ten surviving into adulthood.

- Bessie, 1881–1909
- Annie, 1882–1952
- George, 1884–89
- William, 1885–1957
- Edgar, 1887–1935

---

10 Edgar Lansbury, *George Lansbury: My Father* (London: Sampson Low & Marston, 1934), p. 34.
11 For more on this theme, see Daniel Weinbren, 'Labour's roots and branches', *Oral History*, 24(1) (spring 1996), pp. 30–1, 33–4; also Daniel Weinbren, *Generating Socialism: Recollections of Life in the Labour Party* (Stroud: Sutton Publishing, 1997).

- Dorothy, 1890–1973
- Daisy, 1892–1971
- Nellie, 1896–1980
- Doreen, 1899–1902
- Constance, 1899–1983
- Violet, 1900–72
- Eric, 1905–69

Like many contemporary families, at a time of high infant mortality, the Lansbury household suffered its personal tragedies. Four Lansbury children predeceased their parents: George at age five, in 1889, Doreen (one of twins) at two, in 1902, and their eldest child, Bessie, at twenty-eight, in 1909.[12] In 1922 Minnie, Edgar's first wife, died aged thirty-two, after imprisonment during the Poplar rates revolt. Her husband passed away from cancer at forty-eight, in 1935, shortly after his mother and five years before his father.

As we have seen, George Lansbury later declared that he and his wife 'never trained our children to be socialists'. Edgar, a lifelong socialist, confirmed that his parents did not compel the children in any way to adopt their political views. However, he added that they 'liked to think that we should all grow up into good Socialists'. Edgar believed the freedom of thought and behaviour he and his siblings enjoyed could be seen in the widely different paths they took as adults.[13]

Their father observed that his offspring learned socialism (as he did) 'in the school of experience'. His autobiography reveals how his work as a socialist propagandist in the Marxist Social Democratic Federation (SDF) in the 1890s was a significant influence on his family in acquiring socialist attitudes, beliefs and values:

> All of them went about with me to propaganda meetings, selling literature and generally taking part in the work of helping to gather money for the cause. One time in Victoria Park, the families of my comrades in the Social Democratic Federation and my children sold thousands of copies of *Merrie England* when that fine book was sold at a penny. Books I read they read.[14]

---

12 Bessie (junior) and her husband, Harry Haverson, had three children. In 1938 their daughter, Irene, married the journalist and politician John Dugdale. Elected to Parliament in 1941, he was appointed Parliamentary Private Secretary to Clement Attlee in 1945 and Minister of State at the Colonial Office in the post-war Labour government.

13 Edgar Lansbury, *George Lansbury*, p. 137.

14 George Lansbury, *My Life*, pp. 77–8. Robert Blatchford's *Merrie England* was a book on socialism, published in 1894. The penny edition sold over 750,000 copies within twelve months and two million copies overall in Britain and abroad.

George also noted how his children had engaged in public debates with the theosophist Annie Besant and Stanton Coit of the Ethical Society.

Lansbury's membership of the SDF, when Bessie and their children also moved over to the Ethical movement in London, coincided with a total loss of his deep Anglican faith, about which he said little.[15] He briefly acknowledged that 'Only for a year or two did they as children come under the influence of heterodoxy … [when] they attended the Ethical Sunday School in Bow, organized and conducted by the prince of teachers F. J. Gould'.[16] However, Edgar calculated that his father lost his religious faith for about ten years.[17]

The Lansbury family and the British Communist Party

In 1920 the Communist Party of Great Britain (CPGB) was formed, by which time the surviving Lansbury children were now in their adult years with an age range spreading over twenty-three years. While their parents never formally joined the CPGB they did display a continuing political interest and sympathy for Bolshevism – which probably cost Lansbury a Cabinet post in Ramsay MacDonald's first Labour government in 1924. He twice visited Russia, in 1920, meeting Lenin and other leading Bolsheviks, and again in 1926 with his wife, Bessie, to see their daughter, Violet.[18] According to Edgar, his mother, though 'a quiet spoken, gentle, retiring woman', was a staunch internationalist and an unflinching champion of the Soviet regime.[19]

Five of Bessie and George's family were among the members of the new party in the early 1920s before eventually moving to the Labour Party. However, Annie and Violet were loyal Communists, probably throughout their lives.[20] In addition, other members of the Lansbury family had

15 East London Ethical Society, *First Annual Report* (1890); I. D. MacKillop, *The British Ethical Societies* (Cambridge: Cambridge University Press, 1986).

16 See F. J. Gould, *The Life-Story of a Humanist* (London: Watts, 1923), pp. 76–8.

17 Postgate, *The Life of George Lansbury*, p. 55 (quoting Edgar).

18 George Lansbury, *What I Saw In Russia* (London: Leonard Parsons, 1920); John Shepherd, *George Lansbury: At the Heart of Old Labour* (Oxford: Oxford University Press, 2002), pp. 183–4; for a critical view of Lansbury's 1920 visit to Bolshevik Russia, see F. M. Leventhal, 'Seeing the future: British left-wing travellers to the Soviet Union, 1919–31', in M. W. Bean (ed.), *The Political Culture of Modern Britain: Studies in Memory of Stephen Koss* (London: Hamilton, 1987), pp. 212–13.

19 Edgar Lansbury, *George Lansbury*, pp. 140–1.

20 Violet Lansbury was always a staunch Communist. However, Lansbury descendants doubt whether Annie Lansbury remained a Communist. Interview with Terry Lansbury

Communist partners. Nellie Lansbury, Daisy's younger sister, for a time was employed at the CPGB office and was business manager at the King Street headquarters and later at Collet's left-wing bookshop in London. She married Albert Hawkins, a Communist councillor in Edmonton. As a leading member of the CPGB, he had belonged to the National Union of Ex-Servicemen and various other groupings, such the British Socialist Party, that had been one of the political factions forming the new party.[21]

In 1920 Violet, the youngest of the Lansbury daughters, was also a foundation member of the CPGB and remained an ardent and highly committed Communist.[22] In recalling her parents' support for the Russian Revolution, she observed that 'living in my father's home, I could not fail to know a great deal more than my school friends of what was going on in the British Labour movement'.[23] After elementary school, she was briefly her father's secretary before working in 1920 as a substitute shorthand typist with the newly arrived members of the Russian Trade Delegation in London (later the Soviet Embassy). Andrew Rothstein, also a founding member of the CPGB and the London correspondent for the Soviet news agency ROSTA (later TASS), was an influential associate.

After working at the Soviet embassy for five years, Violet travelled to Russia in October 1925 to study at the University of Svedlovsk, where she developed her formidable knowledge of colonial Russian. She also became an interpreter and later a renowned translator of various Russian publications, including Tolstoy's works. In 1940 her popular autobiography, *An English Woman in the U.S.S.R.*, provided an account of her life in the Soviet Union and her reflections on Russian society and politics. Violet initially stayed in Russia for thirteen years, and arranged her parents' visit in 1926 to review the development of the Soviet Union since the Bolshevik Revolution.[24] Her first husband was Igor Reussner, Professor of Agriculture. In 1938 she married Clemens Palme Dutt, brother of the

---

(Lansbury grandson), 9 December 2015. Oliver Postgate (Lansbury grandson) describes Annie as a 'Christian fundamentalist'. Oliver Postgate, *Seeing Things: An Autobiography* (London: Pan Books, 2001), p. 33.

21 Kevin Morgan, Gidon Cohen and Andrew Flinn, *Communists and British Society 1920–1991* (London: Rivers Oram Press, 2007), p. 11: Keith Laybourn and Dylan Murphy, *Under the Red Flag: A History of Communism in Britain, c. 1849–1991* (Stroud: Sutton Publishing, 1999), pp. 42–5.

22 Violet was probably the unnamed Lansbury daughter who defiantly hid under her bed to protest against the family leaving the Ethical Sunday School and to being baptised in the Anglican Church. Postgate, *The Life of George Lansbury*, p. 55.

23 Violet Lansbury, *An English Woman in the U.S.S.R.* (London: Putnam, 1940), pp. 3–4.

24 *Ibid.*, pp. 122–52.

Marxist intellectual R. Palme Dutt.[25] With her second husband she lived in Moscow and London after the war, working as a journalist with a column on the *Daily Worker*.[26]

Edgar and Minnie Lansbury

Edgar Lansbury was the third son born to Bessie and George Lansbury, in 1887, following their abortive emigration in 1884–85. After school, Edgar briefly joined the Civil Service, but in 1901 joined the family timber business with his brother William. In 1912 Edgar was elected to Poplar Council as a Labour candidate, where he served alongside his father. With other family members Edgar had been actively involved in the so-called 'Suffragettes by-election' campaign in Bow and Bromley in 1912.

According to Raymond Postgate, his brother-in-law was closest in his family to his father and the most likely member of the Lansbury family to follow in George Lansbury's political footsteps.[27] Father and son discussed politics almost daily. In 1918, for example, Edgar advised his father to tread carefully as the editor of the *Daily Herald* in his comments on the international response to US President Woodrow Wilson's 'Fourteen Points'. Edgar wrote: 'You know better than I do that it is always worth while waiting a couple of days before praising or blaming a statesman unduly'.[28] Edgar joined the CPGB when it was founded in 1920 and, like his father, served as Mayor of Poplar, in 1924–25, only the second Communist in Britain to hold the position. He also became the chairman of the Poplar guardians and headed up their struggle with the government over poor relief.[29]

25 Kevin Morgan, 'A family party? Some genealogical reflections on the CPGB', in Kevin Morgan, Gidon Cohen and Andrew Flinn (eds), *Agents of the Revolution: New Biographical Approaches to the History of International Communism in the Age of Lenin and Stalin* (Oxford: Peter Lang, 2005), pp. 186–9; Kevin Morgan, *Bolshevism and the British Left: Labour Legends and Russian Gold* (London: Lawrence & Wishart, 2006), pp. 97–100.

26 *Morning Star*, 14 March 1972.

27 Postgate, *The Life of George Lansbury*, p. 59. Terry Lansbury (grandson) fought two general elections as the unsuccessful Labour candidate in February and October 1974 in Gainsborough, where his grandfather in December 1933 had suffered a near-fatal accident that sidelined him from the party leadership for seven months. Interview with Terry Lansbury, 9 December 2015.

28 George Lansbury Papers, Vol. 8, fol. 4, Edgar Lansbury to George Lansbury, 26 January 1918.

29 *Workers' Weekly*, 15 February 1924.

In 1914 Edgar had married Minnie Glassman, the daughter of Polish immigrants, Annie (née Goodkindt) and Isaac Glassman, a Jewish coal merchant. Born in 1889 in Stepney, Millie trained as a London County Council schoolteacher. An ardent feminist and a highly popular figure in the East End, she campaigned tirelessly for women's suffrage and for war pensions, assisting Poplar widows, the war-wounded and orphan children. As Honorary Secretary she had helped Sylvia Pankhurst establish the East London Federation of Suffragettes (ELFS). The ELFS was supported by most of the Lansbury family (with Edgar as Honorary Treasurer) in promoting women's suffrage, feminism and socialism. In March 1916 the ELFS became the Workers' Suffrage Federation, and Minnie became its Assistant Secretary in 1918.

After the First World War, the Lansbury family continued to play a highly significant role as party officials and activists in the constituency-level politics of the Poplar Labour Party. As Duncan Tanner and Matthew Worley have both shown about Labour's changing political profile, the party's expanded membership base, especially in the new women's sections, was particularly evident in Poplar, Woolwich and Bermondsey, where there was a tradition of women's militant political activity.[30]

In the 1919 municipal elections, based on a trebled local electorate, Labour for the first time gained control of Poplar Borough Council, with thirty-nine out of the forty-two councillors and with the Christian social-ist and pacifist George Lansbury elected as Poplar's first Labour Mayor (who declined to wear the trappings of the mayoral robes). At the outset, the Labour-controlled council co-opted Minnie as one of the four new aldermen (the terminology then for both men and women). Minnie and Edgar, along with Julia and John Scurr, and Nellie and George Cressall, formed some of the formidable political partnerships on the council, de-ploying their municipal powers to promote socialism in their battle against poverty, deprivation and unemployment. The Labour council introduced a £4 minimum wage for employees, started housing and health schemes and campaigned for the equalisation of the rates between the wealthy boroughs and the poorer boroughs like Poplar.[31]

---

30 Duncan Tanner, 'Labour and its membership', in Duncan Tanner, Pat Thane and Nick Tiratsoo (eds), *Labour's First Century* (Cambridge: Cambridge University Press, 2000), pp. 249–52; Matthew Worley (ed.), *Labour's Grass Roots: Essays on the Activities of Local Labour Parties and Members, 1918–45* (Aldershot: Ashgate, 2005), pp. 1–4; see also K. Y. Stenberg, 'Working-class women in London politics, 1894–1914', *Twentieth Century British History*, 9 (1998), p. 337 n. 47.

31 Shepherd, *George Lansbury*, chapter 11; Janine Booth, *Guilty and Proud of It! Poplar's Rebel Councillors and Guardians 1919–1925* (London: Merlin Press, 2009).

Edgar was prominent in the Poplar Council's bold refusal to levy precept rates, which led eventually to the High Court and the imprisonment of thirty councillors for six weeks.[32] In 1921 their rebellious stance mobilised large numbers on the streets and outside Brixton and Holloway prisons in their support.[33] Edgar and Minnie – arrested with the paterfamilias, George – were among the thirty who willingly went to prison to battle for their local community against the government and the national Labour Party leadership.[34] Other Lansbury family members and their friends were embroiled in the Poplar struggle. Daisy, who tireless campaigned outside Brixton and Holloway, wrote to ask the Bishop of Oxford to use his influence with the Home Secretary. She protested: 'In the first place, it is a miscarriage of justice to arrest a few individual members of a corporate body and imprison them as common debtors ... something must be done, and done quickly.'[35]

As George Lansbury observed, the six-week imprisonment adversely affected the councillors' health, particularly Minnie. After her release from Holloway she developed influenza and pneumonia and died tragically aged thirty-two.[36] One of the five jailed women, she was the youngest of the Poplar councillors.[37] Once again, Poplar witnessed large crowds, including women, outside her house to march with her coffin to her funeral.[38] At the crematorium, the Reverend Kitkat paid tribute to Minnie's greatest qualities: 'her intellectual power ... her extraordinary liberal mind and generosity of disposition ... her love of justice, and depth of her sympathy, for suffering and sorrow'.[39]

---

32 Raymond Postgate, *The Life of George Lansbury*, p. 217.

33 See Annie Lansbury, 'The Poplar story', *Daily Worker*, 7 May 1951.

34 For the imprisonment of the Poplar councillors, see John Davis, 'Poplar councillors (*act.* 1919–1922)', in *Oxford Dictionary of National Biography* (Oxford: Oxford University Press, May 2015); Noreen Branson, *Poplarism 1919–1925: George Lansbury and the Councillors' Revolt* (London: Lawrence & Wishart, 1979); Shepherd, *George Lansbury*, chapter 11.

35 Home Office Papers, The National Archive (TNA), HO 45/11233, Daisy Lansbury to the Rt. Rev. Bishop of Oxford, 5 September 1921.

36 *Daily Herald*, 7 January 1922.

37 George Lansbury also declared that imprisonment in 1921 had contributed to the premature deaths of councillors Julia Scurr, Sam March, Charlie Sumner, James Rugless and Joseph O'Callaghan within a few years of their release. George Lansbury, *My Life*, p. 157.

38 For photographs of impressive community support during the Poplar rates revolt, see Minnie Lansbury '*en route* to Holloway Prison' and the Poplar Councillors 'marching to the High Court and Possibly Prison' in Shepherd, *George Lansbury*, photographs 15 and 16, between pages 204 and 205.

39 *East London Advertiser*, 7 January 1922.

Nearly two-thirds of the Poplar population worked in the local economy and formed important parts of neighbourhoods and kinship groups.[40] In taking up his ministry Father St John B. Grose commented on the unique relationship between the Poplar councillors – virtually all local manual workers – and the community who elected them and who they strove so hard to represent.[41]

Daisy Lansbury and Raymond Postgate

Born in 1892, Daisy Lansbury was brought up in a large late-Victorian family of seven sisters and four brothers. She later wrote: 'Nobody asked me what I wanted to be when I grew up. There was very little choice. Two of my sisters became teachers for a short time, another entered the Civil Service in one of the low-grade positions which were open to women.' After leaving elementary school at fourteen, Daisy remained at home for three years, 'learning housekeeping under a skilled and exigent mother' before entering a Civil Service training school – Clark's College – which led to her working as a secretary for her brother, Edgar, for a while in the family timber business.[42]

However, for more than twenty years, Daisy took on the highly significant role as her father's private secretary, first at the *Daily Herald*, before becoming closely involved with his political and parliamentary career in Britain and abroad.[43] Even when, as Labour leader in 1933, George at seventy-four suffered a near fatal broken leg and was seemingly out of action for seven months, Daisy was active in keeping him in touch with Labour Party business. From 1936 to 1939, when her father undertook his peace crusade in the United States, Canada and Europe, Daisy was a crucial figure in planning the arrangements.[44]

Daisy later wrote affectionately about her parents and, in particular, with insight about the influences of community and class on the family's upbringing in the East End. In particular, the Lansbury children soon recognised that their father – who held every elective office – from poor law guardian to East End MP and later Cabinet minister and party leader – was unlike other fathers. George's indefatigable work as

---

40 Weinbren, 'Labour's roots and branches'.
41 St J. B. Groser, *Politics and Persons* (London: SCM Press, 1949), p. 12.
42 Daisy Postgate, 'The private secretary', in Margaret I. Cole (ed.), *The Road to Success: Twenty Essays on the Choice of a Career for Women* (London: Methuen, 1936).
43 Postgate and Postgate, *A Stomach For Dissent*, pp. 102–4.
44 Shepherd, *George Lansbury*, pp. 310–15.

a travelling socialist propagandist in Britain had made him more than a
well known local figure. Daisy shrewdly observed: 'Not that he was not an
extremely affectionate and interested father, but rather he belonged to the
people as well as to us and that we were part of something much bigger
that the mere family'. Aged three years, Daisy was too young to recall her
father as the Marxist SDF parliamentary candidate in the 1895 election,
but other members of the family mentioned his campaign so frequently
that she often thought she did remember it.[45]

Daisy also emphasised the active involvement of the Lansbury children
when their father regularly preached the merits of socialism in the 1890s
in nearby Victoria Park, an important meeting place for political and
religious speakers:

> On Sundays he would take us into Victoria Park, where he addressed
> meetings for the Social Democratic Federation. With my two brothers and
> three sisters there were enough of us to make a crowd, and like a snowball
> it soon gathered more. My father had an enormous voice [after learning]
> elocution at the Band of Hope in Whitechapel when he was a boy.... He
> also believed in what he wanted to say and so said it with all the force and
> assurance of a convinced Socialist of forty years of age.[46]

The young daughter soon took great pride in selling the SDF newspaper,
Justice. 'I can still remember the feeling of satisfaction I had when I took
my first penny and handed over a copy of the paper ... I shouted "*Justice*
one penny" ... and frequently had to be told to shut up because I was
drowning [out] my father...'.[47] It proved the beginning of a lifelong career
of an ardent suffragette and politically active feminist and socialist.

Daisy also provided her own observations of life from their family
home in the East London in her articles on 'A child in George Lansbury's
house', published in *The Fortnightly* in 1948. With a young and growing
family the Lansburys were often in difficult financial circumstances,
particularly as Lansbury's political propaganda work was largely unpaid.
George had worked as a veneer dryer in the timber yard owned by his
father-in-law, Isaac Brine, but even when he took over that family business
after the death of Isaac in 1897, the Lansburys' standard of living and way
of life remained for some time largely similar to that of their working-class
neighbours in the East End.[48]

45 Daisy Postgate, 'A child in George Lansbury' house', *The Fortnightly*, 164 (July–
    December 1948), 393.
46 *Ibid.*, 394.
47 *Ibid.*
48 Margaret I. Cole, 'Daisy Lansbury (1892–1971): socialist', in Joyce Bellamy and John
    Saville (eds), *Dictionary of Labour Biography* (London: Macmillan, 1975), vol. 2, pp. 303–4.

During the Great War, as a member of the socialist Bow Brigade associated with left-wing groups, including the ILP, the Labour Research Department and the National Guilds League, Daisy met her future husband, the intellectual Raymond Postgate, the eldest son of Cambridge classical scholar and university don, John Percival Postgate (known as JP), who promptly disinherited his pacifist offspring as well as his sister Margaret (later Dame Margaret Cole) and always refused to meet Daisy.[49]

Besides being a founder member of the CPGB and editor of the *Communist*, Raymond Postgate was an important historian, classicist and later editor of *Tribune* and eventually gourmet editor of *The Good Food Guide*. After leaving the CPGB in May 1922 he remained a prominent figure on the non-communist left in the 1920s and 1930s. In particular, his marriage to Daisy made him a very close associate and first biographer of his father-in-law, George Lansbury, with whom he worked on the *Daily Herald*, *Lansbury's Labour Weekly* and other books and publications.[50] Others connected with Lansbury during the *Daily Herald*'s early days were a group of principled young journalists – known collectively as 'Lansbury's Lambs' – many of whom were associates of the wider Lansbury family.[51]

Like most members of the Lansbury family, Raymond Postgate also shared Bessie and George Lansbury's unflinching pacifism.[52] During the Boer War, when Lansbury had contested Bow and Bromley in the 1900 election as an SDF candidate he and his young family had been attacked on the streets as 'pro-Boers'.[53] In October 1935 the Lansbury family gathered at the Labour Party conference to support George before he resigned as the pacifist party leader after his famous clash with the trade union leader Ernie Bevin.[54] In the First World War, as a student at the University of Oxford, Postgate had applied unsuccessfully for exemption

49 Postgate and Postgate, *A Stomach For Dissent*, pp. 102–5.

50 J. M. Bellamy, *rev.* Mark Pottle, 'Postgate, Raymond Williams (1896–1971)', in *Oxford Dictionary of National Biography* (Oxford: Oxford University Press, 2004), pp. 996–7.

51 Included among these young associates were Francis Meynell, G. D. H. Cole, Gerald Gould, William Mellor and Harold Laski. Shepherd, *George Lansbury*, chapter 8.

52 The youngest Lansbury child, Eric, had not shared his parent's pacifism – certainly not by 1940, when he joined the Royal Engineers as a driver. David Graham Pole, George Lansbury's close friend, reassured the worried Eric that his father in his last weeks had confessed that as a young man he might also have joined up. David Graham Pole Papers, Borthwick Institute of Historical Research, York, UL/5/6/9, David Graham Pole to Eric Lansbury, 18 December 1940.

53 Postgate, *The Life of George Lansbury*, pp. 53–4.

54 For the Lansbury family leaving the Dome at Brighton after the crucial conference debate in 1935 between Lansbury and Bevin, see Shepherd, *George Lansbury*, photo-graph 26, between pages 204 and 205. See also Shepherd, 'George Lansbury', pp. 162–6.

from military service and spent time in Oxford Prison.[55] In the Second World he worked as a civil servant and served in the Home Guard.

As Dr Janet Shepherd demonstrates in chapter 7 of the present volume, on the Progressive League, the early 1930s were crowded times politically, with new committees and various left-wing groupings of intellectuals and others wishing to revive Labour fortunes after the collapse of the Second Labour government and Labour's catastrophic defeat in the 1931 general election. Around 1933 Raymond Postgate, and other family members, became involved in the Socialist Film Council (SFC), established by the Socialist League and supported by Fabians, Labour MPs and trade unionists. A member of the Lansbury circle and close associate of Edgar Lansbury, the wealthy Rudolph Messel, was the main figure behind the venture to produce propaganda films on socialism for the British labour and co-operative movements.[56] In founding the SFC, Messel was joined by Raymond Postgate and the film critic Terence Greenidge, with Postgate setting out the aims of the new body: 'Making films to make socialists'.[57] The initiative brought together various members of the Lansbury and Postgate families and their associates, both in front of and behind the cameras. George Lansbury, the new leader of the Labour Party, served as the SFC President.[58]

Film-going was an increasingly important leisure activity for many in the inter-war years. The SFC aimed to produce silent 16mm films as alternatives to the weekly newsreels at local cinemas, to offset their bias. As John Postgate observed, his father Raymond shared the views of many left-wing intellectuals that contemporary British and American films largely reflected capitalist outlooks and values.[59]

However, the SFC produced only three films: *What the Newsreel Doesn't Show*, *The Road to Hell*, about the 1930s means test, and *Blow, Bugles, Blow*. However, *What the Newsreel Doesn't Show* was not the beginning of a series but a disappointing single-reel production featuring building works

---

55 For Raymond Postgate's pacifism in the First World War and his difficulties with the military authorities and his Tory father, see Postgate and Postgate, *A Stomach For Dissent*, chapters 4 and 5.

56 As the youngest director of the *Daily Herald*, in 1920 Rudolph Messel had famously smuggled Russian jewels into Britain in a box of chocolate creams to outwit the British Secret Service. Unknown to George Lansbury, the escapade implicated his son, Edgar. See Shepherd, *George Lansbury*, pp. 187–8.

57 Stephen G . Jones, *The British Labour Movement and Film, 1918–1939* (London: Routledge & Kegan Paul, 1987), p. 142.

58 John Postgate, 'Raymond Postgate and the Socialist Film Council', *Sight and Sound*, winter 1990–91, pp. 19–21.

59 *Ibid.*

during the Five-Year Plan in the Soviet Union, and scenes of London and Glasgow slums as well as May Day celebrations in Britain, with George Lansbury at a socialist rally in Hyde Park. The rudimentary nature of the SFC film production was evident in various appeals to borrow 16 mm projectors (including one from Sir Stafford Cripps) and in the recruitment of family and friends, including Daisy Lansbury and celebrated novelist Naomi Mitchison, as cast members. Yet, the dilettante Messel secured some publicity for *The Road to Hell* by filming scenes in the Lansbury family house in the East End.[60]

Dorothy and Ernest Thurtle

In 1912 Dorothy Lansbury married Ernest Thurtle in Philadelphia, USA, the beginning of a significant and long-lasting partnership on the left in British politics spanning the inter-war years and beyond the Second World War.[61] From the outset, Ernest told his future father-in-law, 'We are both looking forward to working together to forward our ideals ... logical trade unionists we believe in strength of unity all the way through'.[62]

From the early 1920s Dorothy and Ernest Thurtle were always associated with the impoverished working-class district of Shoreditch, close to the Lansbury family fiefdom of Poplar. They were both redoubtable and indefatigable campaigners in municipal and national politics. Dorothy was particularly recognised as a pioneer of women's rights, birth control, abortion law reform and family planning. Dorothy became General Secretary of Shoreditch Trades Council and Labour Party, was elected to Shoreditch Borough Council in 1925 and was subsequently Vice-Chairman of the Public Health and Finance Committee. For more than thirty years, Dorothy took a crusading interest in health and social welfare policy for her working-class community. In 1936 she became Mayor of Shoreditch, in the same year her father George was Mayor in nearby Poplar for the second time. In 1960 her long record of service to public life was recognised when she was honoured with the freedom of the Borough.

---

60 *New Clarion*, 27 May 1933, p. 486. On the SFC, see Bert Hogenkamp, *Deadly Parallels: Film and the Left in Britain, 1929–1939* (London: Lawrence & Wishart, 1986), chapter 4.
61 For biographical details of Dorothy and Ernest Thurtle, see Stephen Brooke, 'Thurtle (née Lansbury), Dorothy (1890–1973)', in *Oxford Dictionary of National Biography*, (Oxford: Oxford University Press, May 2006); Shepherd, *George Lansbury*; *The Times*, 23 August 1954 (obituary of Ernest Thurtle); Ernest Thurtle, *Time's Winged Chariot: Memories & Comments* (London: Chaterson, 1945).
62 Lansbury Papers, Vol. 6, fols 124–5, Ernest Thurtle to George Lansbury, 12 July 1912.

During the Great War, Ernest Thurtle had been commissioned and was severely wounded at Cambrai in 1917. After his harrowing experiences on the Western Front, he campaigned untiringly for the abolition of the death penalty for cowardice and desertion. He published two books on the topic: *Military Discipline and Democracy* (1920), with a preface by George Lansbury, and *Shootings at Dawn: The Army Death Penalty at Work* (1929). In 1930, despite the opposition of Lord Allenby and others, Ernest's long campaign, with support from T. E. Shaw (Lawrence of Arabia), was finally victorious. It was considered his greatest parliamentary success.[63]

After unsuccessful attempts to enter Parliament in 1918 and 1922, Ernest had become the Labour MP for Shoreditch in 1923, the start of a political career at Westminster that lasted almost thirty years. He was the Parliamentary Private Secretary to the Labour Minister of Pensions in 1924 and also in 1929, when George Lansbury became First Commissioner of Works in Ramsay MacDonald's second Labour government. Ernest held office as a Lord Commissioner of the Treasury from 1930 to 1931, although he lost at Shoreditch in Labour's most disastrous election defeat to date in 1931, when his father-in-law was the only surviving Cabinet minister on the Labour side. In 1935 Ernest returned to Westminster as the MP for Shoreditch and served the constituency until his death in 1954. During the Second World he had held the post of Minister of Information.[64]

After leaving the local elementary school, at fourteen Dorothy found employment as a clerk and accountant. Her political consciousness was sharpened in the ranks of the Women's Labour League (WLL), the ILP and the Women's Freedom League (WFL).[65] (Ernest had also joined the ILP before the First World War.) There were, however, divisions between Dorothy and her siblings (as well as her father) over suffragette militancy and violence. In 1913 William's two-month custodial sentence for illegal window-breaking had infuriated her. She brusquely advised her brother that his militancy might instead be spent on bettering conditions for the working class.[66] The radical American millionaire Joseph Fels, a naptha soap manufacturer who funded various Lansbury ventures, including the poor law and farm colonies, complained about Dorothy's censorious article on suffragette belligerency. He observed sharply: 'It is a pity that

---

63 Thurtle, *Time's Winged Chariot*, pp. 81, 93, 106–77, 110–11.

64 *The Times*, 23 August 1954.

65 Fenner Brockway, *Inside the Left: Thirty Years of Platform, Press and Parliament* (London: Allen & Unwin, 1942), pp. 26–7.

66 Esme Whiskin Papers (in private possession of the Lansbury family), Dorothy and Ernest Thurtle to William Lansbury, 2 February 1913.

any relative of yours should be so foolish as to condemn a thing without taking the trouble to understand what she is condemning'.[67]

In 1906 Dorothy had joined the National Union of Clerks (NUC), aged sixteen, where she met Ernest, who was Chairman of the London district council of the union. Their first major project was an important political tract on union activity, *Comradeship for Clerks*, which they co-authored in 1913.[68]

In 1910 George Lansbury had been elected as one of the three Labour councillors who formed the Labour bench on the London County Council (LCC). During this time, the LCC began to increasingly employ women clerks to replace boy labourers, as a new and cheaper form of labour in the clerical divisions. In 1911 the NUC established a Women's League on the LCC in its campaign against low pay. As an NUC leader, Dorothy was in the forefront of establishing 'equal pay for [the] same work' and argued for the 'right of [a] woman on the labour market ... to earn a living however she chooses'.[69]

Dorothy was ready to fight her corner in a male-dominated and misogynist party.[70] In 1926 she argued forcibly for equality for women:

> Women are still not regarded as human beings with equal rights and duties. And the reason for this seems to me to be found in the doctrine that the prime function of women is to bring forth children and perpetuate the race. It would be idle to deny that this is an important function that can only be performed by a female. Modern conditions have proved conclusively however that this is not necessarily a full-time occupation and in most cases should not be.[71]

As a married couple the Thurtles were key figures in campaigns for birth control and abortion law reform in the inter-war years. As Pat Thane has observed, the growing numbers and pressure of women was an important factor among the Labour pioneers who prepared the ground of social policy underpinning the post-1945 welfare state in Britain.[72] Their political

---

67 George Lansbury Papers, Vol. 7, fols 62–3, Joseph Fels to Bessie Lansbury, 21 June 1913.
68 Ernest Thurtle and Dorothy Thurtle, *Comradeship for Clerks: An Appeal for Organisation* (London: Clerk Publishing Society, 1913).
69 Dolly Lansbury, 'Equal pay for equal work', *Clerk*, February 1912, p. 25, cited in Susan D. Pennybacker, *A Vision for London 1884–1914: Labour, Everyday Life and the LCC Experiment* (London: Routledge, 1995), p. 43.
70 For George Lansbury's criticisms of the Labour Party, see Lansbury, *My Life*, pp. 268, 274.
71 Dorothy Thurtle, 'Women – an oppressed class', *Labour Woman*, May 1945.
72 Pat Thane, 'Labour and welfare', in Duncan Tanner, Pat Thane and Nick Tiratsoo (eds), *Labour's First Century* (Cambridge: Cambridge University Press, 2000), pp. 93–5.

activism in twentieth-century Labour politics demonstrated what could be achieved, albeit with somewhat limited progress, in a male-dominated political party with entrenched power structures.[73]

In 1912, in the United States, Ernest Thurtle and Dorothy Lansbury had written to George Lansbury on hearing of his Bow and Bromley by-election defeat – largely over the issue of votes for women. From across the Atlantic, they wondered how the male working-class electorate had reacted to the feminist suffrage campaigners who had invaded the constituency. Ernest wrote to his future father-in-law:

> The papers here said you were assisted by a great number many suffragists perhaps their presence in such numbers created a feeling of false security among the regular workers? Dolly [Dorothy] thinks this may have been the case.

He went on to comment:

> Indirectly your coming out & fighting in the way you have done will surely have a beneficial effect on the Labour Party unless they are past praying for, the fact you felt by principle & common honesty to come out and to make a fight is bound to cause all but the most care hardened to do a little hard thinking. If they think long enough they too may realise that in the Party as it stands there is no room for honest men.[74]

A few months later, Ernest wrote in similar terms to his mother-in-law, Bessie, on the imprisonment of her husband, George, and their children, which had made 1913 an *annus horribilis* for her. He sympathised:

> It is not cheerful to be left alone ... of course Mr. Lansbury is a wandering agitator *par excellence*, but I fancy you are rather glad of it, when you think of how he does agitate and what he agitates for.... By this time you will have one of your gaol birds out of the cage and the other won't have much longer to stay.[75]

---

73 Pat Thane, 'Women in the British Labour Party and the construction of state welfare, 1906–1939', in S. Koven and S. Michel (eds), *Mothers of a New World: Maternalist Politics and the Origins of Welfare States* (London: Routledge, 1993), pp. 343–77.

74 George Lansbury Papers, Vol. 6, fols 293–6, Ernest Thurtle to George Lansbury, 29 November 1912.

75 George Lansbury Papers, Vol. 7, fol. 30, Ernest Thurtle to Bessie Lansbury, 21 March 1913. In 1928 the Thurtles visited India, writing home: 'A visit to India throws a flood of light on many things. I wish you and mother could ... come [here] in the next cold season ... a liaison office between India & England is absolutely necessary'. For their support of Indian nationalism, see George Lansbury Papers, Vol. 8, fol. 309, Dolly (Dorothy) Thurtle to George (and Bessie Lansbury), 21 February 1928.

Birth control campaign

In the 1920s Dorothy Thurtle and her husband Ernest were prominent figures in the campaign for free birth control information for working-class women at welfare centres and were founder members of the Workers' Birth Control Group (WBCG) in the Labour Party.[76]

On 2 February 1926 Ernest Thurtle moved the Local Authorities (Birth Control) Enabling Bill in Parliament under the Ten-Minute Rule. *New Leader* proclaimed the bill to be 'the most important subject before Parliament this week'.[77] Thurtle argued it was a measure cutting across ordinary party lines; it would permit local authorities to provide free information on birth control to poor women that was previously available to only the wealthy and middle classes. In the London boroughs of Westminster and Chelsea, for instance, the birth rate was only 11.2 per 1,000 and 14.3 per 1,000 respectively, whereas in his constituency of Shoreditch, the poorest and probably most crowded district in the capital, the birth rate was more than twice such rates, at 25.0 per 1,000.[78] As a socialist he observed: 'I do say that knowledge which would enable working-class people to exercise a wide restriction to the size of their families would have an immediate ameliorative effect on the condition of those workers'.[79]

A Presbyterian minister, the Reverend James Barr Labour MP, a well known pacifist and socialist, spoke against Ernest's Private Member's Bill (only one speaker was permitted for the both sides on the Ten-Minute Bill). However, despite the backing of George Lansbury, Philip Snowden, Frederick Pethick-Lawrence and other leading Labour politicians, Thurtle's Bill was defeated by 167 to 81 votes. Twenty-eight Labour and Co-operative MPs had voted for the measure, but forty-five voted against. And only one woman MP from the small parliamentary contingent of women members in 1926, Ellen Wilkinson, was present in the Commons to support it.[80]

The defeat of her husband Ernest's Private Member's Bill brought a typically powerful response from Dorothy Thurtle about the treatment of women in a male-dominated Labour Party. She complained bitterly about the leadership on this aspect of social policy: 'The attitude of the

---

76 Clare Debenham, *Birth Control and the Rights of Women: Post-Suffrage Feminism in the Early Twentieth Century* (London: I. B. Tauris, 2014), pp. 32–3.

77 *New Leader*, 26 February 1926, p. 2.

78 *Parliamentary Debates, Official Report*, 9 February 1926, cols 849–50.

79 *Ibid.*, col. 851.

80 In 1926 there were only six women MPs at Westminster: Nancy, Viscountess Astor, Mabel Philipson, Katherine, Duchess of Atholl, Margaret Bondfield, Susan Lawrence and Ellen Wilkinson.

Labour Party Executive on the question of Public Welfare Centres and birth control was indefensible, and *shows clearly that the Executive has no use for women except to do the donkey work*'.[81] To which Dorothy added piercingly: 'Some of us do not agree that our function as Labour women is to help a few Labour men to make careers' and she called on women in the Labour Party to fight their corner in the women's sections and divisional party meetings.[82]

Bessie and George Lansbury apparently had not practised any of the more effective modern methods of birth control increasingly available to middle-class and upper-class parents and, to some extent, to the skilled working class. At the beginning of the twentieth century, many working people, especially men, refused to use methods such as the condom, through ignorance, cost or sheer masculine opposition.[83]

In his biography of his father-in-law, Raymond Postgate made only one brief reference to birth control. Although he did not mention Dorothy and Ernest Thurtle directly, he observed that George Lansbury around 1926 'made one exceptionally difficult change: he was convinced by the advocates of birth-control and the columns of his paper [*Lansbury's Labour Weekly* in 1925–27] altered accordingly. It cannot have been easy: he was the father of twelve children, he had a typically Victorian unwillingness to discuss sex, and the mechanics of contraception disgusted him. He was convinced, not by the economic arguments of the neo-Malthusians (which he distrusted), but by the argument that women should be allowed to control what happened to their own bodies. It was once again for him a matter of personal freedom.'[84]

However, in 1920 George Lansbury had given an early hint of a changing attitude with a public statement in the *Daily Herald*: 'I could not help wondering when men will become honest and above-board about the question of the sex relationship'. His new thinking on contraception reflected the important developments in Labour social policy in the 1920s in which members of the Lansbury family had been very influential.

With her husband Ernest, Dorothy was an invited member of the new governing body of the National Birth Control Council in 1930. The Ministry of Health in November 1930 issued the important Memo MCW 153, which permitted local authorities in Britain to provide guidance at

---

81 *New Leader*, 26 February 1926 (emphasis added).
82 *Ibid.*
83 Kate Fisher, *Birth Control, Sex and Marriage in Britain 1918–1960* (Oxford: Oxford University Press, 2006).
84 Postgate, *The Life of George Lansbury*, p. 242.

maternity and child welfare clinics on birth control to nursing and expect-
ant mothers on the grounds of health.[85]

Abortion law reform

In 1936 Dr Joan Malleson, a medical doctor interested in legalised
abortion, convened a meeting for supporters that led to the formation of
the Abortion Law Reform Association (ALRA).[86] Dorothy Thurtle joined
it, alongside other prominent birth control campaigners, Janet Chance,
Alice Jenkins and Stella Browne, as well as Dora Russell and Frida Laski.[87]
Dorothy became Vice-President of the ALRA, a position she held until her
retirement from public life in 1962.

Between 1937 and 1939 Dorothy Thurtle made her greatest contribution to abortion law reform as one of sixteen members of the Home Office
and Ministry of Health Inter-Departmental Committee on Abortion,
chaired by the barrister and Liberal MP Sir Norman Birkett. The Inter-
Departmental Committee, which included Lady Lucy Baldwin, the Prime
Minister's wife, Sir Rollo Graham-Campbell, the chief metropolitan
magistrate and Mr Bentley Purchase, the London coroner, held forty-
seven meetings in two years and took evidence from a wide range of
organisations as well as fifty-five witnesses.[88]

The only untitled woman on the committee, Dorothy, made an outstanding contribution to abortion rights, particularly for working-class
women, which drew on her personal and political experiences as a member
of the Lansbury family in the East End. Her participation in the battle over
birth control in Labour Party politics in the 1920s, as well as her health
and welfare work on Shoreditch Borough Council over many years, had
sharpened her feminism and made her a prominent local politician.[89] Her
socialism underpinned her role in working-class politics for the remainder

---

85 Margaret Howard, 'A pioneer of birth control', *FPA News*, May 1973, p. 4.

86 Lesley A. Hall, *Sex, Gender and Social Change in Britain Since 1880* (Basingstoke:
Palgrave Macmillan, 2013), pp. 113–14.

87 For the abortion campaign, see Ann Farmer, *By Fruits: Eugenics, Population, Control and
the Abortion Campaign* (Washington, DC: Catholic University of America Press, 2005).

88 H. Montgomery Hyde, *Norman Birkett: The Life of Lord Birkett of Ulverston* (London:
Hamish Hamilton, 1964), p. 462.

89 For the birth control campaign in the Labour Party in the 1920s, see Stephen Brooke,
*Sexual Politics: Sexuality, Family Planning, and the British Left From the 1880s to the
Present Day* (Oxford: Oxford University Press, 2011), chapter 2; Lesley Hoggart, *Feminist
Campaigns For Birth Control and Abortion Rights in Britain* (Lewiston: Edwin Mellen
Press, 2005).

of her life. Ahead of her time, Dorothy Thurtle's advanced views were not implemented until David Steel's Abortion Act of 1967.[90]

Highly active and formidable, Dorothy was only member of the Inter-Departmental Committee unmistakably in favour of abortion law reform. Yet, in accepting the invitation to serve, she later revealed she had 'an open mind on the question of abortion, and in fact knew very little about it'.[91] What compelled her onwards – which she shared with her parents, her husband and other family members – was her strong sense of social justice about her impoverished working-class constituents lacking advice and treatment compared with middle-class rich women with relative ease of access to contraception and abortion.

Moreover, in linking the question of abortion with contraception in the late 1930s, Dorothy observed: 'I have always been very active in pressing for contraceptive facilities for all women, and my sense of justice and equality has revolted against the unfairness of the existing lack of a system, which causes the poorest and weakest women to bear the burden of constant child-bearing'.[92]

During her two-years on the committee, hearing a wide range of evidence, Dorothy became increasingly aware of the gulf between herself and her fellow committee members.[93] 'I was disappointed and astonished that my colleagues would not even go so far as to propose that contraception should be made available for all women', she declared. When the final report recommended no major change in the abortion law, Dorothy authored her own dissenting minority report (of one), advocating the legalisation of abortion in certain cases, especially for women with high fertility rates (four or more pregnancies).[94]

The Inter-Departmental Committee did not wish to recommend that contraception be made available to all women. In response, an astonished Dorothy asked her colleagues about the size of their own families. The daughter from a working-class Cockney family of twelve children discovered that, of the fifteen committee members, four were from families of four or more. However, only one was from a family of five or more.

90 *Hackney Gazette*, 2 March 1973.
91 Dorothy Thurtle, 'Abortion – right or wrong?', *Eugenics Review*, 32(1) (April 1940), 11.
92 *Ibid.*, pp. 11, 14.
93 For the proceedings of the Inter-Departmental Committee on Abortion, see The National Archives, TNA/MH, 71/21, which includes Dorothy Thurtle's questioning of the evidence of Professor James Young and Dr Angus Macrae on abortion in Britain and Soviet Russia.
94 'Minority Report By Mrs. Dorothy Thurtle', in Ministry of Health and Home Office, *Report of the Inter-Departmental Committee on Abortion* (London: HMSO, 1939), pp. 139–51.

Legacies and memorials

In 1965 A. J. P. Taylor described George Lansbury as 'the most lovable figure in modern politics', a verdict widely endorsed by his family and often by his political opponents.[95] However, there were also at times considerable differences between Lansbury family members in terms of personality as well as political outlook, as witnessed by the younger members of the family. Professor Postgate has written that his father, Ray, 'refused to have Daisy's sister Violet Dutt (née Lansbury) visit our house in Finchley after she became chief fund raiser for the Communist *Daily Worker*. He also had trouble tolerating the right-wing Labour MP for Shoreditch, Ernest Thurtle....' His political differences with George Lansbury were quite as great, but his affection remained undiminished.[96]

In 1951 a new Lansbury estate was built in Poplar as a 'living architecture' scheme during the Attlee government's Festival of Britain to celebrate the lives of George and Bessie Lansbury. It remains alongside similar memorials in east London to their next generation, particularly the Minnie Lansbury Memorial Clock recently refurbished in Bow, the Dorothy Thurtle Memorial Garden in Shoreditch and in local schools and streets named after the Lansbury family.

Today the Lansbury name is also known through the world-famous Hollywood, Broadway and television actress Dame Angela Lansbury CBE, daughter of Edgar Lansbury and his second wife, Moyna MacGill. Angela's cousin, the animator, puppeteer and writer Oliver Postgate (1925–2008), the son of Daisy and Raymond Postgate, was the notable creator of highly popular children's television series over thirty years, including *Ivor the Engine*, *Bagpuss* and *The Clangers*, currently being successfully continued by his son Dan Postgate.

George and Bessie Lansbury's legacy was one of a continuing contribution to socialism, social provision and humanitarian causes in Britain that added to the evolution of citizenship and modern democracy. The Lansbury marriages into other families, particularly the Lansbury–Postgate connection, produced a next generation of diverse and rich talent in British public life. Bessie and George Lansbury's large family ensured a political legacy of socialist values, even though many of their children operated within, and married into, communism. What emerges from their lives is their great appreciation of their upbringing, a social awareness that

---

95 A. J. P. Taylor, *English History, 1914–1945* (Oxford: Oxford University Press, 1992), p. 191, n. 3.
96 John Postgate, 'Remembering Raymond Postgate: Revolutionary, Pacifist. Classicist & Gourmet' *Encounter*, vol. 71, no.3, September to October 1988, pp. 71–72.

enhanced and enriched George and Bessie Lansbury's contribution. Their role in the advance of socialism and in the history of the modern Labour Party was diverse and significant.

Acknowledgements

I would like to take this opportunity to express my whole-hearted thanks to Chris Wrigley and Keith Laybourn for their magnificent support, wise counsel and unfailing friendship over more than twenty-five years. I am also very grateful to members of the Lansbury and Postgate families for interviews: Dame Angela Lansbury CBE (granddaughter), Terry Lansbury (grandson); the late Esme Whiskin Lansbury (granddaughter); Nigel Whiskin MBE (great-grandson); Dan Postgate (great-grandson); and the late Professor John Postgate (grandson).

I am also most indebted to The National Archives, the British Library of Political and Economic Science and the Wellcome Institute Library for permission to quote from material for which they hold the copyright. Every effort has been made to trace copyright holders and to avoid infringement. I apologise unreservedly to any copyright holders who have been inadvertently overlooked.

11

Comrades in bondage trousers: how the Communist Party of Great Britain discovered punk rock

MATTHEW WORLEY

Speaking in June 1976, Paul Bradshaw, the editor of *Challenge*, the newspaper produced by the Young Communist League (YCL), surveyed the state of British youth culture.[1] Superficially, he reasoned, things did not look good. The youth movements that helped define the 1960s had fragmented; popular music appeared depoliticised. Although glam rock had briefly offered an interesting challenge to masculine stereotypes, and reggae continued to provide a militant protest transmitted to the 'heart of "Babylon"', nostalgia for a 'golden age of rock' was becoming ever more commonplace.[2] If anything, signs of reaction were creeping in, as indicated by the allusions to fascism made by David Bowie in his Thin White Duke persona.[3] Escapism (soul) and 'friendly yobbos from next door' (Slade) appeared to preoccupy the young working class.[4]

Not all was lost. As is well known, the mid-1970s found British politics and the British economy ensnared in domestic and international problems.[5] Inflationary pressures inherited from the 1960s precipitated

---

1 Paul Bradshaw, 'Trends in youth culture in the 1970s', *Cogito*, 3 (1976), 3–13. The article was based on Bradshaw's report to the YCL Executive Committee.

2 The early to mid-1970s saw a rock'n'roll revival; we may think, too, of John Lennon's *Rock'n'Roll* album, released in 1975.

3 Bowie made comments referring to the desirability of a fascist dictator and played with the signifiers of fascism in various interviews and appearances at this time. See David Buckley, *Strange Fascination: David Bowie, the Definitive Story* (London: Virgin, 2000), pp. 289–91. We should note, too, that two months after Bradshaw's speech came Eric Clapton's racist outburst to an audience at Birmingham Odeon. It was this event that acted as the stimulus for Rock Against Racism.

4 Bradshaw, 'Trends in youth culture'.

5 For a comprehensive overview, see Brian Harrison, *Finding a Role? The United Kingdom, 1970–1990* (Oxford: Oxford University Press, 2010).

a steady rise in unemployment and industrial conflict that combined to inaugurate a prolonged period of socio-economic and political strife.[6] The global oil crisis of 1973 had served only to exacerbate matters, tipping the economy into recession and providing the backdrop to a miners' dispute that hastened the fall of Edward Heath's Conservative government in early 1974. Although growth returned in 1975, Britain's erratic and relatively sluggish economic performance fed into a far deeper sense of post-imperial malaise. This, in turn, was articulated in a language of 'crisis' and 'decline' that eventually found embodiment in the Labour government's resort to the International Monetary Fund (IMF) for a loan in 1976 and, later, the strikes that informed the so-called 'Winter of Discontent' (1978–79).[7] Given such a context, Bradshaw readjusted his investigative lens to predict that 'new forms of culture, especially through music', would develop to 'give expression to the problems facing youth'. Unemployment and inner-city tensions born of fractured working-class communities would prompt new cultural trends, Bradshaw suggested. The task for the left, he concluded, was to analyse such tendencies as they emerged; to understand their progressive and reactionary inclinations and prevent them forming conduits to fascism. Boldly and openly, the Communist Party of Great Britain (CPGB) needed to project a 'lively, viable alternative'.[8]

Bradshaw's estimations proved well timed. Coinciding with his speech to the YCL Executive Committee, a new youth culture was indeed gestating

---

6 By 1976, unemployment had moved beyond the symbolic one million mark to reach 1,502,000 (5.7 per cent) in 1977; inflation rocketed to around 25 per cent in 1975 and continued to fluctuate thereafter. See UK Statistics Authority, *Labour Market Review 2006* (Basingstoke: Palgrave Macmillan, 2006), pp. 52–3; Sean Glynn and Alan Booth, *Modern Britain: An Economic and Social History* (London: Routledge, 1996); Richard Coopey and Nicholas Woodward (eds), *Britain in the 1970s: The Troubled Economy* (London: UCL Press, 1995).

7 Jim Tomlinson, *The Politics of Decline* (Harlow: Longman Pearson, 2001); Jim Tomlinson, 'Thatcher, inflation and the "decline" of the British economy', in Ben Jackson and Robert Saunders (eds), *Making Thatcher's Britain: Essays on the History of Thatcherism* (Cambridge: Cambridge University Press, 2013), pp. 62–77; Colin Hay, 'Chronicles of a death foretold: the Winter of Discontent and construction of the crisis of British Keynesian', *Parliamentary Affairs*, 63(3) (2010), 446–70. For contemporary examples of this mood beyond the newspaper headlines, see (for various responses) Richard Clutterbuck, *Britain in Agony: The Growth of Political Violence* (London: Penguin, 1978); Stephen Haseler, *The Death of British Democracy* (London: Elek Books, 1976); Isaac Kramnick, *Is Britain Dying? Perspectives on the Current Crisis* (Ithaca, NY: Cornell University Press, 1979); John Barr, *Derelict Britain* (London: Pelican, 1969); Stuart Hall, *Policing the Crisis: Mugging, the State, and Law and Order* (Basingstoke: Macmillan, 1977); John Harrison and Andrew Glyn, *The British Economic Disaster* (London: Pluto, 1980); Anthony King, *Why Is Britain Becoming Harder to Govern?* (London: BBC, 1976).

8 Bradshaw, 'Trends in youth culture'.

in the streets, art schools and minds of disaffected counter-culturalists. By June 1976, the Sex Pistols' early gigs and interviews had begun to cause a stir in the music press, presenting a challenge to the conceits of the music industry and reconfiguring pop's aesthetic in ways that foregrounded youthful rebellion amidst political signifiers and wilful iconoclasm. The Clash, who offered social-realist ballast to the Pistols' negation, would make their stage debut on 4 July. Come the end of the year, moreover, and the furore that followed the Sex Pistols' 'foul-mouthed' appearance on Thames Television's teatime *Today* programme stoked a media panic that propelled punk into popular consciousness.[9] The kids were revolting: Britain's various 'crises', be they a product of social dislocation, economic decline or imperial hangover, appeared to have found cultural realisation.[10]

Much debate was to follow – both in political circles and in the media – about just what punk *meant*.[11] Punk itself would comprise a contested culture through which diverse expressions became manifest as it evolved over time and permeated beyond London's confines. For Bradshaw, however, writing in early 1977, punk's 'new wave' met his own brief with aplomb: that is, punk served to provide cultural expression for 'working class kids [...] tired of having no voice to shout about unemployment' and 'other rubbish we're being fed'.[12] Indeed, the period that followed was partly defined by leftist attempts to engage with and channel youth culture towards progressive ends. Rock Against Racism (RAR), more closely associated with the Socialist Workers' Party (SWP) than the CPGB, became a staple of the late-1970s struggle against the National Front (NF), building its support on local clubs and punk-influenced bands delivering 'militant entertainment'.[13] Not unrelatedly, the politics of what became known as post-punk were often informed by 'new left' concerns as to questions of gender, sexuality, language, desire and cultural production.[14]

---

9 As is well known, the live programme saw the Pistols' guitarist, Steve Jones, conclude the interview by declaring the presenter, Bill Grundy, a 'fucking rotter'. The best history of punk's emergence and early development remains Jon Savage, *England's Dreaming: Sex Pistols and Punk Rock* (London: Faber & Faber, 1991).

10 For interesting analysis, see Joe Moran, '"Stand up and be counted": Hughie Green, the 1970s and popular memory', *History Workshop Journal*, 70(1) (2010), 173–98.

11 Matthew Worley, 'Shot by both sides: punk, politics and the end of "consensus"', *Contemporary British History*, 26(3) (2012), 333–54.

12 Note from the Editor, *Challenge*, March 1977, p. 7.

13 David Widgery, *Beating Time: Riot 'n' Race 'n' Rock 'n' Roll* (London: Chatto & Windus, 1986); Ian Goodyer, *Crisis Music: The Cultural Politics of Rock Against Racism* (Manchester: Manchester University Press, 2009).

14 Simon Reynolds, *Rip It Up and Start Again: Post Punk, 1978–84* (London: Faber & Faber, 2005); David Wilkinson, 'Difficult fun: British post-punk and the libertarian left

Of course, the extent to which Bradshaw's foresight may be put down to chance, intuition, astute Marxist analysis or wishful thinking is open to question. What remains interesting, however, is the debate underpinning the CPGB's attempts to locate youth culture as a site of political struggle. Running in *Marxism Today* through 1973–75 and into the wider communist press thereafter, the protracted discussion revealed much about the fissures opening up in the CPGB as it travelled towards dissolution in 1991. Cultural changes, the undermining of communist authority in the wake of Soviet actions and revelations, shifting social dynamics, the emergence of identity politics, technological advances and the allure of consumption all conspired to cut a swathe through long-held convictions. As the world changed, so the CPGB struggled to change with it.[15] But while the results of all this are relatively well known, as 'modernisers' and 'traditionalists' did battle over the CPGB's future, so the substance of the party's debate on youth culture – not to mention the relationship between politics and popular music[16] – remains pertinent today.

The purpose of this chapter is twofold: first, to demonstrate how and why a section of the YCL came to embrace punk as a signal of youthful revolt at least somewhat in tune with the objectives of the CPGB; second, to use the party's debate on youth culture as a means to expose tensions that served both to enliven but also to fragment the left over the later twentieth century. Previous accounts of the CPGB's relationship to youth culture have been critical of the party's 'late' response to punk.[17] The SWP's support for and involvement in RAR have, understandably, overshadowed the CPGB's more piecemeal interaction with punk-associated

on the cusp of neoliberalism, 1978–83', PhD thesis, University of Manchester (2013). For a good example of 'post-punk' politics being given full expression, listen to Gang of Four, *Entertainment* (EMI, 1979).

15 Geoff Andrews, *Endgames and New Times: The Final Years of British Communism, 1964–91* (London: Lawrence & Wishart, 2004).

16 See, for example, Simon Frith, *Sound Effects: Youth, Leisure and the Politics of Rock 'n' Roll* (New York: Pantheon, 1981); John Street, *Rebel Rock: The Politics of Popular Music* (Oxford: Blackwell, 1986); John Street, *Music and Politics* (Cambridge: Polity Press, 2012).

17 Jeremy Tranmer, 'Rocking against racism: Trotskyism, communism, and punk in Britain', in Robert Adlington (ed.), *Red Strains: Music and Communism Outside the Communist Bloc* (Oxford: British Academy, 2013), pp. 267–81; Evan Smith, 'Are the kids united? The Communist Party of Great Britain, Rock Against Racism, and the politics of youth culture', *Journal for the Study of Radicalism*, 5(2) (2011), 85–118. See also James Eaden and David Renton, *The Communist Party of Great Britain Since 1920* (Basingstoke: Macmillan, 2002), pp. 167–8.

cultures.[18] But while YCL members may not have seized the initiative as decisively as others on the left, some revealed themselves attuned to punk's early stirrings and engaged in wider debate as to the youth cultural changes over the later 1970s. In fact, Bradshaw's report to the YCL Executive Committee in the summer of 1976 reveals how at least some young comrades had absorbed the analyses emanating from the University of Birmingham's Centre for Contemporary Cultural Studies (CCCS) that, in turn, found expression in the pages of *Marxism Today* and countless academic studies of youth culture thereafter.[19]

The thesis

The CPGB's debate on youth culture was initiated in 1972–73 by Martin Jacques, then a twenty-seven-year-old lecturer in economic history at the University of Bristol and member of the party's Executive Committee.[20] Having reported to the Central Committee in February, Jacques published his analysis in *Marxism Today* the following September under the title 'Trends in youth culture: some aspects'.[21] The objective was to understand the origins, development and nature of post-war youth culture in order to posit connections between overtly political protest (such as demonstrations against the war in Vietnam) and disenchantment with capitalist society displayed at a cultural level. It also formed part of a broader effort to contest the CPGB's traditional emphasis on industrial struggle as the precursor to political consciousness ('economism') and to enact a 'cultural turn' in the party's politics and perspectives.[22]

There were precedents. Not surprisingly, the post-war emergence of distinct youth cultures centred on style and popular music generated

---

18 For CPGB recognition of its 'inadequate' involvement in RAR over 1977, see Communist Party Papers, People's History Museum, Salford, CP/CENT/CULT/2/7, Minutes of the Arts and Leisure Committee, 5 May 1978 (just after the first RAR–ANL carnival, held at London's Victoria Park in April 1978).

19 Bradshaw makes explicit reference to the CCCS in his *Cogito* article (p. 3). The principal CCCS-inspired take on punk remains Dick Hebdige, *Subculture: The Meaning of Style* (London: Methuen, 1979).

20 See the minutes and letters relating to CPGB questions contained in the Communist Party Papers, People's History Museum, CP/CENT/CULT/2/2.

21 Martin Jacques, 'Trends in youth culture: some aspects', *Marxism Today*, September 1973, pp. 268–80.

22 For Jacques' more general argument, see his 'Culture, class struggle and the Communist Party', *Comment*, 29 May 1976, pp. 163–5. For an overview, see Andrews, *Endgames and New Times*, pp. 50–72.

reaction from the party over the 1950s and 1960s. Initially, at least, curt dismissals of all things 'pop' being a product of American imperialism tended to set the tone, although some in the YCL endeavoured to align their communism to youthful disaffection.[23] Folk music, revived through the Workers' Music Association, remained the party's soundtrack of choice.[24] Come the 1960s, however, and a new generation of YCL recruits began to filter their revolutionary impulses through acts of social and cultural transgression. Not only did the widespread student protests of the period generate excitement and allow the YCL a notable foothold in student politics, but the fledgling counter-culture was recognised to provide a youthful challenge to bourgeois morality.[25] In response, and amidst often terse debate, the YCL sought to ride on the crest of youth culture's wave, organising discos, events (including a 1967 youth festival at the Derbyshire miners' holiday camp in Skegness featuring The Kinks) and presenting itself as part of 'The Trend'.[26] To this end, *Challenge* was revamped in accord with the aesthetics of the underground press and a pamphlet – replete with a gently psychedelic cover – put the YCL's case to recruit young 'ban-the-bombers, anti-racialists, folk singers' and others to the party.[27]

---

23 Mike Waite, 'The Young Communist League and youth culture', *Socialist History*, no. 6 (1994), 8–10.

24 Ben Harker, 'Communism and the British folk revival', in Robert Adlington (ed.), *Red Strains: Music and Communism Outside the Communist Bloc* (Oxford: British Academy, 2013), pp. 89–104; Ben Harker, *Class Act: The Cultural and Political Life of Ewan MacColl* (Manchester: Manchester University Press, 2011). The CPGB's Cultural Committee stated in 1962 that folk music was a 'valuable popular weapon with which to combat the brain-softening commercial culture that the masters think fit for the masses'. Communist Party Papers, People's History Museum, CP/CENT/CULT/01/04. Also cited in Smith, 'Are the kids united?', p. 91.

25 See, for youth as a political force, George Bridges, 'British youth in revolt', *Marxism Today*, August 1969, pp. 252–6. For the YCL and the counter-culture, see copies of *Challenge* in the late 1960s and Mike Waite, 'Sex 'n' drugs 'n' rock 'n' roll (and communism)', in Geoff Andrews, Nina Fishman and Kevin Morgan (eds), *Opening the Books: Essays on the Social and Cultural History of the British Communist Party* (London: Pluto, 1995), pp. 210–24.

26 Keith Gildart, *Images of England Through Popular Music: Class, Youth and Rock 'n' Roll, 1955–76* (Basingstoke: Palgrave Macmillan, 2013), p 139. For debate, see Communist Party Papers, People's History Museum, CP/YCL/09/04, YCL's District Congress, December 1967.

27 YCL, *The Trend – Communism* (London: YCL, 1967). That many in the YCL were resistant, or suspicious, of such a strategy was revealed at the 1971 YCL conference, which resolved that *Challenge*'s appeal to the 'mass of uncommitted youth' had been 'proven' incorrect. See *Report of the 28th National Congress of the YCL* (London: YCL, 1971).

Of course, cultural questions had also proven central to debates initiated by the new left, born – in part – from splits in the CPGB following the Soviet intervention in Hungary and Nikita Khrushchev's revelations about Stalin (both 1956).[28] As Marxists explored beyond the remits previously defined by the party (via Moscow), so new influences – from Gramsci and Lukács to Barthes and Benjamin, Althusser and Adorno, Mao and Marcuse – began to shape intellectual discussion across leftist milieus through the 1960s and into 1970s and beyond. Simultaneously, 'new social movements' were forged and celebrated over the terrains of race, gender and sexuality as the personal became political; new parties and protests jostled for position, aligning to student groups and interweaving amidst the emergent counter-culture of the 1960s. As a result, journals such as *New Left Review* gave space to articles examining the political significance of the Rolling Stones and the CCCS pioneered research positing youth culture as a 'site of resistance' to prevailing socio-economic structures, class relations and cultural hegemony.[29] By 1973, therefore, some in the CPGB and YCL felt the need to focus party attention more fixedly on questions of youth, especially as the 1960s began to give way to the harsher sensibilities and intensifying struggles of the 1970s.[30]

Jacques began by outlining what he perceived to be the three determining characteristics of the post-war generation.[31] First, he suggested that an 'ideological framework' defined by full employment and rising living standards (as opposed to unemployment and fascism) ensured that post-war youth bore higher expectations than their forebears. Second, he posited that youth's influence was expanding. The proportion of the population aged between fifteen and twenty-four had increased over the 1950s and 1960s; widening educational opportunities and rising incomes allowed for greater autonomy and spending capacity. Third, Jacques noted how

---

28 Michael Kenny, *The First New Left* (London: Lawrence & Wishart, 1995). An important early example would be Raymond Williams's *Culture and Society* (London: Chatto & Windus, 1958).

29 Such an argument was best expressed in John Clarke, Stuart Hall, Tony Jefferson and Brian Roberts, 'Subcultures, cultures and class: a theoretical overview', in Stuart Hall and Tony Jefferson (eds), *Resistance Through Rituals: Youth Subcultures in Post-War Britain* (London: Hutchinson, 1976), pp. 9–74. See also Phil Cohen, 'Subcultural conflict and working class community', *Working Class Papers in Cultural Studies*, 2 (1972), 4–51. For the Rolling Stones, see the articles by Andy Beckett, Richard Merton and Michael Parsons in *New Left Review* (January–February 1968 and May–June 1968).

30 An early article along these lines came from Tom Bell, 'An analysis of British young people', *Cogito*, no. 1 (1971), 4–6. See also David Forgacs, 'Gramsci and Marxism in Britain', *New Left Review*, no. 176 (1989), 83–4.

31 Jacques, 'Trends in youth culture', 268–80.

youth's social composition was evolving due to changes in industry and the extension of technical, scientific and intellectual labour. As a result, he suggested that working-class youths were becoming more diverse in terms of work and education, feeding into the growing ranks of students and white-collar workers, which allowed 'cross-fertilisation' between classes.

There were, of course, tensions amidst all this. Not only did the young working class remain among the most exploited section of the workforce, but educational opportunities, though extending, continued to be filtered through channels geared towards the needs of capital. Youthful expression, ever more vibrant and self-confident, provoked division in the working-class family, fanning generational conflict; commercialisation, the driver of consumerism, helped shape the ideological content of youth culture. Consequently, Jacques argued, the degree to which youth's cultural tendencies could be deemed either progressive or rebellious had to be evaluated in terms of both form and content.

Before moving on to assess the connotations of such socio-cultural change, Jacques next offered a brief history lesson. Rock 'n' roll, skiffle and the growth of CND (the Campaign for Nuclear Disarmament) were hailed as early tremors that challenged the social, political and ideological 'straightjacket' of the 1950s. The 'pop explosion' triggered by The Beatles in 1963–64 was then deemed to have reinforced generational dislocations manifest in wider society. Not only was popular music recognised thereafter as a cultural vehicle through which young people's feelings and aspirations were expressed, but it helped bind together various identities, attitudes and interests that reflected youth's growing self-assurance. Simultaneously, Jacques suggested, the commercialisation of pop was resisted by the formation of 'underground' scenes centred on folk, jazz or R 'n' B, culminating in the emergence of a recognisable counter-culture towards the end of the decade.

Again there were tensions. The counter-culture's conception of an 'alternative' society was vague, its realisation born of no coherent strategy. Beyond concerted opposition to the war in Vietnam, it inclined towards individualism rather than collectivism.[32] For Jacques, therefore, the counter-culture's focus on freedom and self-expression remained 'immature': utopian-anarchist rather than proto-socialist.[33] This, in turn, explained counter-cultural antipathy to the state *in toto* and distrust of organisational leadership, including the labour movement. It also explained

---

32 We should note that Jacques did not consider the collective impulses of, for example, communal living or squatting.

33 For emergent counter-cultural criticisms of the organised or party-political left see Jeff Nuttall, *Bomb Culture* (London: MacGibbon & Kee, 1968).

the counter-culture's appeal to those detached from the harsher realities of class struggle: to students and white-collar youth susceptible to such 'tendencies' as 'subjectivism [...], leftism, libertarianism and anarchism'.

That tensions should lead to fractures bore Jacques no surprise. As pop music became more commercially successful, so bands detached from their audience. Wealth, fame and a desire to experiment began to separate bands physically and emotionally from those who bought and listened to the music. Notably, too, class antagonisms were reasserted in cultural form, as between skinheads, students and middle-class elements within the counter-culture. Accordingly, by the early 1970s, youth culture was fragmenting as the class struggle intensified. Jacques' question for the CPGB was: how could the party 'translate the progressive developments' of youth culture into 'organised and consolidated form'?[34]

The debate

The upheavals of 1956 required the CPGB to reassert its political identity over the 1960s. By so doing, and in response to contemporaneous socio-economic changes and emergent socio-political forces (most notably feminism and the student movement), divergent tendencies began to develop across the party: one stressing the CPGB's working-class basis within the labour movement; the other seeking to reimagine and extend the party's political reach beyond its core (male) working-class constituency.[35] Though both recognised the need for the CPGB to establish alliances and adapt its approach to changing circumstances, their realisation roused evident friction. Running parallel to the debate on youth culture, therefore, were comparable discussions as to the party's relationship to changing class forces, gender politics, race, sexuality, the Labour Party, the trade union movement and the non-CPGB left.[36] In effect, battlelines were being drawn for the internecine conflict that tore British communism asunder in the 1980s.

Not surprisingly, Jacques' article helped reveal many of the fractures beginning to course through the CPGB. Most obviously, it generated a response from those keen to hold fast to the Marxist–Leninist basis of the party's political and organisational approach. For John Boyd, who invoked Lenin's rejection of 'special cultures' to contest the very premise of Jacques'

---

34 Jacques, 'Trends in youth culture'.
35 Andrews, *Endgames and New Times*, pp. 73–139.
36 See, for example, the debate on class in Alan Hunt (ed.), *Class and Class Structure* (London: Lawrence & Wishart, 1977).

thesis, youth culture was but an invention of capital; it was the 'child of Uncle Sam', a 'fire ship in disguise', a product of cultural imperialism that 'imposed alienation' and destroyed cultural heritage.[37] Rather than providing a conduit for rebellion, Boyd recognised youth culture as revolt 'dressed up' to foster division and redirect young people away from the *real* struggle. The discotheque, Boyd railed, with its darkened room, loud music, Coca-Cola and flashing lights, was designed so that 'every sense [is] taken care of to ensure that not one thought, let alone a social idea, takes place'. A working-class culture could not be built on commercial terms, he concluded: it resided in folk clubs and on street corners, developed – as directed by Lenin – in the spirit of class struggle and forged from 'the stores of knowledge which mankind has accumulated'.[38]

Related arguments were put forward by Brian Filling and Denver Walker. Where Filling accused Jacques of not writing from a 'class position', Walker questioned the use of the term 'culture' in relation to music and styles transmitted through the media.[39] Even the counter-culture, he insisted, was based on acceptance of the system: 'dropping out' and drugs were the 'solipsistic' responses of a bourgeoisie in retreat. Some credence was given to John Lennon for writing the song 'Working Class Hero', though even this was let down in Denver's mind by its failure to offer a 'way forward' for the workers. As for 'Imagine', Lennon's paean to a world without religion or boundaries, its affinity to any future communist society was dismissed as unclear, given that the song contained no reference to the Soviet Union! All in all, Denver concluded, pop culture was divisive and no substitute for the depth and breadth of mass struggle.

As should be apparent, Boyd *et al.* objected to the blurred class boundaries in Jacques' analysis. They reasserted the primacy of economics and recoiled from the idea of revolutionary struggle being pursued through cultural channels that were becoming ever more commercialised.[40] In their stock references to the Soviet Union and reliance on a narrow reading of Lenin, they revealed Stalinist predilections that ensured a rigidly mechanistic interpretation of the relationship between class, culture and capital.

---

37 John Boyd, 'Trends in youth culture', *Marxism Today*, December 1973, pp. 375–8; see also Albert Mills's contribution in *Marxism Today*, December 1974, pp. 79–80.

38 Boyd drew from Lenin's 'On proletarian culture' (1920) and 'Tasks of the youth leagues' (1920).

39 Brian Filling, 'Trends in youth culture', *Marxism Today*, September 1974, pp. 283–6; Denver Walker, 'Trends in youth culture', *Marxism Today*, July 1974, pp. 215–17.

40 See also Mills, 'Trends in youth culture', who insisted that a focus on economics, not culture, was the party's real concern.

Alternative perspectives came from those more sympathetic to Jacques' attempts to broaden the party's realms of engagement. This meant, first, foregrounding culture as a site of struggle in straightforward Marxist terms. So, for example, Jeremy Hawthorn located artistic production, communication and consumption in the context of 'base' and 'super-structure'. Just as religion contained elements of social struggle ('the heart of a heartless world'), so, Hawthorn suggested, culture should also be seen as both 'theirs' and 'ours' – its 'progressive' and 'reactionary' contradictions reflecting social contestations.[41] In other words, Hawthorn began to grapple towards conceptualising youth culture in hegemonic terms that complemented Jacques' analysis and opened a way beyond what were understood to be crudely economistic readings of Marx.

Others brokered similar arguments. Paul Fauvet dismissed the idea of youth culture harbouring some kind of capitalist conspiracy by distinguishing between the making and commercialisation of culture. Culture, he suggested, indicating shifts ongoing across the left in the 1960s–70s, provided a means to challenge 'bourgeois norms' beyond the purely economic.[42] Nick Kettle, meanwhile, recognised that culture could not provide a 'short cut to socialism', but nevertheless cited the later Beatles' work and soul music as examples of pop's political and 'liberating' potential.[43] For Judy Bloomfield, it was pop music's 'celebration of the senses' that gave it political potential. In language that nodded towards debates on pleasure and desire fuelled by feminism and the counter-culture, she defined music and youth culture as 'symptomatic of changing consciousness'.[44]

Surprisingly, perhaps, questions of race and gender were only tentatively brought to the fore. Imtiaz Chounara urged the party to recognise how black youths were caught between two cultures: that of Britain and that of their parents.[45] Bloomfield noted how the family unit helped instil gender roles that passed into broader cultural relations. By so doing, however, both Chounara and Bloomfield raised a further point of contention:

---

41 Jeremy Hawthorn, 'The Communist Party and developments in British culture', *Marxism Today*, December 1973, pp. 363–6. See also Jim Cornelius, 'Trends in youth culture', *Marxism Today*, September 1974, pp. 281–3, who used Lenin to argue similarly and counter Boyd's Leninist credentials.

42 Paul Fauvet, 'Trends in youth culture', *Marxism Today*, March 1974, pp. 93–4.

43 Nick Kettle, 'Trends in youth culture', *Marxism Today*, July 1974, pp. 213–15.

44 Judy Bloomfield, 'Trends in youth culture, *Marxism Today*, February 1973, pp. 61–4. For an obvious example of a counter-cultural text on play and desire, see Richard Neville, *Play Power* (London: Jonathan Cape, 1970).

45 Imtiaz Chounara, 'Trends in youth culture', *Marxism Today*, October 1974, pp. 317–19.

namely, contradictions *within* the working class.[46] Throughout the debate, the relationship between class and culture, between 'progressive' and 're-actionary' elements, proved difficult to contain. But once attention began to fall on 'escapist', racist, sexist or homophobic aspects of working-class culture, so more instinctive (maybe generational) class affinities began to take effect. If hegemony helped explain such, then it did not prevent there developing a sense by which the working class was being presented more as part of the problem than of the solution.

Come April 1975 and the discussion was temporarily brought to a close, with Jacques bolstering his argument and replying to those who criticised his original thesis.[47] This time he began with Marx, quoting from the 'Preface' to *A Contribution to the Critique of Political Economy* (1859) to denote the limited autonomy accorded to ideology within the relationship between base and superstructure. Nodding to Gramsci, Jacques explained the 'consensual' nature of political and ideological hegemony under the rubric of 'advanced capitalism'. The implication, he continued, was that class oppression was multifaceted and should be fought on various levels, including the cultural and ideological. Simultaneously, he understood that the class nature of such a struggle would not be recognised by the majority of participants. The 1960s, however, had revealed 'the first signs of disenchantment with and opposition to the dominant cultural practice amongst sections moving into struggle for, in the main, the first time'.

The relationship between class and culture remained problem-atical. Though recognising the existence of two cultures, 'bourgeois' and 'working class', Jacques insisted that the 'partially autonomous' culture of the working class was nevertheless 'dominated' by bourgeois values. Betwixt this, Jacques continued, distinctive youth cultures had begun to develop as a result of changing historical conditions. These, in turn, combined progressive tendencies with elements of dominant bourgeois ideology (individualism etc.), but retained the potential to stimulate con-sciousness. As for the student-led protests of the 1960s, Jacques accepted they bore petty-bourgeois inclinations. He nevertheless warned against seeing students as inherently petty-bourgeois, maintaining that youth movements comprised manual and white-collar youths among their ranks. For this reason, youth cultures could not be detached – or seen as separate – from the class struggle.

Jacques' reply did not bring with it firm political conclusions. He pre-ferred instead to leave the discussion hanging, positing further enquiry

---

46 Bloomfield, 'Trends in youth culture'.
47 Martin Jacques, 'Trends in youth culture: reply to the discussion', *Marxism Today*, April 1975, pp. 110–16.

into the physiognomy of contemporary youth cultures. Certainly, the debates that preceded the revision of the CPGB's official programme – *The British Road to Socialism* – did not lead to youth featuring heavily in the published resolutions, despite Jacques being one of its co-authors.[48] Only in 1979 did the YCL produce *Our Future*, a statement that spoke to the 'No Future Generation' and came replete with photos of punks, skinheads and young activists. Youth cultural identity, the programme insisted, be it ted, mod, rocker, hippy, skin, teenybopper or punk, served to provide a young person with a 'weapon' to make 'their presence felt', a collective identity through which 'real unity' could develop.[49] As this suggests, the emergence of punk informed the party's youth cultural analysis, enabling young comrades to test their conception of youth culture and explore the possibilities opened up by a cultural form ostensibly committed to 'threaten[ing] the status quo'.[50]

Conclusion

The YCL's embrace of punk has been well documented elsewhere.[51] Following Bradshaw's lead, *Challenge* lent support to the 'new wave' from early 1977 via approving summaries of the emergent scene, positive record reviews and, belatedly, support for RAR.[52] Not only did the paper's language and design transform ever closer to a superficially 'punk' style through 1977–79, mimicking the cut 'n' paste aesthetic of fanzines and the

---

48 CPGB, *The British Road to Socialism* (London: CPGB, 1978). Recognition of the 'specific problems' of young people as a 'social group' was made in the final programme, but very much in political rather than cultural terms. The programme also noted 'areas of oppression' beyond the workplace and provided for the establishment of a 'broad democratic alliance' that linked the class struggle to the 'new social movements'.

49 YCL, *Our Future: Programme of the Young Communist League* (London: YCL, 1979). See also YCL, *Our Future: Draft for Discussion* (London: YCL, 1978), which included Clash song titles among it sub-section headings.

50 *Anarchy in the UK*, no. 1 (1976), p. 8. This was a Sex Pistols' fanzine produced by Jamie Reid, Vivienne Westwood, Ray Stevenson and others in late 1976.

51 Mike Waite, 'Young people and formal political activity', MPhil thesis, University of Lancaster (1992); Worley, 'Shot by both sides', 333–54; Smith, 'Are the kids united?', 85–118; Evan Smith, 'When the party comes down: the CPGB and youth culture, 1976–1991', *Twentieth Century Communism*, no. 4 (2012), 38–75.

52 I. Wright, 'New wave', *Challenge*, March 1977, p. 7. By 1978, under Steve Munby's editorship, Brendan O'Rourke had become the paper's resident punk record reviewer. For RAR, see Communist Party Papers, People's History Museum, CP/CENT/CULT/2/7, Minutes of the Arts and Leisure Committee, 5 May 1978; Dave Cook, 'The British road to socialism and the Communist Party', *Marxism Today*, December 1978, p. 371.

stark graphics of punk record covers, but there were even occasions when YCL debate took place under the title of contemporaneous punk songs: White Riot (race), Love Lies Limp (sex), Complete Control (capitalism), Medium is the Tedium (education), Red London (socialism).[53] For a time, at least, punk groups played YCL-sponsored events (Sham 69 appeared at the 1977 London festival). A few young comrades even formed bands: Tony Friel was a founding member of The Fall; Green Gartside and Niall Jinks initiated Scritti Politti (Gartside served on the editorial board of *Challenge*, 1978–79). Inevitably, too, debate as to punk's meaning continued to find space in *Challenge*, *Comment* and *Marxism Today*. Indeed, the party's 'theoretical and discussion journal' came under the editorship of Jacques in 1977, leading to ever greater space being given to cultural matters, including punk, pop music and youth culture more generally.

None of this could halt or prevent the CPGB's decline. The YCL, for all its attempts to connect with 'the kids on the street', was internally divided and haemorrhaging members by the late 1970s. Over the twenty-year period from 1967 to 1987, those enrolled in the YCL reputedly fell from 6,000 members to just forty-four. In 1974, the YCL comprised 2,576 card-holders; by 1979, its membership stood at 1,021.[54] Nor should too much be read into the YCL's embrace of punk when assessing its (and the CPGB's) decline. True, at least one YCL branch felt moved to complain about the lack of 'Marxist political content' in *Challenge* during Steve Munby's tenure as editor, writing to the CPGB executive in April 1978 to bemoan recent editions 'almost completely devoted to punk rock and homosexuality'.[55] But the YCL was fracturing prior to 1977 and before the adoption of punk founts. More significant, perhaps, was the Conservative general election victory of 1979 – an event that served only to exacerbate fault-lines running through the CPGB. With the party and its Soviet role model appearing ever more anachronistic over the 1980s, so the collapse of communism in Eastern Europe and the USSR sealed its fate.

---

53 For discussion titles, see the advertisement for a YCL event at Charlton House, Greenwich, in *Challenge*, April 1978, p. 8. See also copies of *Challenge* and *Comment* from the period and the materials gathered for YCL publications in the Communist Party Papers, People's History Museum, CP/CENT/CULT/2/6. Even the 1979 YCL General Council report was presented in a punk-style fount and a pen-scrawled cover depicting Margaret Thatcher under the slogan 'Tory Freedom = No Future' (CP/CENT/DC/15/09).

54 Graham Stevenson, 'Anatomy of decline: the Young Communist decline, 1967–86', unpublished manuscript (n.d.); Smith, 'When the party comes down', p. 49.

55 Communist Party Papers, People's History Museum, CP/CENT/EC/16/04, Letter to the National Executive Committee of the Communist Party from the Haringey YCL branch, April 1978.

And yet, to dismiss the debates that accompanied the CPGB's endgame would be a mistake. By contrast, they reveal much about the left's evolution over the later twentieth century, retaining insights and lessons still relevant today. First, the CPGB's ruminations – on pop, youth culture and other related concerns – did not take place in a vacuum. Nor was the substance of debate exclusive to the party. Take out the Soviet genuflections, and key aspects of Boyd *et al.*'s critique were oft-repeated by those inside and out of the CPGB who disavowed 'progressive' readings of youth culture and popular music. Most obviously, the presentation of popular culture as defined by its mode of production evoked the writings of Theodor Adorno and Max Horkheimer on 'the culture industry' that formed the basis of much leftist criticism of mainstream rock and pop.[56] Likewise, the discombobulating spectacle of the disco and rock's fallacious sense of rebellion were more vigorously stated by anarchist groups drawing from situationist ideas.[57] The SWP, too, more than any other leftist party, made a connection to punk through RAR and the Anti-Nazi League, and would later see its conference move against the 'populist' direction of the *Socialist Worker* newspaper, concerned as to the 'dilution' of its traditional focus on overtly political and industrial struggles.[58] Far cruder Trotskyist and Maoist critiques also drew on theories of Americanisation and capitalist conspiracy to define their opposition to popular music and 'capitalist' culture.[59]

---

56 Theodor Adorno and Max Horkheimer, *Dialectic of Entitlement* (1944; London: Verso edition, 1997); Theodor Adorno, 'On popular music', in Simon Frith and Andrew Goodwin (eds), *On Record: Rock, Pop and the Written Word* (London: Routledge, 1991), pp. 301–14; Chris Cutler, *File Under Popular: Theoretical and Cultural Writings on Music* (London: November Books, 1985). See also smaller leftist periodicals such as *Cogs and Wheels* and *Musics*.

57 David and Stuart Wise, 'The end of music', in Stewart Home (ed.), *What is Situationism? A Reader* (Edinburgh: AK Press, 1996), pp. 63–102 (originally titled 'Punk, reggae; a critique', this was published as a pamphlet in 1978 and circulated around anarchist groups in Leeds).

58 Steve Jefferys, 'The politics behind the row on the paper', Modern Record Centre, 242/2/1/3; Ian Birchall, *The Smallest Mass Party in the World* (London: SWP, 1981). Nor was there any obvious *increase* in the SWP membership registered as the 1970s became the 1980s, even if turnover appeared to speed up. John McIlroy suggests the membership remained 'stable' at 4,000 between 1978 and 1980, the peak of RAR. John Callaghan's figures for the International Socialist membership record 3,900 members in 1974. See John McIlroy, '"Always outnumbered, always outgunned": the Trotskyists and the trade unions', in John McIlroy, Nina Fishman and Alan Campbell (eds), *British Trade Unions and Industrial Politics* (Aldershot: Ashgate, 1999), vol. 2, p. 285; John Callaghan, *The Far Left in British Politics* (Oxford: Blackwell, 1987), pp. 105, 205.

59 'Which way for the punk rebellion?', *Young Socialist*, 4 August 1979, p. 4; 'Who is Cornelius Cardew?', *NME*, 10 September 1977, pp. 11–12.

Second, it is interesting to note how Jacques' overview picked up on themes that would later inform academic reflections on youth. Flick through the contextualising segments of important books by Arthur Marwick, Bill Osgerby, Axel Schildt and Detlef Siegfried, and the core themes defined by Jacques as integral to understanding youth culture's emergence and development are all present and correct.[60] More immediately, of course, Jacques and subsequent historians were themselves informed (to varying degrees) by the pioneering research of Stuart Hall and others in the CCCS, many of whom contributed to discussion in *Marxism Today* over the 1970s and 1980s. Dave Laing, who reported to the CPGB's Arts and Leisure Committee in 1976–77, provided one very important link, later writing the most insightful article on punk to appear in the communist press.[61] Certainly, the mission to find (class-based) resistance in the activities of young people dovetailed neatly with the objective of the CCCS: that is, to contest and counter sanguine, pessimistic or 'reactionary' readings of youthful consumption.

Third, and not dissimilarly, both Jacques' and Bradshaw's diagnosis of pop music and youth culture's condition in the mid-1970s would later become entrenched in the cultural narrative of punk. In other words, punk represented a response to rock's detachment from its youthful audience and the banalities of mainstream pop. Thus, to quote The Clash's Paul Simonon, whose dad had held Communist membership, punk's origins stemmed from: 'kids who watch *Top of the Pops*, and they see all these shitty groups, and there's nothing to do. And they see a guy play guitar in a club and they think it takes about a hundred years to learn to play.'[62] Early journalistic accounts (and much popular history thereafter) repeated these tropes, before further adding reference to the Sex Pistols' working-class backgrounds and the political relevance of The Clash's depictions of inner-city tensions. It was only 'natural', Caroline Coon wrote of the Pistols in late 1976, that a group of 'deprived London street kids' would produce music 'with a startlingly anti-establishment bias'.[63]

Fourth, the party's debate on youth culture – and culture more generally – was very much part of a gradual turn away from class as the

---

60 Arthur Marwick, *British Society Since 1945* (London: Pelican, 1982); Bill Osgerby, *Youth in Britain Since 1945* (Oxford: Blackwell, 1998); Axel Schildt and Detlef Siegfried (eds), *Between Marx and Coca-Cola: Youth Cultures in Changing European Societies, 1960–1980* (Oxford: Berghahn, 2006), especially the editors' 'Introduction', pp. 1–35.

61 Communist Party Papers, CP/YCL/21/1Minutes of the Arts and Leisure Committee; Dave Laing, 'Interpreting punk rock', *Marxism Today*, April 1978, pp. 123–8.

62 Quoted in *Negative Reaction*, no. 5 (1977), 5.

63 Caroline Coon, 'Sex Pistols: rotten to the core', *Melody Maker*, 27 November 1976, pp. 34–5.

'master' identity within progressive politics. Put simply, questions of race, gender and sexuality began to contest (or intersect with) the working class's position as the driver of revolutionary struggle. Of course, synchronicity beyond the fragments was aspired to; debates seeking to align Marxism with social movements of various hues were among the most politically stimulating of the period; the struggles of 'new social movements' brought about necessary and positive social change.[64] In the process, however, attention turned towards contradictions *within* the working class as much as without. If 'labourism' and 'economism' were designated drags on the revolution, then so too was a working-class culture now deemed to be imbued with reactionary tendencies absorbed from the ruling class. The fissures and tensions occasioned by such developments remain.

Finally, the CPGB's youth cultural debate revealed that the party was capable of motivating and hosting intellectually vibrant discussion, even as it headed for dissolution. It remains something of a paradox that *Marxism Today* became ever more effervescent as the party fell deeper into decline. The debates presented in the journal make for fascinating reading. Like many a great punk record, they serve as time capsules that provide insight into the tenor and the conflicts of their time. If the Sex Pistols' Johnny Rotten and The Clash's Joe Strummer could not save the CPGB, then their innovations helped reveal tensions that still cut to the heart of the British left.

Acknowledgements

This chapter is dedicated to Chris Wrigley, whose supervision guided me through a PhD at the University of Nottingham. The thesis related to the CPGB, but much time was also given to our mutual interest in the history of popular music. I hope this chapter offers a neat conflation of the two and serves to underline my admiration for a great historian and a true friend. More formally, the chapter stems from a Leverhulme Trust funded project examining the links between punk, politics and youth culture in Britain during the 1970s and 1980s. A longer version of the chapter appears as 'Marx–Lenin–Rotten–Strummer: British Marxism and youth culture in the 1970s', in *Contemporary British History*, 30(4) (2016). My thanks go to Andrew Pearmain, Lucy Robinson, Evan Smith, John Street, Mike Waite and David Wilkinson for their helpful comments.

---

64 I nod here, of course, to Sheila Rowbotham, Lynn Segal and Hilary Wainwright, *Beyond the Fragments: Feminism and the Making of Socialism* (London: Merlin Press, 1979). But see also Lucy Robinson, *Gay Men and the Left in Post-War Britain: How the Personal Got Political* (Manchester: Manchester University Press, 2007).

12

Must Labour lose? Lessons from post-war history

KEVIN JEFFERYS

The labour movement has long contained a pessimistic streak about its electoral prospects. This thread in party sentiment can be detected in good times as well as bad, as one small example from the 'New Labour' era illustrates. In September 2000 Tony Blair's first administration was rocked by an upsurge of protests against sharply rising fuel prices, with disparate groups of truck owners and farmers' action groups organising blockades of refineries and disrupting supply to petrol stations in different parts of the country. Alarmist newspaper stories referred to petrol outlets being forced to close, food shortages in the supermarkets as deliveries stalled and the National Health Service being put on red alert. The whole episode was over in a week or so. The organisers of the blockades backed down, confident their point had been made, and recriminations began as to who was responsible for costing the British economy an estimated £1 billion in lost income. Yet despite being short-lived, the protests prompted considerable anxiety in left-wing ranks. A few opinion polls suggested a narrowing of Labour's lead, and the Prime Minister was less than pleased that one of his own ministers drew attention to *The Sun*'s January 1979 headline 'Crisis ... What crisis?', the phrase that skilfully tapped into the feeling that Jim Callaghan's Labour government was out of touch and heading for electoral defeat, as proved to be the case when Margaret Thatcher swept to power a few months later.[1]

In reality, although anti-Labour tabloid editors were keen to make comparisons, the fuel protests of 2000 were far from being a carbon copy

---

1 Andrew Rawnsley, *Servants of the People: The Inside Story of New Labour* (Harmondsworth: Penguin edition, 2001), especially chapter 20.

of the 'Winter of Discontent'. The differences were much more striking than the similarities. Unlike Blair, Callaghan was faced in 1979 with insurmountable problems. He had knife-edge parliamentary backing rather than the cushion of a huge majority at Westminster. His government lagged in the polls, whereas Blair had enjoyed consistently high ratings over a long period. He was beset by high inflation and rising unemployment and did not have the luxury as Blair did of a stable, growing economy. His opponents had not come together in a spontaneous, short-lived movement for lower fuel tax. Instead, widespread strike action in support of higher wages was co-ordinated in the 1970s by disgruntled trade union leaders who were prepared to maintain picket lines for weeks rather than days.[2] The two Labour leaders also handled the respective crises differently. Whereas Callaghan's reputation suffered from the pictures of 'Sunny Jim' in shirt-sleeves, attending a summit meeting in the Caribbean while disruption mounted back in wintry Britain, Blair maintained a high-visibility media profile and adopted a resolute, almost Churchillian tone, refusing to discuss possible amendments in fuel policy until the protests had been called off.[3]

With hindsight, it is clear that the fuel dispute caused little more than surface ripples on the electoral landscape. Nine months later, in June 2001, the Blair administration was comfortably re-elected. But it remains the case that for a brief period in the autumn of 2000 plenty of Labour activists and commentators were rattled, and readily willing to posit various doom-laden scenarios. With the possibility, however short-lived, of ministers appearing to lose control of events – the spectre that haunts all governments – there were many who lost sight of how the party had won the biggest majority in its history just three years earlier; as it turned out, it performed remarkably strongly in 2001 as well, winning over 400 parliamentary seats again and 40 per cent of total votes cast. Unlike the Conservative Party, of which it has been said that it 'only panics in a crisis', Labour, it seems, tends to fear the worst even in the best of times.

It was thus hardly surprising that Labour's crushing defeat at the general election in May 2015 was followed by dire prognostications. Instead of taking power at the head of a minority government, as seemed likely on the basis of opinion surveys in the weeks ahead of polling day, even before

---

2 John Shepherd, *Crisis? What Crisis? The Callaghan Government and the British Winter of Discontent* (Manchester: Manchester University Press, 2013).

3 Rawnsley, *Servants*, chapter 20. Kenneth Morgan notes ironically of Callaghan: 'One of the less appropriate sobriquets for this sometimes difficult and bad-tempered man was "Sunny Jim"'. Kenneth O. Morgan, *Callaghan: A Life* (Oxford: Oxford University Press, 1997), p. 751.

the counting of votes was concluded Labour leader Ed Miliband conceded defeat, recognising he was soundly beaten. The party lost rather than gained seats compared with the previous election and was humiliated, in particular north of the border, where the Scottish Nationalists swept the board. Miliband resigned within hours. Inquests into the cause of the defeat began amidst dire warnings that Labour might be consigned to permanent opposition, if not oblivion. The 'strange death of Labour Britain' was once more widely aired and reflected upon.[4]

Such inquests and warnings were far from new. After the party suffered three successive setbacks in the 1950s, two respected writers, Mark Abrams and Richard Rose, produced a widely publicised book in 1960 entitled *Must Labour Lose?* The answers it came up with to the question were equivocal, but not encouraging. The authors found that the party was widely perceived as old-fashioned and incapable in a period of rising living standards to persuade large parts of the electorate to abandon the Tory administration of the day.[5] The downbeat tone of *Must Labour Lose?* was to find many later echoes, and this chapter sets out to explore what light can be shed on the party's present-day malaise by its wider post-war performance, which includes other low points, such as those of 1983 and 1992, as well as that of 1959.

A brief overview of Labour's post-1945 electoral record suggests, however, that – despite precarious and dangerous moments – the default tendency towards negativity on the left has not been altogether justified. The authors of *Must Labour Lose?* ultimately held back from describing Gaitskell's party as a busted flush; a substantial core of loyal activists and voters remained and the incumbent government always remained prone to be being blown off course (as was to occur in the early 1960s). In historical terms, the notion of Labour being in terminal decline has been frequently overstated. Whether that remains the case in 'Brexit' Britain is still (at the time of writing) to be worked out. Already facing a mountain to climb after 2015, with collapse in Scotland marking part of a seismic shift in electoral dynamics, party divisions in the wake of the UK's decision to leave the European Union (EU) left Labour facing a possibly irreversible split; it was certainly confronted with the most serious threat to its existence as a governing force in a generation, with senior figures openly acknowledging that it faced an 'existential crisis'.

---

4   For example, Martin Kettle, 'The strange death of Labour Britain has a worrying precedent', *The Guardian*, 15 August 2015.
5   Mark Abrams and Richard Rose, *Must Labour Lose?* (Harmondsworth: Penguin, 1960).

Winning elections

Labour's gloomy streak about its prospects often fails to take account of its electoral performance as a whole since the Second World War.[6] Moments of despair and despondency should not obscure a broadly defensible record at Westminster elections: in total, up to the time of writing (2016) Labour had won nine general elections, compared with ten for the Conservatives (including the Tories being the largest party in the 2010 coalition with the Liberal Democrats). Although some of the party's victories have been narrow in terms of share of the vote and parliamentary arithmetic – for example in 1950 and in 1974 (twice) – this has not always been the case. At different points in time Labour has demonstrated its ability to secure landslide majorities (1945 and 1997); to produce impressive 'follow-up' victories to bolster earlier, narrower, successes, notably when Harold Wilson extended his 1964 majority in 1966; and to secure successive full-length terms in office, as when Blair followed up his initial thumping triumph with comfortable wins in 2001 and 2005.[7] Nor should it be forgotten that at one of the party's defeats, in 1951, Labour – by piling up huge majorities in its working-class heartlands – won more votes, though fewer seats, than the Tories, its massive 48.8 per cent share of the vote standing as an achievement in the realms of fantasy today.

A straightforward summary of the overall picture since the war therefore stands at odds with an unduly harsh reading of the party's performance and potential. Labour does not always lose. But, we might ask, in what circumstances does it tend to win? In view of the relative scarcity of decisive victories, a brief comparison of key landmark triumphs – 1997, 1964 (ending a thirteen-year spell in opposition) and 1945 – suggests the importance of certain common denominators, as well as underlining the scale of the task facing the party in the Brexit era. New Labour's campaign against the beleaguered Major administration culminated in May 1997 in the party's best ever result at a Westminster election, with an overall majority of nearly 180 seats. By contrast, the Conservatives slumped to their lowest share of the vote (around 30 per cent) for over 150 years – an important reminder that both major parties have faced moments in the modern period when permanent wilderness potentially beckoned.

---

6 For an overview, see Nick Tiratsoo, 'Labour and the electorate', in Duncan Tanner, Pat Thane and Nick Tiratsoo (eds), *Labour's First Century* (Cambridge: Cambridge University Press, 2000).

7 Andrew Rawnsley, *The End of the Party: The Rise and Fall of New Labour* (Harmondsworth: Penguin, 2010).

Looking backwards in time, which of Labour's earlier breakthrough victories had most in common with Blair's march to power? There was much talk during the 1997 campaign about echoes of 1964. Sir David Frost devoted an hour-long television special to the subject, and there were clearly some striking similarities. In both cases, the Tories were victims of the rallying cry 'Time for a change', having spent lengthy periods in office. Accusations of economic mismanagement took their toll in both instances, as did association with 'sleaze'. The Profumo scandal of 1963 had hastened the end of Harold Macmillan's premiership; 'never had it so good' was replaced by the satirists' jibe 'never had it so often'. Labour could also claim, in 1964 as in 1997, to have more dynamic leadership. Macmillan's successor, Sir Alec Douglas-Home, was ill-suited to the emerging age of television politics. His grouse moor image and 'matchstick' grasp of economics was skilfully exploited by the arch-meritocratic Wilson, who as opposition leader promised the white heat of the technological revolution. Labour was persuasively presented as the party of the future: Wilson's vision of a 'new Britain' was designed to echo the 'New Frontier' rhetoric of a youthful Democratic President across the Atlantic, Jack Kennedy.[8]

Yet the movement of votes away from the Tories in October 1964 was not on a massive scale. The swing of 3 per cent, though Labour's best in peacetime before 1997, was sufficient to give Wilson only a tiny majority, of four seats. Whereas economic revival in the mid-1990s under the Major administration did little to improve Conservative ratings, the 'Maudling boom' ahead of the 1964 contest allowed the Tories to make up some of the ground lost in mid-term of the 1959 parliament. Although much maligned, 'the fourteenth earl of Home' made various telling attacks on 'the fourteenth Mr Wilson'. If a further small additional number of voters had returned to the Conservative fold, Douglas-Home would have been cast in the unlikely role of saviour. Wilson – with his trademark Gannex mac and pipe – would then have looked like a pale imitation of Kennedy.

In terms of outcome, the 1997 contest stands much closer to the landslide of 1945, when a 12 per cent swing produced a Labour majority of 147 seats. At first sight, little more than the result seems to link these two Labour high-points. The 1945 campaign followed six years of war against Nazi Germany, with Britain led after 1940 by Churchill's cross-party coalition. In the beauty contest between the party leaders, it was the Tories who appeared to hold all the cards. Churchill, the nation's wartime hero, was pitted against the low-profile Mr Attlee – 'Clem the Clam', as the King

8 David Butler and Anthony King, *The British General Election of 1964* (London: Palgrave Macmillan, 1965).

called him. And in 1945 Attlee's party made extravagant claims, or at least used rhetoric alien to New Labour. The manifesto boldly offered to rebuild war-torn Britain with a programme based on extensive nationalisation and welfare reform. In words that made Tony Blair blush, the 1945 manifesto proclaimed 'the Labour Party is a Socialist Party, and proud of it'.[9]

So what does connect 1945 with 1997? Three things stand out, each a prerequisite to Labour winning the keys to Downing Street at any general election. The first was distrust of, and disillusionment with, the Conservatives. As victory over Hitler became more certain after 1942, the desire of the British people to create a better post-war world could not be mistaken. But Churchill had little faith in the idea of building a 'New Jerusalem'. The Prime Minister's coolness towards the famous Beveridge report led to great cynicism and anger about Tory intentions. 'Why', it was asked, 'get Beveridge to make a plan at all if you are going to turn it down?'[10] Churchill, the national figurehead who won the war, was the same party leader who did much to lose the peace. Public disillusionment with John Major in the 1990s was of a similar order: after the economic debacle of 'Black Wednesday' in 1992, Major was never able to recover authority or credibility.

A second link between the two contests was that in 1945, as in the mid-1990s, Tory efforts to scare voters about the prospect of a Labour administration fell flat. The 'fear factor', a traditional ploy of incumbents, could pay handsome dividends in the right circumstances, as Neil Kinnock discovered to his cost amidst claims of a 'tax bombshell' in 1992. But when Churchill provocatively claimed that socialism in post-war Britain would require 'some form of Gestapo', his comments were considered counter-productive and tasteless, coming just as Allied troops were discovering the full horrors of the concentration camps. Anti-German rhetoric had equally little effect when used by Major in 1990s debates over the future of Europe; the idea of Blair as a dummy sitting on Chancellor's Kohl's knee caused dismay even among senior Tories.[11]

The third and perhaps most vital connection between 1945 and 1997 was more positive in nature, and related to trust and credibility. Neutralising the 'fear factor' about Labour intentions was one thing; persuading voters that the party was the most attractive and trustworthy

---

9 Labour Party, *Let Us Face the Future* (London: Labour Party, 1945).

10 Home Intelligence reports, December 1942 and March 1943, cited in Kevin Jefferys, *The Churchill Coalition and Wartime Politics, 1940–1945* (Manchester: Manchester University Press), p. 151.

11 Kevin Jefferys, *Finest and Darkest Hours: The Decisive Events in British Politics from Churchill to Blair* (London: Atlantic Books, 2002), chapters 11 and 12.

proposition – particularly when it came to handling the economy and the nation's defences – was another matter. Harold Wilson managed to pull this off in 1964, though not to the same extent as Attlee, whose reliable image was a direct consequence of his key role as Deputy Prime Minister during the wartime coalition. Nor did Attlee's programme, though couched in the language of socialism, alarm the voters of what later became known as 'middle England'. State intervention in the economy had been seen as essential in wartime, and reforms such as the introduction of a National Health Service were at an advanced planning stage by the time hostilities ceased. Labour's success in the likes of Winchester in 1945 owed as much to reassurance as radicalism. In a similar vein, Tony Blair secured the trust of voters by offering change, but not a leap in the dark. In terms of New Labour campaign slogans, 'Britain deserves better' sat alongside 'we won't promise what can't be delivered', and many party followers were frustrated to find that the first Blair administration stuck rigidly to its promise not to exceed the spending levels proposed by the Tories in the run-up to polling day. What Labour's two great landslides of 1945 and 1997 most have in common was thus the successful combination of hope and reassurance; 'bread and butter plus a dream', as David Howell memorably remarked of Attlee's success.[12]

Losing elections

Although defensible, Labour's record at Westminster elections since 1945 can best be described as mixed. The stunning highs have been interspersed with desperate lows, including several dismal showings in the party's ten defeats. The Conservatives have not only prevailed more often, but also, by virtue of a greater number of solid Commons majorities, have spent more time holding the reins of power: about forty years in total (and rising to forty-five by the time of the next scheduled election, in 2020) compared with thirty for Labour. As with election victories, each loss has been the product of unique circumstances – for example major policy or presentational failures when in office – though common threads can again be detected. Labour often loses when it falls short in the areas outlined above as being preconditions for success: when it has been unable to rely on dislike of the Tory alternative; has struggled to counter the 'fear factor' over its intentions; or when it has failed to inspire credibility and trust. A short overview of Labour's post-war losses also underlines the importance of two further key determinants: disunity and poor leadership.

12 David Howell, *British Social Democracy* (London: Croom Helm, 1976), p. 132.

The issue of how united or divided the party appears in the eyes of the public has always been central to Labour's fortunes; any political strategy or vision, however bold or compelling, can never fulfil its potential if it fails to command the common approval of those charged with conveying it to the electorate. Ahead of the party's 2010 defeat, the three occasions after the Second World War when Labour relinquished its place as the governing party were each followed by outbreaks of internal strife, twice contributing to protracted spells in the electoral wilderness. Attlee's demise at the hands of Churchill in 1951 remains the party's most curious setback in the modern era. Although Labour's landslide 1945 majority all but disappeared at the general election in 1950, and despite exhaustion among the senior figures who built the welfare state out of the rubble of war, Attlee need not have gone to the country when he did in 1951. During 1952 the world economy entered a phase of rapid growth, from which Labour ministers may well have benefited had they remained longer in office. A further irony was that Labour's strong showing in terms of share of the vote left senior figures confident of an early return to power. Hugh Dalton, Attlee's first post-war Chancellor, described the 1951 result in his diary as 'wonderful', believing the Tories would quickly crumble in office.[13]

As it turned out, Dalton was wide of the mark. Thirteen years in opposition followed, marked by increasingly heavy reverses at the elections of 1955 and 1959, primarily because Churchill and his successors proved adept at exploiting steady economic growth during the emerging 'affluent society' of the time. But Labour undermined any chance it had of regaining power by entering into bitter factional quarrels. Bevanite left-wingers advocated building on the nationalisation programme of the Attlee years as the way forward, and clashed sharply with the emerging Gaitskellite revisionists, who placed social equality at the centre of their creed. For voters, the image was of a party that traded in the unity of the immediate post-war era for futile tribal conflict. By 1952 Dalton was singing an entirely different tune. 'More hatred, and more love of hatred', he wrote, 'in our Party than I ever remember'.[14]

In the second example of Labour losing office, Wilson's defeat in 1970 was followed by renewed in-fighting between the inheritors of the old fundamentalist and revisionist traditions. Beset with problems over policy – notably over attitudes towards the European Community (EU), which Britain joined under Tory premier Edward Heath – the party again presented a picture of disharmony in opposition. But unlike in the

---

13 See Ben Pimlott, *Hugh Dalton* (London: Jonathan Cape, 1986), pp. 605–6.
14 Ben Pimlott (ed.), *The Political Diary of Hugh Dalton, 1918–40, 1945–60* (London: Jonathan Cape, 1986), 24–28 October 1952, p. 601.

1950s, Labour this time got lucky. Heath's decision to gamble by calling an election in the shadow of the three-day week in 1974 backfired badly. Wilson's emollient leadership papered over many of the internal cracks and he retained sufficient acumen to steer Labour back to power, though at both the 1974 general elections the party's share of the vote, squeezed by a revival of Liberalism, fell below 40 per cent. This was hardly a ringing endorsement, and confirmed the end of the age in which the two main parties garnered the overwhelming majority of all votes cast.

The third instance of the party surrendering power came when Callaghan's administration was roundly beaten in the wake of the Winter of Discontent. The aftermath of that election remains a painful memory etched into the consciousness of Labour activists. Thatcher's assault on state collectivism got off to a shaky start; by 1981 unemployment had risen as sharply as her personal popularity had sunk. But as the frustrations of the Wilson–Callaghan era came to the surface, Labour pressed the self-destruct button and embarked on full-scale civil war. Instead of mounting a counter-attack on the so-called 'hard left', leading figures on the Labour right decided it was time to jump ship. Within months of its creation in 1981, the Social Democratic Party (SDP) could claim over twenty MPs, mostly defectors from the Parliamentary Labour Party, aiming to replace Labour altogether on the centre left by 'breaking the mould' of politics.

Michael Foot, who replaced Callaghan in 1980, used the backing of moderate trade unionists to begin a fight back against the hard left, beginning moves to expel members of Militant Tendency from the party. But the poisonous atmosphere at Westminster and beyond – combined with savage tabloid attacks on Foot's leadership – meant Labour was in no position to mount an effective challenge in the early 1980s, especially after Thatcher's fortunes were bolstered by victory in the Falklands War. Dogged by personal and ideological divisions, Labour's own research in the run-up to the 1983 election described the party as 'implausible as an alternative government'.[15] So dismal was Labour's performance in 1983, when its vote share slumped to its lowest at any post-war Westminster contest, 27.6 per cent, that the party faced the real prospect of being eclipsed as the official opposition by the SDP–Liberal Alliance. Under Foot's successor, Neil Kinnock, a partial recovery took place, and by the time of the 1987 election the Alliance tide had receded; Labour came in a clear – if distant – second place. Kinnock's party was at least still in business, but the scars of the early 1980s took a long time to heal. Kinnock

---

15 David Butler and Dennis Kavanagh, *The British General Election of 1983* (London: Palgrave Macmillan, 1984), p. 58.

never reaped the reward of his endeavours, suffering a crushing defeat in 1992, and eighteen years in opposition came to an end only when the New Labour project came to the fore in 1997.

Labour's history thus shows that while avoiding disunity is not a sufficient condition of regaining power, it is a necessary one. Equally important is the role of the party leader. The difficulties of preserving unity among various factions was often compounded in the post-war era by concerns over the intentions and perceived shortcomings of individual leaders, ranging from attacks by the left in the 1950s on Hugh Gaitskell's alleged inflexibility to constant sniping at Gordon Brown's inability to emulate Blair's domination of the political agenda in the dying days of the New Labour regime before the 2010 election. By contrast, Labour's finest hours are inextricably linked in the minds of activists and observers with those leaders who have delivered electoral success, though not in an altogether uncomplicated way. Wide-ranging surveys among academics, including historians and political scientists (the most extensive being that carried out by Mori and Leeds University in 2004), generally concur that Attlee – by virtue primarily of his association with the welfare reforms of the late 1940s – is regarded as Labour's most successful leader; indeed, he often comes first in ranking lists of modern Prime Ministers. Controversial decisions such as British involvement in the Iraq War help to explain why Blair – with a stronger election-winning record – ranks below Attlee in these types of survey, often vying with Wilson for the 'runner-up' slot.[16]

The standing of the leader has clearly played a crucial role in setting the tone of the party's public image, in good times as much as bad. While the maintenance of party unity and coherent leadership have been constant imperatives, whether in government or opposition, there are more equivocal answers to the question of whether it has been beneficial to ditch or stick with experienced leaders who have served as Prime Minister. In the aftermath of Labour losing power in 1951 Attlee remained in place, his standing high as the architect of the post-war settlement, but he lost the election in 1955. Wilson, too, stayed on, despite much internal criticism of his 1970 defeat, yet managed to stage a successful comeback four years later. In Callaghan's case, the departure of the leader a year after Thatcher's victory saw the party's plight get much worse before it got better.

What Labour does not have a tradition of (accepting here that Wilson in 1976 and Blair in 2007 went at moments of their own choosing) is of forcing out those who occupy Number Ten, Downing Street. For insights

16 Kevin Theakston and Mark Gill, 'Rating twentieth century British Prime Ministers', *British Journal of Politics and International Relations*, 82(1) (2006), 193–213.

pertinent in this regard to the position of Gordon Brown, whose stock fell rapidly after he took over from Blair in 2007, one has to turn to the experiences of the Conservative Party. In two of the three post-1945 cases where incumbent Tory premiers were ousted by their own followers – Eden, Macmillan and Thatcher (though the first two departed partly on medical grounds) – their replacements managed to revive government fortunes sufficiently to win the general election that followed, in 1959 and 1992. In the third case, Sir Alec Douglas-Home failed to pull off the same trick, though, as noted above, he came close, losing by only a tiny margin as Labour squeaked home in 1964.

There is therefore some historical evidence to suggest a change of guard at the top between elections can improve a party's fortunes in the short term, especially if the new premier appears to mark a fresh start and presents a different persona to the outgoing leader. Macmillan's unflappability when he took over contrasted with the volatility of Eden; Major's diffidence was initially praised as a departure from Thatcher's stridency. But history provides no guarantees. Labour had already 'swapped horses' once during the 2005 parliament, and disgruntled Cabinet colleagues and MPs ultimately held back from openly seeking to remove Gordon Brown. The calculation was that voters might take the view that to lose one Prime Minister in the lifetime of a parliament was unfortunate; to lose two would be extremely careless, though in the end sticking with Brown did nothing to avert a resounding defeat at the polls. As journalist Andrew Rawnsley notes, outside of London the party had gone 'full circle back to the rump representation in the south before the creation of New Labour'.[17]

Conclusion

Internal strife and inadequate leadership have clearly cost Labour dear on numerous occasions, and both feature prominently on the list of contingent, avoidable factors that have contributed to the party's patchy record at Westminster elections. In the 1950s and 1980s especially, Labour seemed willing to prolong its internecine warfare without much regard for the electoral consequences. The party's failure to put its own house in order stemmed partly from poor leadership at points, which suggests that election setbacks were primarily a contingent process, tied to the short-comings of particular groups or individuals. Labour's loss of office in 1970, for example, clearly had much to do with things that alienated core voters

---

17 Rawnsley, *End of the Party*, pp. 738–9.

such as cuts in public spending, pay restraint and the humiliation of de-
valuation (after months, as one observer put it, of 'treating sterling as the
exchange equivalent of the Virgin Mary'),[13] thereby severely undermining
Wilson's reputation for competent economic management.

In Labour's darkest hours, however, the party's malaise has been attributed as much to deep-seated structural forces as to one-off failings
such as internal divisions or faltering leadership. Above all, attention has
frequently centred on how post-war social and economic change appeared
to make the task of securing a Westminster majority ever more difficult.
After Macmillan's 1959 triumph, it was easy to see why commentators
concluded that Labour looked obsolete. As in many other contests where
the party suffered, it fared particularly badly in the south of England
and parts of the Midlands, where the 'affluent worker' seemed to credit
the Tories with delivering wider home ownership and greater access to
new material goods such as cars and domestic appliances. On the basis
of responses from 500 voters, Abrams and Rose observed in *Must Labour
Lose?* that the party was regarded as mainly representing the poor, this
at a time when 'many workers, regardless of their politics, no longer see
themselves as working class'.[19] This perspective reflected the emerging
concept of 'embourgeiosement', popular among social scientists and parts
of the commentariat, implying a steady and by implication irreversible
diminution in support for the left.

Similar emphasis on long-term social change was popular during
Labour's protracted spell in opposition from 1979, which encompassed
four successive defeats. The erosion or at least recasting of class barriers
that came with rising living standards, though an uneven process, inevitably had profound psephological consequences. From the 1970s
onwards the traditionally Labour-supporting groups in the electorate,
strong in Scotland, Wales and parts of northern England, continued
to shrink sharply as a proportion of the electorate; in contrast, Con-
servative-supporting elements such as managers and other middle-class
professionals expanded. While some political scientists believed failings in
policy and personnel remained crucial in explaining election outcomes,
others felt that Labour's inability to secure more than 40 per cent of votes
cast at any election for a generation after 1970 pointed to an enduring
underlying transformation. Whereas unionised council tenants in the
old industrial heartlands remained loyal, they were increasingly eclipsed
and outnumbered by the mainstay of Thatcher's support after 1979: the

---

18 A phrase coined by the journalist Edward Pearce, *The Guardian*, 6 May 1992.
19 Abrams and Rose, *Must Labour Lose?*, p. 23.

new working and lower-middle class non-unionised home-owners and ex-council tenants of southern England.[20]

In practice – despite the painfully long spells in opposition during the 1950s and 1960s and again in the 1980s and 1990s – the threat of Labour going out of business altogether never materialised. The power of what Macmillan called 'events, dear boy, events' helped to expose the shortcomings of the 'embourgeiosement' thesis, whether applied to the 1960s or later years. Without doubt, Labour struggled during the 1950s to find ways of appealing to groups at the heart of social change, such as 'affluent workers' and younger voters. But, crucially, so did the Conservatives, as became clear when such groups deserted the discredited Tories in large numbers in the early 1960s. Labour's defeat in 1959 (when it still captured 44 per cent of all votes and witnessed a swing in its direction in some parts of the country) should consequently be seen not as part of a process of inexorable decay but, more prosaically, as the product of a time when there was no obvious incentive for voters to switch horses. The 1959 result, in other words, owed more to short-term political than to long-term social determinants and, as such, implied that the possibility of renewal remained real. This was why the authors of *Must Labour Lose?* concluded that it was wrong to present the party as being on the way out; the question they posed could not be answered with certainty because 'politics is continually in a state of flux'.[21] It was this 'state of flux' that paved the way for Labour to return to power in 1964; and much the same applied a generation later, when, five years after the 1992 humiliation, New Labour secured 13.5 million votes, a total exceeded only once before in the party's history – ironically, in the defeat of 1951.

By the time the curtain came down on the Blair–Brown era, Labour was once more deeply unpopular. At the 2010 election the party's vote fell drastically, to just 29 per cent, close to the level that caused the alarms and ruptures of the 1980s. When Ed Miliband assumed the leadership following Brown's resignation, the political landscape had of course evolved enormously since the two-party heyday of the early post-war years. The rise of powerful third and fourth parties was attested to by the success of the Liberal Democrats in 2010 and the Scottish Nationalists in 2015; and the election of Jeremy Corbyn as Miliband's successor – the most left-wing figurehead since Foot – did little to bolster Labour's sunken ratings in the polls. There were a few glimmers of hope. The party's share of the vote

---

20 Contrast, for example, Ivor Crewe, 'Voting patterns since 1959', *Contemporary Record*, 2(4) (1988) with Anthony Heath *et al., Understanding Political Change: The British Voter 1964–1987* (Oxford: Pergamon Press, 1991).

21 Abrams and Rose, *Must Labour Lose?*, pp. 97–8.

in the 2015 election increased slightly compared with 2010, despite the collapse in Scotland, and the number of seats won, 232, was higher than at other low points, such as 1983.[22]

Yet there was no disguising the scale of the task ahead. Detailed research by the polling company YouGov in the autumn of 2015 found that, while hugely popular among those activists who provided him with about 60 per cent of ballots cast in the party leadership contest, Corbyn had much less appeal for voters in the marginal constituencies that Labour would have to win if it was to regain power. According to Peter Kellner, who carried out the research, successful leaders to varying degrees bridged the gap between loyalists and the broader electorate, but in the case of Corbyn the gulf between the two groups had never been greater. Among Labour members in the survey, 80 per cent of those who backed Corbyn for the leadership described themselves as 'very' or 'fairly' left wing, favouring policies such as the abolition of the monarchy and of private schools. But only 15 per cent of potential Labour voters among the wider electorate described themselves in the same way, and this at a time when the party needed to win over at least half of those who said they would consider backing the party in the future if it was to have any chance of success in 2020. According to Kellner, Corbyn was in an unenviable position: if he tacked to the centre ground he ran the risk, on the one hand, of being accused of betraying his principles by those who supported him for the leadership, and, on the other hand, of being attacked by the wider electorate for duplicity, hiding his true views to gain the leadership.[23]

Corbyn's supporters pointed to a defensible record in local elections and parliamentary by-elections during his early months in office, but this did not prevent Labour MPs – fearful that the party was drifting towards oblivion – backing by four to one an unprecedented vote of no confidence in the leader following the EU referendum in June 2016. A divisive and protracted leadership contest dragged on into the autumn before Corbyn's position as leader was reaffirmed, though without any noticeable upturn in Labour's dire poll ratings. As one *Guardian* journalist noted, the 'Tory Europhobes have … crashed the country', yet Labour seemed impotent to exploit the opportunity.[24]

---

22 See analysis of the results in *Sunday Times*, 10 May 2015, and *Sunday Telegraph*, 10 May 2015.
23 Peter Kellner, *New Statesman*, 24 September 2015. See also Kellner's findings in *Prospect* magazine, November 2015.
24 Polly Toynbee, 'This Tory chaos won't last. Labour must take its chance', *The Guardian*, 5 July 2016.

If, looking into murky waters ahead, we today revisit the question 'must Labour lose?', the answer – as it was in 1960 – remains uncertain. The prospect of terminal decline cannot not be ruled out, especially if challenges to Corbyn result in lasting factional splits; but, equally, the historical pattern of cyclical revival and recovery is still possible, propelled by as yet unforeseen events such as Conservative implosion over British terms for leaving the EU. Historians should always be wary of predicting the future on the basis of the past. But what recent events allied to the post-war record suggest most powerfully is that, whatever the medium-term chances of rising once more from the ashes, any early return to power is an outside bet. Labour does not always lose; but it's unlikely to win any time soon.

A select list of the publications of Chris Wrigley

Books

As sole or joint author

A. J. P. Taylor: Radical Historian of Europe (London: I. B. Tauris, 2006), viii + 439.

Churchill (London: Haus, 2006), vi + 166 (Portuguese edition, 2008).

British Trade Unions Since 1933 (Cambridge: Cambridge University Press, 2002), viii + 101.

Winston Churchill: A Biographical Dictionary (Santa Barbara, CA: ABC-Clio, 2002), xxvi + 367.

An Atlas of Industrial Protest in Britain, written with A. Charlesworth, D. Gilbert, A. Randall and H. Southall (London: Macmillan, 1996), xvi + 225 (hardback and paperback).

Lloyd George (Oxford: Blackwell 1992), vii + 171 (hardback and paperback).

Arthur Henderson (Cardiff: University of Wales/GPC, 1990), xvi + 211 (hardback and paperback).

Lloyd George and the Challenge of Labour (Brighton: Harvester-Wheatsheaf, 1990), ix + 325.

A. J. P. Taylor: A Complete Annotated Bibliography and Guide to His Historical and Other Writings (Hassocks: Harvester, 1980), ix + 707.

David Lloyd George and the British Labour Movement (Hassocks: Harvester, 1976), x + 298 (2nd edition, Gregg Revivals, 1992).

As editor

The Industrial Revolution: Cromford, the Derwent Valley and the Wider World (Cromford: Arkwright Society, 2015), 200.

Britain's Second Labour Government, 1929–31: A Reappraisal, with J. Shepherd and J. Davis (Manchester: Manchester University Press, 2011), 272.

The Emergence of European Trade Unionism, with J.-L. Robert and A. Prost (Aldershot: Ashgate, 2004), 268.

A Companion to Early Twentieth Century Britain (Oxford: Blackwell 2003), xx + 578.

A. J. P. Taylor: English History 1914–1945 (London: Folio, 2000), xxxiv + 638.

A. J. P. Taylor: Struggles for Supremacy (Aldershot: Ashgate, 2000), vii + 395.

The First World War and the International Economy (Cheltenham: Edward Elgar, 2000), x + 221.

A. J. P. Taylor: English History 1914–1945 (London: Folio, 2000), xxxiv + 638.

A. J. P. Taylor: Struggles for Supremacy (Aldershot: Ashgate, 2000), ii + 395.

A. J. P. Taylor: British Prime Ministers and Other Essays (London: Allen Lane, 1999), xxix + 431 (Penguin paperback, 2000; 2nd edition, Faber & Faber, 2008).

A. J. P. Taylor: A Century of Conflict, 5 volumes (London: Folio, 1998), xci + 1790.

British Trade Unions 1945–1995 (Manchester: Manchester University Press, 1997), ix + 221.

A History of British Industrial Relations 1939–1979 (Cheltenham: Edward Elgar, 1996), vii + 328.

A. J. P. Taylor: From the Boer War to the Cold War (London: Hamish Hamilton, 1995), xxv + 454 (Penguin paperback, 1996; 2nd edition, Faber & Faber, 2008).

A. J. P. Taylor: From Napoleon to the Second International (London: Hamish Hamilton, 1993), xxii, 426 (Penguin paperback, 1995; 2nd edition, London: Faber & Faber, 2008).

Challenges of Labour: Central and Western Europe 1917–1920 (London: Routledge, 1993), xi + 300.

On the Move: Essays in Labour and Transport History Presented to Philip Bagwell (London: Hambledon, 1991), xxv + 261 (with John Shepherd), xxv + 261.

With the International Brigade in Spain, by John Angus (Department of Economics. Loughborough University, 1983; reprinted 1988), viii + 20.

A History of British Industrial Relations 1914–1939 (Brighton: Harvester, 1987), vii + 328 (2nd edition, Gregg Revivals in Economic History, 1993).

Warfare, Diplomacy and Politics: Essays in Honour of A. J. P. Taylor (London: Hamish Hamilton, 1986), v + 247.

William Barnes: The Dorset Poet (Wimborne: Dovecote Press, 1984), xii + 244 (reprinted 1988, 1990 and 2003; University of Massachusetts Press, 1984).

A History of British Industrial Relations 1875–1914 (Hassocks: Harvester, 1982; also University of Illinois Press, 1982), xv + 229.

The Working Class in Victorian England, 4 volumes, with Max Goldstrom (Aldershot: Gregg International, 1973), 1450.

Editor of *The Historian,* 1993–98.

Editor of the Gregg Revivals in Economic History Series (26 volumes, 1992–96).

Editor of Ashgate Studies in Labour History (19 volumes, 1998–present).

Journal articles and pamphlets

'Smoking for King and country: soldiers and cigarettes', *History Today* (April 2014), 20–6.

'The Beaverbrook Library, A. J. P. Taylor and the rise of Lloyd George studies', *Journal of Liberal History,* 77 (winter 2012).

'The making of the people's William', *Journal of Liberal History,* 75 (2012), 14–19.

'Gladstone and the London May Day demonstrators', 1890, *The Historian,* 105 (spring 2010), 6–10.

'UK trade unions: some historical perspectives', *HHIC Journal,* 12 (May 2010), 4–8.

'Trade unions and the 1964 general election', *Contemporary British History,* 21(3) (2007), 325–35.

'The branches of the Historical Association 1906–2006', *The Historian*, 11 (autumn 2006), 45–57.

'The portrait of a branch: the Historical Association and history in Nottingham before the Second World War', *The Historian*, 90 (spring 2006), 36–9.

'Trade unionism in the United Kingdom in the 1930s and 1940s', *New Perspectives on Modern History*, 11(3) (March 2006), 24–7.

'A widening embrace: the Pump House People's History Museum', *Labour History Review*, 70(3) (2005), pp. 346–50 (with M. Walsh).

'Lloyd George and Gladstone', *The Historian*, 85 (spring 2005), 8–17.

'Churchill and the trade unions', *Transactions of the Royal Historical Society*, 6(11) (2001), 273–93.

'William Morris, art and the rise of the British labour movement', *The Historian*, 67 (2000).

'Womanpower: the transformation of the labour force in the UK and the USA since 1945', *ReFresh*, 31 (2000), 1–4 (with M. Walsh).

'From ASSETT to ASTMS: an example of white-collar union growth in the 1960s', *Historical Studies in Industrial Relations*, 7 (spring 1999), 54–74.

'A. J. P. Taylor and the Historical Association', *The Historian*, 55 (1997), 21–5.

'Hill Top, Beatrix Potter and a tale of much merchandise', *The Historian*, 52 (1996), 14–17.

'The First World War and liberal values', *Liberal Democrat History Group Newsletter*, 10 (March 1996), 13–14.

'The red menace? Russian Revolution and Europe', *Modern History Review*, 5(4) (1994), 20–3; reprinted in P. Catterall and R. Vinen (eds), *Europe 1914–45* (London: Heinemann, 1994), 36–44.

'A. J. P. Taylor: a nonconformist radical historian of Europe', *Contemporary European History*, 3(2) (1994), 1–14.

'A. J. P. Taylor (1906–1990)', *Proceedings of the British Academy*, 82 (1993), 493–524.

'Widening horizons? British labour and the Second International', *Labour History Review*, 58(1) (1993), 8–13.

'Labour and trade unions in Britain, 1880–1939', *ReFresh*, 13 (1991), 1–4; reprinted in A. Digby, C. Feinstein and D. Jenkins (eds), *New Directions In Economic and Social History*, vol. 2 (London: Macmillan, 1992), 97–110.

'Arthur Henderson: from north east industrial conciliation to international multilateral disarmament', *North East Labour History Bulletin*, 25 (1991), 5–2.

'Born again socialism', *New Socialist*, 66 (April 1990), 26–9.

'David Lloyd George, 1863–1945', *The Historian*, 26 (spring 1990), 10–12.

'Explaining why so many and so few: some aspects of the development of the Labour Party in small towns and rural areas', *Journal of Regional and Local Studies*, 10(1) (1990), 17–22.

'May days and after' (centenary of red May days), *History Today* (June 1990), 35–41.

'Hung county councils', *Contemporary Record*, 2(6) (1989), 6–8.

'Recent writing on trade unionism in Britain 1875–1939', *History Teaching Review Year Book*, 2 (1989), 49–53.

'The beginnings of the county council', *Leicestershire and Rutland Heritage*, 5 (winter 1989), 66–7.

'The French Revolution a hundred years on', *New Socialist*, 61 (1989), 23–5.

'Cosy co-operation under strain: industrial relations in the Yorkshire woollen industry 1919–1930', *Borthwick Paper*, 71 (1987), iii + 33.

'Historians and their times: the Webbs, chroniclers of trade unionism', *History Today* (May 1987), 51–5.

'Modern labour history and local history', *Local History*, 15 (April 1987), 18–19.

'Trade unions in Britain 1875–1939', *The Historian*, 9 (winter 1986), 10–12.

'William Barnes: paternalism and nineteenth century socialism', *Somerset and Dorset Notes and Queries*, 32(323) (March 1986), 483–6.

'Philip Bagwell: an appreciation', *Bulletin of the Society for the Study of Labour History*, 51(3), (November 1986), 6.

'The factory and the community', *The Historian*, 6 (spring 1985), 15–16.

'1926: social costs of the mining dispute', *History Today* (November 1984), 5–10.

'Eric Hobsbawm: an appreciation', *Bulletin of the Society for the Study of Labour History*, 48 (spring 1984), 2.

'Profile of A. J. P. Taylor', *The Historian*, 2 (spring 1984), 28.

'The General Strike, 1926: the government's volunteers', *The Local Historian*, 16(1) (February 1984), 36–48.

'The General Strike, 1926: the strikers and their families', *The Local Historian*, 16(2) (May 1984), 83–9.

'A. J. P. Taylor's major books', in *Today's History*, supplement to *History Today*, 33 (June 1983), iv.

The General Strike, 1926, in Local History (Surveys in Economics and Social History, Department of Economics, Loughborough University, 1982).

'A. J. P. Taylor at 75', *History Today*, 3 (April 1981), 49.

'Battersea republicans and the 1902 coronation', *Crosscurrents*, 1 (1980), 25–31.

'Municipal socialism in London', *1837–1901*, 5 (1980), 52–60.

'Thomas Hardy in 1978', *1837–1901*, 3 (1978), 57–60.

'William Barnes and the social problem', *Proceedings of the Dorset Archaeological Society for 1977*, 98 (1977), 19–27.

Battersea Republicans and the 1902 Coronation (London: Battersea and Wandsworth Labour and Social History Group pamphlet, June 1977).

'William Barnes and self-help', *1837–1901*, 1 (1976), 14–16.

'The burning of the pope in early nineteenth century Dorset', *Dorset*, 57 (November 1976).

'The improvement of popular festivals', *Dorset*, 45 (August 1975).

'The Symondsbury harvest home 1857', *Dorset*, 45 (August 1975).

'The myths and realities in the career of John Burns', *South Western Star* (September 1970).

Essays and chapters in edited collections

'May days in Britain', in Abby Peterson and Herbert Reiter (eds), *The Ritual of May Day in Western Europe: Past, Present and Future* (Aldershot: Ashgate, 2016), pp. 131–59.

'Arthur Henderson', in Charles Clarke and Toby James (eds), *British Labour Leaders* (London: Biteback, 2015), pp. 124–45.

'Olive Wootton', in Goldmark Gallery, *Olive Wootton: Myth and Legend* (Hemel Hampstead: Goldmark, 2015), pp. 3–4.

'Red May days: hopes and fears in Europe in the 1890s', in Michael Davis (ed.), *Crowd Actions in Britain and France from the Middle Ages to the Modern World* (Basingstoke: Palgrave Macmillan, 2015), pp. 208–22.

'Coalition blues: the Conservatives, the Liberals and Conservative–Liberal coalitions in Britain since 1895', in B. W. Hart and R. Carr (eds), *The Foundations of the Conservative Party* (London: Bloomsbury, 2013), pp. 153–74.

'The fall of the second Labour government, 1931', in T. Heppell and K. Theakston (eds), *How Labour Governments Fall* (Basingstoke: Palgrave Macmillan, 2013), pp. 38–60.

'Gladstone and Labour', in R. Quinault and R. Swift (eds), *William Gladstone: New Studies and Perspectives* (Aldershot: Ashgate, 2012), pp. 51–70.

'Labour dealing with Labour: aspects of economic policy', in J. Shepherd, J. Davis and C. Wrigley (eds), *Britain's Second Labour Government, 1929–31: A Reappraisal* (Manchester: Manchester University Press, 2011), pp. 37–54.

'Errinerungen, Raume und Demonstranten', in W. Maderthaner and M. Maier (eds), *Acht Stunden aber wollen wir Mensch sein: Der 1 Mai. Geschichte und Geschichten*, 1st edition (Vienna: Rot, 2010), pp. 44–9.

'The commemorative urge: the co-operative movement's collective memory', in L. Black and N. Robertson (eds), *Consumerism and the Co-operative Movement in Modern British History: Taking Stock* (Manchester: Manchester University Press, 2009), pp. 157–73.

'The European context: aspects of British Labour and continental socialism before 1920', in M. Worley (ed.), *The Foundations of the British Labour Party: Identities, Cultures and Perspectives, 1900–39* (Aldershot: Ashgate, 2009), pp. 77–93.

'Industrial relations', in N. Crafts, I. Gazely and A. Newell (eds), *Work and Pay in Twentieth-Century Britain* (Oxford: Oxford University Press, 2007), pp. 203–24.

'Trade unions: rise and decline', in F. Carnevali and J.-M. Strang (eds), *Twentieth Century Britain: Economic, Cultural and Social Change*, 2nd edition (London: Pearson Longman, 2007), pp. 279–92.

'Expression et mise en scene syndicales a l'heure de la communication: une mutation delicate' (with M. Pigenet, D. Tartakowsky, G. Deneckere and P. Francois), in M. Pigenet, P. Pasture and J.-L. Robert (eds), *L'apogee des syndicalismes en Europe occidentale 1960–1985* (Paris : Publication de la Sorbonne, 2005), pp. 227–57.

'Churchill and the trade unions', in D. Cannadine and R. Quinault (eds), *Winston Churchill in the Twenty-First Century* (Cambridge: Cambridge University Press, 2004), pp. 47–67.

'Introduction' to A. J. P. Taylor, *The Course of German History* (London: Routledge, 2001), pp. ix–xv.

'Toil and turmoil: trade unions in a changing economy', in Felipe Fernandez-Armesto (ed.), *England 1945–2000* (London: Folio Society, 2001), pp. 215–22.

'"Carving the last few columns out of the Gladstonian quarry": the Liberal leaders and the mantle of Gladstone, 1898–1929', in D. Bebbington and R. Swift (eds), *Gladstone Centenary Essays* (Liverpool: Liverpool University Press, 2000), pp. 243–59.

'Counter-revolution and the "failure" of revolution in interwar Europe', in D. Parker (ed.) *Revolutions and the Revolutionary Tradition in the West 1560–1991* (London: Routledge, 2000), pp. 169–84.

'Organised labour and the international economy', in C. Wrigley (ed.), *The First World War and the International Economy* (Cheltenham: Edward Elgar, 2000), pp. 201–15.

'The war and the international economy', in C. Wrigley (ed.), *The First World War and the International Economy* (Cheltenham: Edward Elgar, 2000), pp. 1–33.

'A harsher economic climate', also statistical appendix and bibliography, in Eric Hobsbawm (ed.), *Industry and Empire*, 2nd edition (London: Penguin 1999), pp. 298–316 and 325–78.

'A. J. P. Taylor: five faces and the man', in Attila Pok (ed.), *The Fabric of Modern Europe: Studies in Social and Diplomatic History* (Nottingham: Astra Press, 1999), pp. 225–38.

'James Ramsay MacDonald 1922–31', in K. Jefferys (ed.), *Leading Labour: From Keir Hardie to Tony Blair* (London: I. B. Tauris, 1999), pp. 15–40.

'Women in the labour market and in the unions', in J. McIlroy, N. Fishman and A. Campbell (eds), *British Trade Unions and Industrial Politics*, vol. 2 (Aldershot: Ashgate, 1999), pp. 43–69. Paperback 2nd edition, entitled *The High Tide of British Trade Unionism* (Pontypool: Merlin, 2007).

'Premiers mai' and 'Les constraintes de la loi' (with G. Deneckere, M-L Goergen, I. Marssolek and D. Tartakowsky; and N. Olszak), in J.-L. Robert, F. Boll and A.Prost (eds), *L'Invention des syndicalismes* (Paris: Sorbonne, 1997), pp. 199–207, 237–54.

'History: current change and future practice in universities', in D. Kerr (ed.), *Current Change and Future Practice* (Leicester: Leicester University Press, 1996), pp. 16–24.

'Introduction', 'The Second World War and state interventions in industrial relations 1939–45' and 'Trade union development, 1945–79', in C. J. Wrigley (ed.), *A History of British Industrial Relations 1939–1979* (Cheltenham: Edward Elgar, 1996), pp. 1–11, 12–43, 62–83.

'The early May Days, 1890, 1891 and 1892', 'The Coal lock-out of 1893', 'Industrial protest 1940–90', 'Coal disputes manufacturing industry', 'The Winter of Discontent' and 'The 1984-5 miners' strike', in C. J. Wrigley, A. Charlesworth, D. Gilbert, A. Randall and H. Southall (eds), *An Atlas of Industrial Protest in Britain 1750–1990* (London: Macmillan, 1996), pp. 112–15, 116–21, 177–80, 202–9, 210–16, 217–25.

'The impact of the First World War on the labour movement', in M. Dockrill and D. French (eds), *Strategy And Intelligence: British Policy in the First World War* (London: Hambledon Press, 1996), pp. 139–59.

'Trade unions, strikes and the government', in R. Coopey and N. Woodward (eds), *Britain in the 1970s: The Troubled Economy* (London: UCL Press, 1995), pp. 237–91.

'Introduction', Joy Cross (ed.), *Memoirs of A Loughborough Man* (Nottingham: University of Nottingham, 1994).

'Now you see it, now you don't. Harold Wilson and foreign policy', R. Coopey, S. Fielding and N. Tiratsoo (eds), *The First Wilson Government, 1964–70* (London: Pinter, 1993), pp. 123–35.

'The state and the challenge of Labour in Britain 1917–1920', in C. Wrigley (ed.), *Challenges of Labour: Central and Western Europe 1917–20* (London: Routledge, 1993), pp. 262–88.

'The TUC 1868–1968', in *Working for Your Future: The TUC 1868–1993* (London: TUC, 1993), pp. 7–29.

'Chi promosse le prime giornate dei lavoratori in Gran Bretagna', in Andrea Panaccione (ed.), *Il I maggio tra passato e future* (Rome: Piero Lacaita, 1992), pp. 181–91.

'The ILP and the Second International: the early years, 1893–1905', in D. James, T. Jowitt and K. Laybourn (eds), *The Centennial History of the Independent Labour Party* (Keele: Keele University Press, 1992), pp. 299–313.

'Lloyd George and the Labour Party after 1922', in J. Loades (ed.), *The Life and Times of Lloyd George* (Bangor: Headstart, 1991), pp. 49–69.

'Trade unionists, employers and the cause of industrial peace 1916–21', in C. Wrigley and J. Shepherd (eds), *On the Move* (London: Hambledon Press, 1991), pp. 155–84.

'Trade unions, the government and the economy 1945–89', in T. R. Gourvish and A. O'Day (eds), *Britain Since 1945* (Basingstoke: Macmillan, 1991), pp. 59–88.

'Il I maggio del 1890 e del 1891 en Gran Bretagna', Andrea Panaccione (ed.), *I luoghi e i soggetti* (Venice: Marsilio Editori, 1990), pp. 137–66.

'Great Britain', in Andrea Panaccione (ed.), *The Memory of May Day* (Venice: Marsilio Editori, 1989), pp. 83–108.

'The First World War and state intervention in industrial relations' and 'The trade unions between the wars', in C. Wrigley (ed.), *A History of British Industrial Relations 1914–1939* (Brighton: Harvester Press, 1987), pp. 23–70, 71–128.

'"In the excess of their patriotism": The National Party and threats of subversion', in C. Wrigley (ed.), *Warfare, Diplomacy and Politics* (London: Hamish Hamilton, 1986), pp. 93–119.

'William Barnes and rural Dorset', in B. Jones (ed.), *William Barnes 1801–1886: A Handbook* (Dorchester: William Barnes Society, 1986), pp. 25–8.

'The trade unions and the Labour Party', in K. D. Brown (ed.), *The First Labour Party* (London: Croom Helm, 1985), pp. 129–37.

'The Ministry of Munitions: an innovatory department?', in K. Burk (ed.), *War and the State* (London: Allen and Unwin, 1982), pp. 32–56.

'The government and industrial relations', in C. Wrigley (ed.), *A History of British Industrial Relations 1875–1914* (Hassocks: Harvester Press, 1982), pp. 135–58.

'Trade unions and politics in the First World War', in B. Pimlott and C. Cook (eds), *Trade Unions in British Politics* (London: Longman, 1982; 2nd edition, 1991), pp. 69–87.

'How trade unions are organised' and 'What the retail price index means', in G. Terry Page and Michael Armstrong (eds), *Personnel and Training Yearbook and Directory 1977* (London: Kogan Page, 1976), pp. 18–22, 27–31.

'The Trade Union and Labour Relations Act 1974', in G. Terry Page and Michael Armstrong (eds), *Personnel and Training Yearbook and Directory 1976* (London: Kogan Page, 1975), pp. 47–52.

'Liberals and the desire for working class representatives in Battersea 1886–1922', in K. D. Brown (ed.), *Essays in Anti-Labour History* (London: Macmillan, 1974), pp. 126–58.

Encyclopaedia and dictionary entries and similar

'Labour, labour movements, trade unions and strikes (Great Britain and Ireland)', in *1914–1918: International Encyclopedia of the First World War* (University of Berlin, April 2015); available online at http://encyclopedia.1914-1918-online.net/article/labour_labour_movements_trade_unions_and_strikes_great_britain_and_ireland (accessed January 2017).

'Churchill and Labour', Churchill Archives website https://www.chu.cam.ac.uk/archives (accesssed January 2017).

'William Barnes', 'Ernest Bevin', 'George Brown', 'John Bruce Glasier', 'Katherine Bruce Glasier', 'Arthur Henderson', 'Thomas Mann', 'James Peddie', 'Robert Smillie', 'Sir Ben Turner', in H. C. G. Matthew and B. Harrison (eds), *Oxford Dictionary of National Biography* (Oxford: Oxford University Press, 2004).

'Unions', in J. Mokyr (ed.), *The Oxford Encyclopaedia of Economic History*, vol. 5 (Oxford: Oxford University Press, 2003).

'John Burns' and 'John Robert Clynes', in G. Rosen (ed.), *Dictionary of Labour Biography* (London: Politicos, 2001), pp. 93–4, 124–5.

'Arthur Henderson', in G. Batho (ed.), *Durham Biographies* (Durham: Durham University, 2000), pp. 68–73.

'British trade unions', 'Margaret Bondfield', 'Arthur Henderson', 'Tom Mann' and 'Ben Tillett', *Encarta Encyclopedia 2001* (Redmond, WA: Microsoft, 2000).

'The welfare state', *Encarta Encyclopedia 1999* (Redmond, WA: Microsoft, 1998).

'The 1997 general election', *Encarta Encyclopedia Yearbook 1997* (Redmond: Microsoft, 1997).

'The Labour Party' and 'The Liberal Party', in *Microsoft Encarta Encyclopedia* (CD-Rom), World English edition (Redmond, WA: Microsoft, 1997).

'The First World War and liberal values', 'The Liberals and the First World War' and 'David Lloyd George', Social Democrat History Group, 1996, available at the website of the Liberal Democrat History Group, http://www.liberalhistory.org.uk/ (accessed January 2017).

'Walter Citrine', 'The Clydsiders', 'The General Strike', 'The Taff Vale judgement', 'J. H. Thomas', 'Trade union legislation' and 'TUC', in F. M. Leventhal (ed.), *Twentieth Century Britain: An Encyclopedia* (New York: Garland, 1995), pp. 152–3, 167, 321–4, 759, 776, 784–9.

'Arthur Henderson' and 'Will Paynter', in K. Robbins, *The Blackwell Biographical Dictionary of British Political Life in the Twentieth Century* (Oxford: Blackwell, 1990), pp. 199–201, 309.

'Robert Smillie', in J. O. Baylen and N. Gossman (eds), *Biographical Dictionary of Modern British Radicals*, vol. 3, part 2 (Hassocks: Harvester, 1989).

'David Landes' and 'A. J. P. Taylor', in J. Cannon (ed.), *Dictionary of Historians* (Oxford: Blackwell, 1988), pp. 232, 406–8.

'Lord Peddie', in D. Jeremy (ed.), *Dictionary of Business Biography*, vol. 4 (London: Butter-worths, 1985), pp. 604–9.

Index